New Babylon

Studies in the Social Sciences

44

MOUTON PUBLISHERS · BERLIN · NEW YORK · AMSTERDAM

William T. Preyer (1841–1897)

Contributions To A History Of Developmental Psychology

International William T. Preyer Symposium

Edited by
Georg Eckardt,
Wolfgang G. Bringmann
and Lothar Sprung

With a Foreword by
Urie Bronfenbrenner
and a Preface by
Karl-Friedrich Wessel

MOUTON PUBLISHERS · BERLIN · NEW YORK · AMSTERDAM

CIP-Kurztitelaufnahme der Deutschen Bibliothek

Contributions to a history of developmental psychology / Internat. William T. Preyer Symposium. Ed. by Georg Eckardt ... With a foreword by Urie Bronfenbrenner and a pref. by Karl-Friedrich Wessel. — Berlin ; New York ; Amsterdam ; Mouton, 1985.
  (New Babylon ; 44)
  ISBN 3-11-009977-2 Pb.
  ISBN 3-11-009976-4 Gewebe

NE: Eckardt, Georg [Hrsg.]; International William T. Preyer Symposium (1982, Jena); GT

Library of Congress Cataloging in Publication Data

International William T. Preyer Symposium (1982 :
  Jena, Germany)
  Contributions to a history of developmental psychology.
  (New Babylon, studies in the social sciences ; 44)

  Includes indexes.
  1. Developmental psychology—History—Congresses.
  2. Preyer, William T., 1841–1897—Congresses.
  I. Eckardt, Georg. II. Bringmann, Wolfgang G. III. Sprung, Lothar.
  IV. Title.
  BF712.5.I56   1982   155   84-27281
  ISBN 0-89925-044-0
  ISBN 0-89925-045-9 (pbk.)

Printed on acid free paper

Contents

Part II: **William T. Preyer – His Time, His Work and His Influence**

List of Contributors

Mitchel G. Ash, Ph. D.
Assistant Professor, Department of History,
University of Iowa, Iowa City, Iowa, USA

William D. G. Balance, Ph. D.
Professor, Department of Psychology,
University of Windsor, Windsor, Ontario, Canada

Peter J. Behrens, Ph. D.
Assistant Professor of Psychology,
Pennsylvania State University,
(Allentown Campus), Fogelsville,
Pennsylvania, USA

Norma J. Bringmann, B. A.
Research Associate
Mobile, Alabama
USA

Wolfgang G. Bringmann, Ph. D.
Professor, Department of Psychology,
University of South Alabama,
Mobile, Alabama, USA

Urie Bronfenbrenner, Ph. D.
Professor, Department of Human Development and Family Studies,
Cornell University, Ithaca, N. Y., USA

John C. Cavanaugh, Ph. D.
Assistant Professor, Department of Psychology,
Bowling Green State University,
Bowling Green, Ohio, USA

Kurt Danziger, D. Phil.
Professor, Department of Psychology
York University, Downsview,
Ontario, Canada

Roger Dixon, Ph. D.
Research Scientist, Max Planck
Institute for Human Development,
Berlin, FRG

Georg Eckardt, Dr. sc. phil.
Assistant Professor, Division of Psychology,
Friedrich-Schiller-Universität,
Jena, GDR

Christina Fritsche, Dr. phil.
Research Associate, Karl-Sudhoff
Institute for the History of Medicine,
Karl-Marx-Universität, Leipzig, GDR

Howard E. Gruber, Ph. D.
Professor, Division of Psychology,
Université de Génève, Geneva, Switzerland;
Rutgers University, New Brunswick,
N. J., USA

Ben Harris, Ph. D.
Assistant Professor, Department of
Psychology, Vassar College,
Poughkeepsie, N. Y., USA

Manu V. Jääskeläinen, Ph. D.
Chief of Educational Affairs,
Finnish Medical Association,
Helsinki, Finland

List of Contributors   IX

Siegfried Jaeger, Dr. phil.
Research Associate, Psychological Institute,
Freie-Universität-Berlin, FRG

Robert T. Keegan, M. A.
Lecturer, Department of Psychology,
Pace University, Kearny, New Jersey,
USA

Ursula Köhler, Dr. rer. nat.
Professor Emeritus, Department of
Labor Science,
Technische Hochschule,
Dresden, GDR

Richard M. Lerner, Ph. D.
Professor, College of Human Development,
Pennsylvania State University,
University Park, Pennsylvania, USA

Richard Lowry, Ph. D.
Professor and Head, Department of
Psychology, Vassar College,
Poughkeepsie, New York, USA

Alexandre Métraux, Dr. phil.
Research Scientist, Psychological Institute,
Universität Heidelberg, Heidelberg,
FRG

Paul Mitzenheim, Dr. sc. paed.
Professor, Division of Education,
Friedrich-Schiller-Universität,
Jena, GDR

Frank Ortmann, Dr. med.
Research Associate, Ernst-Haeckel-Haus,
Friedrich-Schiller-Universität, Jena,
GDR

Robert Richards, Ph. D.
Associate Professor, History of Science,
University of Chicago, Chicago, Illinois,
USA

Eckardt Scheerer, Dr. phil.
Professor of Psychology,
Universität Oldenburg,
Oldenburg, FRG

Hans-Dieter Schmidt, Dr. sc. nat.
Professor, Division of Psychology,
Humboldt Universität zu Berlin,
Berlin, GDR

Helga Sprung, Dr. rer. nat.
Research Scientist, Berlin, GDR

Lothar Sprung, Dr. sc. nat.
Assistant Professor, Division of Psychology,
Humboldt Universität zu Berlin,
Berlin, GDR

Irmingard Staeuble, Dr. phil.
Professor, Psychological Institute,
Freie-Universität-Berlin, Berlin, FRG

Ethel Tobach, Ph. D.
Professor and Curator, Comparative
Psychology,
American Museum of Natural History,
New York, New York, USA

Ryan Tweney, Ph. D.
Professor, Department of Psychology,
Bowling Green State University,
Bowling Green, Ohio, USA

Michael Wertheimer, Ph. D.
Professor, Department of Psychology,
University of Colorado,
Boulder, Colorado, USA

X   List of Contributors

Karl-Friedrich Wessel, Dr. sc. phil.
Professor, Division of Philosophy,
Humboldt Universität zu Berlin,
Berlin, GDR

Joachim F. Wohlwill, Ph. D.
Professor, College of Human Development,
Pennsylvania State University,
University Park, Pennsylvania, USA

William Woodward, Ph. D.
Associate Professor, Department of Psychology,
University of New Hampshire, Durham, New Hampshire, USA

Foreword

It can be said that a scientific field comes of age when it begins to acknowledge its history. If so, then this volume marks the growth of developmental psychology beyond its adolescence. To be sure, that growth has been somewhat retarded. I still recall my dismay, when, in the late 1940s, the chairman of a leading psychology department in one of America's major universities summarily announced that no course in the history of psychology would henceforth be taught, since, in his view, modern scientific psychology had no connection with, and had nothing to learn from, its past. (I hasten to add that the institution in question is not my own; Cornell psychologists take pride in the fact that E.B. Titchener, a pupil of Wundt, founded the first laboratory of experimental psychology at our *alma mater.*) To reach scholarly maturity is to recognize that today's intellectual achievements are based on ideas and approaches that, in retrospect, may appear commonplace and crude, but, in fact, constitute the prototypes of modern science. It is these fateful foreshadowings that are the exciting burden of the chapters in this volume.

The figure appearing most often in these pages is William Thierry Preyer, the nineteenth century German physiologist, in whose honor psychologists from both sides of the Atlantic assembled at Jena in 1982, in order to celebrate the hundredth anniversary of the publication of Preyer's classic biography of infant development, *Die Seele des Kindes* (The Mind of the Child). That study was based principally on Preyer's observations of his infant son over the first three years of life. Seen from the perspective of the scholarly essays that follow, Preyer emerges as the *de facto* definer of a new research paradigm. Prior to the publication of his classic, the study of children's development had been essentially a subjective enterprise. On the one hand, that enterprise consisted of largely unsubstantiated generalizations from broader educational and evolutionary theory; on the other, it relied on anecdotal accounts of infant development in which fact and fiction had been inextricably confounded. Preyer confronted both approaches by introducing and insisting upon careful, systematic methods of observation, in which data were to be distinguished from interpretation. Although, by contemporary standards, his work lacked an adequate statistical base, Preyer was, in effect, setting a new external criterion of validity that, in due course, would revolutionize the field. From this viewpoint, Preyer might properly be called the father of experimental child psychology. Yet even this laudatory description fails to convey the theoretical roots of his methodological concern. The latter is most aptly captured in the original German title of the chapter by H. and L.Sprung: *"Preyer als Methodologe und Methodiker"* (Preyer as a Pragmatic Methodologist). But this scientific pioneer was much more than a methodologist, even in a broad sense; for his insistence on careful systematic observation was only a by-product, a means to the end of his primary goal—acquiring and applying knowledge about human behavior and development. As documented in several essays in this volume, Preyer's scholarly contributions extended far beyond his basic discipline of physiology into such diverse domains as the psychology of perception (H. and L.Sprung), linguistics (Tweney), hypnosis (Fritsche and Ortmann), and the reform of German schools (Jaeger). Preyer was also an active participant in the discussions of evolutionary theory, which also was a key influence on his own work. As Eckardt points out in his chapter on "Preyer's Road to Child Psychology," the "Mental Life of the Child" represented a convergence of vectors from four directions: Preyer's discontent with the unscientific character of earlier descriptions of infant development; his training as a physiologist; his exposure to the burgeoning discipline of experimental psychology; and an evolutionary orientation engendered by Darwinism.

In completing this brief preview of Preyer's scientific achievements, I must add yet one other serendipitous contribution that, paradoxically, was not accomplished until more than a century after his birth. For the symposium celebrating the centenary of *Die Seele des Kindes* also served as the occasion for recognizing and reviving the still-stimulating ideas and research findings of other pioneers in the study of psychological development—among them Rousseau (Mitzenheim), Carus (Köhler), Herder (Schmidt), Darwin (Dixon and Lerner; Keegan and Gruber; Tobach), Lotze (Woodward), James (Richards), and, in our own century, Watson (Harris), Pavlov (Behrens), Koffka (Ash), Muchow (Wohlwill) and Kaila (Jääskeläinen).

Other authors provide an invaluable service by tracing historical developments, in particular developmental domains, including early diaries (Jaeger), pre- and postevolutionary formulations of the nature-nurture controversy (Lowry, Métraux, Staeuble), evolving conceptions of imitation (Danziger, Scheerer), thinking and cognition (Cavanaugh, Wertheimer), and the development of experimental approaches in child psychology (Bringmann, Bringmann and Balance). Especially noteworthy in the last account is a brief description of the work of Adolf Kussmaul, a public health physician, who published, in 1859, what must be regarded as the first experimental studies of the behavior of the newborn.

Taken as a whole, this unusual compendium testifies to two truths more often honored in the breach than in the observance. The first is the truth of what is typically offered only as a truism, that science is in fact a "community of scholars." Two such communities are represented in this volume: those who are written about, and those who write about the former. Both communities have spanned two continents of geography and, what is more consequential, two continents of the mind. This bridge in two directions acknowledges a mutual intellectual commitment to the past as a foundation and inspiration for the future. It is this commitment that testifies to the second truth that animates our scientific work. As I have written elsewhere, "We stand on the shoulders of giants and mistake the broadened vision as our own."[1] Many of the giants are to be found in the pages that follow.

Urie Bronfenbrenner
Cornell University

[1] Bronfenbrenner, U. *The Ecology of Human Development: Experiments by Nature and Design.* Cambridge, MA: Harvard University Press, 1979.

Preface

The publication of this volume of articles on the history of the concept of development in psychology can be regarded as a major event in scholarship. The separate contributions, each quite independent of the others, all carry the conviction of this assertion. Historical studies will likely play an ever-increasing role in the progress of the sciences and will gain respect to the extent that they fulfill their function and make significant contributions. Of course, historical writing must be free from one-sided, artificial notions, as well as from the naive claim that they can directly predict the future. Today one should not doubt the importance of historical writings but should always take a critical stance towards individual historical accounts and theories.

It seems to me to be not so important to debate which of the many historical approaches is the true one. Controversies about this topic are most unproductive, because too frequently such writings are primarily interested in excluding other viewpoints and fail to address the complexity and contradictory nature of history itself.

The writing of history always involves a plan, a theoretical plan for the organization and interpretation of existing historical documents. The quality of this organization and intrepretation depends upon the current state of knowledge in the field, upon the methodological preconceptions, and also upon the individual standpoint of the historian. High standards in writing the history of a science involve interaction with the standards of the science itself, which even in their advanced state constantly interact with their own historical development. The unfolding of the consciousness of a science unfolds with this interplay, and progress in the ontogeny of a scientific discipline is paralleled by progress in its historical consciousness. Almost unnoticeably but quite irrevocably, the history of psychology has joined the cast of specialized histories of science which determine or substantially influence our historical awareness of the development of thought.

The present volume is an event in this process. It is particularly important that developmental psychology is the focus of attention and that William T. Preyer is a key figure—indeed his importance has to date not been sufficiently recognized. The assessments offered here, particularly those of Preyer's child psychology, contribute substantially to the shaping of our attitudes towards the concept of evolution. The theory of evolution now plays a central role in the most important theories of science. In fact, it has become almost an article of faith for natural scientists and psychologists. Yet, it seems that there remains an unfinished task: to give an account of the development of the concept of evolution in history, an account which could serve as yardstick for evaluating individual disciplines and personalities in the history of science. I am referring here not to the mere updating of existing histories of science, but rather to the writing of a completely new history of human understanding. Anyone who takes evolutionary theory seriously—the philosophical notion (Hörz and Wessel, 1983), the specific theories, or the interaction of the two levels—must be aware of and take account of the complexity of events, especially of the contradictions in the development of evolutionary theories and methods. It is hoped that these essays make it clear that one cannot write a good history of evolutionary thinking, and certainly not a history of the heuristic functions of evolutionary theories, without including history of psychology.

To the degree that psychology liberates itself from philosophy and becomes a distinct discipline, its unique character becomes a prerequisite for creative interaction between the two fields. Each field is a sovereign entity only as long as this interaction is maintained and used as a heuristic principle for the field's respective development (Wessel, 1983).

I was pleased to note in this connection that this volume addresses the interdisciplinary attitude which is invoked so often nowadays. The dialectical unity *(widersprüchliche Einheit)* of a single discipline *(Disziplinarität)* and the common problems of all sciences *(Interdisziplinarität)* constitutes a fundamental problem in the context, structure, dynamic, and organization of science (Wessel, 1983). This process is and will continue to be heavily influenced by further development of evolutionary theories.

Preyer was a Darwinian—a necessary prerequisite for his historical achievements in the establishment of developmental psychology. Today's situation offers a parallel: consistent progress in developmental psychology is only possible if the most modern biological theories are taken into account. Moreover, a solid foundation of epistemological consciousness provides a necessary defense against reductionistic oversimplifications.

One final thought. The history of science is indivisible as far as the formation of subspecialties is concerned. It is a tradition for writers in a given country self-confidently to portray their national history of science in its full complexity. Scholars in the German Democratic Republic have dedicated themselves increasingly to this task in recent years, and the William T. Preyer Symposium in Jena is a further expression of this interest. Nevertheless, scholars everywhere also have the right and duty to devote themselves to the history of science independent of territorial constraint.

Altough differences in *Weltanschauungen* among the contributors to this volume are apparent, I believe that efforts to demonstrate the indivisibility of science have been successful.

References

Hörz, H., and Wessel, K.F. (1983) *Philosophische Entwicklungstheorien.*
Wessel, K.F. (1982) Weltanschauung und das Verhältnis von Disziplinarität und Interdisziplinarität. *Deutsche Zeitschrift für Philosophie* 32.
—(1983) Zum Verhältnis von Philosophie und Psychologie. *Wissenschaftliche Zeitschrift der Humboldt-Universität zu Berlin,* 32.

Karl-Friedrich Wessel
Humboldt-Universität

Acknowledgments

The editors wish to express their gratitude, first and foremost, to the authors of the chapters of this volume, whose scholarship, diligence, patience and commitment to the project are the key reasons for the book's existence. We also wish to thank Urie Bronfenbrenner, who arranged a busy schedule to meet with some of the East European participants in the Preyer symposium and to write the foreword for this work.

Thanks are due to our publishers, Mouton Publishers in Berlin (West), whose sense of the importance of timely publication in the history of developmental psychology contributed greatly to our endeavor.

Preparation of this book was aided by course reductions authorized by Jeral Williams, Dean of the College of Arts and Sciences of the University of South Alabama and by the assignment of special typing assistance from the Department of Psychology of the University of South Alabama, which was made available by Larry Allen, Chairman of the Department.

Special thanks are owed to Mary Conwell and Janice Davis of the University of South Alabama, whose fast and accurate typing made our editorial task much easier, to Norma J. Bringmann, who gave unstintingly of her time for the copy editing and to Charles E. Early, Mobile College and Dipl.-Ing. Frank Backes of Pfungstadt, FRG, who assisted with the exacting task of proof-reading. For his assistance in translating the PREFACE by Professor Wessel, we gratefully recognize David Robinson of the Department of History, University of California, Berkeley.

Special gratitude is owed to the Historical Commission for Psychology of the Scientific Council for Psychology and the Society for Psychology of the GDR whose presidents, Professor Friedhart Klix and Professor Adolf Kossakowski, were responsible for the planning and successful implementation of this international conference. The material support of Friedrich-Schiller-Universität in Jena, GDR, where the various sessions of the conference were held, was most appreciated. Last not least, we thank the Ministry of Higher Education of the GDR for its generous financial and organizational support of the 1982 International William T. Preyer Symposium.

Prologue

The belief in the impermanence of the organic world—specifically the birth and death of the individual—belongs to the most ancient experiences of mankind. In contrast, the seeming durability of the firmament and the mountains and valleys of our physical world have provided a sense of continuity. Man has been confronted by these polarities for millennia. How long may it have taken him to discover that one does not have to choose between these extreme views of the world but that there always has been change and development and always will be?

Today we know a great deal about the origin and transformations of the concept of development in the history of human thought. There have been a number of radically different models of development, and it may be useful to consider some of these conceptualizations, beginning with those suggested by Pongratz (1967): (1) The circular model or *Kreismodell* predominated primarily in classical antiquity (i.e. Heraclitus, Empedocles, Plato, Aristotle, and the Stoics). It was patterned after the cosmological model of the sky. The "eternal return of the same," according to which "there is nothing new under the sun," was the guiding idea behind this model of development. (2) The semicircular model or *Halbkreismodell* can also be documented in various historical periods. It follows the biological processes of growth and decay. According to this perspective, all living things and, by extension, cultures, ideas and societies, go through distinct stages of increased and decreased growth. This is essentially a pessimistic model of change. (3) The spiral model or *Spiralenmodell* is cyclical in nature and its general orientation is rather optimistic. Development is viewed as a progressive movement, although, of course, deadend streets and circuitous pathways cannot always be avoided. Thus, world history is transformed into the "Story of Salvation" *(Heilsgeschichte)*. One should not be surprised to discover that the great prophets of world religions and the philosophers of the enlightenment subscribed to this model in their explications of developmental ideas. The philosophers of the eighteen century replaced the idea of salvation with a belief in a progressive development of the world, nature, society, and man (i.e. Montesquieu, Herder, Humboldt). (4) Finally, the dialectical model or *Dialektische Modell* of change (i.e. Hegel, Darwin, Marx, Engels) united the ideas of growth and decay with those of permanence and progress in its conceptualization of development. Since the middle of the nineteenth century the dialectical model has been ever widely accepted by major disciplines as an essential method of scientific thinking and research.

The most fruitful and consequential utilizations of the concept of development in the nineteenth century occured in biology (Darwin) and psychology (Preyer). The history of evolutionary thinking in the biological sciences has been dealt with at length. We are well informed about the predecessors, contemporaries, opponents, collaborators, and successors of Charles Darwin. We also know a great deal about the historical context, the motivations and the controversies (i.e. Haeckel) which facilitated the acceptance of developmental thinking in biology. Unfortunately, much less attention has been devoted to the history of evolutionary thinking in psychology and the beginnings of empirical child psychology, comparative psychology, and developmental psychology.

Fields of science, which have lived through their "childhood" and "adolescence" stages, often begin to become interested in their own history. Such interest begins at first only very tentatively and is represented by a handful of individuals who work in the history of their discipline as a hobby or avocation in addition to their regular responsibilities. Later historical involvement becomes more professionalized. It appears that we have now reached the last-mentioned stage in the history of developmental psychology. Therefore, the centennial of the publication of *The Mind of the Child* (*Die Seele des Kindes*, 1882) by *William T. Preyer* (1841–1897) was a welcome opportunity for historians of science and psychology from many countries to present their research findings in the small East German university town of Jena where, in a manner of speaking, the "birth certificate of empirical child psychology" was officially recorded more than a century ago.

The initial preparations for the international William T. Preyer Symposium and the conference during the fall of 1982 revealed how much information existed about the beginnings of child and developmental psychology. At the same time it became apparent that there were a number of diverse beginnings of this important specialty of modern psychology. More importantly, these complexities in intellectual orientation were not restricted to the origins of developmental psychology, but continue to leave their imprint on the field today. Participants of the conference almost unanimously deplored the lack of a comprehensive history of the field and thus encouraged the present publication.

The papers in this volume are organized in chronological order under three broad headings. *Part I* focuses primarily on the beginnings and early formulations of developmental thinking which bear indirectly upon the establishment of modern empirical child psychology before Preyer. *Part II* concentrates on the life and academic career of Preyer and his impact on his contemporaries. Finally, *Part III* presents a number of contributions dealing with the influence of specific developmental theories and methodologies on various specialties of modern psychology. Attention is also directed to the work of contemporaries and successors of Preyer who continue to influence the course of developmental psychology today.

We cannot, of course, deal with all questions in the field in one volume. We are fully aware that historical linkages between developmental psychology and other related specialties, which have only been mentioned in passing, need to be explored more fully. These include comparative psychology, ethology, child psychiatry, psychoanalysis, history of education, and the history of anthropology.

We do believe, however, that this volume contains the first comprehensive presentation of the theoretical and empirical beginnings of developmental psychology during that period in which, to paraphrase Ebbinghaus, the "long past" of the field had ended and the "short history" of developmental psychology was about to begin. It is hoped that the labors of authors and editors may tempt at least some of our readers to join us in active engagement in historical scholarship in the field. We have found it deeply satisfying.

Lothar Sprung,
Humboldt-Universität

Wolfgang G. Bringmann
University of South Alabama

Georg Eckardt
Friedrich-Schiller-Universität

Part I
The Origins of Developmental Psychology

The Evolution of the Concept of Development in the History of Psychology

by Michael Wertheimer

In his 1880 introductory notes to Shakespeare's *As You Like It*, the celebrated critic Henry Norman Hudson comments (pp. xiv–xv; see also Boyd's magnificent 1980 volume) that the division of human life into stages or epochs, as made by Jaques in his famous speech, also occurs in Greek, Latin, and later Hebrew literature. The Greek, Solon, divided human life into ten ages of seven years each, Proclus distributed it into seven ages, each of which was ruled by one of the planets, and Hippocrates too used seven ages, but with a different number of years allotted to each period. The "Oral Law" of the Jews, in the third century, specified fourteen ages, but the *Midrash*, the Hebrew exposition of the sixth to twelfth centuries, divided life into seven periods again. Hudson notes that Jaques' speech presents a somewhat tarnished version of what for more than a thousand years had been popular lore about the development of the individual. Jaques' jaundiced account, you will recall, goes like this (*As You Like It*, II, vii, 139–165):

> All the world's a stage,
> And all the men and women merely players:
> They have their exits and their entrances;
> And one man in his time plays many parts,
> His acts being seven ages. At first the infant,
> Mewling and puking in the nurse's arms.
> Then the whining schoolboy, with his satchel
> And shining morning face, creeping like snail
> Unwillingly to school. And then the lover,
> Sighing like furnace, with a woeful ballad
> Made to his mistress' eyebrow. Then a soldier,
> Full of strange oaths, and bearded like the pard,
> Jealous in honour, sudden and quick in quarrel,
> Seeking the bubble reputation
> Even in the cannon's mouth. And then the justice,
> In fair round belly with good capon lin'd,
> With eyes severe and beard of formal cut,
> Full of wise saws and modern instances;
> And so he plays his part. The sixth age shifts
> Into the lean and slipper'd pantaloon,
> With spectacles on nose and pouch on side,

14 Wertheimer

> His youthful hose, well sav'd, a world too wide
> For his shrunk shank; and his big manly voice,
> Turning again toward childish treble, pipes
> And whistles in his sound. Last scene of all,
> That ends this strange eventful history,
> Is second childishness and mere oblivion,
> Sans teeth, sans eyes, sans taste, sans everything.

Is the idea of the evolution of each individual member of the human race, then, an ancient one? Yes, of course it is, for our ancestors were neither blind nor stupid. They could see what happens to people with the passage of time. But their conception of development was, paradoxically, quite static—static in a way that the etymology of the word "development," or of "evolution" (Singer 1959: 550–553) or of the French, German, or Spanish counterparts, *développement, Entwicklung,* and *desarrollo,* exemplify. For "development" means, in effect, "unfolding" or "unwrapping;" when the wrappings are removed, what is revealed had been there all along. It is not that something new and different is generated, as more recent conceptions of "evolution" or "development" imply, but that what had been there from the beginning finally becomes manifest.

Such a static conception of the individual is fully consistent with the static conception of history, indeed of the entire world, that dominated Western thought for several millennia. As the distinguished Cambridge historian, Butterfield, points out (1957: 187) when he was describing what was taken for granted in the early seventeenth century, "For two thousand years the general appearance of the world and the activities of men had varied astonishingly little—the sky-line for ever the same—so much so that men were not conscious of either progress or process in history... . Their view of history had been essentially static because the world had been static so far as they could see—life in successive generations played out by human beings on a stage that remained essentially the same." And this sameness applied, of course, not only to social institutions, cities, and rulers, but also to the geographic setting, to the Church, to the heavens (both theological and astronomical), and to the inhabitants of earth: the many plants and animals had continued as fixed and immutable species since the dawn of creation.

This is, of course, a very different conception of development from the one that has dominated Western thought for more than the last century, described by Viktor Hamburger (1967: 49) as "a more or less continuous process which usually involves progressive changes from a more simple to a more complex structure or organizational pattern." Putting it negatively, J.P. Scott (1957: 59) asserts that "It is now generally agreed that the concept of development in its original sense of a process of unfolding or unwrapping is too simple to fit the observed facts."

What happened between Shakespeare's day and our own (or William Preyer's) to change the idea of development from a static to a dynamic one? Among the major intellectual events, of course, was the emergence of the idea of organic evolution, brewing during the first half of the nineteenth century, and culminating in Darwin's synthesis of Lamarckian theory with Malthus' analysis of population dynamics, and the idea of the survival of the fit. Not unrelated were the post-Renaissance expansion of empires, the advent of modern empirical science, and the Industrial Revolution, all of which contributed to the gradual realization that the future need not replicate the past, that change characterizes the world better than permanence does, indeed that there may be such a phenomenon as progress.

These different views of development did not emerge for the first time during the nineteenth century. Pongratz (1967: 7–8) distinguishes three models of history. He identifies the first, the circular model (Kreismodell), with ancients like Heraclitus, Empedocles, Plato, Aristotle, and the Stoics, and quotes Ben Akiba as epitomizing the model with his phrases, Nichts Neues unter der Sonne, there's nothing new under the sun, and Alles ist schon einmal dagewesen, everything has already been here before. Goethe, too, believed that everything sensible had already been said before, and Nietzsche spoke of der ewigen Wiederkehr des Gleichen, the eternal return of the same. Pongratz suggests that the rotating heavens, with their unchanging constellations, are the prototype of this conception of history.

Pongratz's second model, which he somewhat inappropriately calls that of the semicircle (Halbkreismodell), has a biological origin; it emphasizes the transitory nature of everything living, which gradually unfolds, reaches its maturity, and then decays toward death. He identifies it with Oswald Spengler, who applied it to cultures and nations as well as to individuals. This is, of course, the same as the somewhat pessimistic view implicit in Jaques' characterization of the seven ages of man.

The third, the ascending spiral (Spiralenmodell), is a more optimistic model. Pongratz points out that St. Augustine contrasted this Christian theological conception with the cyclic, naturalistic view of the ancients; the history of the world is the history of salvation, determined by God's holy will and deeds: eventually faith will triumph over doubt, the *civitas dei* over the *civitas terrena aut diaboli.* During the Enlightenment, the idea of salvation was secularized into the idea of progress. Giovanni Battista Vico, Charles de Montesquieu, and Johann Gottfried Herder believed in a continuous evolution of humanity; they, like Gotthold E. Lessing, Wilhelm von Humboldt, and Friedrich von Schiller, were inspired by the goal of humanism. For Friedrich Hegel the ultimate goal of history was awareness of the Holy Spirit; for Auguste Comte it was mastery over the material world through natural science; for Karl Marx it was paradise on earth. Pongratz argues that the spiral model is necessary for anyone who believes in natural science: any science which makes no progress negates itself. Indeed, the optimism inherent in the ascending spiral idea reached an excessive degree of enthusiasm in late nineteenth-century neo-Darwinists like G. Stanley Hall, who waxed poetic about how the meachnism of Darwinian evolution necessarily assures the ever-increasing perfection of the human race in the future.

But this is getting ahead of our story. Let us return to the Golden Age of Greece, then trace in somewhat greater detail the evolution of the concept of development from Aristotle and his contemporaries through the early Christian and medieval eras to the Renaissance and beyond, ending with the late nineteenth century, when the distinguished Jena physiologist, William Thierry Preyer, published his painstaking observations of his son's first three years, *Die Seele des Kindes.*

The pre-Socratic Greek natural philosophers were concerned with "coming into being" and "passing away," with change, generation, corruption, life, and death (Hall and Hall 1964: 20), in other words, with Pongratz's "semicircular model." Anaximander conjectured that human beings must have evolved in a retrogressive sense: since human babies are so fragile and require such prolonged nursing, their original, primeval form must have been sturdier and must have been independent earlier, like animal infants (Leahey 1980: 34–35). A major debate concerned the polarity between "being" and "becoming:" Parmenides maintained that beyond the flux of the changing world there are eternal truths and values that exist apart from humanity in a "realm of pure Being;" they exist changelessly apart from the changing physical world. Heraclitus, by contrast, denied that such truths, or such a realm of pure being, exist: things never simply are, they are always becoming something else (Leahey 1980: 35). The "being" approach was, of course, elaborated by Plato, and the "becoming" view by Aristotle.

But Aristotle's conception of "becoming" had very little in common with late nineteenth-century ideas of evolution, or even with Anaximander's. True, Aristotle was impressed with the continuity between man and other forms of life, and recognized man as an advanced product of a developmental process, but his teleological view of evolution was that the process begins with hypothetical formless matter, which moves upward in progressive stages in the direction of "pure form," with rationality at the apex; if we are to understand man and animal, or even any human or animal structures like arms or eyes, we must discover the inherent purpose of that structure, the part it plays in the total plan (MacLeod 1975: 68–69). Everything strives to actualize its potential, its inherent purpose. The growth of life-forms within the great hierarchy of existence is a process by which the forms strive to realize their fullest potentiality; the development of every organic existence is deeply influenced by the teleological end toward which it is self-actualizing (Grinder 1967: 14–15). Two essential ideas of late nineteenth-century evolutionary doctrine are totally alien to Aristotle's hierarchical organization of the world into successively higher levels of form and matter: that species are not fixed, but mutable, and that more complex structures are later than, and develop from, simpler structures (Watson 1968: 54).

According to Robert I. Watson (1965: 4–5), for more than a thousand years, a static conception of the world was taken for granted, including the view of childhood and child development. The child was seen as a future citizen and as a member of a family group. The child was essentially a miniature adult. Children wore small versions of adult clothing, and adult manners and customs were forced upon children even while they were still toddlers. Education was regarded as an indoctrination into the ways of adult life and a means of getting the child to act like an adult as quickly as possible. Indeed, early biologists believed that in mating the male transmits to the female a completely formed but minute adult human being; this homunculus grows in strength, size, and intelligence, and adults differ only quantitatively, not qualitatively, from babies. The Christian era added a new moralistic dimension: as a result of Adam's fall, all humanity is born in sin. This view of the child as innately depraved held sway for many centuries, and justified the attitude, "Spare the rod and spoil the child," and the exploitative, neglectful, and downright abusive treatment of children that persisted for so many centuries and that looks so cruel and inhumane, from today's perspective (de Mause 1974).

Philippe Aries (1962), in a controversial work, argues (p. 10) that in the tenth century, artists were unable to depict a child except as a man on a smaller scale; until about the twelfth century (p.33), medieval art did not know childhood or did not attempt to portray it. "It is hard to believe that this neglect was due to incompetence or incapacity; it seems more probable that there was no place for childhood in the medieval world" (p.33). He suggests (p.47) that "the discovery of childhood began in the thirteenth century, and its progress can be traced in the history of art in the fifteenth and sixteenth centuries. But the evidence of its development became more plentiful and significant from the end of the sixteenth century and throughout the seventeenth." Aries's conclusion (p.128) is unequivocal: "In medieval society the idea of childhood did not exist," in the sense of "an awareness of the particular nature of childhood, that particular nature which distinguishes the child from the adult, even the young adult." Elizabeth Marvick (1974: 291) emphasizes that this lack of recognition of the separateness of childhood may have served a useful psychological protective function during an age when rates of infant and child mortality were so high that the parents "had no better than an even chance of preserving" their offspring.

Authors as varied as de Mause (1974: 5–6) and Kroll (1977) have argued that Aries' thesis is on shaky ground, indeed unreliable, since there are many instances of realistic medieval paintings of children, and since legal documents, medical writings, and church and monastic chronicles support the view that children were indeed perceived as special: fragile, vulnerable, and naive, while also possessing a potential for closeness to God and the supernatural world. But other writers concur in the relative neglect or denigration of the concept of childhood until about the late Renaissance. Thus, J. Tucker (1974: 229) flatly asserts that, "The medieval idea that children were not terribly important persisted into the fifteenth and sixteenth centuries," and (p.252) by early in the seventeenth century, "'a new consciousness of childhood' was beginning." Van den Berg (1961: 23) claims that Jean-Jacques Rousseau "was the first to view the child as a child, and to stop treating the child as an adult." Aries himself (1962: 129) suggests that by about 1700 "a new concept of childhood had appeared, in which the child, on account of his sweetness, simplicity and drollery, became a source of amusement and relaxation for the adult." And it was at about this time, too, that ideas of progress were beginning to make inroads in areas other than child rearing.

Early during the Renaissance, Machiavelli (Butterfield 1957: 211) could still see human beings as "acting throughout the centuries on the unchanging stage of the earth—the whole of nature providing a permanent scene upon which the human drama is superimposed. The human beings themselves are always alike, always made out of the same lump of dough; or, rather, we might say, they are varying mixtures of the constant ingredients of passion, affection, and desire. The texture of historical narrative, therefore, would be fundamentally the same whatever the period under consideration, and to any person taking a bird's-eye view, the total appearance of the world would be very similar in all ages. One city or state might be found to be flourishing in one century and different ones at other periods, but the world in general would present the same picture–indeed, Machiavelli, for his part, explicitly tells us that he inclines to the view that the total amount of virtue in the world is always the same." With this view of the universe, Butterfield declares (1957: 212), "time and the course of history were not considered to be actually generative of anything. On this view also, one had no conception of a world opening out to ever grander things, to an expanding future—there was not even an idea of a civilisation that was supposed to develop indefinitely. Men assumed rather the existence of a closed culture, assumed that there were limits to human achievement, the horizon reaching only to the design of recapturing the wisdom of antiquity, as though one could do no more than hope to be as wise as the Greeks or as politic as the Romans."

Butterfield continues (1957: 218), "The transition to the idea of progress was not one that could be completed in a single simple stage, ... and at the close of the seventeenth century we can neither say that the idea had been fully developed nor feel that its implications had become generalised ... Fontenelle, though he was conscious of the widening vistas which the future promised to the natural sciences, was too well aware of the limitations of human nature to share the illusions of many of the *philosophes* concerning the general improvement of the world." By late in the seventeenth century, though (p.218), "the idea is asserting itself that a general improvement is taking place in conditions, and particularly in the things that concern the welfare of ordinary human beings.... Writers were able to address themselves to this idea of a general progress in human conditions as though it were a matter generally understood."

By the eighteenth century (Butterfield 1957: 219–220), "the attempt to embrace the whole course of things in time and to relate the successive epochs to one another—the transition to the view that time is actually aiming at something, that temporal succession has meaning and that the passage of ages is generative—was greatly influenced by the fact that the survey became wider than that of human history, and the mind gradually came to see geology, prehistory and history in due succession to one another. The new science and the new history joined hands and each acquired a new power as a result of their mutual reinforcement. The idea of progress itself gained additional implications when there gradually emerged a wider idea of evolution. . . . The history of the idea of evolution is connected with the development of systems of classification in the realm of plants and animals," starting perhaps "with the work of *John Ray* in the closing years of the seventeenth century," who elaborated on the notion of species and supported "the traditional view which regarded the various species as having been absolutely fixed since the day when God rested from the work of Creation." The same view was adopted by Linnaeus, whose classifications "in the 1730s gave him a remarkable reputation that lasted down to the time of *Darwin*. He assumed that all individuals in a given species could be traced back to an original pair produced at the Creation, and . . . he gave the weight of his great authority to the idea of the immutability of species." Before Linnaeus, the German philosopher Leibnitz "had emphasized the continuity of creation and the unbroken gradation of organisms in nature" (p.220); indeed the eighteenth century brougth (p.221) "to a climax in scientific thought, in philosophy, and in literature, the notion of 'the Great Chain of Being'—the idea of an infinitely graded series of creatures stretching down to inanimate nature and up to God Himself, with man standing somewhere near the middle." What was remarkable about "the course of the eighteenth century was the transformation of the 'Chain of Being' into historical terms, into a ladder by means of which the living world had come to its present state" (p.222). In the latter half of the eighteenth century Buffon's huge natural history contained views which hovered (p.224) between Biblical Creation and the ideas of evolution, showing "a remarkable sense for the continuous flow of things in time" (p.226). As for the evolution of the geologic structures on the surface of the earth, James Hutton, late in the eighteenth century, pointed to the igneous origin of rocks; he "preferred to interpret the past in the light of the known present and sought to account for the earth's present condition by references to processes still observable, forces still in operation and principles already familiar" (p.229). But the preformation theory—that the male or, by this time, more frequently the female, contained the germ of all later generations, not merely in germ but in the miniature form of adult individuals—was still widely held, including such eminent scientists as Charles Bonnet (pp.222–230). These developments culminated early in the nineteenth century with Jean Baptiste de Monet, alias Lamarck, whom Butterfield calls the founder of invertebrate, and Georges Leopold Cuvier, whom Butterfield calls the founder of vertebrate, paleontology (p.230). Both changed the chain of being into a tree-like structure, and it was but a small further step to Darwin's version of evolutionary theory. By early in the nineteenth century, "all the ingredients of Charles Darwin's theory had already been discovered save the idea of the struggle for existence. The work of Malthus and the economic writings of the industrial revolution were soon to supply what was needed here, and the development of geological study—the work of Lyell, for example—prepared the minds of men for the *Origin of Species* in 1859" (Butterfield 1957:233).

Butterfield has been quoted and paraphrased so extensively because his account of the fundamental changes in the history of science from the early days of the Renaissance to the middle of the nineteenth century is masterful. Other accounts, such as that of Kearney (1971) confirm the gradual evolution of the concept of evolution, pointing out, for example, that "Malthus, in stressing the continual pressure of population upon food supply, provided the key for Darwin's theory of natural selection" (p.22). Robinson (1974: 310–322) elaborates on the roots of the idea of progress in many Enlightenment figures, including Voltaire, Diderot, and Condorcet, and writes (p.311) that the latter "set to paper the idea that powered that entirety of the nineteenth century: the idea of progress." And there are many other similar responsible accounts.

But this revolution in the conception of the development of the species was distinct from changes in the conception of the development of the individual. As summarized above, various writers place the emergence of the concept of childhood as fundamentally different from miniature adulthood in the seventeenth or eighteenth century. What happened, between this time and the mid-nineteenth century, to the idea of childhood itself?

Van den Berg (1961: 72) points out that the word *Flegeljahre*, or awkward age, first appeared in a German dictionary in the year 1808, and had been used in the title of a book four years before that by Jean Paul Richter; but the historian John R.Gillis (1974) implies that the new stage, adolescence, emerged somewhat later: one of the chapters in his book *Youth and History* is entitled "Boys will be boys: Discovery of adolescence, 1870–1900." The fashion of describing the *Sturm and Drang* of the age after childhood but before full maturity, epitomized by Goethe's immensely successful novel about the sorrows of young Werther, already flourished in the latter half of the eighteenth century. So by the early nineteenth century, at least three qualitatively different developmental stages of human existence were clearly distinguished: childhood, adolescence, and adulthood.

Early in the nineteenth century, Karl Ernst von Baer helped establish the new field of embryology with extensive studies of mammalian ova, and hinted at the idea that the early development of the individual parallels to some extent the developmental stages of lower animals. This idea was to be picked up and combined with speculations of Fritz Müller by the distinguished Jena Darwinian biologist, Ernst Heinrich Haeckel, who formulated the "biogenetic law," popularized by Herbert Spencer, James Mark Baldwin, and G.Stanley Hall and others as "recapitulation theory:" ontogeny recapitulates phylogeny. This theory (which was to be repudiated by early writers in the present century), that the individual goes through stages in which it resembles all the major phyletic predecessors of its own species, constituted a complete fusion of the evolution of the species and the development of the individual. The approach was even extended to psychological and cultural development, with the expectation (Diamond 1974: 469) that the study of early child development should yield information about the development of the human mind from its "primitive" to its "civilized" form. As Kessen (1965: 115) puts it, "Species develop, societies develop, man develops." From the publication of *The Origin of Species* to the end of the nineteenth century, there was a riot of parallel-drawing between animal and child, between primitive man and child, between early human history and child. The developing human being was seen as a natural museum of human phylogeny and history; by careful observation of the infant and child, one could see the descent of man."

It was natural, therefore, that the late nineteenth century should witness the emergence of a spate of "baby biographies." Indeed, Wayne Dennis (1949) found more than forty detailed observational accounts of the early development of normal infants published before 1882, the year in which Preyer's book appeared. Diamond (1974: 470–471) quotes such observations even by St.Augustine, and many others deserve recognition as early astute recorders of child development: Tiedemann, Taine, Kussmaul, Darwin himself, and Bernard Perez, whose *The First Three Years of Childhood*, almost as long and thorough as Preyer's *The Mind of the Child*, and in several ways more scholarly, was published in France four years before Preyer's work. Preyer was aware of some of these works, and cites several himself, but dismisses Perez as too fanciful; since for Perez "'the glance' is associated with 'the magnetic effluvia of the will,'" Preyer believed he "must leave" this work "out of consideration" (Preyer 1909, vol.2: 260). While "scientific child psychology is commonly said to have begun with the publication of Preyer's *Die Seele des Kindes* (Dennis 1949: 224), then, many other possible "beginning dates" and "originators" could be defended. And Preyer's work did not receive universal acclaim. As Watson (1968: 272) points out, Wundt categorically rejected the beginning of a child psychology in Preyer's work, since the conditions of study were far too uncontrolled. Kessen (1965: 132) comments that while Preyer set a pattern for child study that persisted for a long time, he was not really original, and his book contained some surprising errors, such as that all children are born deaf; Kessen's ungenerous evaluation is (p.147) that "Preyer's reputation probably outruns his contribution to child psychology."

Whatever posterity decides about how William Preyer's contribution is to be judged, he at least was inadvertently responsible for the present gathering, and I am personally grateful to him for that. And he clearly has a place in the history of the concept of development, whose evolution, however, has taken a major turn since Preyer's time. In those days, the assumption was that evolution is inexorable, and that everything will continue to get better, if not bigger. Now we recognize the continuing inevitability of change, but not necessarily of progress. What comes later is the necessary consequence of what came before—but the population explosion, resource depletion, industrial pollution, decay of cities, and insane worldwide deployment of ever scarcer resources into incredibly destructive and sophisticated military devices do not bode well for the future of the human race. Let us hope that the human intellect has evolved sufficiently by now to solve these worldwide problems before they make the species extinct.

References

Aries, P. (1962) *Centuries of childhood: A social history of family life.* R. Baldick, translator. New York: Knopf.

Boyd, E. (1980) *Origins of the study of human growth.* Eugene: University of Oregon Health Sciences Center.

Butterfield, H. (1957) *The origins of modern science, 1300–1800.* New York: Macmillan.

de Mause, L. (1974) The evolution of childhood. In L. de Mause (ed.), *The history of childhood.* New York: Psychohistory Press.

Dennis, W. (1949) Historical beginnings of child psychology. *Psychological Bulletin,* 46: 224–235.

Diamond, S. (ed.) (1974) *The roots of psychology: A sourcebook in the history of ideas.* New York: Basic Books.

Gillis, J. R. (1974) *Youth and history: Tradition and change in European age relations 1770–present.* New York: Academic.

Grinder, R. E. (1967) *A history of genetic psychology: The first science of human development.* New York: Wiley.

Hall, A. R. and Hall, M. B. (1964) *A brief history of science.* New York: New American Library.

Hamburger, V. (1967) The concept of "development" in biology. In D. B. Harris (ed.), *The concept of development: An issue in the study of human behavior.* Minneapolis: University of Minnesota Press.

Hudson, H. N. (1880) Introduction and notes to *As You Like It.* New York: Ginn.

Kearney, H. (1971) *Science and change 1500–1700.* New York: McGraw-Hill.

Kessen, W. (1965) *The child.* New York: Wiley.

Kroll, J. (1977) The concept of childhood in the middle ages. *Journal of the History of the Behavioral Sciences,* 13: 384–393.

Leahey, T. H. (1980) *A history of psychology: Main currents in psychological thought.* Englewood Cliffs, N. J.: Prentice Hall.

MacLeod, R. B. (1975) *The persistent problems of psychology.* Pittsburgh: Duquesne University Press.

Marvick, E. W. (1974) Nature vs. nurture: Patterns and trends in seventeenth-century French child-rearing. In L. de Mause (ed.), *The history of childhood.* New York: Psychohistory Press.

Perez, B. (1892) *The first three years of childhood.* A. M. Christie, translator. London: Swan Sonnenschein.

Pongratz, L. H. (1967) *Problemgeschichte der Psychologie.* Berne: Francke.

Preyer, W. T. (1909, 1914) *The mind of the child.* 2 vols. H. W. Brown, translator. New York: Appleton.

Robinson, D. N. (1974) *An intellectual history of psychology.* New York: Macmillan.

Scott, J. P. (1957) The genetic and environmental differentiation of behavior. In D. B. Harris (ed.), *The concept of development: An issue in the study of human behavior.* Minneapolis: University of Minnesota Press.

Shakespeare, W. (1880) *As You Like It.* The New Hudson Shakespeare. New York: Ginn.

Singer, C. (1959) *A short history of scientific ideas to 1900.* London: Oxford University Press.

Tucker, J. (1974) The child as beginning and end: Fifteenth and sixteenth century

English childhood. In L. de Mause (ed.), *The history of childhood.* New York: Psychohistory Press.

Van den Berg, J.H. (1961) *The changing nature of man: Introduction to a historical psychology (Metabletica).* H.F. Croes, transl. New York: Norton.

Watson, R.I. (1968) *The great psychologists: From Aristotle to Freud.* 2nd ed. Philadelphia: Lippincott.

—(1965) *Psychology of the child.* 2d ed. New York: Wiley.

Pre-Evolutionary Conceptions of Imitation

by Eckart Scheerer

1. Introduction

One characteristic feature of late nineteenth-century evolutionary psychology is that it accorded the concept of imitation a central role in the explanation of the development and socialization of the human mind. This fact is so obvious that it has found a somewhat exaggerated reflection in the historiography of psychology. When reading the few available historical sketches of the imitation concept (Miller and Dollard 1941; Allport 1968) one gets the impression that imitation was "discovered" only during the period that was dominated by the theory of evolution. In the present essay, an attempt is made to correct this over-simplified picture by describing some pre-evolutionary uses of the imitation concept. For pragmatic reasons, a certain emphasis is given to the German-speaking tradition; however, no claim is made that the German tradition occupies a special place in the history of the imitation concept.

2. The philosophical background

Throughout European intellectual history up to the eighteenth century, the concept of imitation was used in a great variety of contexts, most of which ultimately go back to the classical period of Greek philosophy:

(a) *Cosmology.* In everyday Greek language, "mimesis" had roughly the same meaning as "imitation" and its equivalents in the modern European languages, that is, it referred to a process occuring between people. However, as a philosophical term it had a very broad meaning, encompassing any kind of similarity between two entities, provided that one of them is somehow subordinated to the other. This broad meaning is best exemplified in Plato's cosmology, where the visible world is conceived as an "imitation" of the world of ideas (e.g. Timaios 48e). The cosmological conception of imitation has a certain relevance for anthropology, inasmuch as the human body is formed in imitation of the universe (op.cit., 44d), and men are enabled to think in an orderly fashion by imitating the harmony and regularity of the cosmos (op.cit., 47c).

(b) *Theory of art.* Plato had already described th activity of the artist as imitation, but he did so in a derogatory fashion, stressing the derived nature of artistic representations as compared to the productions of artisans and the works of nature (*Republic* 597a–598d). As a positive principle, the theory that art imitates nature was formulated by Aristotle. The Aristotelian theory, which was destined to dominate esthetic theory up to the early eighteenth century, is based on the anthropological premisses that from childhood on, man has a penchant to imitate, that of all animals man is most inclined to imitate, and that he begins to acquire knowledge through imitation (*Poetics* 1448b). However, it should be noted that when Aristotle says that man derives great pleasure from imitations, he is referring to pictorial representations and dramatic performances.

(c) *Anthropology and education.* On the other hand, there can be little doubt that in classical antiquity the imitation of people and other living beings was considered as a natural characteristic of man which plays an important role in the acquisition of knowledge and skills. In the Pseudo-Aristotelian *Problemata Physica*, imitation is described as a property of the mind, while the body does not have the ability to imitate (*Prob. Phys.* XXIX 10, 951a). According to Democritos, man has learned many important things, such as weaving, building houses, and singing, from the animals through imitation (fragment A154). As a special case of imitation, language learning attracted the attention of philosophers and historians (cf. *Prob. Phys.* XI 27, 907a). An "imitation theory" of language acquisition clearly lies at the basis of Quintilian's (*Inst. Orat.* I 1, 4–5) injunction to employ wet nurses who speak correctly, because it is the nurse's words that a child will first imitate.

(d) *Ethics.* The imitation concept has a long theory in ethics, again going back to the pre-Socratic philosophers: "People ought either to be good or to imitate a good man;" "it is bad to imitate a bad man and not even to be willing to imitate a good man" (Democritos, fragments 39, 79). Here, imitation is considered to be neutral in an ethical sense, and it acquires a value dimension only according to the "examples" that are being imitated. To imitate good examples, of course, has always been a popular moral precept. In late antiquity, it is occasionally coupled with the admonition to avoid imitating the anonymous crowd and to turn inward instead (Seneca, *Epistles* I, 7–8).

(e) *Religion.* Due to the absolute incomparability of God, there was no place for an "imitation of God" in the Old Testament. The concept plays a certain role in pagan religious thinking, but there it was most probably a special case of the cosmological imitation theory (Michaelis 1942). It is only in early Christianity that "imitation" assumes a specific religious meaning, owing to the fact that the Apostle Paul at various places exhorts the believers to imitate Christ. While in these contexts "imitation" is best interpreted in the sense of "obedience" (Michaelis 1942), subsequently the doctrine of the Imitation of Christ acquired a rich variety of meanings which are scarcely comparable to any present-day meaning of "imitation." Nevertheless, it should be noted that during the Middle Ages "imitation" was most frequently used in a religious context.

Within the philosophical tradition, it is extremely difficult, up to the eighteenth century, to find any attempt to conduct a functional analysis of imitative behavior which would bear even a remote resemblance to the late nineteenth century, not to speak of the present-day, efforts in that direction. The only exception known to me are some observations in F.Bacon's *Sylva Sylvarum* (1627/1859: 423–425). Bacon wonders "how children, and some birds, learn to imitate speech." This achievement is a "thing strange in nature," because "the sounds of speech are very curious and exquisite." He notes that the imitation does not depend on observation of "the motion of the mouth of him that speaketh," because birds learn to imitate in darkness, and that no reward need be given in order to produce learning by imitation. Among all animals, only birds are able to imitate human speech; and this is not due to any "conformity" (i.e. anatomical peculiarity) of their speech organs, but rather to their attention to speech. In general, "labor and intention to imitate voices, doth conduce much to imitation." Compared to his astute observations, Bacon's explanatory efforts are somewhat obscure. With some hesitation, he considers "that there is some transmission of spirits; and that the spirit of the teacher put in motion, should work with the spirits of the learner a predisposition to offer to imitate."

3. The imitation concept in eighteenth-century German empirical psychology

3.1 *A changed perspective on imitation*

When Bacon states that "there is in man and certain creatures a predisposition to imitate," he simply echoes the views of Aristotle, and as far as the innateness of a "drive," "faculty" or "disposition" to imitate is concerned, the Aristotelian tradition was to remain unchallenged for another two centuries. In fact, among the eighteenth-century writers I have consulted, I did not find a single one who would have doubted the presence of a "natural" tendency to imitate. While in the eighteenth century some real changes in the conceptualization of imitation occurred, these changes cannot be subsumed under the simple label "From the imitation drive to imitation as learned behavior." Rather, they are tied to a changed perspective on the traditional (mainly Aristotelian) notions of imitation, which resulted in the introduction of certain distinctions within the imitation concept and ultimately in its transformation into a psychological concept. Certain highly debated philosophical issues tended to involve, partly owing to the classical tradition, the imitation concept, and in attempts to resolve them there arose the necessity for a more detailed consideration and even, to a certain extent, empirical investigation of imitative behaviors.

It is more convenient to sketch the anthropological re-evaluation of the classical imitation doctrine by its results rather than by its beginnings, and for this purpose we quote some statements by Immanuel Kant. For instance, in his *Critique of Esthetical Judgment* we read that "everybody will agree that genius is totally opposed to the spirit of imitation" (1793/1922: 183)—a statement which, however, is restricted by Kant to the genius in arts, while in the sciences the "greatest inventor" differs from the "toilsome imitators and apprentices" by degrees only.

The opposition between "genius" and "imitator," especially with reference to the arts, reflects the outcome of a protracted criticism of the imitation theory of artistic production (Ritter 1974). This criticism had begun in England, at the end of the seventeenth century, and received a forceful impetus in Germany during the second half of the eighteenth century, most notably through the *Sturm and Drang* movement. According to the traditional doctrine, art was not only imitation in the sense that it was supposed to be a quasipictorial representation of reality, but also in the sense that it could be learned by following classical examples. Against this concept of learning-by-imitation as an essential prerequisite of artistic production, the "new" esthetics put forward the idea that artistic genius is defined by originality, rather than by knowledge of traditionally transmitted rules. The opposition between "originality," "inventiveness" etc. and "mere imitation" was destined, in one form or the other, to play a great role in the nineteenth century, to such an extent that even today we find it difficult to believe that during most of our history a good artist was considered to be a good imitator.

Again, in Kant's *Anthropology* we read that "the imitator (in moral matters) is no character; for the latter consists precisely in the originality of one's way of thinking. A character draws from a source of his behavior which he himself has opened." Kant goes on to explain that a man of reason depends on principles which are valid for everyone, and then he uses the German pejorative term for "imitation" (*Nachäffen*, "aping") in order to denounce the crank *(Sonderling)* as somebody who imitates a man of character (1800/1922:185).

Statements of this type obviously represent the ethical equivalent of the esthetic contrast between genius and imitation; but the history of the imitation concept in ethics is more difficult to trace than in esthetics. At any rate, it seems safe to say that in both fields of philosophical inquiry, the imitation concept became subjectivized and thus psychologized during the eighteenth century. Just as in the theory of art imitation was transformed from the objective result of artistic production into a subjective impediment to true artistic genius, in ethics imitation was no longer evaluated according to its objects, but according to the mental processes underlying it. The first process-related distinction between "good" and "bad" imitation I was able to locate is found in Christian Wolff's *Philosophia Practica Universalis*. Wolff contrasts "reasonable" and "empirical" imitation. The former obtains when we inquire into the reasons for people's actions and imitate them only when we find that they conform to reason. The latter consists in neglecting the reasons for people's actions and in acting (or acting in some way) only because other people act (or act in some way). Reasonable imitation is laudable, empirical imitation is blind and dangerous (Wolff 1739, §208).

It is remarkable that we find the imitation concept in Wolff's ethical works only; I have not been able to locate it in his German or Latin writings on psychology. Nevertheless, in distinguishing between "reasonable" and "empirical" imitation, Wolff made several important steps towards the psychologization of imitation. First, he appeals to the motives and to the more or less complex mental organization underlying imitation, rather than to the (good or bad) examples that are imitated. Second, he insists that specific actions form the object of imitation, rather than the *habitus* (i.e. dispositions) from which these actions arise. Third, contrary to the everyday use of the term, but antedating an important development in the nineteenth century, he insists that "imitation" should include "self-imitation" (op.cit., §204). And finally, when speaking of "blind" imitation, he implies that imitation in itself, independent of the properties of the "example", may be rewarding.

3.2 *Imitation as a drive; its relation to sympathy*

In the German empirical psychology *(Erfahrungsseelenkunde)* of the late eighteenth century, imitation was acknowledged as a motivational process by assigning it to the appetitive faculty *(Begehrungsvermögen)* and postulating a drive to imitate. However, while everybody agreed that imitation was a drive, no consensus could be reached when it came to subordinate the imitation drive under one of the major human drives. The eclectic philosopher, J.G.H. Feder, attempts a compromise between the divergent opinions by counting imitation among the "drives of very mixed relations." He thinks that the motives to imitate must be "deeply rooted in the nature of man;" such motives are "involuntary stimulations arising from sympathy," "need to keep oneself busy," "inclination to please others" and "hope ... to obtain the same advantages that others have procured themselves" (Feder 1785: 428f.). The moral ambivalence of imitation is underscored by Feder when he describes imitation as one of "the most natural, most beneficial and most dangerous drives of man" (ibid.).

It is obvious that by and large Feder's inventory of motives to imitate expresses commonsense opinions and has no scientific value, even according to the standards of the psychology of his day. There is one exception to this, however: his inclusion of sympathy as an involuntary stimulus to imitation. As Feder himself acknowledges, it reflects the influence of the British moral philosophers, and specifically of Hutcheson and of Adam Smith, whose *Theory of Moral Sentiments* (first edition 1759) had been translated into German in 1770. So far as I have been able to ascertain, the concept of imitation does not play a very important role in Smith's thinking. However, in German writers after 1770, a connection between sympathy and imitation is frequently established. One peculiarity of the relevant dicussions in Germany is that some writers at least considered the possibility that sympathy was an effect of imitation, rather than the other way round. In at least two writers, I have found a line of argument starting with the received opinion that imitation derives from sympathy and ending with the conclusion that, after all, sympathy is a "fruit of our drive to imitate" (Weikard 1798, Vol.2: 116), or that our sympathies with other people arise from a certain kind of imitation (Tetens 1777: 677).

3.3 Imitation and the origin of language

Approximately at the same time at which the sympathy concept began to attract the attention of German psychologists, an even more powerful impulse to clarify the nature and effects of imitation was given by the controversy concerning the divine vs. human origin of language. In 1756, J.P. Süssmilch—a member of the Berlin Academy of Sciences—had defended the thesis that the orderliness, regularity, and complexity of language defied the possibility that it could have been "invented" by man himself. This thesis was controversial within the Academy itself, because its former president, Maupertuis, had sketched a theory of the origin of language which did not appeal to the necessity of divine intervention. Accordingly, in 1770, the Academy offered a prize for the best essay on the question whether man, left to his natural faculties, would be in a position to invent language, and by which means he would arive at such an invention (see Aarsleff 1974, for the debates antedating the setting of the topic by the Academy). The question posed by the Academy provoked or occasioned a numer of important essays (e.g. Tetens 1772/1971, Tiedemann 1772); best known among these is J.G. Herder's prize-winning essay *On the Origin of Language,* which answered the question in the affirmative. The whole controversy is interesting to us because all participants adhered to the position that the first speech sounds occurred on the basis of imitation, rather than as an expression of strong emotions, as was maintained by some French writers of the period (at least as they were understood by their German contemporaries).

In the earlier debates, a human origin of language had been rejected on the basis of the supposedly vicious circle that on the one hand language is the main instrument of reason, and on the other hand the "invention" of language presupposes reason. Herder cut through this vicious circle by deriving language not from reason, but from man's sensory life. Language is "invented" when man uses a certain sensory feature of an object to differentiate it from other objects and transforms it into an internal token *(Merkwort)* for the object. As Herder's example for this process is that the bleating of a sheep is taken as the sheep's name, one might expect him to wholeheartedly support an imitation theory of the genesis of words. In fact, however, Herder expresses a rather low opinion about the contribution of imitation to the origin of speech. At least the mechanical imitation ("aping") performed by animals is not conducive to language; what is needed is a reflective imitation *(besonnene Nachahmung)* which is peculiar to man, in that it depends on man's unique ability to freely select any feature of the environment for his own purposes and in the interest of perfecting the human species. In sum: "Invention through mere imitation, without a human mind, is nonsense" (Herder 1772/1980:81).

Several considerations may have contributed to Herder's critical statements about the imitation theory of the origin of language. He was strongly opposed to the faculty psychology of his time, and so we cannot expect him to acknowledge imitation as an inborn faculty of the mind. Moreover, he maintained a basically individualistic approach to the origins of language; man is transformed into a social animal because of the invention of language; he did not invent language because he was a social animal (and thus, one might add, was prone to imitation). And finally, Herder establishes the relation between listening and speaking at a very abstract level: because the objects of audition are connected with movement, they become expressible by speech. In various respects audition occupies a "middle position" among the senses, between vision on the one hand and "feeling" (i.e. touch) on the other hand. Again, the internal token marking the acquisition of language is a product of inner listening, rather than inner speech. Herder's statements about the privileged position of audition in the phylogenesis of language and reason are occasionally interpreted as an epochal breakthrough, as a highly original criticism of the preoccupation of the enlightenment philosophers with vision and touch; but it should be noted that in their curious naiveté they could have been taken, in part, from Aristotle's natural philosophy, not to speak of more contemporary forerunners (see Pross 1980, for the latter).

J.N. Tetens's essay *On the Origins of Language and Writing* (1772/ 1971) was more representative of the viewpoints prevalent in German empirical psychology of the time. As a cautious, empirically-minded thinker, Tetens contented himself with showing the possibility of a natural origin of language, without affirming the actual necessity of answering the question in the affirmative. Tetens draws up a list of the "natural faculties of the mind:" "somatic mechanical instincts," sensibility and irritability, "the feeling of one's own internal activity," the imitative faculty, and the "productive faculty" *(Dichtungsvermögen,* i.e. the ability to actively analyze ideas and to produce new combinations of them). Imitation "belongs to those faculties the effects of which we can note first." The exercise of the imitative faculty does not only depend on imagination, but presupposes the entire animal nature. Its preconditions are (1) a vivid idea of the movement that is to be imitated, (2) a mental state which is similar to the mental state in which the model is felt to be, and (3) the desire to be active in conformity to this mental state, i.e. to express it externally. Potential objects of imitation are not only men and animals, but also inanimate objects (op.cit., pp.34ff.).

Tetens describes the first beginnings of language in a way that bears some similarities to Herder's description. The basic ability required is the selective attention to some sensation; however, contrary to Herder, Tetens believes that the process first occurs with reference to internal sensations, like thirst and hunger, and serves communicative functions. The "material" of the first speech sounds is furnished by a variety of sources. First come the "natural sounds" emitted by man as part of his "mechanical instincts;" at this level imitation is not a necessary part of language acquisition. Imitation gets into the picture at the later stages: imitation of animal sounds and of inanimate objects. The latter are not only imitated with respect to the sounds emitted by them, but also by virtue of what today is called "phonetic symbolism:" certain qualities of objects are expressed by similar qualities of sounds. The idea goes back to Plato's *Kratylos*, an influence acknowledged by Tetens. The further development of language, as viewed by Tetens, is not relevant in the present context.

Why did language originate from the the production and imitation of sounds and thus evolve into a system of spoken signs which only secondarily is supplemented by a system of written signs? Tetens's answer to this question considerably differs from that given by Herder. In rough outline, it is already contained in his *Essay* of 1772, but it was formulated more comprehensively in 1777, when Tetens had become acquainted with Herder's essay. He rejects Herder's idea that audition occupies a "middle position" among the senses; instead, he draws attention to two "remarkable properties" of audition: (1) Among all sensations, auditory sensations can be most easily and completely reproduced in the absence of the object from which they have arisen; for instance, it would take a long time to produce a pictorial representation of an animal, while the auditory representation of the sounds emitted by an animal is done quickly and with high accuracy. (2) The sounds which we utter in order to express our emotions are unique in that they are heard by others in exactly the same form in which we themselves hear them. The first property explains why audition is "the sense most natural for language," the second accounts for the fact that "the way from heart to heart without exception is shortest through audition, provided that we want to arouse such sympathies which naturally erupt into sounds" (Tetens 1777: 678). Both properties are advantageous only if language is considered in its communicative function, and indeed Tetens was, in contrast to Herder, convinced that language ultimately had a social origin. Tetens also differs from Herder with respect to the general approach taken to the "Origin of Language" question. Herder stays more closely to the task of reconstructing the genesis of language in the history of mankind, including its natural history. In fact, he has often been considered as a forerunner of evolution theory. While he insists that man differs from the brutes not only quantitatively but qualitatively, he does so from a biological perspective, stressing the instinctive nature of animal behavior and man's freedom from instinctual constraints. Tetens, on the other hand, keeps man and animal both more separate from and more close to each other than Herder does. Man differs from the animals because he has reason and is a social creature; he is similar to the animals in that he shares with them such "faculties" like the "mechanical instincts," sensibility, and imitation. Indeed, for Tetens animal and human imitation differ from each other not *per se*, but by virtue of the fact that in man the "material" provided by imitation is subjected to further processing by his higher cognitive functions, such as the "productive faculty" and especially reason. He thus may be said to combine a nonevolutionary biologism with an idealistic insistence on the autonomous activity *(Selbsttätigkeit)* of the human mind—a perspective frequently found in German psychologists of the time and reflecting their intellectual indebtedness to the Leibniz-Wolff tradition. Perhaps as a consequence of this orientation, Tetens tends to transform the ("phylogenetic") "Origin of Language" problem into the ("ontogenetic") problem of the acquisition and use of language by individual human beings. Inasmuch as imitation is an important subprocess of language acquisition, it shares this change of perspective and turns into an empirical research problem in, anachronistically speaking, child psychology and general cognitive psychology.

"To the observer of the mind, the beginning and the development of child language is more noteworthy and important than all speculative investigations on the origin of language as such"—these words of a contemporary psychologist (Pockels 1785: 75) succinctly express the attitude which gave rise, between 1780 and 1790, to several attempts at gathering systematic observations on the development of language in children. Of these, only D. Tiedemann's *Observations on the Development of Menal Abilities in Children* (1787) are still known today, owing to their rediscovery in the late nineteenth century. In 1772, Tiedemann had already published an *Attempt at Explaining the Origin of Language*, where he propounds views similar to those held by Tetens, except that they are couched in the language of association psychology. His *Observations* are historically important because they provide the first reasonably accurate information on the chronology of the emergence of various imitative behaviors. In the process of language acquisition, imitation intervenes at two distinct periods: in the first months after birth in the form of babbling, and in the first half of the second year in the form of imitative speaking, which begins with the imitation of natural sounds and then proceeds to the imitation of single words. At least with respect to the acquisition of "word language," the imitation theory had gained universal acceptance; Pockels (1785) again expresses a commonly held opinion when he states: "If we take notice of how children by and by learn to express themselves through words, we find that their speech is nothing but the imitation of the speech of those who interact with them" (1785: 79f.). So-called "inventions" of words by children were interpreted as the result of imperfect imitation. There certainly was no place for any "creativity of child language"!

3.4 *The taxonomy and functional analysis of imitation*

One drawback of imitation theories in the eighteenth century empirical psychology was that they operated with a totally undifferentiated concept of imitation. While the concept generally was applied to the imitation of observable behavior, rather than of internal states or dispositions, little attention was given to a taxonomy and functional analysis of imitative behavior. Perhaps the only exception to this rule, for a long time to come, was J.N. Tetens. In his *Philosophical Essays on Human Nature and Its Development* (1777), he included a brief section on the faculty of imitation. Space limitations prevent a reasonably complete review of his somewhat complicated arguments; my presentation will therefore be restricted to some highlights.

For Tetens, imitation (*Nachahmung* in the strict sense of the word) is always voluntary; it requires actions that are patterned after the actions of others, and it is concerned with the **form** of an action, i.e. with the "way in which it is performed and with its effect as far as it depends on the way in which the action is performed." In copying we are concerned with the **matter** of an action; depending on whether the action itself or its material effect are of interest, Tetens uses two different terms (*Nachtun* and *Nachmachen*) which seem to have no equivalents in English. Finally, the category of copying also includes cases of involuntary imitation, such as yawning—the classical example given already in the Pseudo-Aristotelian *Problemata Physica* (VII 1; 886a).

Thus, Tetens orders imitative phenomena along two dimensions: form vs. matter, and process vs. product. It is remarkable that he did not apply, at least with respect to terminology, the process vs. product dimension to imitation in the proper sense, i.e. to the imitation of the "form" of actions. This may reflect his intuitive insight that actions have the same "form" only inasmuch as they are directed towards producing the same effect. However, there is no textual evidence on this. At any rate, Tetens certainly was the first psychologist to point out that the imitation of movements ought to be distinguished from the imitation of actions.

Historical priority belongs to him in another respect, too: He saw that the ability to "copy" somebody else's movements is by no means self-evident. He opens his discussion of imitative phenomena with the following sentences: "How is it that we can copy an action which somebody else performs before our eyes, even though we can see nothing of it except its outward appearance ...? We do not look into man's innermost [life], we do not feel his efforts, but only their external effects; how are we made fit to put ourselves in his position, to feel internally exactly like he does, and to direct our powers in the same direction as he does?" (1777: 665). Thus, because all movements result from the application of "internal powers" and can only be understood with reference to them, even the copying of movements necessarily operates at the level of internal representations ("ideas," in the language of the time)—a feat that is difficult to explain because we cannot know directly the internal representations underlying somebody else's overt behavior.

In tackling this problem Tetens discusses two main cases. In the first case, the movements of the model and its effects are simultaneously visible with one's own movements; for instance, when learning to paint under the supervision of a painter. Here, the products of one's own behavior can be compared to those of the teacher's behavior, and imitation proceeds in a way that today would be called "negative feedback:" "Whenever the externally visible side of his own action deviates from the visible external side of the model's [action], the imitator gives his power a direction to the opposite side" (op.cit., p.666). But how does copying occur in the second case, i.e. in the absence of visual control of one's own movement? Tetens briefly considers the possibility that the similarity of one's own movements to those of the model is registered by looking into a mirror; but he quickly dismisses it in favor of a "labelling" explanation: "The way of nature is shorter.... A child is crying. He is told that he is crying, his action is denoted by a word. The same child sees that somebody else is crying, and again he is told that this person is crying. This is sufficient. The similar word teaches him the similarity of the actions...." The auditory "idea" of the word is merged with the visual "idea" of the seen movement. As a result, an image of one's own action is formed, and imitation can occur, because "copying requires an idea of that which is to be copied." The actual instigation of an imitative act is explained by a principle akin to the later "law of ideomotor action:" "The image of an act is already the genuine beginning of the act from within" (op.cit., pp.671f.).

A final point that interests Tetens is the question of to what extent the perceived action of a model can produce an action that the imitator himself never has performed before. The elicitation of a "new" act by imitation is a special case in that the very fact that the act has never been performed before means that the imitator does not have an "idea" or image of it. For this special case, Tetens acknowledges that a "direct" physical influence of the model on the imitator can occur; it consists in an effect of "sympathy" where certain general movement patterns of the environment provoke similar movement patterns in the nervous system of the imitator. However, such cases are rare, and sympathy more typically works at an ideational level; it then actualizes actions that have been performed in the past. Such ideational effects fall under two cases. In one of them, the components of an action which is to be imitated are known already; they are then combined, via an "assimilatory connection" (verähnlichende Verbindung), into a new pattern, according to the pattern of the model's action that works as a "standard" (Ideal) for coordinating the initially undirected component acts of the imitator. The case of learning painting by copying belongs to that category. In another case, the action to be imitated is already in the imitator's repertoire in the form of a skill (Fertigkeit), which means that an idea of it is available to the imitator. Here, the action of the model only provides an occasion for reawakening the idea of one's own action, which then is executed by virtue of the movement-producing forces of ideas.

If considered with respect to the relation between the actions of the model and the internal representation of the imitator's actions, then, imitation may be divided in three cases: It is based on a similar sensation ("physical" effect of sympathy), on a "fiction" that is formed under the influence of an external standard, or on the reproduction of a similar "idea" (1777:677).

4. The "imitation drive" in nineteenth-century pre-evolutionary psychology
4.1 *The received opinion, as found in textbooks*

When turning to the first half of the nineteenth century, we find nothing comparable to the vivid interest displayed in imitation by the psychologists of the enlightenment period, not to speak of subtle analyses like that performed by Tetens. Despite Herbart's and later Lotze's attacks on the "faculty psychology," the typical textbooks of the period are still organized around the principle that the mind has two or three main faculties (cognitive, appetitive, and/or emotional) which are subdivided into a higher and a lower level (e.g. reason or understanding and sensation within the cognitive faculty) and operate, within each level, through specific "powers."

In a textbook representative of this approach, we find that the imitation drive is subsumed under the "drive for mental nourishment, activity and occupation" which in turn belongs to the "reasonable drive for perfection" (Scheidler 1883: 469). Despite its basically reasonable nature, the imitation drive may become perverted, and then it appears as the "obsession to imitate" (op.cit., 483). Twenty years later, another textbook writer still assigns the imitation drive to the appetitive faculty, but he treats it as a subdivision of "sociability" *(Geselligkeitstrieb)* which belongs to the lower, instinctual level of the appetitive faculty: "The blindness and merely instinctive nature of the imitation drive explains why precisely the most nonsensical and ridiculous actions are imitated most frequently" (Esser 1854: 563). Only a more extended study of the average textbook of the time could show whether these different sortings and evaluations of the imitation drive reflect a change in the received opinions, or merely an idiosyncrasy of some particular textbook writer.

The usual psychology textbook of the time makes only passing reference to the development of mental faculties; but this does not mean that child psychology was not cultivated. Relevant information can be found, as one might expect, in treatises on education, but also (more unexpectedly) in textbooks of physiology or "physical anthropology." They usually contained lengthy sections on development across the life-span, organized along the lines of the old theory of "life ages" *(Lebensalter)* and covering not only physical, but also mental development. In the few educational (Schwarz 1829) and medical (Gruithuisen 1810, Burdach 1830) treatises I have been able to consult, I find that nobody challenges the "imitation drive." When actual observations on imitative behaviors are quoted, as Burdach does, they are taken from Tiedemann. In general, imitation is considered to be most prevalent in early childhood; language acquisition is still the context in which most allusions to imitation occur.

In a sense, the widespread acceptance of the imitation drive is remarkable, because it found its place in authors of very divergent theoretical outlooks. For instance, the educators and physicians just mentioned were influenced by the *Naturphilosophie* movement, and looked with disdain at the old empirical psychology of the preceding century. Just to document the ubiquity of the imitation drive, it should be noted that imitation was included in the phrenological list of mental faculties; in fact, it belonged to the original list of faculties drawn up by Gall before he left for France (cf. Bischoff 1805, Ackermann 1806).

Despite this terminological uniformity, it would be erroneous to assume that everybody meant the same when speaking of an "imitation drive." In fact, under the verbal umbrella of the imitation drive the two major alternative interpretations of imitation were already formulated that have preoccupied earlier historians of the imitation concept (Miller and Dollard 1941: 289–326): the learning theory and the instinct theory. That both theories could be lodged under the same term is due to the fact that, at least in the older philosophical usage, the German word *Trieb* is neutral with respect to the innate vs. acquired dimension and refers to a consciously felt urge arising from the actualization of some firmly established mental disposition.

4.2 First steps towards a stimulus-response analysis of imitation

Miller and Dollard (1941:305) credit A. Bain with being "one of the first to have taken a decisive stand against the instinctive theory of imitation." They then criticize him for having held "a simple associationist theory based on repetition." Their assessment of Bain's role in the history of the imitation concept is inaccurate in more than one respect. First, they consider Bain's *The Senses and the Intellect* (1855) only, where he indeed based his views on imitation on repetition only; but in *The Emotions and the Will* (third edition 1888) he basically resorts to the reinforcement principle which Miller and Dollard miss in his account of imitation. Second, Bain certainly was not the first to reject the instinct theory of imitation. In a sense, Miller and Dollard acknowledge this by saying that he was "one of the first" to do so, but they do not inform us who the others were. The present section is intended to supply, with respect to German psychology, the information not given by them.

That association takes part in the acquisition of imitative acts had already been a common assumption of the empirical psychologists of the eighteenth century. For instance, Tetens' "assimilatory connection" was conceived as an effect of the "imaginative faculty" *(Einbildungsvermögen)* which at the time usually was considered to be the locus of the association of ideas. The general approach was that imagination, through the association of ideas, supplies our mental powers with the material needed for their "formation" *(Ausbildung)*. This approach can still be found in J.F. Fries, the philosopher who wanted to reform Kant's critique of reason on an anthropological basis. In many ways, he still reflected the spirit of the *Erfahrungsseelenkunde*. To him, the imitation drive is "the first educator of the human mind under the reign of habit;" in imitation, "the associations guide our voluntary activity" (Fries 1837:223).

The first German psychologist I have found who explicitly rejected the notion of an innate imitation drive is F.E. Beneke. At first sight, this may seem strange, because Beneke was strongly influenced by the common-sense philosophers of Scotland (who counted imitation as one of the faculties of the mind; see Brooks 1976), and in his arguments with Herbart he defended the usefulness of the "mental faculties" approach. But Beneke pictured mental faculties not as fixed entities but as mere potentialities which for their gradual development needed to be "filled in" by external stimulation. One special case of the "'filling in" of a yet undeveloped mental faculty is that the faculty in question enters into cohesion with an already developed mental "formation" *(Gebilde)*. If such cohesion occurs with respect to the strongest of similar formations, imitation obtains; on empty minds, like those of children, what others present to them usually makes the strongest impression (Beneke 1833:128f.).

Beneke explains the acquisition of movements by imitation in the following way: "The child sees a certain movement or hears a certain sound. These visual or auditory ideas, or at least similar ones, have entered into connection with certain muscular activities, owing to previous co-existence or succession. What is more natural than that ... this mobile conscious power, a rich supply of which is given to them, should by transferred to the muscular activities?" (Beneke 1827: 629). A British association psychologist would have couched the same explanation in the terms "contiguity" and "similarity;" the substance of it would have remained the same.

Beneke acknowledges that certain innate connections between auditory ativities and the speech musculature might support the acquisition of speech by imitation; but in man, at least, such connections are very general and lack the specificity required to elicit definite articulations. In sum, "it is erroneous to call the imitation drive innate" (op. cit., p.630). Moreover, even the label "drive" may be too narrow, because imitation frequently occurs by "mere transfer of stimulation" (i.e. elicitation of muscular activity by stimulation) without implying any conscious "striving" *(Streben)* to imitate (op.cit., p.633 note). In Beneke's uncertainty as to whether or not the drive concept should be applied to cases of involuntary imitation, we notice a reluctance to part with the older way of thinking, according to which a drive should be guided by some conscious representation of its object. L. Noack, who in 1858 wrote a brief paper on the *"Imitation Drive and its Epidemic Perversion,"* no longer has any qualms about reducing the drive concept to a stimulus-response connection. According to Noack, every drive presupposes some sensory impression generating excitations that are capable of being transferred to the nervous fibers eliciting muscular movements. In order that the sensory-motor transfer of excitation does not remain a mere possibility, a peculiar tension is needed which originates either from external or internal sensations signalling a disturbance of the equilibrium of our somatic condition. Such a tension involves displeasure, and it leads to the activity called "drive." Without any attempt to justify the claim, Noack subsumes imitation under the drive category: "The imitation drive, then, may be called the result of a sympathy which transforms itself into movement or action" (Noack 1858: 50). Imitation is an "automatic and instinctive activity," which intrudes into all aspects of our somatic sensory life long before any conscious motives arise. Even in the adult, conscious motives only incidentally accompany or direct the imitative activity; more frequently, the latter determines man's actions at an unconscious level and against his will. Imitation is the guiding principle in the acquisition of abilities and skills. It is the "original bond of society," inasmuch as it provides a counterweight against activities tending to social isolation; but it also can produce mental epidemics, such as the "democratic illness of the year 1848," which as a "new mad form of the imitation drive" of late has attracted the attention of psychiatrists (op. cit., p. 52).

Although it is a piece of "popular science" writing rather than a serious psychological analysis, Noack's paper is significant in that it represents a merger of two distinct lines of thought in pre-evolutionary nineteenth century German psychology. One of them reveals itself in the reduction of drive to a sensory-motor connection. It reflects the physiologization of the type of "empirical psychology" propounded by Beneke, who already had proclaimed psychology to be a part of natural science. But there is also another strand in Noack's "theory" of the imitation drive which cannot be put into that quarter. It shows itself in Noack's allusion to "sympathy" and in the fact that he draws something like intellectual satisfaction from pointing out that imitation works at an unconscious level most of the time.

4.3 The primacy of unconscious imitation

As was noted above, "sympathy" and "imitation" had been brought very close to each other by at least some psychologists of the Enlightenment. But this close alliance had been severed by their intellectual successors in the nineteenth century. At best, a mere parallel was drawn between sympathy and imitation, such that sympathy was assigned to the emotional and imitation to the volitional department of the mind (e.g. Fries 1837). The idea that imitation is caused by sympathy was upheld, not by the epigones of the *Erfahrungsseelenkunde*, but by at least one representative of the Romantic Movement in psychology.

In his *Lectures on Psychology*, C.G. Carus described imitation as one "branch" of sympathy, the other branch being love. Because sympathy is an "attraction produced by an essential inner conformity along with a certain outward dissimilarity" (Carus 1831/1931: 377), one expects Carus to insist that inner dispositions are imitated rather than external behavior; and while he takes this for granted, he really is not interested in the issue at all. The framework in which he puts the imitation concept is brought out in the following (freely translated) quotation: "Perhaps we ought to mention another branch of sympathy. Though it takes an entirely different course than love, it grows from the same roots, and with its first sprouts it remains in the animal world. But in its higher developments it becomes the sole property of man, and on the top it produces one of the most beautiful blossoms of human social life: I refer to imitation and its development into art" (op.cit., p.412). Thus, Carus maintains an evolutionary approach to imitation, and the type of evolution he has in mind is exemplified by the metaphor of animal growth. His evolutionary orientation renders him receptive of Herder's ideas, and indeed he quotes Herder as an authority on imitation.

Carus discusses imitation on the background of his general "formula" of mental evolution: An initial state of unconsciousness first gives way to "consciousness of the world" *(Weltbewusstsein)* and then, in man only, to "self-consciousness" *(Selbstbewusstsein)*. At the level of world-consciousness (or at the unconscious level), imitation is involuntary, and then it is best called "copying" *(Nachmachen)*. In its proper sense, the term "imitation" should be restricted to the level of self-consciousness.

The distinction between two levels of imitation bears a certain resemblance to what Herder had said on the topic, especially because Carus, like Herder, reserves the higher form of imitation to man. But there are several point at which we can note disagreements between Carus and Herder. First, Carus criticizes Herder for applying the pejorative term "aping" to imitation by animals; for an animal, it is quite as natural to imitate at its own level of mental functioning as it is for man at the level of self-consciousness. Second, while Carus along with Herder sees a distinguishing mark of higher-level imitation in the conscious decision about whom, what, and when to imitate, he explains the ability to imitate reflectively not so much by man's particular type of world-knowledge (as Herder had done), but by his ability to measure external appearances against the internal standard of "mind looking into itself" (op.cit., p.413)—an idea he supports by appealing to the etymology of the German word *Nachahmung*, which according to Adelung contains a root meaning "to measure". Third, Carus emphasizes that the lower form of imitation, which is the only form of imitation existing in animals and young children, continues to be present throughout human life, and transforms itself, through imperceptible transitions, into self-conscious imitation. And finally, when Carus links artistic production to imitation, he may be said to go back to a pre-Herderian conception of art; on the other hand, he derives art from the joint effects of imitation and of creative imagination, and thus he may be said to have produced a synthesis of the imitation and of the genius theories of art.

Among Carus' views on imitation, the most noteworthy is his high opinion of nonreflective imitation. Though strictly speaking it is contingent on "world-consciousness," he occasionally calls it "unconscious." In general, a high opinion of unconscious imitation may be expected from a writer who held the principle that "the key to knowing the nature of conscious mental life lies in the region of the unconscious" (Carus 1851:1). But the way in which this general principle is applied to the imitation concept should nevertheless attract our attention. As a synonym for nonreflective imitation Carus employs the term "contagion." Although when he introduces it he wants to restrict it to what today would be called psychosomatic interactions, the cases of mental contagion he adduces include, for instance, the acquisition of language by children. Now, mental contagion, as exemplified by the traditional yawning example, has always been a piece of evidence for the existence of an imitation drive; but before Carus I have not encountered a single writer who would have drawn a direct link between "yawning by contagion" and the acquisition of language and other higher-level skills. It is true that Tetens had discussed the yawning example in the context of "copying." But his objective was exactly opposite to that of Carus: Tetens wanted to show that even in yawning a mental representation of one's own behavior must be formed before imitation can occur. Carus, on the other hand, does not feel obliged to find an explanation for the acquisition of skills by copying; he contents himself with a vague metaphor: The child is supposed to copy his mother like a piece of iron gets magnetized by being attracted by a magnet (Carus 1831/1931:451). In sum, when Carus states that imitation "advances our first development in the most natural and most beautiful manner" (op.cit., p.417), we must understand him to mean that imitation conforms to nature precisely because it basically is irrational.

5. The evolutionary approach to imitation: Some continuities with traditional notions

In one respect, the imitation concept underwent a profound change after the advent of evolution theory. Like any other mental function, imitation was now considered in terms of its adaptive value, and attempts were made to elucidate its place among the two chief factors of adaptation: instinct and intelligence. But there were also remarkable continuities with the pre-evolutionary conceptions of imitation. They will become evident when we briefly sketch the history of the imitation concept in evolutionary thought.

A **first** phase is characterized by inferences from human consciousness to animal behavior and by a predominantly Lamarckian approach to the inheritance of instinctive behavior. According to this line of thought, which is best exemplified by G.J. Romanes, imitation is a kind of lower intelligence. Like other forms of intelligence, it may "change or deflect an instinct" (Romanes 1884: 219). Even more: Imitation is involved in the formation of instincts, which are then transmitted to future generations by way of the inheritance of acquired traits. Romanes even believes that among the more intelligent animals the parents employ the "faculty" of imitation in order to "intentionally educate their young in the performance of quasi-instinctive actions" (op.cit., p.226).

Besides Darwin, the authority on imitation most frequently quoted by Romanes is W.Preyer. In fact, Preyer (1882) provided the first reliable observations on imitation in children. But contrary to a popular stereotype, he did not remain on a purely descriptive level. To him, imitative movements have a very deep theoretical significance, because they are always guided by some mental representation. When they first occur, they are always conscious, and thus their presence constitutes evidence that the cerebral hemispheres are functioning. Instinctive movements, on the other hand, are not mediated by the cerebral hemispheres. In a **second** phase, imitation is subsumed under the category "instinct." Among psychologists, the best known proponent of this approach was W.James (1890). It should be noted, though, that among biologists the instinct theory of imitation never reigned with absolute sovereignty. A case in point is C.Lloyd Morgan, who exhibited considerable oscillations in his treatment of imitation. In his earlier works, he still calls imitation "a lower form of intelligence" (Morgan 1891: 453ff.). Later on he considers the genetically earliest forms of imitation to be instinctive; more specifically, "biological imitation" is instinctive with respect to its effects, but not with respect to the animal's intentions (Morgan 1900: 190). But Morgan never reduced all forms of imitation to instinct. When the child displays the ability to profit from chance experience, he has reached the stage of "intelligent imitation", and as soon as he realizes that he is imitating somebody, he is said to exhibit "reflective imitation", and his imitative behavior now is based on a "schema of behaviour" (op.cit., pp.191f.).

The sociological counterpart of the biological instinct theory of imitation, in its most extreme form, is represented by G.Tarde and his *Lois de l'Imitation*. The spirit of Tarde's "theory" is best transmitted by his (in)-famous aphorism: *"La société, c'est l'imitation; et l'imitation, c'est une espèce de somnambulisme"* (Tarde 1896/1911: 95). For Tarde, imitation is the social expression of a universal tendency to repetition, which appears in inanimate nature in the form of oscillatory movement and in living matter in the form of heredity. At a psychological level, every action that has become habitual is a repetition of itself and therefore an imitation of itself. Social imitation develops on the basis of self-imitation, but arises as a consequence of involuntary suggestion. Tarde later extended his theory by assuming a tendency named "counter-imitation," but the latter functions in exactly the same mechanical and involuntary fashion as imitation. The real opposite of imitation is not counter-imitation but "invention"—an original achievement which is possible only because the inventor flees society and occupies himself with "bizarre problems devoid of any actuality" (op.cit., p.XIII). The polarity between invention and imitation concisely expresses the main tendency of Tarde's sociology, which is built on the contraposition of the "hero" and the passively responding "crowd."

In the **third** phase, the instinct theory of imitation fell victim, as it were, to the decline of Lamarckism and the advent of neo-Darwinism. Once the instinct concept was restricted to innate behaviors mediated by strictly fixed anatomical pathways (e.g. Ziegler 1920), it could not be applied to imitation, because the latter is characterized by the acquisition of "new" stimulus-response connections and cannot be realized by prewired anatomical pathways. As a result, many psychologists adopted a "hybrid" theory of imitation: The innate contribution to imitation was reduced to a mere disposition, while the actual execution of imitative behaviors was made contingent on learning. The chief candidate for an innate disposition underlying the acquisition of overt imitation was the principle of ideomotor action (cf. Groos 1923: 48f.).

A "hybrid" theory of imitation was also propounded by J.M. Baldwin. From a behaviorist perspective, Baldwin's reduction of imitation to circular responses is remarkable in that it "anticipates" both the classical conditioning and the instrumental conditioning "explanation" of imitation, and the fact that he still adhered to some innate dispositional basis of imitation appears as a deplorable concession to the *Zeitgeist*. In fact, Baldwin's principle of "organic selection" (which works through circular responses) was destined to remove an anomaly of the evolution theory of his time: its inability to explain the speed and directedness of adaptive changes in the absence of inherited acquired traits. But Baldwin's real significance in the history of the imitation concept lies somewhere else. With his concept of "persistent imitation," he opened the way to view imitation in the context of the internalization of behavior. In persistent imitation, the child compares the results of his efforts at imitation with the model that is imitated (Baldwin 1896/1898: 343). Persistent imitation is coupled with a feeling of effort which corresponds to the seen movement; it thus allows the child to segregate the inner from the outer with respect to his own body, and to emerge from his earlier "projective" stage into the "subjective" stage of development (op.cit., p.314), which later on is replaced, on the basis of the perceived similarity between one's own actions and their results with those of others, by the "ejective" stage where the inner-outer dualism is extended to all persons. In sum, for Baldwin imitation allows the child to form his own self on the basis of his social experience, and to use his self to gain a deeper understanding of his social experience (op.cit., p.317).

To what extent have the evolutionary conceptions of imitation been anticipated by the pre-evolutionary thinking on imitation? We can look for an answer to this question at two levels, either with respect to specific concepts, or with respect to the overall approach.

If we look at specific concepts, we make an experience that is all too familiar to every historian of psychology: Again and again, ideas are discovered anew, without the discoverer's knowledge (or acknowledgment) that they have been found before. For the area of imitation, there are three obvious examples. (1) The concept of self-imitation, so prevalent and characteristic, e.g. in Tarde's and Baldwin's theories, is already found in Christian Wolff. (2) In 1896, C.Lloyd Morgan recommends that a distinction should be made between the imitation of actions and the imitation of the results of an action (1896/1909: 190f.). Tetens had already hit on the same distinction. (3) The rough distinction between two forms of levels of imitation—the first unconscious, automatic, involuntary, the second conscious, goal-directed, intentional—must have been rediscovered several times. How many later imitation theorists were aware of the fact that originally the distinction had an ethical significance?

The distinction between "unconscious" and "conscious" imitation is a good starting point to discuss an overall continuity between pre-evolutionary and evolutionary conceptions of imitation. It seems that two distinct trends can be identified in the evolutionary theories of imitation; one of them—the older one—is connected with the names of Romanes and Preyer. Here, imitation is an act of elementary intelligence, it somehow mediates between instinctive behavior and higher forms of intelligence, it is based on internal representations. The other found its most extreme expression in Tarde, but it was quite widespread at the end of the last century. Imitation is involuntary, it is identical with suggestion or even "somnambulism," it reflects the operation of some universal "repetition principle." Compared to the customary principle of organizing the history of the imitation concept—"from the imitation drive to imitation as learned behavior"—the opposition between a "cognitive" and a "motivational/emotional" perspective on imitation provides a much more informative picture of the history of the concept. Taking the era dominated by evolution theory as a reference, it can be projected backward and forward. If we look back, we notice that the "cognitive" approach has its forerunners in Tetens, also in Herder, and it found some followers, such as Fries, in early nineteenth century; the "emotional" approach basically goes back to Adam Smith, and in Carus we find an anticipation of several principles of the Tarde-type imitation theory; "mental contagion" and "sympathy" are the historical keywords of the "emotional" approach. Looking forward from evolutionary psychology, we notice that the early behaviorists, despite their protestations against the drive-conception of imitation, preserve several important characteristics of the Tarde approach, most notably the involuntary nature of imitation and its dependence on (and assimilation to) mere repetition. The cognitive approach to imitation was rediscovered by Piaget. Attempts at a synthesis between the two lines of thought are extremely rare; an early example is Tetens, perhaps the only serious attempt has been made by Baldwin, in whose thinking the two variants of the evolutionary imitation concept coalesced; to Baldwin, the most primitive forms of imitation depend on suggestion, but in its higher forms imitation was very much the function assigned to it by Romanes or Preyer—it provides a link between instinct and intelligence.

The present review has a strictly descriptive and doxographic character; I have not been concerned with explaining the historical data except by pointing out some intellectual affiliations. Nevertheless, I should like to point out two potential areas of research suggested by the material that I have presented. The first is biographical. To what extent were the earlier conceptions of imitation known to the evolutionary imitation theorists? On the basis of their printed works, one gets the impression that none of them was aware of any attempt to classify and explain imitation before the advent of evolution theory. On the basis of biographical information we could perhaps find out whether or not such an idea like "imitation is an intermediary between instinct and intelligence" could have resulted from a cryptomnesia of the philosophical teachings received in the student days. Another point is meant as a challenge to social historians. One important difference between the pre-evolutionary and the evolutionary perspective on imitation is that only the latter, in some of its variants, lifted imitation to the status of a universal principle underlying the totality of man's social experience. A conception like that of Tarde may have some forerunners, but in its totality it has no equivalent in the history of the imitation concept. It is significant that in Tarde it is coupled with a hero/crowd antinomy. In the German tradition, there are several symptoms that the emotional, passivist concept of imitation received a strong impulse after 1848, the year of the abortive revolution. Could it be that the imitation concept was used to discredit the revolutionary movement as the expression of a mere "folly," as a case of irrational "mental contagion"? I think it is pretty obvious that the social meaning of Tarde's "laws of imitation" can be deciphered broadly along the line that mass movements were to be exposed to the contempt of the intellectual heroes. But what is the social meaning of Baldwin's synthesis between emotionalism and cognitivism? Answers to this and similar questions will eventually be found, but they will be considerably more complicated than in the case of Tarde.

References

Aarsleff, H. (1974) The tradition of Condillac: The problem of the origin of language in the 18th century and the debate in the Berlin Academy before Herder. In: D.Hymes (ed.): *Studies in the history of linguistics*, pp.93–156. Bloomington, London: Indiana University Press.

Ackermann, J.F. (1806) *Die Gall'sche Hirn-, Schedel- und Organenlehre vom Gesichtspunkte der Erfahrung aus beurtheilt und widerlegt.* Heidelberg: Mohr and Zimmermann 1806

Allport, G.W. (1968) The historical background of modern social psychology. In: G.Lindzey and E.Aronson (eds.): *The handbook of social psychology*, 2d ed., pp.1–80. Reading, Mass.: Addison-Wesley.

Bacon, F. (1859) Sylva Sylvarum: or a natural history (1627). In: J.Spedding, R.L. Ellis

52　Scheerer

and D.D. Heath (eds.): *The works of Francis Bacon*, Vol.2, pp.331–680. London: Longmans.

Bain, A. (1855) *The senses and the intellect.* London: Longmans.

—(1888) *The emotions and the will,* 3d ed. London: Longmans, Green.

Baldwin, J.M. (1898) Mental development in the child and in the race (1896). German translation: *Die Entwickelung des Geistes beim Kinde und bei der Rasse.* Berlin: Reuther and Reichard.

Beneke, F.E. (1827) *Über die Vermögen der Seele und deren allmälige Ausbildung* (Psychologische Skizzen, Bd.2). Göttingen: Vandenhoek and Ruprecht.

—(1833) *Lehrbuch der Psychologie.* Berlin, Bromberg: Mittler.

Bischoff, C.H.E. (1805) *Darstellung der Gallschen Gehirn- und Schädel-Lehre, nebst Bemerkungen über diese Lehre von C. W. Hufeland.* Berlin: Wittich.

Brooks, G.P. (1976) The faculty psychology of Thomas Reid. *Journal of the History of the Behavioral Sciences* 12: 65–77.

Burdach, K.F. (1830) *Die Physiologie als Erfahrungswissenschaft,* Vol.3. Leipzig: Voss.

Carus, C.G. (1931) *Vorlesungen über Psychologie* (1831); E.Michaelis (ed.), Erlenbach bei Zürich: Rotapfel.

—(1851) *Psyche,* 2d ed. Stuttgart: Scheitlin.

Esser, W. (1854) *Psychologie.* Münster: Cazin.

Feder, J.G.H. (1785) *Untersuchungen über den menschlichen Willen,* Pt.1. Linz: Trattner.

Fries, J.F. (1837) *Handbuch der Psychischen Anthropologie,* Vol.I, 2d ed. Jena: Cröker.

Groos, K. (1923) *Das Seelenleben des Kindes,* 6th ed. Berlin: Reuther and Reichard.

Gruithuisen, F.v.P. (1810) *Anthropologie.* München: Lentner.

Herder, J.G. (ca.1980) Abhandlung über den Ursprung der Sprache (1772). Quoted after: W.Pross (ed.): *J.G. Herder: Über den Ursprung der Sprache; Text, Materialien, Kommentar.* München: Hanser. no date.

James, W. (1890) *Principles of psychology,* Vol.2. New York: Macmillan.

Kant, I. (1799) *Kritik der Urteilskraft,* 3d ed. Riga: Hartknoch.

—(1922) Anthropologie, in pragmatischer Absicht (2d ed., 1800). In: E.Cassirer (ed.): *I.Kants Werke,* Vol.3. Berlin: Bruno Cassirer.

—(1922) *Kritik der ästhetischen Vernunft,* Berlin: Cassirer.

Michaelis, E. (1942) Mimeomai, mimetes, symmimetes. In: G.Kittel (ed.): *Theologisches Wörterbuch zum Neuen Testament,* Vol.4, pp.661–678. Stuttgart: Kohlhammer.

Miller, N.E. and Dollard, J. (1941) *Social learning and imitation,* New York, London: Yale University Press.

Morgan, C.L. (1891) *Animal life and intelligence,* 2d ed. London: Arnold.

—(1909) Habit and instinct (1896). German translation: *Instinkt und Gewohnheit.* Leipzig, Berlin: Teubner.

—(1900) *Animal behaviour.* London: Arnold.

Noack, L. (1858) Der Nachahmungstrieb und seine epidemische Ausartung. *Psyche: Zeitschrift für die Kenntniss des menschlichen Seelen- und Geisteslebens* 1: 49–52.

Pockels, C.F. (1785) Über den Anfang der Wortsprache in psychologischer Hinsicht (Fortsetzung). *Magazin zur Erfahrungsseelenkunde* 3: 75–88

Preyer, W. (1882) *Die Seele des Kindes.* Leipzig: Grieben.

Pross, W. (ca.1980) *J.G. Herder: Über den Ursprung der Sprache; Text; Materialien und Kommentar.* München: Hanser, no date.

Ritter, J. (1974) Genie (III). In: J.Ritter (ed.), *Historisches Wörterbuch der Philosophie,* Vol.2, cc. 285–309. Basel, Stuttgart: Schwabe.

Romanes, G.J. (1884) *Mental evolution in animals.* New York: Appleton.

Scheidler, C.H. (1833) *Handbuch der Psychologie*, Pt.1. Darmstadt: Leske.

Schwarz, F.H.C. (1829) *Erziehungslehre*, Vol.2, 2d ed. Leipzig: Göschen.

Tarde, G. (1911) *Les lois de l'Imitation* (1896). 6th ed. Paris: Alcan.

Tetens, J.N. (1971) Über den Ursprung der Sprachen und der Schrift. In: J.N. Tetens: *Sprachphilosophische Versuche*, pp.26–92. Hamburg: Meiner.

—(1777) *Philosophische Versuche über die menschliche Natur und ihre Entwickelung*, Vol.1. Leipzig: Weidmann and Reich.

Tiedemann, D. (1772) *Versuch einer Erklärung des Ursprungs der Sprache.* Riga: Hartknoch.

—(1787) Beobachtung über die Entwickelung der Seelenfähigkeiten bei Kindern. *Hessische Beiträge zur Gelehrsamkeit und Kunst* 2.

Weikard, M.A. (1798) *Der philosophische Arzt*, Vol.2, 2d ed. Frankfurt/M.: Andreä.

Wolff, C. (1739) *Philosphia practica universalis, methodo scientifica pertractata*, Vol.2. Frankfurt, Leipzig: Renger.

Ziegler, H. (1920) *Der Begriff des Instinktes einst und jetzt*, 3d ed. Jena: Fischer.

The Importance of Rousseau's Developmental Thinking for Child Psychology

by Paul Mitzenheim

In the introduction to his famous book, *Die Seele des Kindes* (The Mind of the Child, 1882), William Preyer characterized his new specialty of "physiological pedagogy" by the shorthand formula "First untame nature, then culture." He also added as an afterthought "The art of letting infants become (what they are) is much more difficult than training them prematurely." With such ideas Preyer gives us the key to understanding his work, which echoes the command of Rousseau to "love childhood..." (1979, vol. 2:79). Although the recent *Wörterbuch der Psychologie* (Clauss 1981) does not mention the name of Rousseau under the heading of "Developmental Psychology" (pp.159–161), we wish to draw attention to the genetic principles found in his educational philosophy. His psychological insights, derived from his extensive observations of child and adolescent development, were components of his educational theory which in turn was closely connected with his political ideas. It is well known that Rouseau both stimulated and disturbed his contemporaries in many ways. He accomplished this by his thesis that man was good by nature. He also cleared the way for psychology to take on the functions of an auxiliary science for education. Rousseau's accomplishments were possible because of the powerful impact of his original and courageous inquiries about the function of culture, the origin and role of property, the best forms of government, and the corresponding educational systems. They have a central place among the ideological and theoretical antecedents of the French Revolution.

The publication of his prize-winning essay, "Has the restoration of the sciences and arts tended to purify morals?" in 1750 brought Rousseau fame and enthusiastic admiration, as well as envy, disdain, material suffering and political persecution. According to Rousseau, his major writings (*Social Contract* 1762, *Emile* 1762) formed a "perfect whole." The main thread in these works was protest against the social structure of the feudal–absolutist state. Consequently, the primary concern of Rousseau's life became the struggle for the new "bourgeoisie" and its relationship to state and society. After reading the *Social*

Contract, Robespierre called Rousseau his teacher. Goethe characterized *Emile* as "nature's gospel of education" but Pestalozzi considered it "education's impractical handbook of dream interpretation." Voltaire was convinced that Rousseau was an insane "madman." Tolstoy, on the other hand, regarded Rousseau and the Gospels as the two "great beneficial influences" in his life and added that Rousseau never became outdated. Such evaluations are fully deserved as far as Rousseau's claim of adult responsibility for childhood is concerned. The same is true with regard to his firm conviction that educators must prepare themselves for their practical task by studying in depth the developmental stages and important characteristics of childhood. Rousseau's view of education differed most radically from traditional, feudal ways of child-rearing in his understanding of the child's individuality, which he based on his own systematic observations. In the letter-novel, *The New Heloise* (1761) and the educational utopia, *Emile* (1762), he showed us how children must be approached and how we can learn to understand age-specific characteristics by comparing the behavior of children with that of adults. In *Emile* we discover Rousseau's basic orientation towards childhood (1979:90):

> Nature wants children to be children before being men. If we want to pervert this order, we shall produce precocious fruit which will be immature and insipid and will not be long in rotting. We shall have young doctors and old children.

Rousseau made strong arguments in favor of letting children develop their natural talents freely. His views on this topic, expressed in *Emile* and *The New Heloise,* correspond to his philosophy of education. He saw man as good by nature and radically rejected feudal culture in all of its manifestations. Like other bourgeois ideologists of his time, Rousseau believed that the laws of society and those of nature were interconnected. Specifically, he viewed nature as the chief regulating force of social organization. For this reason his disciple, Emile, is to feel from early on the "hard yoke" which nature imposed upon man (1979, vol.2:90).

Rousseau demanded that teachers who want to study the "nature of children" must have high qualifications. For example, the understanding of the most complex mental processes of his students is an intrinsic part of the educator's art. Following the sensualistic epistemology of John Locke, Rousseau took the position that the child's abilities unfold in successive stages. First, the child must train his senses to gain an accurate and dependable view of his world. By these techniques Rousseau hoped to avoid premature intellectualization of the child (1979, vol.1: 73):

The greatest harm from the hurry one is in to make children talk before the proper age is not that the first speeches one makes to them and the first words they say have no meaning for them, but that they have another meaning than ours without being able to perceive it; so that, appearing to answer us quite exactly, they speak to us without understanding us and without our understanding them.

The core of Rousseau's model of education is contained in the "gardener" image used in the first volume of *Emile* (1979, vol. 1 : 83):

Plants are shaped by cultivation and men by education. Everything we do not have at our birth and which we need when we are grown up is given by education.

Rousseau called the ideas, which he discussed at length in *Emile,* the dreams of a visionary. In his *Confessions* (1951) he evaluated *Emile* as one of the most important books ever written, "as well as the most important and best of my writings." If we consider that Rousseau's education was that of an autodidact and that he did not raise his own five children but turned them over to a foundling home shortly after birth, it is remarkable that he devoted himself to an investigation of childhood and assigned major educational responsibilities to the father. He appears, however, clearly aware of his own shortcomings as a parent when he wrote (1979, vol. 1 : 49):

He who cannot fulfill the duties of a father has no right to become one. Neither poverty nor labors nor concern for public opinion exempts him from feeding his children and from raising them himself.

Rousseau demanded from the educator that he rely on the positive developmental tendencies in the child and fight against harmful influences. Even this frequently misunderstood call for a type of "negative" education was used by him to accentuate the unique value of childhood and the special laws of its development (1979, vol. 2 : 80):

Humanity has its place in the order of things; childhood has its in the order of human life. The man must be considered in the man, and the child in the child.

Rousseau was not yet able to fully accomplish this on the basis of exact empirical research methods due to the primitive developmental status of science and the general conditions of life. Instead he based his conclusions on the memories of his own childhood and on a series of projected methodically exact observations based upon the strong interest of the observer, as well as considerable impartiality, a sensitive heart, and sufficient leisure. Rousseau even wanted to have a special book written on the art of observing children because he was aware of the errors caused by the awareness of being observed.

Rousseau organized his educational ideas through his description of various developmental stages. Infancy consisted, for him, of the period from birth to the beginning of the second year. He defined childhood as the time from the second to the twelfth year of life. Adolescence comprised the years from twelve to fifteen, and young adulthood was counted by Rousseau as the years from fifteen to twenty-five, a traditional age of marriage. Modern psychology distinguishes different phases, periods, and stages of development than Rousseau did. However, his conviction that children are not "miniature editions" of adults and that they go through interrelated stages of development comprised an intuitive vision of human development which has provided much stimulation for the growth of psychology. Rousseau's descriptions of infancy and childhood included many finely-detailed descriptions of child behavior. Apart from some disagreements on specific points, his picture of the physical development of the infant is accurate. Rousseau also transmitted a wealth of pertinent information about the beginnings of intellectual development. Infants need the assistance of educators from birth because of their physical and mental weaknesses. This system of indirect guidance of the child's activity drive begins immediately after birth (1979, vol.1:62).

> I repeat: the education of man begins at his birth; before speaking, before understanding, he is already learning. Experience anticipates lessons.

The importance of Rousseau's method of "negative" education depends on the developmental level of the pupil and the educational intentions of the teacher. Rousseau believed that the child learns at about the same time to eat, to walk, and to speak, and he expressed these views in the following guidelines (1979, vol.1: 68):

> *First Maxim.* One must aid them and supplement what is lacking to them, whether in intelligence or strength, in all that is connected with physical needs.

> *Second Maxim.* One must, in the help one gives them, limit oneself solely to the really useful without granting anything to whim or to desire without reason; for whim, inasmuch as it does not come from nature, will not torment them if it has not been induced in them.

> *Third Maxim.* One must study their language and their signs with care in order that, at an age which they do not know how to dissimulate, one can distinguish in their desires what comes immediately from nature and what comes from opinion.

During infancy, nature is the teacher of the child and much effort is needed at this time to let children persist in their natural condition.

During childhood, however, the teacher discreetly becomes the advocate of nature and provides developmental assistance to help the child prepare for the next stage of development. Rousseau's critical comments about opportunities and limitations for achievement during childhood are noteworthy (1979, vol.2:78):

> Our didactic and pedantic craze is always to teach children what they would learn much better by themselves and to forget what we alone could teach them.

Rouseau protested the overemphasis on verbal teaching, which was gaining popularity during the eighteenth century. He stressed the need for the formation of useful ideas during childhood and warned against stuffing children's heads with meaningless words and concepts. To lose, rather than to gain time, as we would say, was the most important rule of childhood for him. Such paradoxical statements can frequently by found in his educational writings. By their dialectical nature, they tend to make the genetic perspectives in Rousseau's thinking more explicit (1979, vol.2: 92, 94):

> Do not give your pupil any kind of verbal lessons; ... Exercise his body, his organs, his strength, but keep his soul idle for as long as possible. Be afraid of all sentiments anterior to judgement which evaluates them.

In this respect Rousseau clearly differs from John Locke (1979, vol.2: 89–90):

> To reason with children was Locke's great maxim. It is the one in vogue today. Its success, however, does not appear such as to establish its reputation; and, as for me, I see nothing more stupid than these children who have been reasoned with so much. Of all the faculties of man, reason, which is, so to speak, only a composite of all the others, is the one which they want to use in order to develop the first faculties! The masterpiece of a good education is to make a reasonable man, and they claim they raise a child by reason! This is to begin with the end, to want to make the product the instrument. *If children understood reason, they would not need to be raised.* By speaking to them from an early age a language which they do not understand, one accustoms them to show off with words, to control all that is said to them, to believe themselves as wise as their masters, to become disputatious and rebellious; and everything that is thought to be gotten from them out of reasonable motives is never obtained than out of motives of covetousness or fear or vanity which are always perforce joined to the others.

Rousseau wanted to preserve the simplicity and spontaneity of childhood. The child who is in control of his senses is a happy child, one who gradually discovers himself and his environment. In this context, the educational importance of play was emphasized. The games of childhood help develop the abilities that give content and direction to the future life. The training of the limbs by regular, physical exercises also helps the child to strengthen his senses. The child is to be taught as early as possible to deal independently with difficult situations. Thus, the child learns to harmonize his abilities and wishes, as well as his desires and needs. Nothing is more inappropriate for children than to be condemned to passivity. Rousseau wanted to encourage the child to act autonomously during all stages of development, and he was convinced that children will remember permanently only what they have acquired on their own. From his knowledge of the child's nature, Rousseau concluded that both excessive severity and excessive leniency are to be avoided in child-rearing.

The joy of discovery and eagerness to learn are characteristics of the next developmental period which begins at the age of twelve. During this adolescent stage, the skillful educator encourages his pupils to acquire the methods of learning and not just the accumulation of subject matter. During this time of life the individual must also be prepared for work—the natural responsibility of man. Moderation and work were two natural healers of man for Rousseau: work stimulates his appetites and moderation guards against excess (1979, vol. 1: 62).

When one begins to look at expressions of developmental thinking in Rousseau's work, one discovers other psychological topics and problems which are still relevant to our quite different social conditions. These include, for example, Rousseau's recommendations for the training of the emotions and of willpower in young children, his astute analysis of early childhood learning, the important distinction between cognitive and character *(Herzensbildung)* education, and, last but not least, his stress on the role of emotions in the field of learning. Unfortunately, we do not have enough time to discuss these important topics in detail.

Our study of the developmental perspectives in Rousseau's work makes it very clear that his writings are major sources for the history of developmental psychology, and that his name must have a place in any competent history of modern psychology. Rousseau's vital importance for the establishment of child and developmental psychology becomes readily apparent when one traces the influence of his work. His impact had begun already during his lifetime and is especially notable in the publications of Pestalozzi, Fröbel, Herder, Herbart and other educational thinkers. Both the pedagogy of the Enlightenment and the educational reform movements at the beginning of the twentieth century based their programs on essential aspects of Rousseau's educational philosophy. His major importance for the new field of developmental psychology lies in the wealth of original ideas and suggestions he offers the modern reader. Rousseau's chief accomplishment was his recognition of the central place of the child in the educational process, which places him consequently among the forerunners of modern scientific psychology (Ahrbeck 1978, Hofmann 1976, Röhrs 1957). He was a pioneer in strong support of close cooperation between the fields of education and psychology. Rousseau's importance for our own time resides in his insistence that the physical and psychological processes in the child must be monitored continuously and his insightful reminder that (1979, vol. 2 : 120):

> The child usually reads his master's mind much better than the master reads the child's heart.

References

Ahrbeck, R. (1978) *Jean-Jacques Rousseau.* Leipzig.

Clauss, G. (1981) *Wörterbuch der Psychologie.* Leipzig. Bibliographisches Institut.

Hofmann, F. (1976) Erziehungsweisheit. *Paedagogia-Pädagogik.*

Rohrs, H. (1957) *Jean-Jacques Rousseau.* Heidelberg.

Rousseau, J.J. (1951) *Confessions.* (2vols.) London: Dent. (Original work published in 1782 and 1789).

—(1959). *The confessions of Jean-Jacques Rousseau.* (J.M. Cohen, Trans.) Baltimore, MD: Penguin Books.

—(1979) *Emile.* 2vols. (A.Bloom, Trans.) New York: Basic Books. (Original work published, 1762).

—(1761). *La nouvelle Heloise.* Paris: Hachette.

—(1947) *Social contract.* New York: Hafner. (Original work published in 1762).

The Origin of the Diary Method in Developmental Psychology

by Siegfried Jaeger

Philosophi etiam ad
incunabula accedunt
Cicero

The German education reformer Joachim Heinrich Campe (1746–1818) included in his famous 16-volume encyclopedia, *Allgemeine Revision des gesamten Schul- und Erziehungswesens* (General Revision of the Entire School and Education System, 1785) an invitation for the preparation of a diary by a trained psychological observer about the physical and mental development of a child from birth. Since diary records have remained important sources of developmental information well into our century—one only has to think of authors like Preyer, Shinn, Stern, Bühler, and Piaget—it may be interesting to pay some attention to the origin of this research tradition. Despite the meritorious work of von Fritsche (1910), Götz (1921), Schumann (1921), Bühler and Hetzer (1929), Dennis (1949, 1972), Höhn (1959), and Reinert (1976), there are still gaps in documenting the beginnings of this approach in the eighteenth century which our work will hopefully help to fill.

I

As one of the main representatives of the Philanthropists and the editor in chief of the *General Revision*, Campe tried to unite the "brightest heads among the applied educational philosophers of his time" into one organization which would subject the entire field of education to a critical review. One by-product of this endeavor was to be the publication of the most complete and detailed pedagogical handbook ever. The individual sections, which Campe submitted to members of the public for subscription, who were "enlightened" and "interested in the well-being of posterity," were to be written by different authors. However, each section was to be discussed and, if necessary, revised after approval by the team of contributors. Campe apparently hoped to find competent authors for the unassigned segments or topics of the project by awarding financial stipends to potential new contributors. The topics, which did not immediately find volunteer authors, included the preparation of the "baby" diary. Nevertheless, it is clear from the prospectus to the handbook that Campe regarded this assignment as important, although he was fully aware that it would not be an easy undertaking (1785a: xxiii f.):

> Among the proposed topics for the prize competition there is one, in particular, which I would like to support myself, if I were wealthy with a thousand thalers. The subject requires that the individual who accepts the assignment dedicate to it all of his time and energy. If a truly psychologically-minded observer were to undertake this task, the resulting benefit would be indescribably great. *This is the preparation of an exact diary about all observed physical and mental changes of a child* (emphasis by Campe), which would begin at birth and continue without interruption. How much information would such careful and continuous observation of a child provide for the psychologist and educator! For one person this task is almost too great. Two equally astute observers would be needed to divide the responsibilities among themselves. One would always remain with the child, while the other would record his observations.—Where is the friend of man who would like to contribute something to enable us to offer a relatively encouraging award for the completion of this unpopular task.

The actual assignment was described as follows (1785a: xxvi f.):

> NB. 9. Journal of a father about his child containing: a faithful presentation of the entire physical and moral treatment of the child including the observed effects and consequences; observations of the first expressions of independence, attention, joy and pain; advances in physical and mental development; gradual formation of language and the child's own very simple grammar; the beginnings of individual differences and emotions; basic patterns of the future personality etc.

In addition, Campe expressed the hope that several observers would start such diaries and offered himself as editor of the completed works. The prize for the best diary was to be awarded after the notes for the first year of life had been received and evaluated. Further observations would be published year-by-year as long as a careful study of the child appeared possible and useful.

Corresponding to the forty-six sections of Campe's theoretical master plan of educational reform, the practical part of the project was to consist of a carefully planned series of textbooks about all aspects of education. After a general introduction to the principles of physical and mental education, the following specific educational problems were to be discussed with concrete examples from the different periods of children's lives: development and instruction in observational and memory skills; the stimulation, direction, and control of needs and skills; the encouragement of moral behavior by natural means and the role of reward and punishment; and methods for maintaining an equilibrium between physical and mental aptitudes. This educational encyclopedia also included discussions of: character training aimed at avoiding extremes; the facilitation of physical strength and mental well-being by gymnastic exercises for boys and girls; and instruction in pleasant and useful hobbies and games. Considerable space focused on the treatment of physical, mental, and moral deviations, including even sexual problems. The objectives, subjects, and methods of instruction for the different fields of learning were to be adapted to the needs of the different social classes and the anticipated future work of each child. Special attention was also devoted to the educational needs of the daughters of farmers, skilled tradesmen, middle-class townspeople, soldiers, and noblemen. The program concluded with a discussion of the possibilities and limitations of education at home with a tutor, in institutions and public schools, and the special responsibilities of the state as well as a brief history of education and school systems. A supplement was to contain a German translation of the pedagogical writings of Locke and Rousseau with critical comments.

II

It was the objective of the entire project to offer a systematic foundation of pedagogy with the practical intention of improving the inadequate educational institutions and, for the first time, to establish a public school system. The Philanthropists believed that such reforms were the best means for creating middle-class conditions in the economically underdeveloped dwarf states of Germany.

It is not clear why the invitation for the preparation of a baby diary was included in the proposed program of educational reform. Why was it not published in one of the specialized psychological journals? What was the intellectual and philosophical background which encouraged Campe to support the diary project? Evolutionary thinking about history, the development of language, philosophy, the natural sciences, and other cultural phenomena was widespread during the second half of the eighteenth century. The parallels between individual and societal development had been widely accepted and included the view that the general development followed natural and lawful stage which the individual must recapitulate in his own life. However, there were clear limits placed upon the psychological and educational applications of these general theoretical views. If one viewed the existing societal conditions as alien to the nature of man, as was the case with Rousseau and others, education could not derive its norms from an existing society but had to rely upon its understanding of human nature for guidance, specifically the laws of psychological development. The Scottish philosopher and founder of the common-sense school, Thomas Reid (1710–1796), articulated the need for a dependable source of information about child development in the Introduction to his *Inquiry into the Human Mind* (1764:99):

> Could we obtain a distinct and full history of all that hath past in the mind of a child, from the beginning of life and sensation, until it grows up to the use of reason—how its infant faculties began to work, and how they brought forth and ripened all the various notions, opinions, and sentiments which we find in ourselves when we come to be capable of reflection—this would be a treasure of natural history, which would probably give more light into human faculties, than all the systems of philosophy about them since the beginning of the world. But it is in vain to wish for what nature has not put within the reach of our power.

In other words, self-observation or introspection, the desired medium of understanding, was only available at the end of the developmental sequence which it was to decipher. Hence, it was almost impossible to separate social conventions and individual characteristics from the original forces and laws of mental nature. One existed, so-to-speak in a theoretical blind alley and it should not come as a surprise that the most important psychological publication of that period, the *Philosophische Versuche über die menschliche Natur und ihre Entwicklung* (Philosophical Experiments on Human Nature and its Developments) by Johann Nicolas Tetens (1736–1807) paid almost no attention to the development of children!

Despite these theoretical and methodological problems, a few investigations existed which contained occasional observations, conversations, and reports about the effects of novel educational methods on children. Forerunners of this type of literature also were found in published accounts of child prodigies, the feebleminded, feral children, and "savages." The latter were typically compared to young children in their mental capacity, and in turn, the young children were often perceived as "savages." Practical interests in improving the school system, improved the quality of these "educational histories" which now began to focus increasingly on normal children. The fact that man educated young males, who did not want to become civil servants or ministers, earned their living as private tutors for the sons of the nobility and the wealthy, may well have played a role in the writing of these educational histories. The preparation of reports about the progress of their charges and a substantial amount of free time, which could be used in preparation, for a literary or academic career, were additional causal factors (i.e. Tiedemann, Herbart, Campe).

First attempts towards a standardization and systematic evaluation of educational histories were initiated by Carl Philipp Moritz (1756–1793) within the context of his theory of semiotics. Another important publication outlet for this material was the journal, *Pädagogische Unterhandlungen* (Educational Treatises) which the Philanthropists Basedow and Campe founded in 1777. In this publication Johann Karl Wezel (1747–1819) discussed at length the difficulties of gaining psychological understanding from the observations of one's own students. Man's complexity permits us to make only educated "guesses about the probable causes" of certain events. Difficulties with the observation of others are almost insurmountable because they require that the observer be sophisticated in psychological matters and be trained as an observer. The traditional study of obsolete metaphysical systems does not prepare scholars for this work. The observation of others leads to self-observation, because one must compare one's own inner experiences with the phenomena perceived in others. Self-observations, in turn, require the talent to "... be two persons, one of which observes while the other one acts ... heavens! What demands" (Wezel 1778:27)! Even if all these specifications have been met, the educator still needs to avoid influencing his ward unconsciously. Therefore, he must carefully study his life history and learn to distinguish between facts and speculations. Although none of the methodological problems were solved at that time, Wezel still believed that educational histories would eventually provide a stable psychological basis for educational practice in a manner analogous to that of case histories in medicine. Specifically, he hoped that the discussion of case histories by several observers would reduce errors and improve methods. According to Wezel, an educational history was to include an account of the student's previous life, a description of his parents and other important figures in his life, an autobiography of the teacher, and a description of the student himself. This information was to be used in the formulation of a well-designed plan of education and the eventual description of all major pedagogical techniques, as well as their impact on the physical, mental, and characterological development of students.

Wezel suggested that educators should not function merely as neutral observers but should actively test the character of their students by "trials and experiments." This seminal idea was pursued further by Ernst Christian Trapp (1745–1818). He suggested that the lack of an "experimental psychology" was the reason that "... doubts in psychology cannot be resolved as well as in science..." (1780: 64). Still, he reasoned that one could carry out experiments with children between two and 16 years of age. These experiments should have educational objectives and focus on the "external phenomena of the human nature." Thus, he proposed "listening to children everywhere when they do not know about it" and to follow up these informal observations with interviews about the hidden thoughts and motives of the children. In addition, special monitors, who could be seen by teachers or students, were to keep records of classroom interactions to determine the most economical use of resources (Wezel 1780)! He encouraged his readers to "collect experimental information through all possible combinations of childrens ... and objects" (Wezel 1780: 66) in the hope that the analysis of these data might yield outstanding and lasting relations among interests, ideas, and actions. In this connection, Trapp voiced the opinion that these "objectives" could also be living persons and that "a child sometimes becomes an object for another one" (1780: 68). Today we would, of course, regard his views as social-psychological perspectives.

Trapp (1760: 43) and the other Philanthropists viewed education as the development of abilities, which are present at birth but which do not grow stronger on their own. They have to be stimulated until maturity has been reached, if one wants to overcome the results of false pedagogical interventions. But how could one gain dependable information about the abilities of the newborn? Trapp still regarded this problem as insolvable but he hoped that an answer would eventually come from the field of physiognomy. We have already shown that the development of the child was not believed accessible to empirical, psychological study due to the limits of the introspective method with small children. In the field of education, where there was much pressure to deal with these problems for practical reasons, novel approaches for a solution were developed and improved. First, attention was redirected to the entire postnatal stage of development and not just the first year of life. In addition, a distinction was made between teachers who are primarily interested in practical applications and researchers who wish to gain a general understanding of the developmental processes following the model of the natural sciences. The unsolved methodological problems and the difficulties encountered in generalizing the empirical results now become the province of specialized organizations of scientists.

Campe's call for the preparation of a diary by a psychological observer can be viewed as the culmination of this development. He showed a basic scientific interest in the problem and was fully aware of the relevance of the method to the field of education. In this respect his work differed sharply from other forms of the infant diary in which the development of the child was presented as an autonomous process which hides the concrete, material conditions of human development behind an undifferentiated concept of stimulus and response relationships. The Philanthropists always included their speculations about the possibility of human progress within the context of society's progress as a whole in their understanding of human nature. We can only fully understand the achievements of the Philanthropists, if we recognize their enthusiastic reception of the psychological writings of the English empiricists and the French materialists which allowed them to overcome the narrow boundaries of the German faculty psychology. The advent of nationalism and the theoretical systems of the early nineteenth century made the Philanthropists and their eclectic and cosmopolitan empiricism suspect. Their contributions to the history of child and developmental psychology became forgotten. Philanthropism was replaced as an effective educational philosophy by Humanism (Niethammer 1808).

III

Following the proposals of the Philanthropists, a number of baby diaries were prepared and actually published. The best known of these works are the *Beobachtungen über die Entwickelung der Seelenfähigkeiten bei Kindern* (Observations on the Development of Mental Abilities in Children, 1787) by the German philosopher Dietrich Tiedemann (1748–1803). As a subscriber to the leading philanthropist publications, he was, of course, familiar with their objectives. His own psychological publications were an additional qualification. The diary was published in a journal, which Tiedemann co-edited. It contained observations about his son Friedrich Tiedemann (1781–1861), who later taught as a respected physiologist and iatrochemist at Landshut and Heidelberg Universities. The article presented information for the first three and a half years of life in chronological order about Tiedemann's son. It impresses us still because of his accurate descriptions and specific interpretations. Overall, however, this diary did not really meet the requirements of the Philanthropists, since little attention was focused upon the relationship between developmental patterns and the treatment of the child by his parents. It was Tiedemann's primary goal to collect data for a comparative analysis of the natural, mental development of an average child. This information was to serve as the basis for future educational planning.

The full theoretical orientation of Tiedemann can hardly be discerned in the awkwardly organized diary form. It can be reconstructed, at least partially, from a reading of his *Handbuch der Psychologie* (Handbook of Psychology, 1804: 401–431) in which he used observations of his son as the basis for a systematic account of the development of the soul. In this context, he sharply criticized the belief in innate ideas and was convinced that even his limited observations were proof that development arises from sensations. These initially form a chaotic mass, which changes almost constantly with the accretion of new impressions. At this early stage of life, inner and outer sensations are not yet distinguished nor are they associated by the child with the objects from which they originated. The mass of sensations becomes differentiated only by the comparison of repeated sensations. Consequently, initial ideas develop which, in turn, help organize new sensory experiences. The associative linkage of ideas becomes the basis for the first, vague memories around which the concept of the individual's identity is formed. The generalization of the sensory experiences of impermeability and extension leads to the awareness that the external world is something distinct and different from the individual self. Since the child knows nothing better than himself, he initially holds an anthropomorphic view of external objects. The first beginning of reflexive thinking can be observed when the child becomes familiar with a variety of images or ideas and learns to recognize their similarities and differences. Language helps the child to broaden his discoveries and to draw conclusions about longer and more complex series of objects and events.

The reception of Tiedemann's work in the nineteenth century became the model for other diaries. In 1799 the physician Johann Friedrich Posewitz (1766–1805) used Tiedemann's account as the standard against which he compared a case of abnormal sensory development in a young child. He believed that it would be possible eventually to diagnose the presence of organic brain damage from deviations in the normal sensory development of children. Tiedemann's account was also briefly mentioned by Schwarz (1804: 371) and Burdach (1830: 180, 750), but his real contributions to child study remained unrecognized until the late 1800s. Interestingly, Tiedemann was rediscovered abroad. Two French (Michelant 1863, Perez 1881) and one English translation (Soldau 1890), republished the original diary, before Ufer (1897) gave Tiedemann credit as one of the founders of developmental psychology in Germany.

Campe and Trapp published two of the many manuscripts which they had received with brief commentaries. The *Tagebuch eines Vaters über sein neugeborenes Kind* (The Diary of a Father about his Newborn Child, 1789, 1790, 1791) by Major A. von Winterfeld contained the description of the treatment and development of his daughter up to her fifth year. According to the editors, the book was an exceptional work because (Campe and Trapp, 1789: 405):

> . . . the author had the courage to model the treatment of his child after Rousseau's prescriptions. . . . He even dared to apply some extreme procedures, the outcome of which could not always be predicted . . . his hopes were not disappointed, however. . . . In the future such methods can be used without danger as long as one avoids all extremes and only gradually helps a child adjust to hardship.

Winterfeld attributed the good health and proper behavior of this daughter and his other children to his educational methods which provided them with ample opportunities to grow without restrictions and punishment. In contrast to the dominant traditions of child-rearing of his time, he made arrangements for his daughter to be nursed at first by her mother and afterwards to receive only very simple and wholesome food. The child was not swaddled which provided her more opportunities to move freely and made it easier to keep her clean. Winterfeld's daughter was bathed in cold water from the first day of her life. It was also forbidden to rock her in her cradle when she cried. Instead, she was included in all activities of her parents which took place outside the home, including their extensive travels. Under the influence of the medical writings of Tissot and Unzer, the father treated the illnesses of his own children without medication. During a smallpox

epidemic in 1790, he vaccinated his own children. Winterfeld's observations about motor behavior, perception, attention, fear, and speech
development are rather limited. Nevertheless, he sincerely tried to show
how child-rearing methods influenced his child's efforts to gain control
over her physical and social environment.

The second published diary was written by the teacher and later
minister, Friedrich W.Dillenius (1789, 1790, 1799). This work is interesting as a psychological document because it relates to a greater degree
to the existing literature. The "natural drives for self-preservation" in
man are described in the order in which they appear. Curiosity,
sociability, sympathy, activity, pleasure, imitation, defensiveness,
revenge, and pity were identified through observations of his daughter.
Dillenius also wrote about the methods which he used to strenghten or
weaken these drives. By providing children with opportunities in which
they could observe all manner of objects, while these were being named,
education was begun in the first year of life. Specifically, he hoped to
encourage the development of clear ideas, the precise use of language,
the development of artistic taste and moral principles, control over
emotions, and the learning of appropriate behavior patterns for males
and females. Dillenius did not really challenge the traditional values and
methods of education. He made it clear, however, that only those
persons who possessed the necessary psychological and pedagogical
qualifications for this work should be given access to children.

Finally, Immanuel David Mauchart (1764–1826), who published two
further installments of the Dillenius diary in his journal (1790, 1791),
printed another diary in 1798 about the first year of his daughter,
explicitly acknowledging the influence of Campe.

The baby diaries, which were written under the influence of the
German Philanthropists, share the view that psychological
development begins much earlier than had previously been assumed.
Moreover, it was clearly recognized that the course of development
could be influenced by educational interventions and that physical
deprivations and other forms of punishment were not necessary. The
sheer scope and complexity of the research problem, posed by Campe,
indicates why none of the published diaries adhered fully to the master
plan in the search for basic patterns of child development.

The publication of baby biographies by the nineteenth-century scholars, Pestalozzi, Alcott, Darwin, Strümpell, and others, is often interpreted as evidence for continuity in the use of this research technique.
Actually, these noted writers whose interest in developmental matters is

well-documented, appear to have collected information about the early development of their own children as a personal hobby and in quite an unsystematic manner. For the most part, they did not publish their observations until many years later, and they do not seem to have integrated their empirical observations with their theoretical writings on child development. Actually, the baby biography by the American E. Willard, which was published in 1835, is the only diary which was printed immediately following its preparation. Thus, the caustic comment of Friedrich Albert Lange (1828–1875) about the developmental psychology of his time is pertinent (1875: 390):

> The speculations of our philosophers about the origins of consciousness are astounding. Apparently they never felt the need to enter a nursery and personally observe what goes on there.

References

Bühler, C., and Hetzer, H. (1929). Zur Geschichte der Kinderpsychologie. In E. Brunswick et al. (Eds.) *Beiträge zur Problemgeschichte der Psychologie.* (Bühler Festschrift), Pp. 204–224. Jena: Fischer.

Burdach, K. F. (1830). *Die Physiologie als Erfahrungswissenschaft* (Vol. 3). Leipzig: Voss.

Campe, J. H. (Ed.) (1785–1791). *Allgemeine Revision des gesamten Schul- und Erziehungswesens von einer Gesellschaft praktischer Erzieher* (16 Vols.). Hamburg: Bohn After Volume 5 (1786) Wolfenbüttel: Schulbuchhandlung.

—(1785a) Vorrede, welche zugleich den Plan des Werkes enthält. *Allgemeine Revision* (Vol. 1), Pp. III–LVI.

—(1785b). Über die früheste Bildung junger Kinderseelen im ersten und zweiten Jahre der Kindheit. *Allgemeine Revision* (Vol. 2), Pp. 3–296.

—(1786). Über die große Schädlichkeit einer allzufrühen Ausbildung der Kinder. *Allgemeine Revision* (Vol. 5), Pp. 1–160.

Dennis, W. (1949). Historical beginnings of child psychology. *Psychological Bulletin, 46,* 224–235.

—(Ed.) (1972). *Historical readings in developmental psychology.* New. York: Meredith.

Dillenius, F. W. J. (1789) Fragmente eines Tagebuchs über die Entwickelung der körperlichen und geistigen Fähigkeiten und Anlagen eines Kindes. *Braunschweigisches Journal philosophischen, philologischen und pädagogischen Inhalts, 6,* 320–342.

—(1790). Fragmente eines Tagebuchs über die Entwickelung der köperlichen und geistigen Fähigkeiten und Anlagen eines Kindes—Fortsetzung. *Braunschweigisches Journal, 1,* 279–298.

Engel, J. J. (1785). *Ideen zu einer Mimik* (Part I.). Berlin: Mylius.

Fritzsch, T. (1910). Die Anfänge der Kinderpsychologie und die Vorläufer des Versuchs in der Pädagogik. *Zeitschrift für pädagogische Psychologie, 11,* 149–160.

Götz, H. (1921). Zur Geschichte der Kinderpsychologie und experimentellen Pädagogik. *Zeitschrift für pädagogische Psychologie, 19,* 257–268.

74 Jaeger

Höhn, E. (1959). Geschichte der Entwicklungspsychologie und ihrer wesentlichen Ansätze. In H.Thomae (Ed.) *Handbuch der Psychologie* (Vol.3): *Entwicklungspsychologie*. Göttingen: Hogrefe, 21–45.

Kussmaul, A. (1859). *Untersuchungen über das Seelenleben des neugeborenen Menschen.* Heidelberg: Winter.

Lange, F.A. (1875). *Geschichte des Materialismus und Kritik seiner Bedeutung in der Gegenwart*(Vol.2).Iserlohn: Baedeker.

Mauchart, M.I.D. (1798). Tagebuch über die allmählige körperliche und geistige Entwickelung eines Kindes. Geboren am 7.April 1794. Nach Campe'scher Methode. *Allgemeines Repertorium für empirische Psychologie und verwandte Wissenschaften, 4,* 269–294.

Michelant, H. (1863). Observations sur le Développement des Facultés de l'Ame chez les Enfants. *Journal Général de l'Instruction Publique,* Pp.251–291, 309, 319.

Niethammer, F.I. (1808). *Der Streit des Philanthropismus und des Humanismus.* Jena: Fromann.

Perez, B. (1881). *Thierri Tiedemann et la Science de l'Enfant.* Paris: Bailliere.

Posewitz, J.F.S. (1799). Ätiologische Entwicklung der Äußerungen des Sensoriums beim Foetus und beim jungen Kinde sogleich nach seiner Geburt bis zum 247.Tage. *Journal für Medizin, Chirurgie und Geburtshülfe, vorzüglich mit Rücksicht auf Ätiologie und Semiotik, 1,* 94–175.

Reid, T. (1764). Versuch über die Wichtigkeit der Untersuchungen, die den menschlichen Verstand betreffen. *Berlinisches Magazin, 3,* Pp.583–599.

Reinert, G. (1976) Grundzüge einer Geschichte der Human-Entwicklungspsychologie. In H.Balmer (Ed.) *Geschichte der Psychologie. Psychologie des XX.Jahrhunderts* (Vol.1, Pp.862–896). Zürich: Kindler.

Schumann, P. (1921) Aus den Anfängen der Kinderpsychologie. *Zeitschrift für pädagogische Psychologie, 22,* 209–218.

Schwarz, F.H.C. (1804). *Erziehungslehre* (Vol.2). Leipzig: Göschen.

Soldau, F.L. (1890). *Tiedemann's record of an infant* (B.Perez, Trans.). Syracuse, NY: Bardeen.

Tiedemann, D. (1787). Beobachtungen über die Entwickelung der Seelenfähigkeiten bei Kindern. *Hessische Beiträge zur Gelehrsamkeit und Kunst, 2,* 313–333, 486–502.

—(1804). *Handbuch der Psychologie zum Gebrauch bei Vorlesungen und zur Selbstbelehrung bestimmt.* Leipzig: Barth.

Trapp, E.C. (1780.) *Versuch einer Pädagogik.* Berlin: Nicolai.

Ufer, C. (1897). Dietrich Tiedemanns Beobachtungen über die Entwicklung der Seelenfähigkeiten bei Kindern. Altenburg: Bonde.

Wezel, J.K. (1778). Über die Erziehungsgeschichten. *Pädagogische Unterhandlungen, 2,* 21–43.

Willard, E. (1835). Observations upon an infant during its first year. By a mother. In A.A. Necker de Saussure (Ed.), *Progressive Education,* Boston: Ticknor, 323–348.

Winterfeld, M.A.v. (1789) Tagebuch eines Vaters über sein neugeborenes Kind. *Braunschweigisches Journal philosophischen, philologischen und pädagogischen Inhalts, 5,* 404–441.

—(1790). Beantwortung einiger Entwürfe des Herausgebers des Tagebuchs eines Vaters von dem Verfasser des Tagebuchs. *Braunschweigisches Journal, 7,* 322–332.

—(1791). Fortsetzung des Tagebuchs eines Vaters. *Braunschweigisches Journal, 12,* 476–484.

The Concept of Development in Herder's Philosophical Anthropology

by Hans-Dieter Schmidt

My topic is closely associated with the location of this symposium. I shall deal with a chapter in the history of eighteenth century science in the Jena-Weimar region, which focused on the phenomenon of "development" and its explanations. To no one's surprise, perhaps, the names of Schiller, Goethe and, *most of all*, Herder will appear quite frequently in my presentation.

The concept of development is a historical category and, thus, belonged to the province of Schiller, who held an appointment as Professor of History at the University of Jena. Schiller viewed development as an intrinsic part of human existence, that incorporated both man's organic nature and his social needs. As a young medical student at the *Württemberg Military Academy* in Stuttgart, Schiller had pondered "The Relationship between Man's Animal and Spiritual Nature" and published the resulting essay in 1780. His work on "Grace and Dignity" elaborated upon this comparison and elevated it to the rank of an heuristic principle of esthetic knowledge. Schiller reiterated his ideas in his lectures on "universal history" at Jena. He also stressed the necessity for interpreting regional historical events within the context of national and world history. Today we would consider Schiller's approach as similar to that of ethnohistory or historical psychology.

Goethe's relationship to the evolutionary thinking of his time requires little verification, since this aspect of his work is well known. His work on the topic ranges from biological studies of the development of plants and animals (including his empirical contributions to the problem of homology), his discovery of the evolutionary meaning of the *os intermaxillare* (in Jena), his work on the so-called "vertebral theory" of the skull to his growth-decay philosophy of history and human life. It may well have been Goethe who best expressed the principle of development with its sequence of differentiations into hierarchical structures (e.g. Spencer 1864, Werner 1926), as we read (1966: 199):

> The less perfect an organism may be, the more equal or similar are its parts and the more they resemble the whole. The more perfect an organism becomes, the

more dissimilar become its parts.bs1.. The more the parts resemble each other, the less they are subject to each other. The subordination of parts is a characteristic of a perfect organism.

It must be recognized that Goethe, despite his progressive skill in describing developmental sequences, did not make the full transition to a materialistic interpretation of evolution, although quite a few "heretical" thoughts for his time are to be found in his work (Schmidt 1970: 25f.).

Goethe's idea of development has importance for my topic, because it was the focus of his communications with Herder from their joint student days in Strassburg, finding even more intense expression in conversations, debates and letters after Herder was appointed to head the Protestant churches in Weimar in 1776. One result of this relationship, which was not without conflict, was the completion of the book, which gives us the clearest understanding of Herder's philosophical anthropology and the model of development it implies. I am, of course, referring to his *Ideas on the Philosophy of Human History* (1965), hereafter abbreviated as *Ideas*.

We know that Goethe encouraged the author to complete this work. His influence may have been partly responsible, as well, for the supplementation of the social-historical content of the *Ideas* with a foundation from the natural sciences (Suphan 1909; Stolpe 1964, 1965a).

My own continuing interest in Herder's anthropology derives from a recognition that his anthropological contributions to biological and developmental psychology and to the theories of personality have largely been neglected in the history of psychology. I shall address myself specifically to three broad questions: (1) To what extent is Herder's anthropology the product of his tendency to think in developmental categories throughout his life? (2) What is Herder's concept of animal organism and what, in turn, is his image of man? (3) What contradictions can be found in Herder's anthropology and why?

I

Herder's anthropology, expressed in the *Ideas*, grew out of numerous preliminary studies, dating from his Königsberg student days and the influence of Hamann and Kant. A sketch of his thinking as it "converged" eventually in the *Ideas* follows (Suphan 1909, Stolpe 1965a):

(1) *Notes from the Student Years* (1765–1766). *Themes:* changes of the physical world, of nations; laws of change (differentiation, formation

of developmental stages, developmental process as a spiral); "main springs" of change (attraction and repulsion, interaction between natural and social elements); comments on the origin of man.

(2) *An Account of my Journey in the Year 1769. Themes:* Plan of a "Universal History of the World;" recognition of the individual characteristics of people and epochs, these to be conceptualized as the totality of conditions, institutions, laws and philosophies; stages of child development.

(3) *Award-Winning Essay on the Origin of Language* (1770). ("Was Man able to invent language when left to his natural resources? And how was this achieved?") *Themes:* Animal-human comparison; image of animal vs. image of man; reason and language as special features of man; "basic laws" of human nature, including the invention of language and its social-societal "perfection;" the identification and recognition of the characteristics of objects are the roots of language (in the sense of a monocausal explanation of the origin of language, H.S.).

(4) *Yet Another Philosophy of History on the Origin of Mankind* (1774). *Theme:* Impulsive, ecstatic storm-and-stress sketch of human history, analogous to the stages of childhood-youth-adulthood.

The next stage in Herder's anthropological thinking consisted of plans, preliminary manuscripts, and a final draft of the *Ideas* (ca. 1774). After their publication, he researched and published the *Letters for the Promotion of Humanity* between 1792 and 1797. The *Humanity Letters* should be regarded as a continuation of the *Ideas* and a substitution for the unwritten fifth part (Stolpe 1971: 617) and must be included in an analysis of Herder's anthropological work. He was the center of a group that was vitally interested in the idea of development. Herder contributed to the evolutionary thinking of his associates and was, in turn, also influenced by them. As was the case with other thinkers during the period of Enlightenment, his support for the political emancipation of the bourgeoisie was one important consequence of his position on development. Herder regarded this support as an obligation, as we can see in his evaluation of the French Revolution (1971). He was also deeply interested in the progress of the natural sciences and, in particular, in their contributions to epistemology.

II

An appropriate answer to my second set of questions requires preliminary discussion of the overall plan of the *Ideas,* as well as the general principles and laws of the development of the universe as envisioned by Herder. We must, in other words, investigate the methodological and theoretical premises which are widely dispersed among Herder's writings.

The outline of the *Ideas* reveals the author's reasoning and underlying logic. Herder followed two lines of thought. The first describes developmental events, and the second traces the origin of general principles and laws of development (including respective comparative methodologies):

(1) Cosmological development

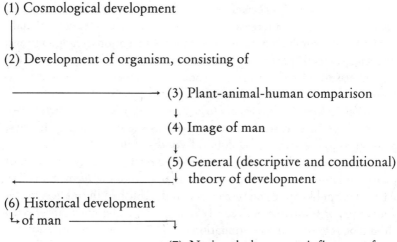

(2) Development of organism, consisting of

(3) Plant-animal-human comparison

(4) Image of man

(5) General (descriptive and conditional) theory of development

(6) Historical development of man

(7) National character; influence of religion, forms of government, *Zeitgeist*, etc., on man.

The laws of development, proposed by Herder, belong to two classes. They pertain either to regularities in the sequence of developmental events (sequential laws) or to the production of developmental phenomena (causal laws). I will give some illustrations for both types of principles from natural rather than from social history.

Sequential Laws. (1) "Nothing in nature stands still;" "everything strives and moves on" (*Ideas*, vol.1: 174). The higher levels include the lower forms and stages as well. Development in nature and society follows qualitatively different stages. (2). The original state of development is uniformly undifferentiated; development involves a process of differentiation and a "simplification" of organization, which is species-specific (p.105). (3) Inorganic matter precedes organic matter. Plants are genetically older than animals and these, again, are older than man. (4) Despite numerous modifications by climatic, cultural and other conditions, one can discover prototypes of organic formation which can be considered as invariable. Herder calls these "analogies." We call them "homologies" today.

Causal Laws. (1) The idea and will of the creator is realized in each development and can be recognized in the prototypes and the "organic force" which is the endogenous source of developmental dynamics. This "organic force" is "an idea (of God, H.S.), which has been realized in the eternal design of creation" (p.173f.) It existed before matter and makes use of matter. (2) After their creation, the prototypes and the "organic force" continue to develop autonomously. Each new level of development, in other words, does not need to be created anew.

> When the gates of creation were closed the chosen organizations existed as distinct pathways and gates through which, in the future, the lower forces were to ascend and further develop within the limits set by nature. New forms were no longer created; instead they change and transform themselves by these (natural, H.S.) forces, and what we call organization is only their *guide to higher development* (p.174).

This observation is especially true for the social-historical development of man, which results from his actions, the institutions he has created, his norms and laws, etc. (3) The ultimate purpose of development is the protection of reproduction and the "preservation of families" (p.57) under the conditions of space limitations and the struggle for life (p.64). (4) The "kingdoms" of plants, animals, and man are connected through their metabolism and form an ecological unit which exists in a state of equilibrium (p.62). (5) "Always and everywhere we can see that nature destroys by rebuilding and that it separates by uniting again" (p.52). (6) Organic development is neither based on preformation nor on "mere" additive-mechanical epigenesis. It is the "formation" or genesis which results from "inner forces for whose use nature has prepared a formless substance, in which they can express themselves and become visible (p.170).

What conclusions can be drawn from these laws? Although Herder's general theory of development has an endogenous-Platonic character, he achieved an understanding that has implications for the dialectics of development. Whether the same holds true for his comparative account of human and animal development is quite another matter.

Herder first proposed his image of animal nature in his award-winning essay, and he refined his views further in the *Ideas:*

(1) The organic forces are arranged in a species-specific manner in animals which thus assures the instinctive operation of the senses and determination of behavior, as well as specialized "mechanical instincts" (in the sense of Reimarus) and other innate skills. (2) The instinctive organization in animals functions without learning and practice. When it leads to external products (i.e., spiderwebs), these are "extensions of the self" (p.100). (3) The senses of animals, their psychic forces and their behavior patterns are specific to the "sphere" or "circle" of each species (p.101). Lower organisms in the evolutionary chain display more specialized "mechanical instincts" and live in a more restricted and impoverished environment. (4) The "irresistable needs" and the "error-free skills" become less frequent at the higher levels of the evolutionary scale. Learning supplements the repertoire of instinctual behaviors and allows the animal "a more liberal and varied use of its forces and limbs" (p.102). (5) The organization of the more complex animals, especially those living in social groups, has implications for man, and one must be cautioned against interpreting their behavior mechanistically.

> Everywhere are models of human behavior, which animals also practise. It is a sin against nature... to regard them as machines, when we see their nervous systems, their similar needs and ways of life before us. Therefore, it is not surprising that the more one approaches the human level, the more it loses its mechanical skills (p.107).

As Gehlen noted in 1941, Herder anticipated ideas which are found more than a century later in the work of von Uexküll (1921), and in the "classical" ethology of Lorenz and Tinbergen (1952: 88). Herder was sharply opposed to mechanical explanations of animal behavior (cf. Descartes), in accordance with his ecological-biological orientation. His emphasis on a net of endogenous and exogenous determinants of behavior bears similarities to a dialectical view of life.

Herder's paradigm of a general schema of the physical and psychic nature of animals is an intrinsic part of his anthropology. Comparisons between animals and man have the purpose of more clearly defining the contrasting image of man. Herder's point of departure is the conviction that "Animals are the older brothers of Man" (p.63).

The first result of this comparison is the identification of components in man which are shared by and stem from plant and animal life. Physico-chemical processes and substances as well as behavior patterns need to be examined in this context. Herder is interested in the "absorption" of the "lower realm" of organic nature in human existence and action.

For this reason, he describes, at length, the instinctive mechanisms of human behavior to be identified in the early stages of individual life.

> The child in his mother's body appears to go through all stages (of development) through which earthly creatures can pass. . . . As soon as it is born, it gasps for air, and sucking is its first, unlearned performance. All of the processes of digestion and nourishment, of hunger and thirst, occur instinctively or are controlled by drives, which we do not understand well. The muscular and reproductive powers strive for development and a person needs only to become insane, as the result of intense emotions or illness, to perceive his animal needs. . . . The needs have not been taken away from man . . . rather they have been suppressed and subjected to the control of the nerves and the complex senses. Without them, the creature, which is still largely an animal, could not live at all (p. 140f.).

We read further:

> And how do they become suppressed? . . . Let us follow their course beginning with childhood; it will show us what is often foolishly called human weakness from quite a different side. (p. 141)

This "different side", to Herder, meant that man "must be born weak to learn reason" (p. 142).

Gehlen has claimed erroneously (1955: p. 89) that Herder conceptualized man as an "organism that is, by nature, characterized by lack of instincts" and "biological helplessness" and needs reason and language as a substitute for these inadequacies. Gehlen exclusively quoted from the essay on the *Origin of Language* (1770). He neglected the *Ideas* which provide a more solid foundation. Herder was convinced that man possesses a system of instincts which is transformed during ontogenesis. Herder describes how this takes place in a manner that impresses us with its modernity. He emphasizes the importance of the newborn child's perceptual, rather than his motor system (Thompson and Grusec 1970). He is particularly aware of the relevance of this phase for cognitive development in children.

> The baby is placed at the mother's breast. . . . His finest senses—eye and ear— awaken first and are guided by configurations and tones . . . Gradually . . . he focuses on the eyes of the people around him . . . his ear becomes attached to human language and learns to discern the first concepts . . . he gradually learns to grasp. Now his limbs desire exercise of their own. At first he was an apprentice of the two finest senses . . . The artificial instincts that he is to be taught are reason, humanity, and a human life style, which no animal possesses nor can acquire (p. 142).

We can draw another conclusion from Herder's work about man's social nature and its importance as a *natural condition* of development. Social growth of the child becomes, for Herder, the earliest:

> ... foundation of a necessary, human society without which no man can grow up and without which the majority of people cannot live. Man is born into a social life, and he learns this from the sympathy of his parents during long years of his childhood (p.157).

Herder views man's special place among the organisms to be a result of the dialectical resolution of the plant and animal components in his morphological, physiological, and psychological constitution. The "lower" components become weakened, inhibited, and restructured due to the transformation of the human design. Thus, man becomes able to place himself at the head of the other organisms and to dominate them.

Man's status as a biological organism is seen in the structure and texture of the cortex, the dominance of distance senses, his upright position and walk, and the consequent liberation of his hands. Herder also points to the prolongation of childhood and the relative autonomy from environmental conditions as special learning conditions for man's biological organization.

Man's unique *psychological condition,* according to Herder, consists of aptitudes which will be summarized under five subheadings:

(1) *Rationality:* reason, language, writing, deliberate action and freedom of self-determination and self-control; dominance of learning; tool use and invention.

(2) *Lack of specialization:* "indeterminate life-style," "unrestricted (expression) of needs;" "a general interest in everything;" "no uniform or narrow sphere (of life)."

(3) *Sociability:* social ties, feelings, traditions and institutions.

(4) *Participation in society:* consciously created norms, laws and institutions.

(5) *Potential for being human.* Peacefulness, love and sympathetic participation, decency, religiosity. Actualization of this potential for being human depends on the historical stage of development of a nation, the general cultural and educational conditions of each respective society, and the form of government under whose control the individual lives and acts. Herder does not mince words:

> (Man) apparently has characteristics which no animal has and has produced effects which, good or bad, remain uniquely his . . . no animal murders its family at the command of another in cold blood! (p.108)

A critical analysis of Herder's image of man leads us to the conclusion that rational consciousness is not the only human characteristic. Sociability and the participation in society are also intrinsic parts of human nature. Herder's *Ideas* appear to lack the direction, which has been so cogently expressed by Marx and Engels (1972):

> One can distinguish humans from animals by consciousness, by religion or whatever else one wishes. They themselves (Men) begin to make this distinction as soon as they begin to *produce* their own food, a step which is determined by their physical organization. By producing their food, humans indirectly produce material life itself (p.207).

Did Herder perhaps overlook work as the constitutional characteristic of man, which Marxists regard as the essential feature (Leontjew 1964: 156ff.)? Was Herder perhaps bound by the "spiritual axiom" of the bourgeoisie image of man, as Hiebsch has suggested (1960, 1966)? If we accept the statements in the *Ideas* alone, we must answer these questions in the affirmative. I myself have given the same answer in the past (Schmidt 1970: 247). This view is false, however, because it depends on an interpretation of Herder's *Ideas* without the evidence Herder gives us in the *Humanity Letters*.

Herder offered pertinent information in the section of the *Ideas*, in which he discussed the relationship between a sense of shame and prehistoric production of clothing:

> ... Thus Man received clothing, and, as soon as he was expert at this and other arts, he was able to endure all climates of the earth and take it in possession. A few animals were able to follow him into all regions but with what change in their appearance, with what change in their innate temperament! Man alone has changed least and not at all in essential parts. One is surprised how completely and uniformly his nature has been preserved ... (p.148).

How does Herder solve this problem? He does not, as could have been expected, refer to the invention of clothing, which made life easier. He points instead to man's upright position, his homeothermic nature, and similar biological characteristics in the *Ideas*.

Herder took a giant step forward in the *Humanity Letters*. I refer specifically to the twenty-fifth letter in the Second Collection, published in 1793. Herder describes "the laws of human nature" to his fictive correspondence partner and discusses "the lasting character of man and his species:"

> If a man departs from here, he takes nothing more along than the knowledge of having done his duty being human. Everything else remains behind him with the other humans. The use of his abilities, all interest from the capital of his forces,

which often greatly exceed the borrowed inheritance, become the property of his family. Young and energetic men take his place, who continue to trade with these goods; they too depart, but mankind continues immortally. Its main asset, the use of its powers, the training of its skills, is a common and lasting benefit and must continue to grow naturally by its continuing use.

Exercise strengthens these powers. . . . Humans create more and better tools for themselves; they learn to use themselves more and better as tools. The physical power of Man increases as well; the ball of human progress becomes bigger; the men who drive it on become more experienced, artistic, skillful and refined.

All objects in this realm . . . can and will be explored, known and applied by man. . . .

The result is a contest between human forces which becomes stronger the more the realm of knowledge and practice increases. Elements and nations make contact which previously did not appear to have known one another; the more they are in conflict, the more the opponents grind each other down, and finally common productions of several nations come into being (p. 118 ff.).

In view of the above statements, I maintain that Herder provided an answer to the questions asked above—How can man increasingly adapt himself and achieve more without changes in his biological constitution? In addition, I also maintain that Herder again anticipated later thinkers—like Adam Smith in his *Investigations on the Nature and Origin of the Wealth of Nations* (1776)—in his *Humanity Letters*. His ideas directly relate to the intellectual core of the historical-materialistic image of man. The quoted passages imply the process of work and its cultural objectivation, the acquisition of which made possible the mental, scientific, and technological progress of subsequent generations. If Marx and Engels had taken note of Herder's writings, they would have found rich and impressive support for their own position.

Finally, I maintain that Herder's image of man reaches farther and has more depth than that of the bourgeois-philosophical anthropology of today, which continues to interpret the relationship between society and the individual as one of confrontation and alienation. Contemporary anthropology is familiar with the individual will and mind that invents tools, but it does not know man as *Homo faber*, who works in a collective for the production and transmission of culture—the twin sources of man's historical progress. Eibl-Eibesfeld and Lorenz accept the restricted image of man, when they write (1974: 620):

Herder's question as to why the ape—the most human-like animal–did not become human can now be answered in two ways. . . . First, the apes lacked the close interchange between action and cognition . . . and, consequently, the fundamental prerequisite for language. Secondly, Man retains his curiosity well into old age.

We are astounded when we read such statements. Herder gave than two answers!

III

Herder's text presents readers with substantial difficulties. Problems begin with his use of language—the mixture of scientific description or argumentation and poetic, exaggerated, even ecstatic symbolization. The difficulties are compounded by the frequent, anthropomorphic interpretations of animal sensation and behavior, which identify him as a representative of the anecdotal tradition in comparative psychology. His tendency to combine causal and teleological explanations is confusing to say the least.

The problems are most substantial where the objective conflict in his life situation—he was both a practising theologian and a philosopher with scientific ambitions–resulted in subjective, ideological contradictions. The latter are most obvious in his treatment of the phenomenon of humanization. When we consult Herder's basic statements in the *Ideas* and avoid being blinded by poetic metaphors like the fraternity of man and animals (p.12), we realize that he was adhering to a Platonic and anthropocentric concept of development. He always remained loyal to the Biblical account of creation. As Suphan noted (1909:666):

> In this Herder always remains the same: Only a human beginning is acceptable for our species, never a simian one.

Stolpe (1964, 1965b) followed Herder's controversy with the Scottish anthropologist Lord Monboddo in the fourth volume of the *Ideas*. Herder discussed the conflict with Monboddo as follows (1965b: 439):

> Monboddo stressed that Man differs only by his perfectability and the level of skills and aptitudes he has reached. He does not differ qualitatively from animals. . . . Thus Monboddo was convinced that the orangutangs should be included among the human species.

Herder disagreed with this point. Man, for him, as well as for Rousseau, could not be descended from lower organisms (p.441). Siegel (1907: 159) noted that Herder met three premises of modern evolutionary thinking—adherence to the homology, continuity, and succession principles—but he rejected the hypothesis of "genetic descent."

Althoug he occasionally appears to use phylogenetic formulations, he explicitly insisted on "the constancy of species" (Günther 1967 : p.43). In conclusion, as far as biological principles of evolution are concerned, we must recognize that, while Herder's position was quite flexible, he is best characterized as "conservative." On the other hand, he anticipated modern concepts of "natural dialectics." His philosophy of becoming deserves special mention. Its developmental principles are still valid today, as well as his anticipation of thinking in terms of ecological systems. Herder's humanitarian creed, with its derivation of human progress from the process of labor and its cultural objectivation, are also relevant today. I wish to plead for an intensification of research on Herder, because this free-thinking parson out of psychology's past promises an even greater wealth of surprising and rewarding ideas than have been discussed so far.

References

Bielschowsky, A. (1911). *Goethe. Sein Leben und sein Werk* (23rd ed., Vol. 1.) München.

Eibl-Eibesfeld, I., and Lorenz, K. (1974). Die stammesgeschichtlichen Grundlagen menschlichen Verhaltens. In G. Heberer (Ed.), *Die Evolution der Organismen* (3rd ed.), Stuttgart.

Gehlen, A. (1941). *Der Mensch. Seine Natur und seine Stellung in der Welt*. Bonn.

Günther, K. (1961). Zur Geschichte der Abstammungslehre. In G. Heberer (Ed.), *Die Evolution der Organismen* (3rd ed.), Stuttgart.

Herder, J.G. (1959) *Über den Ursprung der Sprache*. Berlin.

—(1965) *Ideen zur Philosophie der Geschichte der Menschheit*. Berlin & Weimar.

Hiebsch, H. (1960) Die Bedeutung des Menschenbildes für die Theoriebildung in der Psychologie. *Probleme und Ergebnisse der Psychologie.*

—(1966) *Sozialpsychologische Grundlagen der Persönlichkeitsforschung*. Berlin.

Leontjew, A.N. (1964). *Probleme der Entwicklung des Psychischen*. Berlin.

Marx, K., and Engels, F. (1972) *Ausgewählte Werke in sechs Bänden*. Berlin.

Nohl, J. (Ed.) *Herder, Journal meiner Reise im Jahre 1769*. Weimar.

Reimarus, J.A.H. (1773). *Allgemeine Betrachtungen über die Triebe der Tiere.* Hamburg.

Schiller, F. (1838). *Schiller's sämmtliche Werke in zwölf Bänden*. Stuttgart, Tübingen.

Schmidt, H. (1970). *Allgemeine Entwicklungspsychologie*. Berlin.

Siegel, C. (1907). *Herder als Philosoph*. Stuttgart.

Smith, A. (1776). *An inquiry into the nature and causes of the wealth of nations*. London: Strahan & Cadell.

Spencer, H. (1864). *Principles of biology.*

Stolpe, H. (1964). Herder und die Ansätze einer naturgeschichtlichen Entwicklungslehre im 18. Jahrhundert. *Neue Beiträge zur Literaturwissenschaft.*

—(1965). Entstehungsgeschichte der "Ideen zur Philosophie der Geschichte der Menschheit." In J.G. Herder, *Ideen zur Philosophie der Geschichte der Menschheit* (Vol. 2). Berlin & Weimar.

—(1971). Herder's Ideen zur Vervollkommnung der Humanität und sein Verhältnis zur Französischen Revolution. Nachwort zu J.G. Herder, (1971). *Briefe zur Beförderung der Humanität* (Vol.2). Berlin & Weimar.

Suphan, B. (Ed.) *Herder's Sämmtliche Werke*. Berlin.

Thompson, W.R., and Grusec, J. (1970). Studies of early experience. In P.H. Mussen (Ed.), *Carmichael's manual of child psychology* (3rd ed., Vol.1). New York & London.

Tinbergen, N. (1952). *Instinktlehre*. Hamburg.

Uexküll, J.v. (1921) *Umwelt und Innenwelt der Tiere* (2nd ed.). Berlin.

Werner, H. (1926). *Einführung in die Entwicklungspsychologie*. Leipzig.

The Relationship Between Nature and Society in Early Conceptualizations of Developmental Psychology

by Irmingard Staeuble

In 1777, in the second volume of his *Philosophical Considerations on Human Nature and its Development,* Johann Nicolaus Tetens drew up a comprehensive progam of developmental psychology:

> The question: what can become of man, and what can be made of him and how? can only be answered substantially once there is a clear and distinct answer to the theoretical question: what does become of man, and how does he develop under the impact of the moral and physical conditions among which he finds himself in this world? (Tetens 1979, vol.2: 373)

While the polemical undertone is directed against moral norms and educational practices insufficiently grounded in a theory of human nature and its development, the core of this program raises problems far more sophisticated than the ones treated in what was later to become developmental psychology.[1]

I

In this paper I would like to reassess Tetens' program by analyzing its achievements and limitations. My interest is in the problems raised by Tetens and his contemporaries but dropped later on by developmental psychologists, and in the theoretical potential that was available for dealing with these problems in more detail, but had already vanished from the horizon of psychology when the discipline took roots in the nineteenth century. In short, I would like to ask what might have, but did not become of developmental psychology.

The scope of Tetens' program may be formulated in terms of two interdependent tasks: (1) to establish rational criteria and standards for accomplished human development; (2) to conceptualize human development in a way that accounts for the realtionship between human nature and society, and for the relationship between individual history and the history of mankind.

Tetens tried to accomplish these tasks in a lengthy and subtle discussion of the development and perfectibility of man.[2] His concept of man comprises an empirical and a normative or, rather, possibilistic notion.[3] Empirically, man is an active being as well as a product of physical and social circumstances. The term "self-determined activity" refers to the choice or selection among alternatives in physical and mental activity, the range of alternatives being determined by the circumstances in which man finds himself.

Tetens' normative, or possibilistic notion of man refers to specifically human traits, which distinguish man from animals. As he clearly saw, the identification of such traits depends on some choice of values; reason or language, freedom or perfectibility have been singled out by philosophers as essential traits. Tetens tried to differentiate between essential traits that are basic, and traits that indicate the direction of human development in the cours of human history. Throughout he presupposes men living in society, man as a social being. The basic trait, man's self-determined activity and concomitant consciousness, is the basis of reason and language, which thus get somewhere in between the empirical and normative notion of man. The direction of development, on the other hand, is indicated by freedom and perfectibility. Freedom, for Tetens freedom of the soul, is conceived as the power of man over his own nature, analogous to the positive social concept of freedom.[4] Perfectibility, though sometimes used as an empirical term,[5] is primarily related to the history of mankind, a history which indicates the possibility of manifold improvements in human capacities.

Tetens' concept of human history and his notion of the historical stages of mankind are quite in line with the philosophy of history which emerged in the last third of eighteenth century and gradually substituted the cyclical view of events for a progressivist view. Tetens' stage-model of primitivism, barbarianism, and civilization as well as his sparse references to the relationship between social and political forms and the structure of human capacities in each stage indicate some familiarity with French and British theories of history, and there is some Rousseauian touch in his argument that any estimate of future prospects of the perfectibility of mankind must reckon with progressive as well as regressive forces. However Tetens had neither theoretical criteria for the conception of stages nor did he take a clear position with regard to the debate on unilinear or dialectical progress (cf. section II).

Though Tetens' allusions to the philosophy of history remain vague in essential points, his concept of human nature may be said, in a sense, to be a historical concept, for it refers to the empirical realization of generically human traits at a given historical stage. In his review of current debates on human nature and development, this concept allowed him to dismiss quite a few controversies—e.g., determinism/indeterminism and mind/body dualism—as metaphysical pseudoproblems from the point of view of practical experience and historical evidence. In the current debate on epigenesis and evolution[6] Tetens took the position that the development of human physical and mental capacities is to be understood as an epigenesis in the course of the evolution of preformed dispositions. Departing from this thesis, his argument is structured in a way that highlights individual development by referring to the history of mankind, and vice versa. This strategy is not used to prove that individual development is an abbreviation of the development of mankind—in fact, Tetens indicates clear limits to that analogy[7]—, but rather to demonstrate the complex conditions of development and the manifold forms, which the perfectibility of man and mankind can take. In the last instance, this demonstration is meant as a political warning: efforts at the improvement of mankind may easily turn fanatical and disastrous if they enforce but one specific form of perfectibility (cf. Tetens 1979, Vol. 1: xxxvi).

In Teten's philosophy of history, conceptualizations of social formations are absent. This absence became a stumbling block for some of his contemporaries, who approached the problems of human nature, society, and history with a view to establishing educational and therapeutical practices.

This may be illustrated with two examples: the authors of the *Allgemeine Revision des gesamten Schul- und Erziehungswesens* (1785–1791)[8] who sought to derive general principles of education from a "correct knowledge of human nature;" and Carl Philipp Moritz, editor of the *Magazin zur Erfahrungsseelenkunde* (1783–1793)[9] who sought to derive a psychopathology and psychotherapy from empirical materials on the psychological development of social deviants.

While the empiricist notion of human nature was conceived by all of these authors in terms of Lockean sensualism, they differed with regard to the meaning of the *tabula rasa*. The authors of the *Allgemeine Revision* shared the wax model, assuming the unlimited modifiability of the human mind and the chance to direct mental development by external control of sense impressions. Moritz, on the other hand, assumed some self-acting force in the individual, which resists external control.

This empiricist notion of human nature is embedded in a notion of essential generic traits of man, the list of which, quite in line with Renaissance anthropology,[10] comprises sociability, self-determination, and perfectibility. With these notions, which are not propounded in a historical context, the authors of the *Allgemeine Revision* tried to establish standards of what may be regarded as accomplished individual development. The problem was most intensively discussed by P.Villaume in a paper entitled "Whether and to what extent education is to sacrifice the perfectibility of the individual in favor of his utility" (*Allgemeine Revision*, vol.3, pp.291ff.), in which he posed the alternative of perfectibility or utility in terms of the education of citizens in a certain state, or of cosmopolitans.

The *Allgemeine Revision* lacks any conceptualization of society or social formations. As far as social conditions are considered with regard to educational practice, this is done in common-sense terms, which accept the factual estate order and various local circumstances. Moritz, on the other hand, formulated a criticism of feudal and bourgeois society, identifying the social division of intellectual and manual labor as the source of all social and psychological problems. But the problem of developmental standards is not a key issue for him. Only implicitly he indicates that, with regard to social deviants, the criterion of a successful therapy or self-therapy would be immunization against suffering, in the sense of a self-preservation of the individual for better social conditions still to come.

Neither the philanthropists nor Moritz can solve the problem of the dichotomy between abstract notions of human nature (empirical and generic), on the one hand, and an incomprehensible social facticity, on the other hand. Their educational purpose required a compromise in favor of the citizen rather than the cosmopolitan, citizen meaning the member of a particular estate in one of the petty German states. Ernst Christian Trapp formulated this compromise quite realistically: one must consider both "what may become of man with regard to his nature" and "what must become of man with regard to the society for which he is destined" (*Allgemeine Revision*, vol.2, p.45).

II

Some of the problems posed by these pioneers of developmental psychology might have been stated more clearly with the aid of other theoretical models of the period, which approached a sociohistoric concept of human nature from different angles.

(a) The social constitution of human nature is most clearly stated by Adam Ferguson and John Millar, representatives of the Scottish historical school,[11] who sought to establish an explanatory theory of history.

For Ferguson, the analysis of human nature is not to depart from the isolated individual, but rather from men living in societies:

> Mankind are to be taken in groups, as they have always subsisted. The history of the individual is but a detail of the sentiments and thoughts he has entertained in the view of his species: and every sentiment relative to this subject should be made with entire societies, not with single men (Ferguson 1969: 6).

Departing from societies primarily means departing from the mode of subsistence prevailing at a given historical stage. This approach to history, inspired by the emerging science of political economy, was the first to emphasize the activities by which the means of living are procured.

Also departing from the mode of subsistence, Millar tried to describe the structure of human needs, capacities, and attitudes as derivations from a specific way of securing material subsistence. For each socio-economic stage—hunting, pasturage, agriculture, commerce and industry—he tried to proceed systematically from the capacities involved in the mode of subsistence, the chances of expanding and refining needs and pleasures, and the attitudes people form in relating to one another, to the social relations between men and women, fathers and children, masters and servants.

This approach sounds like a deterministic version of historical materialism, but it is neither perfectly materialistic nor strictly historicist. There is no explanation of the transition from one mode of subsistence to the next. Since each mode of subsistence is more closely defined by its technique of production, Millar's account starts with the "invention" of some new technique. Some "need of perfectibility," explicitly claimed by Ferguson as the motor of progress, still remains the hidden assumption in Millar's outline. On the other hand, there is a limit to their historicization of man and society. Civil society is conceived as the end and perfection of the history of mankind; the future remains a prolonged present. Thus, there is some remainder of a cyclical model, though it is attached to the model of unilinear progress. Civilized man, man as conceptualized in the seventeenth and eighteenth centuries, is a product of history. This is a criticism of abstract classical anthropology; but with civilized man history comes to a standstill.

(b) In contrast to this unilinear concept of the sociohistoric constitution of human nature, Rousseau[12] provides an outline of a dialectical model. It is only in society that man can acquire his specifically human traits. But while social development can be seen for some time as progress, it later begins to become antagonistic; as soon as there is division of labor between agriculture and industry, and as soon as there is institutionalization of property, progress for some people develops at the expense of the degeneration of the majority of people.

For Rousseau, there is no steady enlargement and refinement of human capacities and needs. Human nature is sociohistorically formed as well as distorted. Thus the *citoyen* is not the fulfilment of man.

Rousseau's social criticism is twofold; it is directed against both French society, which at present is not yet civil society, and against existing civil society in Britain, which provides the model for the future of French society. Since a strictly historical conception of the future does not emerge before the social conditions for an alternative to bourgeois society,[13] the joint criticism of the present and future (present prolonged) results in a past-oriented social alternative[14].

(c) With regard to the problem of theory and practice in the philosophy of history, Kant[15] may be said to offer a sophisticated outlet to the dilemma of either accepting civilized man (bourgeois and *citoyen*) as the present reality of man or despairing of mankind. He tried to demonstrate the possible transition to a cosmopolitan society by departing from men's antagonisms in present society and using the hypothesis of a "natural purpose," which forces mankind to realize reason. Reason is here understood as a natural faculty of the human species for the intelligent choice of means and ends. With the dichotomy between nature and reason thus undermined, a transition from unintelligible to intelligible history is conceivable. The mere concept of an intelligible course of history toward a cosmopolitan society is, however, not sufficient to motivate the practical intention of promoting it. Where could this motivation come from? Before the French Revolution Kant did not answer this question, but when in 1798 he resumed discussion of the problem, there was a glimpse of an answer. The motivation for promoting cosmopolitan society can be drawn from experience; for, even if the French Revolution were to fail, if social conditions remained the same, people would never forget it:

> ... this revolution incites a wishful participation in the mind of the observers (who are not themselves involved in the play-acting), nearly an enthusiasm. .... Such a phenomenon in the history of mankind will never be forgotten, as it

revealed in human nature a disposition or faculty for something better, which no politicvian could have designed from the previous course of events, which could only be promised by nature and freedom . . . (Kant 1964: 358, 361).

(d) In these models, then, there was a theoretical potential, which would have allowed Tetens, Moritz and others to pose the problems and questions of early developmental psychology more sharply: First, if the basic structure of human capacities and needs is sociohistorically constituted as well as "distorted," the conceptualization of individual development should proceed from social concepts and social theories. For the pioneers of developmental psychology, who did not yet abstain from social analysis, this would have meant transforming their social phenomenology and criticism into theoretical concepts. Second, the problem of the relationship between the development of mankind and individual development would have gained an indispensable intermediary dimension. In the history of mankind, the present social order was a distinctive formation, the analysis of which would allow answers to the question of what capacities and needs could be developed at all in this society, and why they developed unequally in the different social groups. Finally, the dichotomy between an abstract ideal of man and his concrete social reality could have been given a Kantian form: what evidence is there of people striving for the perfectibility of mankind and of conditions suitable for these efforts? The Kantian model would also imply an awareness of the distinction between empirical historiography and the philosophy of history. Any project of the emancipation of mankind involves a philosophy of history, which can but demonstrate the *possibility* of improvement and thus leaves the open question whether the possibility will actually be seized.

III

In fact, this theoretical potential has not been used by developmental psychologists, neither by the pioneers nor by their proud successors. The division of labor and specialization in social theory and the social sciences brought about the emergence of a psychology which increasingly disengaged itself from the theorization of society and history. Herbart's reminder that human nature, as analyzed by psychology, is a product of world history may already be taken as an empty phrase, as it was of little consequence for his systematic foundation of psychology.

Quite unlike Ernst Christian Trapp, William Preyer and his contemporaries did not hesitate to define the aims of individual development in terms of social utility. Finally, in our time the question of the aims and ends of individual development has advanced to the status of a nonscientific issue. Because normative questions have to be kept apart from questions of fact, it is said they have been excluded from science. However, the proclaimed scientific neutrality does not and cannot work; thus any developmental theory has its hidden unreflected standards for accomplished development.

The question remains, why have the eighteenth century approaches to a developmental psychology not been pursued, why has the "development" of developmental psychology taken a quite different direction?

The usual hint at the "German misery" is of little help. For the course of developmental psychology, German social conditions were not decisive. There is only one problem I would like to mention with regard to the German pioneers. All of them had a more or less substantial knowledge of British and French social theory and philosophy of history. There is, however, no evidence that they were familiar with the theoretical formulations of the political economy of capitalism, which was an inspiring source as well as a paradigmatic core of social and historical theories in France and Britain;[16] nor would familiarity with political economy have made much sense in the semifeudal conditions of Germany.

More important, I think, are some social and intellectual conditions, which also apply to developmental psychology in Britain and France. When developmental psychologists had just begun to draw on eighteenth century social theory and historical anthropology, the interest of social theorists shifted, and the scope and questions of social analysis rapidly changed. The paradigm of the social mode of subsistence was given up as soon as the social conflicts produced by capitalist society became obvious and the gap between wealth and poverty was registered. When the emerging working class movement began to formulate the radical perspectives of a potential majority of the population, the present and future were turned into history proper, and it remained for the privileged minority to secure the prolongation of the present, practically and theoretically.

With the shifting away from a materialistic theory of history and, after Ricardo, from classical political economy,[17] there was hardly a chance for the pioneers of more scientifically orientated theories to identify the substance and limits of their heritage. On the other hand, the immanent limitations of classical social theory itself smoothed the way for the renaturalization of man. By presenting bourgeois society as a "natural social order," classical theory concealed the significance of the historical question of the relationship of human nature and society even while explicitly posing it.

The social conflicts of the nineteenth century brought about a deep-reaching split in social theory as well. The aim of maintaining the existing social order raised other questions and necessitated other approaches than did the aim of a radical social transformation.[18] Reviewing this split in social theory, we find that the problems posed by early developmental psychologists have been pursued by the radical critics of bourgeois society rather than by social scientists. From Fourier and Owen to Marx the sociohistoric constitution of human capacities and needs has been conceptualized in the context of a critical theory of objective conditions and subjective forces which open up the possibility of improving the developmental conditions for mankind. The perspectives to be gained from this tradition for a developmental psychology could be a promising issue for further investigations.

Notes

[1] In his *Outline of a History of Developmental Psychology*, Günther Reinert (1976) states quite justly that the program of a psychology of human development was never before or after Tetens formulated more comprehensively. Reinert's emphasis is on the scientificity, methodological scrutiny, and Tetens' view of development *processes* and their conditions. While I regard this construction of a predecessor of modern trends in developmental psychology as justifiable, I prefer to emphasize those aspects of Tetens' program, which are in line with the most advanced eighteenth century social and historical theorizing and have not yet been pursued by developmental psychology, but, hopefully, will in the future.

[2] "On the Perfectibility and Development of Man" is the last chapter of Tetens' work (Tetens 1969, vol.2, ch.14). It is described in the Preface as "the goal where most of the preceding considerations get united." The chapter covers nearly 500 pages. In my summary account I try to relate its substance to the presuppositions developed earlier in the work.

[3] For the empirical notion of man cf. esp. vol.1, ch.11, and vol.2, ch.14/4; for the possibilistic notion vol.1, ch.11 and vol.2, ch.14/4/6.

[4] Cf. vol.2, ch.12.

[5] Cf. vol.1: p.740.

[6] For Ch.Bonnet and F.Haller development was the evolution of qualities wholly

preformed in the germ cell. In contrast, Ch.Wolff had propounded the epigenetic thesis of the development of new forms on phylogenesis or ontogenesis.

7   While Tetens allows some analogy from individual development to a modified linearity of the progress of mankind, the chances of improvement of new generations of people are primarily determined by social conditions. Cf.1979, vol.2, ch.14/6.

8   *Allgemeine Revision*, the main journal of the philanthropists, was edited by J.H. Campe; among the members of the editorial board were K.F. Bahrdt, J.Stuve, P.Villaume and E.C. Trapp. For an analysis of the journal see Jaeger and Staeuble (1978: 99–124).

9   For a systematic account of Moritz's approach see Jaeger and Staeuble (1978: 71–84).

10   For a lucid and comprehensive analysis of the concept of man in Renaissance philosophy and emerging anthropology proper see A.Heller (1981).

11   An outline of the social and intellectual development of the "Four-stages-theory" of history is given by R.Meek (1971). For a more recent marxist discussion of Ferguson's theory cf.J.Rohbeck (1981).

12   My interpretation is mainly based on the 1755 *Discours sur l'origine et les fondements de l'inégalité parmi les hommes* (Rousseau, 1978).

13   While F.Bacon may be said to mark the beginning of an orientation towards the technological future, a notion of the social future was not developed before the nineteenth century. A strictly historical notion of the future would imply fundamentally new developments of social and technical conditions. Thus it was more likely to be first formulated by those critics of bourgeois society who, like Marx, tried to identify the transitory character of capitalist social relations.

14   In the *Social Contract* (Rousseau, 1957) the conditions listed for the possibility of establishing real democracy are conditions, which can only apply to small self-sufficient societies subsisting mainly from agriculture and handicrafts.

15   My interpretation is based on "Ideas to a General History in Cosmopolitan Intention" (1784) and "The Contest of the Faculties" (1798). This line of interpretation was first suggested by M.v. Brentano in an unpublished lecture on Kant's writings on the philosophy of history.

16   Adam Smith's *Wealth of Nations* (1776) was translated into German in the year of its first publication by J.F. Schiller, and again 1794–96 by C.Garve. The established system of Cameralism, however, took little note of it. Cf. Staeuble and Jaeger (1978: 84–87).

17   Cf. R.Meek (1950).

18   Marx's critique of social theory emphasizes the inevitable link between social class positions and social theory. With regard to their cognitive substance, social theories are not to be taken as representations of facts, but rather as expressions of the active life process of people. This criterion is also explicitly applied by Marx to his own theory; e.g., "Just as the *economists* are the scientific representatives of the bourgeois class, so the *socialists* and *Communists* are the theoreticians of the proletarian class" (Marx-Engels, *Collected Works*, International Publishers, New York, vol.6, 1976, p.177). More systematically, Marx's theory is in this sense a theory *of* revolution, a formulation of revolutionary aspirations of his period, rather than a theory *about* revolution. This aspect of Marx's break with the theoretical tradition (and, we may add, with the later predominant marxist tradition as well) is discussed in G.Markus (1980).

References

Campe, J.H. (Ed.) (1785–1791). *Allgemeine Revision des gesamten Schul- und Erziehungswesens von einer Gesellschaft praktischer Erzieher.* Hamburg.

Ferguson, A. (1969). *An essay on the history of civil society.* (4th ed.). Gregg International Publishers.

Heller, A. (1981). *Renaissance man.* London & Boston.

Jaeger, S., and Staeuble, I. (1978). *Die gesellschaftliche Genese der Psychologie.* Frankfurt-New York: Campus.

Kant, I. (1964) *Werke in sechs Bänden.* Frankfurt: Insel.

Markus, G. (1980) Die Welt menschlicher Objekte—zum Problem der Konstitution im Marxismus. A. Honneth, & U. Jaeggi (Eds.) *Arbeit, Handlung, Normativität.* Frankfurt: Suhrkamp.

Meek, R. (1950). The decline of Ricardian economics in England. *Economica.*

—(1971). Smith, Turgot, and the four stages theory. *History of Political Economy, 3.*

Millar, J. (1960). *John Millar of Glasgow.* Cambridge University Press.

Moritz, C.P. (Ed.) (1783–1793). *Magazin zur Erfahrungsseelsorge* (10 Vols.).

—(1962). *Schriften zu Aesthetik und Politik.* Tübingen.

Reinert, G. (1976). Grundzüge einer Geschichte der Human-Entwicklungspsychologie. In *Die Psychologie des XX. Jahrhunderts,* Pp. 862–896. Zürich: Kindler.

Rohbeck, J. (1981). Zum Verhältnis von Menschheits- und Naturgeschichte in der Fortschrittstheorie des ausgehenden 18. Jahrhunderts. *Materialistische Wissenschaftsgeschichte.* Berlin: Argument.

Rousseau, J.J. (1957). *The social contract.* New York: Hafner.

—(1978). *Schriften zur Kulturkritik.* Hamburg: Meiner.

Tetens, J.N. (1969). *Philosophische Versuche über die menschliche Natur und ihre Entwicklung.* Hildesheim & New York: Olms.

Victor de l'Aveyron and the Relativist-Essentialist Controversy

by Alexandre Métraux

1. Introduction

The first decade of nineteenth-century science in France reveals itself to be a rewarding field of investigation for the historian of science interested in the emergence of evolutionary theories.

Indeed, in 1809, Lamarck published his *Philosophie zoologique*, which offers a coherent and well-argued approach to the evolution of animal species. In retrospect, this publication presents itself not only as the culminating point of Lamarck's own year-long study in natural science, and especially in zoology, but also as a result of a major trend of thought which attracted a lot of intellectual attention in the period of Enlightenment. Evolutionary ideas had been discussed and debated in various disciplines, whether philosophic or scientific, throughout the eighteenth century. To mention but a few instances:

—In his natural history of mind, Julien Offray de La Mettrie (1745) has attempted to account for the organization of matter into animate beings and—with respect to man—into moral agents from a thoroughly materialistic stance, which outrageously scandalized all the *bien-peasants* of the church and the court;

—Denis Diderot and his friends had welcomed Locke's principles and interpreted them in such a way as to make them the ground on which to build up an ontogenetic theory of knowledge. This explains the relevance of comparative analyses in the study of the growth of cognitive functions, and hence the importance of differential methods taking into account the conditions under which men born with some perceptual deficiency would fill the *tabula rasa* (cf. Diderot 1749/1987a and 1751/1978b), on the one hand, and of comparative ethnographic studies, on the other (for an excellent survey, cf. Landucci 1972 and Duchet 1977).

Bernard Le Bovier de Fontenelle (1702 sqq. and 1766), Anne Robert Jacques Turgot (1750/1842–1853), and Marie Jean Antoine Caritat, marquis de Condorcet (1804/1970) had each tried to impose an evolutionary rationale upon their accounts of the history of science, thereby justifying and popularizing the notion of progress through education, enlightenment, and political reform.

And yet, it seems that the decisive breakthrough of evolutionism proper took place with Lamarck, whose work, as it were, concluded the period of scientific and philosophic maturation of the eighteenth century and opened up a promising horizon for the nineteenth century. Thus, depending on the standpoint the historian takes, the first decade of French science in the nineteenth century can be regarded *either* as the closing chapter of the prerevolutionary period (which was rich of social, political, philosophical, and ideological antagonisms), *or* as the opening chapter of a new period (with even stronger political, social, philosophical, and ideological antagonisms, except that the historical significance of the latter differs notably from that of the eighteenth century).

Most historians of science—with the exception of Gillespie (1956) and Barthélémy-Madaule (1979)—have focused nearly exclusively on the first part of Lamarck's *Philosophie zoologique.* They thus have taken implicitly a more or less moderate presentistic standpoint. The ideas contained in the first part of Lamarck's major work have indeed been more often than not contrasted with Darwin's theory of evolution and/or with some neo-Darwinian or neo-Lamarckian approach. The historians have therefore tended to somehow legitimize this or that theoretical standpoint. But in doing so, they have underestimated (or simply overlooked) what, at closer examination, may be regarded as a very strong heritage of the Enlightenment in Lamarck, namely the innovative and explanatory power of the concept "system of nature" *(système de la nature).* This concept cannot adequately be dealt with from the standpoint of the history of a single science—be it chemistry, physiology, or zoology. In other words, Lamarck's evolutionism outreaches the boundaries of zoology (or even biology), and more specifically the boundaries traditionally attributed to the theory of the evolution of animal species. Instead of a lengthy interpretation in support of this view, suffice it to mention that Lamarck literally exploited within the frame of the "system of nature" the principle of individual adaptation to changing environmental conditions and of the inheritance of individually acquired characteristics in order to explain the morphogenesis of the perceptual apparatus, thus laying the grounds for a comparative theory of *psychological functions.* Indeed, he claimed that "if ideas, thought and even imagination are only natural phenomena, and therefore dependent on organization, then it must be chiefly the province of the zoologist, who makes a special study of organic phenomena, to investigate what ideas are, and how they are produced and preserved" (Lamarck 1963: 287). This makes clear that Lamarck's program aimed at a synthesis of anatomy, physiology, zoology, and psychology.

In the same decade in which Lamarck published his *opus magnum*, a controversy about the cultural or social conditions of human ontogeny was initiated by the capture of a twelve- or thirteen-year-old boy who had lived in almost total solitude until his capture in the forest of Lacaune in Southwest France. The year-long observation of the effects society would have upon this child through the mediation of a systematically designed education was expected to settle the old problem concerning the relationship between nature and nurture. Moreover, the case of Victor—as the boy came to be called—is indicative, from a methodological point of view, of the status of observation and of experimentation in the rise of the anthropological sciences following that of the institutionally already-established biological sciences.

Beast children or *homines feri*, as they were called according to the classificatory label popularized by Linné, have been reported and more or less accurately described ever since the discovery of the *Juvenis lupinus Hessensis* in 1344 (in this context, I do not take into consideration the mythical, but socially and politically relevant cases of beast children like Romulus and Remus). However, up to the early nineteenth century, such children had nearly always been regarded as mere curiosities or as queer anomalies of nature.

Symptomatic for the embarrassment caused by beast children in scientifically trained minds is the attitude of both Boerhaave and Linné. In his lectures on medicine, Boerhaave used to mention the case of a child, later labelled as *Johannes Leodic. Boerhaavi*, who seems to have been abandoned at the age of five and to have lived alone for some sixteen years in the woods around Liège (today Belgium). This boy—or rather, this young adult—attracted Boerhaave's attention, for when he was found, his sense of smell was extremely well developed (it is said that he could recognize humans by mere smell), whereas the longer he lived in society, the more this sense lost its accuracy. Boerhaave's interest thus focused above all upon a phenomenon that was held to be nonnormal from the medical or physiological point of view; his interest did not at all focus upon the theoretically not less intriguing question whether social factors could have some impact on the development of perception; such questions were later raised in connection with the case of Victor and systematically analyzed in the twentieth century, e.g. by Luria (1974).

On the other hand, the classification of beast children in Linné's *Systema naturae* also reveals the embarrassment which arose in a scientific mind when confronted with nonnormal cases of human development. Indeed, though fully recognized as belonging to the species of *homo sapiens diurnus,* they constitute a separate class and are listed individually as exemplars of *homo ferus.* Interestingly, however, the description of the *homines feri* is followed by that of several classes like *homo affricanus, homo europaeus, homo asiaticus,* etc., which, in turn, precedes the description of several monsters (Siamese twins, giants, dwarfs, etc.), who also constitute a separate class of *homo monstrosus* (see Linné 1788: 21–24; see also the commented classification in Linné and Müller 1773: 61–109). The parallelism between the treatment of beast children and that of monsters illustrates the role which socially mediated images of the nature of man (and thus also of nonnormal cases thereof) could play in the classificatory attempts of the time.

A shift of interest from that of anomalous curiosities to that of theoretically interrelated and cogent issues took place around the turn of the eighteenth to the nineteenth century. To be sure, this shift had been gradually prepared by several convergent trends of thought in the eighteenth century. The problem of the origin of cognition, emotion, and language had been raised in different contexts by the *philosophes* within the framework of Locke's critique of Cartesian nativism and of the Lockean empiricist epistemology. This framework allowed one to construe theoretically nontrivial hypotheses about the development of human ideas as well as about the causes and conditions of this development. Yet, although the Lockean framework, which had been made quite popular by Voltaire in France, turned out to be very fruitful for theoretical purposes, the *philosophes* were aware of the fact that none of their hypotheses could really be verified or falsified by empirical evidence. This explains why so many thought experiments were carried out, on the one hand, and why more or less keen suggestions were made about how the hypotheses could be tested, on the other hand.

Both Buffon (1749: 364) and Condillac (1754/1947: 222sqq.)—to mention nearly arbitrarily two authors only—imagined a man (or rather a statue) whose organs were supposed to be fully developed, but who, instead of growing up under normal conditions, would suddenly awake as an adult in a given environment. This philosophical stratagem would then permit the theorist of cognition to observe "by imagination" how the statue would progressively come to know the world on the basis of the sensory input. Thus, as C.Solomon-Bayet (1978: 204) points out, experimental fictions are a common logical and rhetorical topic in the biological and social sciences of the eighteenth century, which in the absence of experimental possibilities, replace Newton's *hypothetes non fingo* by *experientias fingo*.

And regarding what one could call the progam of designs of experiments which in all likelihood would provide some data that could confirm this or that hypothesis, Maupertuis (1752) ought to be mentioned here among many others. He suggested that two or three young children be isolated, so that one could observe the development of both linguistic competence and linguistic performance—Maupertuis obviously believed that speech develops spontaneously. Moreover, he made the suggestion of creating artificial societies in order to allow the observer to grasp differentially the effects of culturally determined behavior patterns on the development of children—an idea in comparison to which the Skinnerian version of a behavioristic design appears to be rather timid after all.

It is not surprising, then, that the discovery and capture of the beast-child Victor was enthusiastically welcomed, since finally an opportunity existed to study the ontogeny of cognition and emotion *in vivo*, instead of constantly debating about more or less plausible answers to this crucial question.

2. The history of the case

The second part of this paper is entirely devoted to the chronological reconstruction of the case of *Victor de l'Aveyron;* this reconstruction is based upon the archival material recently edited by Gineste (1981) as well as upon the most important printed sources published between 1800 and 1830.

– 1797: Some hunters catch a glimpse of a naked boy in the wood of Lacaune (situated at the eastern border of the *département du Tarn*). It is reported that the boy, when seen by the hunters, immediately flees.

– April, 1797: The boy is captured near the hamlet La Bassine, not far away from Lacaune. Some days later, the boys escapes.

– 1798 (June/July): The boy is captured again and is taken care of by a widow. A week after, he escapes once again.

– January 9, 1800: The boy is captured for the third and last time in the village of Saint-Sernin-sur-Rance close to the southwest border of the *département de l'Aveyron.*

– January 10, 1800: In order to carry out some medical observations, the local authorities decide to transfer the boy into a home *(hospice)* at Saint-Affrique.

– January 25, 1800: A brief report about the capture of the boy is published in the newspaper *Les Débats*. Thanks to this article, the central administration of the department, the Secretary of the Interior in Paris, as well as the scientific community are made aware of the extraordinary discovery of a beast-child. The prefect (i.e., the chief administrator of the department) orders the immediate transfer of the boy to the main home of Rodez; there, the natural scientist P.J. Bonnaterre is requested to carefully observe the boy.

– January 29, 1800: On behalf of the *Société des Observateurs de l'homme*, L.F. Jauffret sends a letter to the administrators of the home at Rodez and asks for the transfer of the boy to Paris, so that the members of the Society of the Observers of Mankind may be able to study the case.

– February 1, 1800: Lucien Bonaparte, then Home Secretary, orders the transfer of the boy to Paris.

– February 2, 1800: Second letter of Lucien Bonaparte, repeating his order.

– February 14, 1800: Rogery, Cambon, Passelac, Daude, and Combes of the city administration of Rodez note in their reply to Lucien Bonaparte, that the boy seems to be an abandoned child who ought to be examined, that the observation by Bonnaterre is likely to take some time, and that the boy will be kept in Rodez if the government does not give new and explicit orders to transfer him to Paris. In addition, the members of the administration emphasize that the child should receive "a special attention on the part of the government, for he is of interest to mankind as such" (see Gineste, *op. cit.*, pp. 110–111).

– June 7, 1800: Sainthorent, the prefect of the departement, in a letter to Lucien Bonaparte, suggests that the boy be handed over to Sicard, head of the home for the education of deaf and mute children in Paris; in addition, he mentions the fact that the boy has kept "wild habits," that he has not yet learned to speak, although he is able to utter sounds, and that his mental capacities seem to be normal (see Gineste, *op. cit.*, p. 115).

– June 23, 1800: Lucien Bonaparte urges the prefect to organize immediately the transfer of the boy to Paris, and informs Ambroise Sicard that Bonnaterre will soon deliver the child.

– July 12, 1800: Sainthorent signs the departmental order according to which Bonnaterre is going to take care of the child throughout the voyage to Paris, for which the government pays the sum of 740 francs.

– End of July/beginning of August: Journey to Paris, interrupted at Châlons-sur-Saune due to the fact that the boy fell ill (most probably of smallpox).

– August 6, 1800: A report on Victor is read before the *Société des Observateurs de l'homme.*

– August 9, 1800: Sicard published an account of the case of Victor in the *Gazette de France* (see Gineste, *op. cit.,* pp.119–121).

– August 29, 1800: Lucien Bonaparte invites Sicard to show him the boy.

– August 30, 1800: Victor is shown to Lucien Bonaparte.

– August, 1800: G. Feydel initiates a controversy in the *Journal de Paris* (see Gineste, *op. cit.,* p.123). This controversy will last until the end of the year. Feydel argues that Victor is but an impostor; Sicard and some other authors attempt to show that the boy ought to be regarded as a beast-child.

– September, 1800: Publication of Bonnaterre's report, which contains the history of the case and a detailed description of Victor's physical and mental constitution as far as it could be examined at Rodez (see Bonnaterre 1800).

– November, 1800: An anonymous article, *Réflexions sur le sauvage de l'Aveyron, et sur ce qu'on appelle en général, par rapport à l'homme, l'état de nature,* is published by the journal *La Décade philosophique* (see Gineste, *op. cit.,* pp.173–179). According to Gineste (*op. cit.,* p.319), this text has most probably been written by J.J. Virey.

– End of Autumn, 1800: J.J. Virey defends the culturalistic thesis in his *Dissertation sur un jeune enfant trouvé dans les forêts du départment de l'Aveyron, avec des remarques sur l'état primitif de l'homme* (see Gineste, *op. cit.,* pp.179–197).

– November 29, 1800: Philippe Pinel, at that time the leading French psychiatrist and a member of the *Société des Observateurs de l'homme,* reads a report before the members of this society. Though he refrains from giving a final diagnosis—the second part of his memorandum will be read in May, 1801 only—, the way in which he presents the case invites the audience to believe that the beast-child of the Aveyron is but a congenital cretin. Thus, the biologistic thesis is spelled out for the first time in public (see Pinel 1800).

– February 24, 1801: The administrators of the *établissements de bienfaisance* in Paris ask that the Home Secretary appoint Jean Marc

Gaspard Itard as educator of Victor. The sum of 150 francs per year is requested for the payment of Itard's educational work.

– April 8, 1801: In the meantime, the rather liberal Lucien Bonaparte has been replaced by the politically conservative chemist, Jean Chaptal, as Home Secretary. The latter rejects the request submitted in February and advises the administrators of the home for the education of deaf and mute children (where Victor stays as patient) to transfer the boy to the mental hospital of Charenton, since he is convinced that the case is totally hopeless, and that a psychiatric treatment is preferable to an expensive and useless education by Itard.

– May, 1801: Pinel's report, second part, is read before the members of the *Société des Observateurs de l'homme* (see Pinel 1801). This time, the diagnosis of the psychiatrist is unambiguous.

– June 20, 1801: Itard protests against Pinel's conclusion in a brief note addressed to the *Mercure de France.*

– September/October, 1801: Itard writes his first report, in which he describes the case as well as the training which he has set up for Victor.

– October 7, 1801: Chaptal finally agrees to fund the special training of Victor for the next six months.

– October 20, 1801: Degerando reads a summary of Itard's report (see above) during the meeting of the *Société des Observateurs de l'homme.*

– March 14, 1802: Chaptal wants to know from Itard how far Victor has progressed.

– May 3, 1802: Instead of Itard, Sicard sends a report to Chaptal, pleading for the continuation of the training.

– October 6, 1802: Chaptal complains about the number of daily visitors who want to see Victor at Sicard's home. This indicates—in absence of any administrative document between May 3 and October 6, that new funds have been allocated by the administration, despite Chaptal's decision of October 7, 1801 (see above).

– May 2, 1804: Chaptal orders interruption of the payment for Victor's training. This decision is most likely due to the critical financial situation prevailing in France at that time.

– June 9, 1804: In reaction to Chaptal's order, Itard sends his second report to the Home Secretary and asks for new funds.

– June 20, 1804: Chaptal informs the administration of Sicard's home that Itard's request is going to be rejected.

– July 21, 1804: The administration of Sicard's home submits another request for funding.

– June 13, 1806: Champigny, who has replaced Chaptal (the latter could no longer agree with Napoleon's policies), is willing to reconsider the case and asks for another report.

– June 15, 1806: The report, provided by the administration of Sicard's home, is submitted to Champigny (cf. Gineste, *op.cit.*, pp.267–270).

– September 18, 1806: In order to influence Champigny's attitude toward the case, Itard submits his third report (see Itard 1807).

– September 23, 1806: Champigny is obviously impressed by Itard's third report. In a note to the *Institut National,* he suggests that the memorandum be printed. The positive reaction of Champigny has most probably been reinforced by one of his advisers, Degerando, a member of the *Société des Observateurs de l'homme* (see above).

– End of 1806: Finally, new funds are allocated by the Home Office.

– March 5, 1811: Montalivet, Champigny's successor, gives orders to interrupt Victor's training.

– May 2, 1811: Mme Guérin, who has helped Itard during the past years at the *Institution des Sourds-Muets de Paris,* agrees to take care of Victor; she will be paid a very modest sum for this duty.

– Beginning of 1828: Death of Victor; the exact date has remained unknown to this day.

In retrospect, the entire history of the case of Victor turns out to have evolved on three analytically distinguishable levels:

(1) the level of the press, the literary circles, the theatre, ect.; the events pertaining to this level are not very relevant for the historian of science, but they obviously would have to be taken into account in a sociohistorical reconstruction;

(2) the level of the central and local administration; the events pertaining to this second level are relevant for the historian of science insofar as the attitude of the French Home Secretaries and of their advisers either promoted or obstructed the empirical examination of the case;

(3) the scientific level, on which two groups of experts with more or less outspoken opinions and beliefs opposed each other.

3. The controversy between the culturalistic and the biologistic theses

Two main theses concerning the ontogeny of intelligence and of moral sentiment or emotion conflicted with one another during the period under consideration. The protagonists of the controversy relied on data collected by some few observers and sought to defend their positions by showing that their interpretation of the data was theoretically more convincing than that of the opposing side. There was, on the one hand, the culturalistic thesis, defended by Bonnaterre, Virey, Sicard, and above all by Itard, who was later to become an internationally reputed specialist of orthology. On the other hand, there was the biologistic position, argued for by Pinel (although with some hesitation), and by Jean Etienne Dominique Esquirol and some other physicians.

The culturalistic thesis maintains in line with some central ideas developed in the eighteenth century, e.g. by Rousseau, that a man without education, i.e. without having been subject to some cultural influence, is not a man, and that he is not even comparable to an animal endowed with instincts. On the other hand, the biologistic thesis maintains that the development (or maturation) of human behavior of whatever kind is primarily determined by the physical or biological constitution, although education is said to play some role in the development of cognition, emotion, and language. Indeed, I have not found any remark of the proponents of the biologistic position denying the importance of education as such. The touchstone of the whole controversy is, therefore, not education, but the way in which the relationship between the physical constitution of man and the effects of education through the mediation of social agents ought to be construed in a theoretically satisfactory manner. For the proponents of the culturalistic thesis believe that education *necessarily* determines all mental functions of man (including the elementary perceptual abilities), whereas the proponents of the opposing thesis maintain that mental functions develop spontaneously and that the cultural factor is only *contingently* decisive for a man's speaking Chinese rather than French or English, for a man's counting in the decimal rather than the duodecimal system, etc., but not for a man's speaking, counting, acting, etc., as such.

Now, all participants in the controversy agree that the perceptual abilities of the *juvenis averionensis* Victor were partly damaged. He seems to have been able to hear, but he reacted only to some noises—such as the cracking of nutshells, but not the firing of a pistol. His sight was more or less intact, but he was not capable of fixating on an object longer than some instants. He easily discriminated between hot and cold. According to Virey and Itard, olfaction and gustatory perception were exceptionally well developed, while the haptic sense was quite deficient. Victor's memory seems to have been rather poor.

This manifested itself repeatedly in his being incapable of recalling the simplest items during the painful training designed by Itard in order to teach Victor the French language. Conversely—and this is a crucial point emphasized by the culturalistic position—the speechlessness of Victor is made causally responsible for the deficiencies of his memory. With regard to habits and social behavior, the observers note that Victor did not modify his food habits, that he kept a preference for raw potatoes, nuts, vegetables, and roots of different kinds, refusing to consume meat, fruits, and sweets. His social behavior showed no constancy whatsoever; thus, sympathy for a person could rapidly change without any externally visible cause into antipathy, and vice versa. His manual skills for certain tasks revealed themselves to be extraordinary, but in general his physical and social skills remained far below average, despite the years-long training. In other words, the observers agree that there is something in Victor that is an obstacle to the process of acculturation. And it is precisely this unknown something hidden behind a phenomenally noncontroversial collection of observable facts, which constitutes the subject matter of the controversy which started, as was indicated before, in 1800, and lasted until the eighteen-thirties.

Thus, Esquirol sweepingly asserts in the entry *Idotisme* written for the *Dictionnaire des Sciences médicales* (1818) as well as in his treatise on mental illnesses (see Esquirol 1830: 373–375), that the *juvenis averionensis* was an idiot because (1) his physical constitution resembled that of the young cretins living in mental hospitals, and because (2) a years-long pedagogical intervention would have modified Victor's behavior and led to the acquisition of language had his constitution been that of a normal person. Esquirol's *explanation* rests, as it were, on two different arguments: on the one hand, he argues physiognomically and construes a kind of syllogistic reasoning which implies that Victor must be an idiot since he is *like* persons recognized by the medical profession to be mentally ill; on the other hand, he assumes that the impact of social agents upon Victor's behavior would have had some observable effects if his organic constitution did not determine cognition, emotion, behavior, etc. But in both cases, Esquirol unhesitatingly ignores the fact that, unlike the children whom he could examine in mental hospitals, Victor had been abandoned in early childhood and therefore had lived under conditions which fundamentally differed from those of idiotic children under care of physicians.

Similarly to Esquirol, another physician, Bousquet, maintains in the *éloge* of Itard read before the Academy of Medicine in Paris briefly after Itard's death, that Victor was but an idiot, and that Itard had wasted his time in devoting so much effort to the education of the beast-child. This judgment indicates that at least the medical profession was deeply convinced by 1840 that the case was settled in favor of the biologistic position. And before that, the German physiologist Karl Asmund Rudolphi had already carried out the inductive generalization in saying that *"schwachsinnig war und blieb der Knabe, dessen sich E.M. Itard so väterlich annahm"* (Rudolphi 1821: 25) like all *homines feri* about whom there exist trustworthy reports. . . .

In sum, the biologistic position asserts that all mental functions undergo a process of spontaneous maturation if the biological constitution of an individual permits this process to take place; it further asserts that the development of cognition and emotion follows a certain lawlike pattern independently of social conditions. The latter are merely contingent in that they shape the development of mental functions, i.e. to say, in that they superimpose culturally determined patterns of speaking, behaving, acting, etc., upon a process which in itself is causally determined by the constitution of the organism.

In contradistinction, the proponents of the culturalistic position argue that a congenital idiot could not have survived and that Victor, had he been what the medical profession is believing him to be, would certainly not have acquired some extraordinary skills in adapting himself to a rough environment. Indeed, in a way similar to Lamarck's phylogenetic theory, Itard and his friends were convinced that the environment has selectively favored the development of some skills and repressed that of others, and that when the boy was captured the mental functions were already fixed. This explains why the years-long training called out almost no behavioral or cognitive modification. In other words, had Victor not been abandoned, another—social—environment would have enabled him to undergo a normal development.

In sum, the culturalistic position asserts that mental functions do not develop spontaneously and that in order to develop normally they necessarily require some monitoring through a social environment.

4. Conclusion

There is no doubt that ideological aspects impinged upon the controversy about Victor. Indeed, both groups of scientists argued in a context in which empirical data allowed the drawing of divergent, or even opposite, conclusions. The physicians (Pinel, Esquirol, and some others) tended from the outset to exclude the possibility of interpreting the empirical data as an indication of the existence of inter- or intracultural specificities and differences; instead, they postulated a one-to-one relationship between mental functions and organic constitution. Their culturalistic opponents, on the other hand, tended to overcome the difficulties of an empirically well-founded proof of the adequacy of their thesis by using moral arguments. They implied the normalcy of the physiopsychological constitution of the *juvenis averionensis* and established a causal relationship between the nonnormal development of the child and a crime committed by society. Thus, they mixed theoretical with moral arguments.

But there is more to it. A parallelism exists—as noted before—between Lamarck's evolutionary theory and the theory of the culturalistic thinkers who dealt with the case of Victor. Both theories put the emphasis on the *adaptation* of the *individual* to the environment and consider the environmental differences to be the cause for interindividual differences. To put it differently, the idea of adaptation is the explanatory schema *par excellence* for both theories.

On the other hand, there exists a parallelism between the biologistic theory of Esquirol—to mention only him—and the anti-Lamarckian theory of Cuvier. Indeed, Cuvier, a personal *protégé* of Napoleon, turned out to be an opponent of Itard, too. His pseudoevolutionism implies an essentialistic notion of the animal species. The reasons why he opposed Itard cannot be reconstructed in detail on the basis of the available documents. However, the "family resemblance" between his position and that of Esquirol and other physicians is striking, for the latter also revealed itself to be essentialistic. In other words, the rejection of the idea of the individual adaptation to the natural and/or social environment went hand in hand with the affirmation of the central notion of an immutable (or nearly immutable) species on the phylogenetic level, and that of an immutable (or nearly immutable) physiopsychological constitution on the ontogenetic level. Finally, to the rejection of Lamarck's environmentalism (and relativism)—a politically useful rejection since it permitted the legitimation of a nondemocratic structure—there corresponds the rejection of Itard's environmentalism (and relativism), which permitted the desocialization of cases like that of Victor by making them an issue of psychiatry.

The controversy about Victor was undoubtedly stimulated by a strong scientific interest. Yet, the longer it lasted, the more it seems to have become a fight between the relativism of the Enlightenment and the essentialism of the new conservatism of the eighteenth century, and a prelude for much stronger controversies which have been going on ever since.

References

Barthélémy-Madaule, M. (1979). *Lamarck ou le mythe du précurseur.* Paris: Seuil.

Bonnaterre, P. (1800). *Notice historique sur le sauvage de l'Aveyron et sur quelque autres individus qu'on a trouvés dans les forêts, à différentes époques.* Paris: Panckouke.

Buffon, G. (1749). *Histoire naturelle, t. III: Histoire naturelle de l'homme/Des sens en général.* Paris.

Condillac, E. (1947). Traité des sensations. In *Oeuvres philosophiques de Condillac* (Vol.1). Paris; Presses Universitaires de France, pp.219–335. (1754).

Condorcet, M. (1970). *Esquisse d'un tableau historique des progrès de l'esprit humain.* Paris: Librairie philosophique J.Vrin. (1804).

Diderot, D. (1978a). Lettre sur les aveugles à l'usage de ceux qui voient. In *Oeuvres complètes* (Vol.4). Paris: Hermann, pp.15–72. (1749).

—(1978a). Lettres sur les aveugles à l'usage de ceux qui voient. In *Oeuvres complètes* (Vol.6). Paris: Hermann.

—(1978b). Lettre sur les sourds et les muets à l'usage de ceux qui entendent et qui parlent. In *Oeuvres complètes* (Vol.4.). Paris: Hermann, pp.129–228 (1751).

Duchet, M. (1977). *Anthropologie et histoire au siècle des Lumières.* Paris: Flammarion.

Esquirol, J. (1818). "Idiotisme." In *Dictionnaire des Sciences médicales* (Vol.23). Paris: Pankouke, pp.50–511.

Esquirol, J. (1830). *Des maladies mentales* (Vol.2). Paris: Baillère.

Fontenelle, B. (1702). *Histoire de l'Académie royale des sciences avec les mémoirs . . . tirés des registres de cette Académie.* Paris.

—(1766). Sur l'histoire. In: *Oeuvres de Monsieur de Fontenelle* (Vol.6.). Paris: Les Libraires associés. pp.391–411.

Gillespie, C. (1956). The formation of Lamarck's evolutionary theory. *Archives Internationales d'Histoire des Sciences. 35,* pp.322–338.

Gineste, T. (1981). *Victor de l'Aveyron. Dernier enfant sauvage, enfant fou.* Paris: Le Sycomore.

Itard, J. (1807). *Rapport fait à S.E. ministre de l'Intérieur sur les nouveaux développements et l'état actuel du sauvage de l'Aveyron.* Paris: Imprimerie impériale.

Lamarck, J. (1809.) *Philosophie zoologique.* Paris: Dentu.

La Mettrie, J. (1745). *Histoire naturelle de l'âme.* La Haye: Jean Neaulme.

Landucci, S. (1972). *I filosofi e i selvaggi: 1580–1780.* Bari: Editori Laterza.

Linné, C.v. (1788) *Systema naturae* (Vol.1.). Leipzig: Beer.

Linné, C.v. and Muller, P. (1773). *Des Ritters Carl von Linné . . . vollständiges Natursystem nach der zwölften lateinischen Ausgabe.* Nürnberg: Raspe.

Luria, A. (1974). *Ob istoričeskom rezvitii poznavatel'nykh protsessov.* Moskva: Izdatel'stvo "Nauka."

Maupertuis, P. (1752). *Lettre sur le progrès des sciences.*

Pinel, P. (1800). *Rapport fait a la Société des Observateurs de l'homme sur l'enfant connu sous les nom de sauvage de l'Aveyron.* (Gineste, 1981, pp.197–206).

—(1801). *Deuxième partie du rapport fait à la Société des Observateurs de l'homme sur l'énfant connu sous nom de sauvage de l'Aveyron.* (Gineste, 1981, pp.211–217).

Rudolphi, K. (1821). *Grundriss der Physiologie* (Vol.1.). Berlin: Dümmler.

Solomon-Bayet, C. (1978). *L'institution de la science et l'expérience du vivant.* Paris: Flammarion.

Turgot, A. (1750). *Discours sur les progrès successifs de l'esprit humain prononcé de 11 décembre 1750.* Paris.

The Concept of Development and the Genetic Method of C.G. Carus

by Ursula Köhler

The noted physician, scientist and philosopher of German Romanti-cism, *Carl Gustav Carus* (1789–1869), offered informal, public lectures on a variety of anthropological topics in Dresden, the captial of the German Kingdom of Saxony, during the academic year of 1827–1828. During the winter of 1829 he was invited to extend his popular *Vorlesungen* (lectures) to the field of psychology. Carus was at that time a forty-year-old Professor of Obstetrics at the *Chirurgisch-Medici-nische Akademie* (Surgical Medical Academy) in Dresden where he had recently received a prestigious appointment as physician to the royal court.

1. Origin of the genetic views of Carus

The *Lectures on Psychology* began in December of 1829 before a select audience of "diplomats, civil servants, scientists, physicians and artists" (Carus 1831: iv). Carus did not offer a "formal system" of psychology in his lectures but instead expressed his personal "views, observations, and opinions" about the subject matter to his audience as a basis for group discussion (1831: v).

He critically revised his lecture notes, when the opportunity arose for publication, removing misleading terms like *Teile der Seele* (parts of the soul) or *Sitz der Seele* (seat of the soul) (1831: vii). Carus believed that it would be possible to present his ideas more correctly and more clearly by adhering to the following strategy (1831: ix):

> if one were to apply the theory of biogenesis to psychology, which has yielded such immensely important information for the sciences, one should trace the development of the soul from its darkest and simplest manifestations to the most complex, highest and purest expressions of life.

During the revision of his notes, Carus carefully reviewed his quotations from other authors "on our inner world" (1831: ix) which he had collected for his lectures. Unfortunately, he had to conclude that genetic ideas had been relatively neglected in the history of psychology, although Aristotle and Dante described successive stages of the soul's development. Plato also used a similar model in his discussions of cognition. Carus was convinced that his own approach to psychological questions was influenced by the genetic method, which "Goethe and Herder first proposed ... and which Oken first applied systematically to the subject [matter] of the outer senses ..." (1831: xi). Oken's influence is quite obvious in the *Lehrbuch of Zootomie* (Textbook of Zootomy) which Carus published in 1818. In his autobiography, he specifically acknowledged "the important effect" which this "comparative anatomy" exerted on his own thinking by its "thoroughly genetic organization" (1865:156).

Although Carus cited many authorities in his *Vorlesungen* (1831), he included no specific references to the relevant literature which could support his claims. The documentation of his *Lebenserinnerungen und Denkwürdigkeiten* (Autobiography and Memorabilia, 1865–66) is just as informal. There are many allusions to the literary and scientific works of Goethe and a few comments about his personal contacts with Herder but a direct influence of their ideas cannot be shown. On the other hand,

Table 1.

Content summary of "Psychological Lectures by C.G. Carus (1831)"

Major Topics	Lectures
Introduction: (Theoretical basis and phylogenetic consideration)	I – III
Part I: General psychology of man	
1. History of the development of the human soul	III – X
2. About the health of soul	X – XI
3. About the illness of soul	XI – XIII
Part II: Special psychology of man	
1. Sleep and related conditions	XIV – XVI
2. Wakefulness and related conditions	XVI – XXI

Carus repeatedly described the lasting influence of Ludwig Oken on his own thinking. Oken's *Lehrbuch des Systems der Naturphilosophie* (Systematic Textbook of Natural Philosophy, 1809–1811) had aroused the interest of Carus when he was a twenty-year-old medical student (1865–66:66ff).

Thanks to the repeated revisions of the 1829 lecture notes, the 21 *Vorlesungen über Psychologie* (Lectures on Psychology, 1831) provide their subject matter in a clear and systematic order (see Table 1).

We are primarily interested in the *Introduction* and *Part I* in which Carus dealt at length with the developmental perspective and its application to the study of a previously inaccessible subject matter.

2. Introduction to the genetic method

In *Lecture I* Carus unambiguously stated that his method depended on both "the nature of the subject matter" to be studied and the "developmental level of the individual background of the observer" (p.4). Unfortunately, "observation becomes more difficult ..." the less the subject matter is "accessible to the external senses" (p.4f.). The "human soul" as an object of study, of course, pertains "to the world of the inner sense" (p.4f.) and not to the "phenomena of outer life" (p.3). In a manner of speaking, the ego itself becomes the subject matter of our investigation in this context. Still, one must not be satisfied with the "subjective nature of all knowledge" (p.8) which results from the individual background of the observer. This bias can be overcome, according to Carus, by increasing the number of cases studied and by resorting to "the genius of mankind which over many thousand generations has gradually increased the accuracy of measurement" (p.9). Consequently, the exploration of the soul does not have to be merely a casual reflection of the individual researcher without any objective truth" (p.9f.).

This cognitive dilemma can be overcome by a careful choice of methods, which "are suitable to the intrinsic nature of the subject matter" (p.11). Hence, useful methods must be identified according to the criterion of appropriateness. Specifically, Carus suggested that the methods should be tested not "with the elusive phenomena of the inner sense but ... where the inner sense can be guided, promoted and corrected with the help of the outer senses, i.e. the phenomena of nature" (p.10). In modern terminology, Carus seems to be calling for a validation by external criteria!

Next, he presented three traditional methods which have been used to study nature. Table 2 briefly summarizes the advantages and disadvantages of each technique.

Table 2.

Methods of observation

Methods	Natural phenomena (pp. 11–13)	Human soul (pp. 21–24)
Descriptive	Partial	Partial utilization recommended
Analytic	utilization	
Teleologic	recommended	Not to be applied
Genetic	Proper scientific procedure	

According to Carus, the descriptive and the analytic methods contribute "useful knowledge for many kinds of applications" and the "most beneficial results for the understanding of nature" (p.12). The teleological method, on the other hand, which Carus included for pragmatic reasons, was "assigned a significantly lower rank" than the first two methods (p.13).

The genetic method, however, inspired Carus to the following eloquent paragraph (p.13f.)

> If then there is a certain truth in all the depicted methods . . . and if, therefore, all of them merit partial application, we must look for still another method for our scientific study, which is likely to go to the root of natural phenomena. Such a method is the genetic one. We call it genetic after (the Greek word) genesis— generation, origin—because it follows a sequence . . . which is similar to the course in which natural phenomena arise and emerge.

In the above passage Carus explicitly emphasized the scientific utility of the genetic method and its superiority over other approaches. Next, he illustrated the usefulness of the genetic method by describing how it can be used to make one comprehend the development of a simple plant. In other words, logical arguments for the usefulness of the genetic method can actually be tested and confirmed by sensory experiences!

3. The concept of development according to Carus

Carus provided many specific examples of the application of the developmental method to the understanding of natural phenomena, yet he never offered a formal definition of his concept of "development." In spite of this, we shall try, in this section, to summarize his writings about formal characteristics of the developmental process.

Carus defined the development of natural phenomena in the *Lectures on Psychology* (1831: 14) as follows:

> . . . the phenomena of nature are first preceived as something simple and undifferentiated. Next we notice a restless rush towards greater complexity. Finally, we see them reach a more diverse and higher structure within a stable unit.

We can now isolate the characteristic patterns of the initial and final stages of development, the process of change, and the principles which underlie this process (see Table 3).

To some extent, Carus had taken the view that natural phenomena develop from a "simple" initial state to "greater complexity" in his writings on comparative anatomy. This orientation was even recognized by Goethe, who commented about the first issue of *Erläuterungstafeln zur vergleichenden Anatomie* (Notebooks on Comparative Anatomy, 1826) that "this publication of Mr. Carus . . . traces all evidence of growth from the simplest to the complex forms of life" (Carus, 1865–66: 462). Additional recognition is found in a personal letter, which Goethe wrote to Carus in July of 1828, thanking him for sending him a copy of his recent book on the developmental anatomy of the skull (1828). Although Goethe's terminology is strikingly similar to that of Carus, it is more likely that Carus adapted these terms in the 1829/31 Lectures from Goethe, whom he idolized.

A "lack of differentiation" was the second characteristic of the initial stage of development, according to Carus. As the process continues, however, increasingly more complex structures develop. Carus clearly anticipated Spencer, who defined evolution in a strikingly similar manner about a quarter of a century later. In his *First Principles* (1855:

Table 3.

Characteristics of the concept of development of C.G. Carus (1831) and H. Spencer (1855/80)

Focus	*C.G. Carus (1831)* Natural phenomena	*H. Spencer (1855/80)* *Matter – motion*
Initial/final state	*Simple state* leads to greater complexity within the unit	
	Undifferentiated state is replaced by complex and heterogeneous structures within the unit	Indefinite, incoherent homogeneity to definite, coherent, heterogeneity
Process of change	Restless move forward	Retained motion undergoes a parallel transformation
		Integration of matter, concomitant dissipation of motion
Underlying lawfulness	Results of development are influenced by base level of natural phenomena	

347) Spencer characterized the evolution of matter and motion as follows:

> as an integration of matter and concomitant dissipation of motion: during which the matter passes from an indefinite, incoherent homogeneity to a definite, coherent heterogeneity; and during which the retained motion undergoes a parallel transformation.

Time and direction are the chief components of the process of change, according to Carus.

Carus also believed that the final degree of complexity which is reached during development is predetermined for each organism (Carus 1831: 14). However, in 1831 he did not subscribe to a naive belief in the preformation of organisms. It is not enough to begin one's study of the development of plants with an individual seed, but one must start (p.15):

with the most fragile germ of the seed as it develops within the maternal blossom of higher plants, . . . it appears in the most undifferentiated form as a globe. In this undifferentiated state the seed has the consistency of liquid and is largely permeated by water—the most undifferentiated element of all. As the progress of life continues, an internal structure of this drop develops.

Carus then proceeded to describe the developmental process of more advanced forms of plant life in detail and concluded that (p. 16):

within these extreme contrasts, yet still enclosed in a single unit, the first beginnings of the new seed emerge. Thus plant life organizes itself into a chain which is continuous throughout terrestrial life.

In this context Carus paid tribute to the "primordial plant" (p. 19) but he was forced to acknowledge that "all plants . . . are only members and different levels of development of one and the same organism" (p. 19).

While the genetic method allowed Carus to represent the developmental sequence of biological organisms spontaneously in a dialectical manner, he utilized idealistic philosophical terminologies when he tried to explain the origin of the developmental processes themselves (p. 30):

. . . the existence of a mental image of an organism—its defining idea must be considered its primary causal condition. . . .

Elsewhere he speaks of the "primordial beginnings of things and the form and manner in which they emerged from the eternal source of the world spirit" (p. 26) and he stated that "all life . . . is merely a self-representation of the idea in nature" (p. 274). Interestingly such intimations of Hegel's dialectics and "objectivation of the idea" are not attributed to Hegel, whom Carus mentioned only briefly in his autobiography (1865/66).

4. Application of the genetic method to psychology
a. *The genetic method and the inner sense*

At the beginning of *Lecture III* Carus emphasized that only the descriptive and the analytical methods can be used, and these only partially, to study the life of the soul. Since the teleological method was "least useful" (p. 22), Carus decided to utilize the genetic method "during psychological observations" (p. 24) to explore the "developmental history of the psyche" which he regarded as the chief task of psychology (p. 26).

Although the "origin of the soul," according to Carus, "is not directly accessible to our understanding, it can be indirectly examined by going back, as far as possible, into our own consciousness." Unfortunately, not much useful information can be obtained in this manner because this approach relies on the recollections of events which we really cannot remember well (p.27). Carus was quite aware of the natural limits of retrospective self-observation.

The second approach involved "the conclusion that a simple and incomplete life of the soul must be possible because observable expressions of psychic life exist even in very imperfect organisms" (p.27). After extensive study of living plants and animals, Carus believed that one was justified "to make definite statements about the souls of lower organisms, as long as one based his conclusions on careful observations of nature" (p.38). Furthermore, he believed that in this manner he would be able to draw dependable conclusions about "the secret of the beginnings of psychic development in man" (p.38). In his search for a "comparative theory of the soul" (p.38), Carus fully endorsed Burdach's 1829 call for the development of a "comparative psychology" (p.39).

b. *The developmental history of the soul*

In *Lecture III,* Carus distinguished between three different levels or stages of psychological development (p.41). The first stage consists of the "unconscious souls of plants and the lowest mammals" (p.41f.). Among these he included mussels and starfish. Carus regards these unconscious souls merely as "the spiritual principle and model of the organic formation . . . the primary cause of growth, nutrition and reproduction" (p.41).

A second stage in the development of the soul is reached in "the souls of higher animals, which possess a sense of the existence of the external world" (p.41f). Here, he counted snails, insects, and vertebrates. This group of organisms is objectively distinguished from the first class by the presence of "a structured nervous system, sense organs [and] more elaborate movement and perception" (p.43). Carus believed that "a distinct consciousness of the external nature, a consciousness of the world" emerged at this level (p.43).

Finally, the third developmental stage is characterized by the addition of "self-awareness in the soul of man" who, in this manner, differs from lower animals that are only aware of their environment (p.41).

The developmental history of the soul can be viewed as a phylogenesis of consciousness. However, Carus makes it clear that for him (p.48):

> The development of the soul is only possible through the interaction of the individual with the phenomena of the world (in the sense of environment, U.K.) . . . and the truly human development of the human soul depends on the relation of the individual to mankind.

c. *Developmental history of the human soul*

Carus described the conditions under which the individual, human soul develops and the "first sources of our mental life" in rich detail (Lectures

Table 4.

Early nineteenth century periodization of human life

F. A. Carus (1808)	K. F. Burdach (1829)	C. G. Carus (1831)
Childhood	*Immaturity*	*Youthful immaturity*
Lives mainly in the present, extends from intrauterine "plant life" to beginnings of mental education	7 years, 34 weeks first dentition	
	15 years, 17 weeks adolescence	Life takes place in the present (p. 183 ff.)
Youth		
First perfection in young man and woman	23 years	
Adulthood	*Height of Life*	*State of maturity*
First existence as adult man and woman, period of earned merits and recognition	68 years, 1 week (contains six subperiods)	Life in the past and the present, preparation for the future (p. 186 ff.)
Senescence	*Old Age*	*Advanced age*
Completion of intensive life, existence as mature male and female	75 years, 36 weeks and above	Orientation toward the past and to eternity

III to VIII). In Lectures IX and X he described the personality development of the child (p.158) and offered his own periodization of human ontogenesis (see Table 4).

Carus suggested that the first psychic impulses begin even before birth, and that they are derived from sensory functions and memory (p.158).

To provide an overview of the developmental sequence, Carus briefly discussed the assumption of "certain, distinct periods" of human life (p.179). He critically examined the ten periods, which Burdach (1828) used to describe human development, accepting only the "three major divisions" for his own work. *Lecture X* summarized the typical perspectives, attitudes and behavior patterns for each stage of life.

d. *Developmental psychopathology*

Although Carus briefly focused on problems of abnormal behavior in *Lecture X* he commented at length on the development of psychic abnormalities in Lexture XII. In this context he used a number of illustrations and case histories to show how physical conditions can affect the soul and how the soul, in turn, interacts with the body. For example, bad habits may lead to a false system of values and eventually to an illness of the soul. Carus also shared his ideas about the origins of mental illnesses and how mental health can be regained (Carus 1831:235ff.).

The applications of the developmental ideas of Carus show his skill in adapting the genetic method to psychological questions. One regrets that his original approach did not have an impact on nineteenth century German psychology.

References

Burdach, K.F. (1826–1840). *Die Physiologie als Erfahrungswissenschaft.* Leipzig. Voss.
Carus, F.A. (1808). *Nachgelassene Werke* (7 vols.). Leipzig: Barth & Kummer.
—(1831). *Vorlesungen über Psychologie.* Leipzig: Fleischer.
—(1865/66). *Lebenserinnerungen und Denkwürdigkeiten.* Leipzig: Brockhaus.
—(1939). *C.G. Carus, seine philosophischen, psychologischen und charakterologischen Grundgedanken.* Berlin: Bernard and Gräfe.
Spencer, H. (1855). *Principles of psychology.* New York: Appleton, 1855.

Charles Darwin's Unpublished "Diary of an Infant": An Early Phase in his Psychological Work

by Robert T.Keegan and Howard E.Gruber

As in many creative lives, Darwin's work was organized in a set of enterprises of long duration, some tightly coupled with each other, some loosely. In Darwin's case, due to the synthesizing nature of his main effort, the enterprises were quite diverse, comprising various domains of biology and geology. The duration of each enterprise tended to equal the remainder of his lifetime from that point at which it was begun.

Darwin's interest in psychology is reflected in many documents. Moreover, at least one enterprise which was not originally psychologically oriented became so in the course of his work: his first paper on earthworms, given in 1837, dealt purely with their contribution to soil formation. But by the time his book appeared 40 years later, its title had become *The Formation of Vegetable Mould, Through the Action of Worms, with Observations on Their Habits*—a pioneering contribution to the study of invertebrate behavior. However, Darwin's main interest in the behavioral sciences was at the vertebrate level, and especially *Homo sapiens*. This was necessarily the case, since it was the import of evolutionary theory for the origin and psychology of human beings that generated the greatest interest and controversy.

Charles Darwin never wrote a systematic account of his psychological ideas. But in many places he recorded them: in the *Beagle Diary* (Barlow 1946), in *Descent of Man*, in *Expression of the Emotions in Man and Animals* (Darwin 1871, 1872), in his autobiography (Barlow 1969), and in his biography of his grandfather (Krause 1880). One of the most important sets of records can be found in his early notebooks. The M and N notebooks[1] written during 1838–1839 contain much of the material later found in *Descent* and *Expression* (although it was completely reworked and vastly augmented in these books). As this early phase (1837–1839), in which Darwin kept his B, C, D, and E notebooks on transmutation (De Beer et al. 1960) and the M and N notebooks on "Man, Mind, and Materialism" drew to a close, he married (29 January 1839) and became a father within the year. In the month before his engagement to Emma Wedgwood, in anticipation of the changes to come in his personal life, Darwin jotted down these questions for later consideration:

> Natural History of Babies
> Do babies start (i.e. useless sudden movement of muscles) very early in life. Do they wink, when anything placed before their eyes, very young, before experience can have taught them to avoid danger. Do they know frown when they first see it? (M notebook, p.157).

On 27 December 1839, Charles and Emma Darwin's first child, William Erasmus, was born. While undoubtedly an event of great personal joy, Charles also saw the birth as an opportunity to extend his work as a naturalist by studying the development of a child. He apparently began a diary of his son's development on the day that William was born. Thus, this work was a direct continuation of his notebooks on organic and mental evolution. This document not only gives us a picture of Darwin's ideas on child development, but also reveals a very loving, relaxed, and playful Charles Darwin, a portrait that his formal autobiography doesn't quite capture. More important for our present purposes, together with the other documents, it makes possible the reconstruction of a Darwinian developmental psychology. The M and N notebooks contain a number of scattered questions regarding the nature of babies and their development, but these queries were not pursued in a systematic manner.

The diary clearly shows Darwin's strong interest in questions of mental functioning in the early 1840s. It is a prime example of the great continuity of one of his enterprises, the study of psychological functioning. The integration and compatibility of his personal and professional life can be observed in the connections between these early questions on infant development, engagement and marriage to Emma, and as far as one can tell, an actual plan to observe his own babies for scientific reasons.

The format and timing of the passage cited above are interesting for several other reasons. The way in which Darwin capitalized the first line suggests that it might have been the working title for a proposed work: *Natural History of Babies*. Some notes for such a work appear beneath this title. Darwin wrote these words within days of reading Malthus and formulating the theory of natural selection (Malthus 1826). The study ·of babies could help define which behaviors were inborn and therefore attributable either to inherited habits or to natural selection, and which behaviors were learned. Darwin was still working through the many implications of this new theory of natural selection. The birth of William (referred to as both Willy and Doddy in the diary) presented the opportunity to observe the "natural history" of one infant's development.

The biography of William is generally known by way of Darwin's 1877 article in *Mind* entitled, "A Biographical Sketch of an Infant" (Darwin 1877). The article is an abstract of the diary. It seems as though Darwin wrote this article in response to the earlier appearance in *Mind* of H.A. Taine's article on language acquisition in children (Taine 1877). Darwin opened his article by stating that Taine's article had reminded him of his own efforts to track the development of skills in William. But there were other compelling reasons for Darwin to dust off this diary and publish its contents. In *Descent* Darwin had relied heavily on the role played by language in the mental evolution of our species, arguing that language had natural origins and that precursors of human language existed in the rudimentary forms of communication in animals. Professor Max Müller had disagreed (Müller 1873), arguing that there could be no language without thought and that animals could not think. Darwin had replied to Müller's criticisms in the second edition of *Descent* which was published in 1874. Taine had also read Müller's critique of Darwin and rejected it. Taine presented a case of the natural origin and development of language *in a child* by means of her own activity. Darwin saw an opportunity both to corroborate the view of Taine and again refute the ideas of his critic, Max Müller.

Darwin's 1877 article is, by and large, a faithful but impersonal rendition of the diary. In the article, he rearranged the chronological order of the diary material into a topical discussion. Where the diary asked questions, the article made assertions. The most striking difference between the two documents is not in their view of child development, but in their picture of Charles Darwin as a father. If one read only the article in *Mind*, Darwin might appear as rather cool, clinical, and possibly even exploitative. Anyone who reads the diary would come away with a far different impression. The diary shows him gentle, loving, and playful: interested in his child's development and well-being. It also provides us with a record of Darwin's thought *as it developed* and therein lies its chief value.

In order to clarify the context in which the diary was written, the following chronology is offered:

DATE	EVENT
July 1837–July 1839	B, C, D, and E notebooks on species written
July 1838–April 1840	M and N notebooks on mental evolution written
September 28, 1838	Upon reading Malthus, Darwin grasps the principle of natural selection
October 1, 1838c.	Questions on "Natural History of Babies" written in M notebook
November 11, 1838	Charles's engagement to Emma Wedgwood
January 29, 1839	Charles's marriage to Emma Wedgwood
End of March, 1839	Probable date of William's conception
December 27, 1839	William is born and the diary is begun
November 24, 1859	Publications of *Origin of Species*
February 24, 1871	Publication of *Descent of Man*
November 26, 1872	Publication of *Expression of Emotions*
1877	H.A. Taine's article on the acquisition of language in children appears in English in *Mind*
1877	Darwin's biographical sketch of William appears in *Mind*

Nature-Nurture

Darwin's implicit argument runs as follows: if a behavior appears before there has been any opportunity for learning it, it must be inborn and hereditary; if it is inborn and hereditary it has been shaped either through natural selection or heredity habit. He opened the diary by listing his child's earliest actions (e.g. hiccoughing, sneezing, yawning, etc.) and questioning their purpose and origin. For instance, on the first page[2] he asked, "What can be origin of movement from tickling" (Diary, p.1). It was certainly linked to a greater sensitivity of the skin's surface in certain areas, but not in all cases (e.g. he remarks that the tips of the fingers are sensitive but not ticklish). Other apparently inborn reactions such as hiccoughing were easier to understand:

> Hicchoughing is convulsive movement, caused by irritation of same muscles, which depress diaphragm,—so as to allow gas to escape from stomach.—a person trying to liberate air from stomach, inspires voluntarily in same manner, as that stronger/stronger instinctive/ movement which causes hiccough (p.2v).

The hiccough differed quite substantially from the more subtle voluntary method of manipulating the diaphragm. This idea that instinctive reactions could be distinguished from voluntary, learned behavior on the basis of the abruptness of the movement was also applied to the eye blink:

> He never could have learnt from experience to close his eyes very suddenly from sudden noise near his head.—. If it had been experience he would have done it from visible object—This blinking of eyes, I don't doubt instinct to protect eyes.—I think he has *acquired* habit of closing eyes gently, from being washed (pp.13–14).

Both these examples pointed out the clearly adaptive nature and characteristically abrupt appearance of instinctive reactions. In Piagetian terms, Darwin observed his infant exercising readymade sensorimotor schemata and he saw the adaptive utility of these earliest behaviors. However, there were some very simple reactions which definitely enhanced the chances for survival that had to be learned. Darwin apparently questioned the prominent physician, Dr. Henry Holland, about the extent of inborn behaviors and their survival value. Seeking a medical man's opinion on this matter conforms with Darwin's general pattern of using doctors (beginning with his own father) as important informants on psychological questions.[3] With some degree of surprise, Darwin wrote:

> D.Holland informing me children do not *learn* to blow their noses, or clear their throats, till several years old: curious, when so may analogous actions are performed *instinctively* (good contrast) from earliest days. (p.3)

Though born with a set of adaptive reactions, learning came into play very early and in a very basic way.

Although Darwin saw utility in these earliest instincts, he also recognized that reactions which seemed to lack immediate utility may also mark instinctive behavior. Such behavior could not have been learned since it had no plausible function at that point in the life cycle. It my, however, be useful at a later point in the life cycle. As an example, Darwin recorded an incident in which thirteen-month-old Willy became quite angry with his nurse for attempting to take a piece of cake away from him: "He tried to slap her face, went scarlet, screamed & shook his head—How has he learnt that slapping tends to give pain,—like the just-born crocodile from egg learns to snap with its weak jaws,—i.e. instinctively" (p.29). The slap of a thirteen-month-old and the snap of a newborn alligator are not very effective actions, but they will be so at a later age. Darwin took similar note of Willy's earliest leg movements when he was held upright. The legs moved alternately, not together, as if Willy were attempting to walk although he was only four months old at the time (p.12). Instincts, therefore, consisted of both inborn reactions with immediate utility and behaviors that would become effective when the organism reached adulthood. Other adaptive behaviors had to be learned. The emerging picture of development was a complex one.

The above quotation also provides an insight into the parental style of the Darwins. If they had used any sort of corporal punishment to discipline their child then Willy could have *learned* that slapping had a rather definite impact. Darwin would not then have questioned how the behavior could have arisen. Since it was not learned, it must be instinctive.

The other notable aspect of Willy's slap was its plainly aggressive character. Darwin experienced other manifestations of Willy's aggressive behavior and generated bold hypotheses to explain its origin. One incident in particular captures the very human, familial, nonacademic spirit of this baby biography written by an attentive father. It also reveals the everpresent scientist observing natural behavior in a natural environment and trying to make sense of it. Doddy was two years three months and his sister Annie was one year-old when the following incident occured:

> Doddy is a great adept ad throwing things & when choleric he will hurl books or sticks at Emma. About a month since; he was running to give Annie a punch with a little wooden candlestick, when I called sharply to him, & he wheeled round & instantly sent the candlestick whirling over my head.—He then stood resolute in the middle of the room as if ready to oppose the whole world.—peremptorily refused to kiss Anny, but in short time, when I said "Doddy wont throw a candlestick at Papas head" & he said "no wont—kiss Papa"—I shall be curious to observe whether our little girls take so kindly to throwing things when so very young. If they do not I shall believe it is hereditary in male sex in the same manner as the S. American colts naturally amble from their parents having been trained (pp.33–34).

Darwin raised the question as to whether a specific aggressive trait occurs solely in the male. This question was not of mere passing interest to Darwin, soon to be forgotten. A year later he observed, "Annie shows no signs of skill in throwing things either as an amusement, or as an offensive act, in same ready way as Willy did, nor does she so readily gives slaps" (p.38v). Here was natural, if limited, support for the hypothesis that specific behaviors may be linked to gender. Gender-linked behavior would later become an important topic in his very psychologically oriented work, *Descent of Man*.

In addition to gender specific behavior, Darwin's analogy between Willy's penchant for throwing things and South American colts knowing how to amble because their *parents* were *trained* to do so indicates that Darwin still seriously considered, three and a half years after his discovery of natural selection, the possibility that acquired habits could be transmitted across generations. On the page following his descriptions of Willy's pitching prowess, Darwin continued to note behavior that seemed to consist of inherited habits, "Elizabeth remarked his careful politeness at meals towards his guests was like his granpapa the Doctor" (p.35). This statement is reminiscent of Darwin's observation in the M notebook that his own handwriting was like that of his grandfather (M notebook, p.83). Obviously, natural selection had not become the sole mechanism of descent with modification in Darwin's thinking (Gruber 1981).

Aggression could clearly be an adaptive response to threatening situations, but the *Beagle* voyage had opened Darwin's eyes to other adaptive mechanisms such as camouflage coloration and the tendency to take to flight at the first sign of possible danger. Darwin thought early flight was connected with an animal having an instinctive fear of another animal. He recognized that some birds in the Galapagos Islands had no instinctive fear of human beings which apparently was a result of their long separation from mankind. The lack of this protective instinct proved very unfortunate for some of these species when *Homo sapiens* arrived in the islands (Barlow 1963). Darwin speculated on how they might acquire this adaptive instinct to fear and flee from members of our species.

Darwin's firsthand observations of animal behavior did not end with the *Beagle* voyage. He was fond of going to the zoo, observing the animals, talking to the keepers, and conducting informal experiments (Note 1; Gruber 1981). The diary notes that Willy accompanied him on occasion. Darwin seemed particularly interested in determining whether Willy, as a naive representative of *Homo sapiens*, had any instinctive fears of certain animals and wished to avoid them. He found some evidence to support his conjecture when Willy was two years three months:

> Doddy having this kind of instinctive feeling of fear . . . [of] most quadrupeds, except those somewhat like animals to which he is accustomed . . . whilst he had no fear of any bird, though large, like the ostriches & noisy like the gulls—This fear has certainly come without any experience of danger or hurt, & may be

compared to young mice trembling at a cat the first time, they see one.—During
the succeeded, he was constantly talking of the Z.Gardens & wished very much
to go again & see the birds, but not the "beast in house" (Diary, p.37).

Under an evolutionary point of view, Willy's differential reaction to
birds and quadrupeds made sense; *Homo sapiens* and its progenitors
would have competed for survival much more directly with quadrupeds
than with birds, so an inherited caution of these animals was not
surprising.

The diary reveals that Darwin's interests went well beyond the simple
discernment of instinctive responses. He was genuinely interested in
development. What skills emerged at what age? What changed during
development? What distinguished the human child from its simian
counterparts? These and other intriguing questions passed through the
young father's mind as he watched his firstborn grow.

The growth of competence

The picture of Willy's development painted by Darwin in the diary is one
of gradually increasing competence. New skills do not appear full
blown, but emerge from a rudimentary pattern of behavior that foreshadows the new skill. One skill is added to another and integrated to
form a higher level skill. Development of this sort is not strictly additive
in the way one coral skeleton is added to another coral skeleton in
forming a reef. Differences between individual coral skeletons or
earthworm castings are inconsequential in the structures they form.[4]
Mental constructs (e.g. ideas), on the other hand, are each like distinct
individuals; they cannot be simply heaped up additively but must be integrated into a pattern to be useful and have an effect. This process implies
transformation as well as addition. The system of the individual mind
and its development portrayed by Darwin is quite compatible with the
view elaborated by Jean Piaget over three-quarters of a century later.
Piaget described how one idea was assimilated to another and transformed into a new organization or "schema." New schemata arose
from old ones and development proceeded in a continuous fashion.
There were no inexplicable jumps in development. The following
description of Willy's development of a particular sensorimotor coordination (at four and a half months of age) illustrates the similarity
between Darwin's view of the emergence of competence and the views
later espoused by Piaget: "May 9th a watch held close to face: he

extended his hand to it—Had made feeble trials for two or three days before" (p.16). The skill of coordinating the hand with the eye emerged through a series of increasingly successful approximations to the desired activity—*grasping* an object that is within reach. The experience of recording the gradual but not strictly additive process of change (in which genuine *transformation* occurs) during the mental development of one individual (his son) made a lasting impression on Darwin and influenced his thinking on the phylogenetic development of mind in our species when he came to write *Descent.*

The diary reveals a second aspect of Darwin's thinking on mental development that is highly compatible with the views elaborated by Piaget over three-quarters of a century later—the idea that the earliest thought of an individual is constituted in action. At four months of age Willy demonstrated the sort of coordination of simple actions that reveal the growing intellect of the child:

> Took my finger to his mouth & as usual could not get it in, on account of his own hand being in the way; then he slipped his own back & so got my finger in.—This was not chance & therefore a kind of reasoning (p.12).

As Willy developed, Darwin recorded many instances of his growing competence with the world of objects and his increasing intellectual acumen. We will illustrate Darwin's view of intellectual development by tracing Doddy's continuing encounter with one object, a mirror. It serves as a model for his interaction with all objects.

Darwin's first note on his son's encounter with a mirror occurred when Doddy was four and a half months of age. Unfortunately, there is no way of knowing whether this incident was Doddy's first contact with a looking glass:

> Three or four days ago smiled at himself in glass—how does he know his reflection is that of human being? That He smiles with this idea, I feel pretty sure—Smiled at my image, & seemed surprised at my voice coming from behind him, my image being in front (p.18).

Although one might suspect Darwin of reading too much into his son's experience, especially with respect to his speculation about Doddy having some notion of belonging to a certain species, his assumption is borne out by modern research.[5] The mismatch between Darwin's image appearing in front of Doddy while his voice came from behind clearly confused the young child. In contrast, just two months later, Doddy's reaction was substantially different: "When looking at mirror, was aware that the image of person behind, was not real & therefore, when any odd motion or face was made, turned round to look at the person behind" (pp.21–22). Doddy had solved the puzzle, but Darwin, with characteristic thoroughness, continued to note his son's reactions to surfaces that reflect.

Like Piaget, Darwin recognized that something newly learned is fragile and cannot always be generalized to slightly different situations. Piaget's investigation of children's acquisition of the concept of conservation highlights this point. When a child discovers that altering the shape of a ball of clay does not change its amount, he cannot immediately apply this insight to the analogous situation of pouring a given volume of water from a short wide beaker into a tall thin beaker. The child will report what there is "more" in one beaker than in the other. Thus, even concepts discovered spontaneously by the child can take weeks, months, or years to generalize. Doddy showed this same pattern of cognitive development in his efforts to understand the concept of reflected images. Just two weeks after Doddy learned to look behind him in order to find the person connected with the image in front of him, Darwin observed, "Towards the end of July seemed puzzled at seeing me first through one window & then through another.—did not appear to know whether it was reflection in mirror or reality" (p.22v). Over the next two months, Doddy's idea of mirrors consolidated. When Doddy was nine months of age Darwin reported, "When one says to him, 'where is Doddy?' [he] turns & looks for himself in looking-glass" (p.23). Doddy had come to associate his image with his name, thus displaying a sense of self. A week after this incident, Doddy showed definite signs that his experience with mirrors could be generalized and applied to very different situations. On 2 October 1840 Darwin wrote, "He was aware that the shadow of a hand, made by a candle, was to be looked for behind, in same manner as in looking glass' (p.23). A principle had been learned: twodimensional images in front of you may be caused by threedimensional objects behind you. Although shadows and reflected images seem quite different phenomena at first, their inclusion under the same principle can be understood when intellectual development is conceived of from the gradualist point of view utilized by Darwin.

Mirrors evidently had a certain fascination for Darwin as a tool for experimentation. He continued to note Doddy's encounters with them, but from other passages in the diary it is clear that Darwin extended his mirror experiments to other subjects. As noted above, the zoo was a place for Darwin to explore his ideas, and even conduct simple experiments. One of these experiments involved observing an orangutan's interaction with a mirror. When Doddy was a year old Darwin recorded, "Kissed himself in the glass & pressed his face against his image very like Ouran Outang [did] when could not take up drops he protruded his mouth to do so" (p.26). Darwin had extended his mirror experiments beyond the investigation of ontogenetic development to a comparative analysis of behavior.

Darwin made two additional notes concerning Doddy's habit of kissing his image in a mirror, noting that the habit continued for a number of months. At the same time however, a more interesting piece of behavior occurred. On 12 January 1841 when Doddy was just over a year old, Darwin observed another instance where Doddy was able to generalize the knowledge gained from his mirror episodes to a new situation: "He observed & gave cry of recognition at seeing the image of himself in the pupil of my eye.—I feel sure there was no error in this" (p.27). Doddy's competence with the world on objects was growing. Reflections need not come solely from flat shiny surfaces.

The mirror also provided occasions for observing individual differences in behavior. Throughout the diary Darwin commented on Doddy's fine observational skills. When Darwin's second child, Annie, was born, it provided an opportunity to compare Willy's observational skills with those of Annie. In a passage describing the contrast between Annie's amusement at having something stick to her fingers and Willy's anger when the same thing happened to him, Darwin reflected:

> Annie has infinitely less observation & animation—She now hardly understands a person coming up behind her when she is standing in front of the glass, & looking at her image—She perceived her image in the polished case of my watch (p.29v).

Annie was a year old at the time. Recall that Doddy solved the mirror puzzle around six months of age. While Annie was still having trouble understanding the mirror, she was able to recognize herself in a different reflecting object. Darwin suspected this sort of difference was due to individual factors, not gender, which distinguished it from the skill of throwing. Based on his personal observations, Darwin did not think that a universal schedule of cognitive development could be constructed. Some infants would outpace others with respect to specific skills.

Social competence

Darwin observed Willy's development of social skills with the same care that he used in observing Willy's progress in dealing with the world of objects. From Willy's first days, Darwin closely noted his expressions. When Darwin wrote his article for *Mind,* he said that his "chief object" in the diary had been to attend to his infant's expression (Darwin 1877: 285). By the time he started the diary, Darwin had already identified the topic of expression as having high importance in the M and N notebooks, and had worked through the evolutionary implications of many of his ideas on this subject. Willy's birth provided the chance to verify or refute these ideas.

Darwin thought expression could be used to show the link between our species and others by pointing out the residue of animal behavior in humans and the rudiments of human behavior in animals. Darwin also recognized that expression had a communicative function and Doddy's birth allowed Darwin to study this at first hand. He noted the instinctual expressions of his infant with an eye to their functional significance. On page two of the diary Darwin wrote:

> At his 8th day he frowned much & I believe earlier—now his eyebrows are very little prominent & with scarcely a vestige of down,—therefore if frowning has any relation to vision it must now be quite instinctive; moreover vision at this age is exceedingly imperfect (Diary; p.2).

Since the expression (the squinting of the eyes which are a part of a frown) seemed to have no *immediate* functional value in helping the infant to see better, it must be instinctive. However, Darwin was careful not to read too much into every expression, as if each and every movement had a definite significance. An example of this attitude can be seen in the following observation of Willy's behavior: "When little under five weeks old, smiled but certainly not from pleasure, but [illegible] as chance movement of muscles without a corresponding sensation" (p.3). However, for the most part, expressions had meaning.

Willy's early expressions communicated his state of well-being or discomfort. On the pleasurable side, Darwin observed his son's expression while feeding:

> Long before 5 weeks old it was curious to observe expression of eye during sucking change into vacancy & then into a swimming expression with half closed eyelid like drunken person. curious when the eye is being so imperfect an organ of vision.—being used as means organ of expression (p.3B).

This expression is in stark contrast to one showing discomfort, "In crying—wrinkles & depresses eyebrows—wrinkles skin on nose, & draws up under eyelids into strongly marked line—opens mouth—closes eyes—" (p.4v). Darwin viewed these earliest expressions as signalling Willy's inner state in a clear but general way. He traced how the expressions became more and more explicit as Willy developed. Smiles changed from simply reflecting an inner feeling of comfort to being directed at individual persons in the external environment (p.4). Crying became more specific, signalling whether he was in pain or simply hungry (p.7). Gradually over the first year of life Willy continued to gain competence in revealing his feelings by way of expression, but at eleven months he showed clear evidence that expression had become a two-way means of communication. Darwin described Willy's reaction to children's clapping games such as "Batter-cake:" "He looks very much pleased after the performance [of] any of these accomplishments: he evidently studies expression of those around him, especially if anything new is done before him" (p.26). Willy had learned to take his cue from the expressions of those around him. At the same time Willy exhibited this ability to make sense of the information contained in the expressions of those around him, he also started to show the first signs of substantive verbal communication.

The earliest vocalizations reported by Darwin were Willy's accompaniment to his pain and pleasure states. Darwin thought Willy changed the form of his utterances when his mother came to nurse him, even at the age of nine weeks (p.5). Darwin's first extended observation on his son's verbal behavior occurred when Willy was sixteen weeks of age:

> [He] was exceedingly amused at Bo-Peep, and as often as my face approached his, gave a broad smile, and made a noise somewhat different from any that I have hitherto heard, resembling in a small degree, a laugh; the noise resembled that kind of O, or bleating which he has very long made, when comfortable, but apparently modified by the form of his open and smiling mouth, and likewise by a kind of sob, or interruption, almost the same as that which makes the bleating noise.—The pleasurable sounds appear always to be those of expiration; can noises, expressing pain, be modifications of the O, of pain and surprise, which, it is easy to see, are those of inspiration (p.11).

The analogy between physical (especially facial) expression and vocalization is clear: both convey information on inner feeling states and both gain specificity over time. Darwin also hinted that the noises accompanying pain and pleasure were based on physiological opposites; inspiration and expiration. This observation paralleled his discussion of the marked difference in the use of the face muscles when smiling or grimacing.

At 11 months, Willy started to say "ouchy" to a number of objects (p.26), but his first stable word appeared in the next month. Willy's emerging ability to use verbal utterances occurred at the same time that Darwin noted Willy's ability to study expression and gain meaning from it. Both verbalization and expression seemed to be part of an expanding faculty for communication. The appearance of Willy's first true word signalled the shift to the verbal mode of communication so characteristic of our species, but, to Darwin, it did not mark a dramatic departure from earlier forms of communication, or from the type of communication used by other species:

> In January or earlier, he ceased crying for food, but instead cries "mum"—his word for food & to this word he gives the *most strongly marked* interrogatory sound at end—stronger sound than that (i.e. by inspiration at close of sound) which one ordinarily gives to 'what?'—It is very curious this interrogatory note thus coming, as it appears, instinctively.—He gives the tone of exclamation to the cry of 'ah', which he chiefly uses, & at first, I think, exclusively used, when recognizing any person or his own image in glass.—analogous to cry for food of nestling-birds, which certainly is instinctive & peculiar to that time of life (p.28v).

A word, therefore, replaced a cry. The cry was accompanied by an instinctual inflection that paralleled an instinct linked to infancy in another species. Later in the diary Darwin wrote, "I suspect many expressive modulations of tone, come to children before appropriate expressions for their feelings" (p.31v). Here Darwin is suggesting that language is a natural process, and minimizing the gap between our species and the rest of the natural world. Although singularities in mankind (e.g. a highly developed system for verbal communication) need not have disturbed Darwin, they did. From a modern perspective, with evolutionary thought accepted, there is no difficulty in believing that some species (e.g. *Homo sapiens*) has evolved in ways that are totally new and unprecedented. But in Darwin's perspective, any such singularity seemed to give aid and comfort to the doctrine of special creation and weaken the case for evolution. He *must* find continuities everywhere. The more the better, since continuities provide only a logically weak argument against special creation. If even a single nonnaturally arising function is still suspected, Darwin's whole case would be weakened. So "positive instances" (continuities) help only if they are numerous enough to overwhelm the opposition.

On the very next page of the diary, Darwin made his first comment regarding Doddy's moral development. Doddy was thirteen months old at the time. Although Darwin, in the M notebook, had instructed himself to analyze how language might affect the development of the moral sense (M notebook, pp.150–151), he did *not* explicitly do so in the diary. Despite the fact that Darwin described his son's first word and first sign of a moral sense on facing pages of the diary, Doddy's moral and linguistic development were described separately, without comment on how they might interact. This feature of the diary is surprising since all the early events showing Doddy's development of a conscience involved verbal interactions. Doddy's moral sense did not manifest itself until he created his first word and then it appeared promptly. When Doddy was thirteen months old, Darwin observed the first signs of his son's emerging conscience:

> I repeated several times in reproaching voice "Doddy wont give poor Papa a kiss,—naughty Doddy." He unquestionably was made slightly uncomfortable by this, & at last, when I had returned to my chair, protruded lips, & shook his hands in rather angry manner & made me come receive a kiss—a week afterwards appeared certainly annoyed, when I said "I *wont* give Doddy a kiss."—The first case showed something like first shades of moral sense (Diary, p.28).

As the child's general cognitive abilities developed so did his capacity to consider the moral aspects of a situation. In Darwin's view, conscience arose with the ability to understand the communications of others. Darwin implied that conscience stemmed from the child's observation of the reactions of his primary caretakers. By about one year of age, the child has gained the ability to anticipate these parental reactions and thus conscience is born.

Darwin's view of moral development is another example of his effort to understand change as a gradual process. There are no "catastrophes," marked events such as an Oedipal conflict, in Darwin's discussion of Doddy's moral development. Unlike the cognitive theory of moral development proposed by Lawrence Kohlberg, Darwin considered the very young child to be capable of moral judgments. In fact, Darwin even saw evidence of an incipient altruism when Doddy was two years and three months of age:

> Doddy was generous enough to give Anny the last mouthful of his gingerbread & today he again put his last crumb on the sofa for Anny to run to then cried in rather a vain-glorious tone "oh kind Doddy" "kind Doddy" (p.36).

Darwin clearly saw that Doddy's act of kindness had strong elements of self-interest in it, and that altruistic behavior emerged from earlier forms of behavior without dramatic shifts. Four months later, Doddy showed the delicate nature of the developing conscience:

> This day I met him coming out of dining room, with his pinafore folded up care-fully & he eyeing it—I asked him what he had got there: he said "nothing" looking all the while to see that his pinafore was well folded & as I came nearer he cried "go away" "Doddy going to sand" "go away"—from his odd manner I determined to see what was concealed, when I found he had stained with yellow pickle his pinafore, when taking pickle, like he had done sugar—Here was natural acting & deceit (p.39v).

Doddy's attempt to conceal his theft was clear evidence to Darwin that the sense of right and wrong was present even at this very young age.

Willy's birth provided Darwin with an ideal opportunity. He could *observe* a process of natural development in an individual while he actively *thought* about this issue as it related to species. Questions of pressing importance to him about the evolution of species had parallels in the area of child development. Which behaviors were innate and which were acquired? How was all behavior, instinctive and learned, coordinated? How did development take place and at what rate? Darwin used the parallels he saw between ontogeny and phylogeny to stimulate his thinking on development. In his view, both revealed a process of gradual yet significant change.

It is significant to note that Darwin did not treat morality as having an instinctual aspect in his description of Doddy's moral development. In the M and N notebooks, Darwin speculated on the possible origins of the moral sense. He seemed to think that it was contingent upon possessing both a degree of mental capacity sufficient to make a comparison (e.g. recognize that a conflict exists between two choices) and social instincts. In *Descent* Darwin clearly described the adaptive value of a moral sense and outlined its relationship to instinctual behavior. However, both the comments in the M and N notebooks and *Descent* are concerned with morality at the species level. The diary was a record of *individual* development and apparently at this level moral behavior did not appear particularly instinctive. By keeping this diary, Darwin came to understand more clearly that an individual's moral and intellectual development were interconnected. Connecting the moral sense with general cognitive development clearly placed the topic of morality within a developmental, and by analogy, an evolutionary framework.

Acknowledgement

The authors acknowledge the generous assistance of Mr. Peter Gautrey of the Cambridge University Library in deciphering difficult sections of the diary and for other assistance in the preparation of this article. We thank Mr. George Pember Darwin for his kind permission to reproduce pages from the diary. We also thank Marion J.Keegan for her editorial suggestions and assistance in preparing the manuscript.

Notes

1 The main outlines of the development of Darwin's thought are given in Gruber, Howard E. *Darwin on man: A psychological study of scientific creativity together with Darwin's early and unpublished notebooks* transcribed and edited by Paul H.Barrett, New York: Dutton, 1974. This work has now been republished as two books: Gruber, H.E. *Darwin on man: A psychological study of scientific creativity*, 2nd ed., Chicago: University of Chicago Press, 1981; and Barrett, P.H. (transcriber and annotater) *Metaphysics, materialism, and the evolution of mind; early writings of Charles Darwin: With a commentary by Howard Gruber*, Chicago: University of Chicago Press, 1980.
 The M and N notebooks, referred to in the present essay, are printed both in Gruber, 1974 and Barrett, 1980. We refer to them here as Darwin designated them, and give the manuscript page numbers. There same editions contain a reprint of Darwin's 1877 article in *Mind* which was based on the diary of Willy that Darwin began in 1839.

2 Item 210.17 in the Darwin Papers at the University Library Cambridge is identified as, "Biographical Sketch of a Child." A substantial portion of this document consists of Charles Darwin's observations and thoughts on the development of his first child, William Erasmus, during the infant's first two years of life. The latter portion of this diary spans the years from 1843 to 1855. It contains observations on the behavior of the Darwin children who were born after William.
 This diary contains a number of different handwritings. The great majority of the notes on William (referred to as both "Willy" and "Doddy" in the diary) appear in Charles Darwin's hand. However, none of the entries made between August 1942 and May 1854 were written by Charles. Charles' wife, Emma, recorded her own observations on a very occasional basis during these years. Charles resumed writing in the diary at about midyear 1854 and continued to make entries until July 1856.
 The diary is a bound notebook with a khaki-colored cover measuring approximately 6 × 8 inches. "A W Trin. Coll." appears on the front cover. Inside the back cover, printed very small is, "Albert Way April 29, 1822." Francis Darwin, Charles' son, inserted a note in this document explaining that the notebook originally belonged to Albert Way, a Cambridge undergraduate friend of Charles Darwin (the sketches of Darwin rinding on the back of a beetle reproduced in Gruber, 1981 were drawn by Albert Way). A number of pages are missing from the notebook. Despite the fact that pages were torn from this document, all the pages containing observations on the children seem to be intact. The back pages of the notebook contain notes of a geological/engineering nature which are written upside down in relation to the notes

on the children. There are a total of nine sides of this material. The middle portion of the notebook contains many blank pages. The paper in the notebook is a light gray. The system of pagination used in this notebook is inconsistent and sometimes confusing. In the first part of the notebook, Charles Darwin usually used the right hand page (recto) to begin his entry. If the entry was long, he usually continued it on the next recto. The left hand page (verso) was generally used as a place to calculate Willy's age, record miscellaneous comments, and make notes on the development of the children who were born after Willy. There are, however, exceptions to this pattern. In contrast, Emma Darwin used the pages in consecutive order. When Charles resumed writing in the diary, he adopted Emma's style. Charles Darwin only numbered pages in the upper right hand corner of the recto. In this article, we have used Darwin's own pagination to identify the location of material quoted from the diary. Page numbers that are followed by a "v" indicate that the quoted material is located on the verso.

3 A medical education and career was often the path to scientific work, e.g. Erasmus Darwin, Charles's grandfather and renowned physician.

4 By the time Darwin began the diary of Willy's development, he had already written papers on the formation of coral reefs and the formation of "vegetable mould" through the activity of earthworms. In both these papers, Darwin described change as a gradual process of adding (almost) identical components. He recognized that this simple additive model was insufficient for describing the mental development of a child.

5 For a modern discussion of investigations in various primates of this relation between self-awareness and reactions to the mirror world, see G.G. Gallup. Toward a comparative psychology of mind, in R.L. Mellgren (ed.), *Animal cognition and behavior,* North-Holland Press, 1983. When the Gardner's chimpanzee, Washoe, who was reared with humans, first saw other chimpanzees, she referred to them in sign language as "black bugs." In other words, she "knew" that she was human and they were not!

References

Barlow, N. (Ed.). (1946) *Charles Darwin's diary of the voyage of H.M.S. Beagle.* New York: Philosophical Library.

—(1963) Darwin's ornithological notes, with an introduction, notes, and appendix by Nora Barlow. *Bulletin of the British Museum (Natural History) Historical Series 2,* no.7.

—(1969) *The autobiography of Charles Darwin, 1809–1882.* New York: Norton.

Darwin, C.R. (1871) *The descent of man, and selection in relation to sex.* London: J.Murray.

—(1872) *The expression of the emotions in man and animals.* London: J.Murray.

—(1877) A biographical sketch of an infant. *Mind: Quarterly Review of Psychology and Philosophy 2:* 285–294. See Note 1 for information on modern reprints of this article.

—(1881) *The formation of vegetable mould, through the action of worms, with observations on their habits.* London: J.Murray.

De Beer, G., Rowlands, M.J., and Skramovsky (Eds.) (1960) Darwin's notebooks on transmutation of species. *Bulletin of the British Museum (Natural History) Historical Series 2,* nos.2, 3, 4, and 5.

Krause, E. (1880) *Earsmus Darwin, with a preliminary notice by Charles Darwin.* New York: D.Appleton.

Malthus, T.R. (1826) *An essay on the principles of population; or, a view of its past and present effects on human happiness with an inquiry into our prospects respecting the future removal or mitigation of the evils which it occasions,* 6th ed., 2vols. London: J.Murray.

Müller, M. (1873) *Lectures on "Mr. Darwin's philosophy of language."*

Taine, H.A. (1877) Taine on the acquisition of language by children. *Mind: Quarterly Review of Psychology and Philosophy* 2:252–259.

Hermann Lotze's Concept of Function: Its Kantian Origin and Its Impact on Evolutionism in the United States

by William R. Woodward

A substantial secondary literature (e.g., Kuklick 1977, Wiener 1949) points to the source of pragmatic philosophy and functional psychology in the so-called Metaphysical Club which met informally in Cambridge, Massachusetts during the 1860s and 1870s. The leader of this Club was Chauncey Wright, a gifted philosopher without academic position whom Charles Darwin had personally asked to extend his theory into "the evolution of self-consciousness." Wright combined John Stuart Mill's inductive logic with natural-selection theory to account for the development of our reasoning powers. A key factor for Wright was language, which he connected with the "empirical memory" for signs of objects (Madden 1963). Another factor was behavior: here Alexander Bain's definition of belief as an idea on which we are prepared to act was emphasized by several younger members of the Club. These three ingredients—language, behavior, and belief—were brought together in an inductive psychological process which explained the development of mind by analogy to the mechanisms of variation and selection in natural evolution.

As compelling as was this theory of mental development, Wright's younger proteges Charles Peirce and William James found it deficient in one respect. Wright's theory was based on an inadequate account of induction. To remedy this defect, Peirce and James turned to the German philosophical tradition. The interface between Mill's "induction" and Kant's "transcendental deduction" became on important source for American functional psychology. This coalescence of British, German, and American philosophical traditions around the problem of the evolution and function of mind offers a spectrum of solutions which are well worth reconsideration in modern developmental psychology (cf. Riegel and Meacham 1976, Otto 1981).

The crux of my account of this methodological problem and its historical solutions concerns the origin and impact of the Göttingen philosopher of science and culture, Hermann Lotze (1817–1881).[1]

Lotze was recognized in the nineteenth century as a leading figure, as documented by his call to succeed Herbart at Göttingen in 1844 (Woodward and Rainer 1975) and by subsequent calls to Leipzig, Bonn, Tübingen, and Berlin (three times). The scope of his impact is best portrayed by Merz (1904–12) and Passmore (1968), while his thought has been sensitively reinterpreted recently in a commemorative volume in the German Democratic Republic (Pester, in press; Sprung and Sprung, in press).

A major component in my own reinterpretation of some sources of functional psychology is Lotze's debt to the school of Jakob Friedrich Fries at Jena University. Lotze studied at Leipzig in the mid-1830s, but he came to know Fries personally through a close friend from his home town of Zittau, Ernst Friedrich Apelt (1813–1857). Apelt was then a student, and eventually the successor, of Fries. He is recognized today among philosophers of science for representing the Friesian school at midcentury, and especially for his answer to William Whewell's *The Philosophy of the Inductive Sciences* in 1847 with his book, *Die Theorie der Induction,* in 1854.

Apelt's two major contributions to the logic of science were his theory of rational induction based on "leading maxims" and his expression of this theory by means of mathematical functions. His theory of rational induction may be most briefly explained by noting that Sir Karl Popper's theory of falsificationism is almost a carbon copy of Apelt's. For example, Apelt based induction on two types of hypothetical inference called *modus ponens* and *modus tollens,* which reconstruct the experimental ideal of verification and falsification. In Popper's recently published original manuscript for his *Logic of Scientific Discovery* (Popper 1979), this debt to Fries and Apelt is made explicit. Even the motivation of combating logical positivism was similar to Apelt's quarrel with Whewell. But the important point for our story is that a falsificationist logic of scientific method was available to Lotze, and through him to the exponents of Darwin's theory in psychology. In addition, and this is Apelt's second principal contribution, he expressed induction in terms of mathematical functions of the form $y = f(x)$. he proposed this simplified functional equation after reconstructing the logical pattern of discovery of Kepler, Newton, Laplace, and Lagrange. Thereby he demonstrated that both a deductive principle or "leading maxim" and an inductive principle or "series of observations" were required to establish scientific laws (Apelt 1854).

Although Hermann Lotze did not acknowledge Fries and Apelt to a significent extent, his surviving correspondence with Apelt from 1834 to 1841 clearly reveals some Friesian sources of his own philosophy of science (Gresky 1937–1938). Drawing publically on Herbart and Hegel as the prestige philosophers of the day, Lotze in fact incorporated both of Apelt's themes into his critique of their accounts of scientific explanation. Both mathematical philosophy and dialectical philosophy dealt in abstractions, he argued. As Timothy Lenoir has recently shown, Lotze was a leading figure in the reformulation of the Kantian teleomechanical program for research in the biological sciences. The basis of this program was the replacement of vitalistic concepts of *Lebenskraft* and *Gestaltungskraft* with regulative concepts of life, mind, and biological organization in general, not as teleological explanations *per se*, but as an expression of the goals of scientific research (Lenoir 1981). Lotze called these regulative principles "natural purposes," "functions," "values," and "drives" depending on the context, keeping close to Kant's terminology (cf. Löw 1980). In addition, Lotze stressed that scientific explanation required two other factors, mechanical "laws" and empirical "facts," which taken together give a constitutive account of how systems function. In this way, Lotze incorporated the inductive and deductive aspects of Apelt's theory of science. Although he also expressed explanation in terms of "constitutive equations," we shall not deal with this here because it was not picked up by psychological writers. A recent monograph on Gottlob Frege, however, has shown conclusively that Frege's concept of function was derived from careful study of Lotze's *Logik* (Sluga 1980).

By examining these and other features of Lotze's *Logik* in its 1843 and 1874 editions which American philosopher-psychologists drew upon, we can discover some important epistemological and theoretical elements of post-Darwinian evolutionary theories. Charles Peirce's career revolved around a metaphysics of "evolutionary love" which went through four stages (Murphey 1961). In each stage his central concern was an archetectonic to relate our knowledge to the "community of investigators" who determine it. In 1866 he discovered that deduction, induction, and hypothesis could be correlated with the three figures of the syllogism. This is of interest because it involved roughly the same concern as Apelt's and Lotze's, namely the conclusion that every syllogism can be put into the hypothetical form. From his remarks about Lotze's "subtle misconception ... [of] extension as a species of comprehension" in 1867, we gather that Lotze and William Hamilton were among the sources of his recognition that signs have a different nature from the objects wich they represent. A later article on "modality" in Baldwin's *Dictionary* (1901) expressed admiration for Lotze's demonstration that the necessity of scientific laws can be expressed in the universal judgment, the conditional judgment, or the disjunctive judgment. Thus the reading of Lotze helped Peirce to a new understanding of Kant's "functions of judgment" and led toward symbolic logic. Both men belonged to the transformation of philosophy, as Karl-Otto Apel (1973) has recently termed it, from transcendental logic to a linguistic community in which hypotheses (abductions) are tested through inductions "in the long run." It is this community aspect of the origin of scientific knowledge which is captured in Peirce's phrase "evolutionary love." One finds similar themes in Hegel and Lotze.

Another American who was thoroughly conversant with Lotze is William James. From the marginal comments in James' copy of Lotze's *Logik* we can trace James' search for an alternative to Chauncey Wright's inductive account of the operation of mind. James' essay in 1878 on "Brute and Human Intellect" shows the first results of this recourse to the Kantian tradition. Paraphrasing Lotze's repeated point that "the judgment expresses a relation of two contents, not two ideas" (Lotze 1874: 57, 36), and we justify this relation by specifying the conditions *x* under which *S* is *P* (Lotze 1874: 564, 347), James argued that humans reason by choosing the "reason" or "means," *m*, which connects two otherwise dissimilar ideas, A and Z; he went beyond the "ideally perfect" diagram of the subsumption of S under P (Fig. 1) when he pointed out that "only *so far as we are right* in identifying in our thought the total A and the total Z, with their ingredient, *m*, and in ignoring the outlying portions of the circles, can we reason from one to the other" (Fig. 2) (1878: 242–43). Thus James provided a psychological interpretation of the rational induction which we have traced through Apelt, Lotze, and Peirce. While James was not very receptive to the expression of propositions as mathematical functions, his marginal notes to Lotze's *Logik* also contain the equation "$S = f P$" and a running summary of the hypothetical inference underlying it (Lotze 1874: 114, 142).

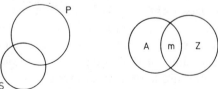

Fig. 1 + 2

The Principles of Psychology in 1890 contain two chapters in particular which show the result of James's study of Lotze's *Logik*. In "The Methods and Snares of Psychology," James repeated Lotze's argument for replacing the association of ideas with the function of judgments; he warned of the "psychologist fallacy" or the "*confusion of his own standpoint with that of the mental fact* about which he is making his report" (1890, I: 196). In the final chapter on "Necessary Truths and the Effects of Experience," James applied this methodological insight to the evolution of scientific knowledge; citing Lotze (1874: 550–572, 342–351), he wrote: "What we experience, what *come before us,* is a chaos of fragmentary impressions interrupting each other; what we *think* is an abstract system of hypothetical data and laws" (1890, II: 634).

The hints of James were developed into a program for functionalism by James Rowland Angell and John Dewey at Chicago. Angell spent time in Germany and wrote a dissertation in the German language on Kant's three critiques and their systematic interrelationship.[2] His declaration "On the Province of Functional Psychology" in 1907 lacked any methodological concern with hypothesis and induction, preferring a biological definition of function as self-regulation. But his colleague, Dewey, took the Kantian tradition in the direction of an instrumentalist view of theories, and he did so with explicit reference to Lotze.

In the lead chapter to his *Studies in Logic* in 1903, John Dewey accepted Lotze's distinction in the *Logik* between the antecedent conditions of thought, the datum of thought, and the content of thought. From these three factors he constructed his own formula of thought as a response to stimuli in a certain situation. But he detected an ambivalence in Lotze between construing theories as "a mere tool" versus "the *action* of erecting the building" (1903: 79). Dewey was critical of Lotze's "separation between an independent thought-material and an independent thought-function," for this implied an absolute reality to which thought adjusts and eventually throws away the scaffolding. For Dewey, theories were rules for symbolically representing the relation between carpenter and building, between thinker and the particular situation. As Ernest Nagel described instrumentalism, "the pertinent question about theories is not whether they are true or false but whether they are effective techniques for representing and inferring experimental phenomena" (1961: 133). For Apelt and Lotze, by comparison, mechanical laws in the deductive-nomological sense of Hempel (1965) and Nagel do combine with empiricial observations to generate predictions which are true or false. Meanwhile, Apelt and Lotze employed leading maxims and functional systems as the goal of inductive investigations. This principle distinction between mechanical laws and functional goals is vitiated by instrumentalism.

Whereas Dewey seemingly collapsed the distinction between reasoning, theory of scientific method, and theory of knowledge, James Mark Baldwin preserved Lotze's systematic divisions in the three volumes of his "study of the development and meaning of thought" entitled *Thought and Things, or Genetic Logic.*

Table 1.

Comparison of Lotze's and Baldwin's Views of Logic

Lotze's *Logik* (1874)	Baldwin's *Genetic Logic*
I. Thought (pure logic)	I. Functional logic, or genetic theory of knowledge (1906)
II. Investigation (applied logic)	II Experimental logic, or genetic theory of thought (1908)
III. Cognition (methodology)	III. Genetic theory of reality (1915)

Baldwin's quotations from Lotze at key transitional points in his volume confirm the appearance of systematic parallels.[3] Baldwin recognized better than anyone else, for instance, that Lotze had three separate questions deserving of separate answers. To the first question of how thought functions (functional logic), Baldwin credited Lotze with showing that the actual movement of thought is hierarchical: according to the canons of Baldwin's genetic logic, mental events are characterized by continuity, progression, and quality, as opposed respectively to the fallacies of discontinuity, causation by other mental events, and equality to other mental events (1906, I: 22–23).

To the second question of how knowledge functions (experimental logic), Baldwin answered that predication established intersubjective meaning. "The identity of the shooting star seen by different observers," wrote Baldwin, "can be rendered in a judgment only through the generalization of the experiences of these observers, whereby the event is pronounced the same for all of them" (1908, II: 99). Again he seems to have borrowed the underlying distinction from Lotze, who insisted upon the difference of the meaning of a judgment and the existence of the content judged. After quoting Lotze to this effect (pp.34–35), Baldwin put this point into two examples illustrated by diagrams. In the sentence "Romola is a woman," the particular subject (S) is related to the general predicate (P) by a relation (R) which characterizes the meaning between them; notice that the meaning of the judgment is also identified as the content (C), and that this content is located within a certain sphere of existence (E) in Fig.3. By comparison, the sentence "The woman Romola really existed" loses this so-called "envelope of belief" and becomes an existential judgment, as shown in Fig.4 by the overlap of the new content (C') and the circle of existence.

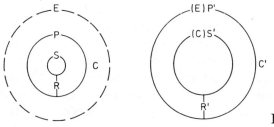

Fig. 3 + 4

Finally comes the question of Baldwin's third volume (genetic theory of reality): What are the possible constructions of knowledge? The answer requires a "genetic epistemology" comparable to what Lotze had called a "real logic" and what Hegel had termed a "speculative logic" (1906, I: 7). Baldwin is dealing at a very abstract level with the issue of the relationship and "value," as Lotze would say, of the various disciplinary approaches to understanding reality. Remarking on the justification of treating the social sciences differently from the natural sciences, Baldwin wrote that "the attempts, notably that of Lotze, to sublimate the physical in the social, rest in fact on the ground of the inconceivability of mechanical interaction in nature" (1915: 183). In other words, he believed that Lotze had hinted at a "communal idealism" based on social interaction, thereby abandoning the quest for a mechanical or scientific psychology and pointing to a new mode of comprehending reality which "while 'extra psychic' (foreign to the individual) is not 'trans-subjective' (foreign to society)" (1915: 183). Esthetic experience, he concluded, has this "synthetic value" of transcending individual experience, as recognized by "the poet Schiller and Lotze" (1915: 215). Baldwin is trying here to elucidate Lotze's point that each individual has a way of comprehending the whole which is at once unique and shared with others.

It has become increasingly clear that Lotze's concept of function is not merely that of self-regulation in living systems. Nor is it the adaptation of the organism to the environment in the sense of evolution by natural selection. The elaboration of Lotze's suggestions into a semiotic community (Peirce), a mental development of natural science (James), an instrumental theory (Dewey), and a genetic logic (Baldwin) reveal a very simple point about functional explanations. They are all doomed to failure, as Carl Hempel has indicated (1965), insofar as one hopes through them to attain the apodicticity of the deductive-nomological explanatory model. Yet as Fries pointed out in clarification of Kant and Schelling, it is a mistake to hope for such certainty from any inductive method, for by definition, induction involves an infinite regress. Acknowledging this negative point from his friend Apelt, Lotze turned it into the positive proposal that regulative concepts of life and value become the building blocks of a social order. This fecund insight took hold among the psychologists seeking to explain mental evolution because they realized the limits of a theory of natural evolution (Richards 1982a, 1982b; Woodward 1982).

Notes

[1] Woodward, W.R. (1975) The Medical Realism of R.Hermann Lotze. Unpublished dissertation, Yale, University. University Microfilms Order No.76–14, 576.

[2] Angell, J.R. (1896) Unpublished dissertation. Yale University Archives.

[3] Wozniak, R.H. Metaphysics and Science, Reason and Reality: the Intellectual Origins of Genetic Epistemology. In J.Broughton and J.Freemann-Moir (eds.) *The Cognitive Developmental Psychology of James Mark Baldwin: Current Theory and Research in Genetic Epistemology.* New York: Ablex, in preparation.

References

Angell, J.R. (1907) The province of functional psychology, *Psychological Review* 14: 61–91.

Apel, K.-O. (1967) *Der Denkweg von Charles S.Peirce. Eine Einführung in den amerikanischen Pragmatismus.* Frankfurt: Suhrkamp.

—(1973) *Transformation der Philosophie,* 2vols. Frankfurt: Suhrkamp.

Apelt, E.F. (1854) *Die Theorie der Induktion.* Leipzig: Engelmann.

Baldwin, J.M. (1906, 1908) *Thought and things. A study of the development and meaning of thought or genetic logic.* Vol.1. *Functional logic, or genetic theory of knowledge.* Vol.2. *Experimental logic, or genetic theory of thought.* London: Swan Sonnenschein.

—(1915) *Genetic theory of reality.* New York: Putnam's.

Buchdahl, G. (1973) Leading principles and induction. The methodology of Matthias Schleiden. In R. Giere and R. Westfall, eds. *Foundations of scientific method.* Bloomington, Ind.: Indiana University Press, pp.23–52.

Dewey, J. (1903) *Studies in logical theory.* Chicago: University of Chicago Press.

Gresky, W. (1937, 1938) 21 Briefe von Hermann Lotze an Ernst Friedrich Apelt (1835–1841). *Blätter für deutsche Philosophie* 10: 319–37; 11: 184–203.

Hempel, C. (1965) *Aspects of scientific explanation.* New York: Free Press.

James, W. (1878) Brute and human intellect. *The Journal of Speculative Philosophy,* 12: 236–276.

—(1890) *The principles of psychology* (2vols.) New York: Holt.

Kuklick, B. (1977) *The rise of American philosophy. Cambridge, Massachusetts, 1860–1930.* Hew Haven, Conn.: Yale University Press.

Kuntz, P.G. (1971) Introduction. In George Santayana, *Lotze's System of Philosophy.* Bloomington, Ind.: Indiana University Press, pp.3–105.

Lenoir, T. (1981) Teleology without regrets. The transformation of physiology in Germany: 1790–1847. *Studies in the History and Philosophy of Science* 12: 293–354.

Lotze, R.H. (1843) *Logik.* Leipzig: Weidmann.

—(1874) *Logik. Drei Bücher vom Denken, vom Untersuchen und vom Erkennen.* Leipzig: S.Hirzel.

—(1885) *Grundzüge der Logik.* 2d ed. Leipzig: S.Hirzel.

Löw, R. (1980) *Philosophie des Lebendigen. Der Begriff des Organischen bei Kant, sein Grund und seine Aktualität.* Frankfurt: Suhrkamp.

Madden, E. (1963) *Chauncey Wright and the foundations of pragmatism.* Seattle, Washington: University of Washington Press.

Merz, J.T. (1904–1912) *A history of European thought in the nineteenth century,* 4vols. London: Blackwood.

Murphey, M.G. (1961) *The development of Peirce's Philosophy.* Cambridge, Mass.: Harvard University Press.

Nagel, E. (1961) *The structure of science.* New York: Harcourt, Brace, Jovanovitch.

Otto, K. (1981) Entwicklungstheorien. In G.Claus, ed., *Wörterbuch der Psychologie.* Leipzig: VEB Bibliographisches Institut, pp.163–169.

Passmore, J. (1968) *A Hundred Years of Philosophy.* Harmondsworth: Penguin, 1st ed. 1957.

Peirce, C. (1967) Upon logical comprehension and extension. *Proceedings of the Amer. Acad. of Arts and Sciences* 7: 416–432. In *Collected papers,* vol.2, pp.237–253.

156 Woodward

—(1901) Modality. In J.M. Baldwin, ed., *Dictionary of philosophy and psychology.* 3vols. New York: Macmillan, 1901–05. Vol.1 (1901). In *Collected Papers,* Vol.2, pp.229–236.

Pester, R. (In press) Zur Stellung von Rudolph Hermann Lotze in der Geschichte der Philosophie und in der Geschichte der Naturwissenschaften. In *Denkschrift an R.H. Lotze.* Berlin-East: Verlag der Wissenschaften.

Popper, K.R. (1979) *Die beiden Grundprobleme der Erkenntnistheorie.* Tübingen: Mohr. First published 1930–1933.

Richards, R.J. (1982a) Darwin and the biologizing of moral behavior. In W.R. Woodward and M.G. Ash, eds., *The problematic science: Psychology in nineteenth century thought.* New York: Praeger, pp.43–64.

—(1982b) The personal equation in science: William James's psychological and moral uses of Darwinian theory. *Harvard Library Bulletin* 30: 387–425.

Riegel, K.F. and J.A. Meacham, eds. (1976) *The developing individual in a changing world,* 2vols. The Hague: Mouton.

Sluga, H. (1980) *Gottlob Frege.* London: Routledge and Kegan Paul.

Sprung, L. and H.Sprung (In press) R.H. Lotze. In *Denkschrift an R.H. Lotze.* Berlin-East: Verlag der Wissenschaften.

Wiener, P. (1949) *Evolution and the founders of pragmatism.* Cambridge, Mass.: Harvard University Press.

Woodward, W.R. and U.Rainer, eds. (1975) Berufungs-Korrespondenz Rudolph Hermann Lotzes an Rudolph Wagner (13 Briefe: 1 Dezember 1842–11 April 1844), *Archiv für Geschichte der Medizin (Sudhoffs)* 59:356f.

Woodward, W.R. (1982) The "discovery" of social behaviorism and social learning theory. *American Psychologist* 37:396–410.

—(1983) Introduction. In *Essays in psychology. The works of William James.* Cambridge, Mass.: Harvard University Press.

Figure1. The subject S is subsumed under the predicate P in the second figure of the universal affirmative judgment, e.g., "All gold is yellow." (From Lotze 1885: 37).

Figure2. Two data, A and Z. In the theoretic sphere *m* is the "reason" for "inferring" Z; in the sphere of action it is the "means" (or the instrument) for "attaining" Z. (From James 1878: 241).

Figure3. "The entire meaning of the Judgment [with presupposition] is an acknowledgment of the Content (C) comprising the Relation (R) between the General (P) and the Particular (S), as holding in a sphere of existence (E)." (From Baldwin 1908, II: 35).

Figure4. "In the Existential Judgment the sphere of Existence (E) has become predicate (P') and the former Subject-matter (C) has become subject (S') of the new relation R', now made Subject-matter or Content (C'). The factors are just the same as in Fig. 1, except that the existence presupposition (E) has now become predicate." (From Baldwin 1908, II: 36).

Experimental Approaches to Developmental Psychology before William Preyer

by Wolfgang G. Bringmann, Norma J. Bringmann, and William D.G. Balance

Historians of psychology generally subscribe to the adage of Hermann Ebbinghaus (1850–1909) that modern "psychology has a long past but a short history" (1911). Following this point of view, four stages can be distinguished in the literature about the history of developmental psychology. There is, however, some disagreement about the exact dating of these periods.

1. *Unsystematic stage.* The first or unsystematic stage, includes the period before the beginning of the nineteenth century. Diamond has characterized this stage in his sourcebook, *The Roots of Psychology* (1974:469), as follows:

> Before Darwin, child psychology was limited to occasional bits and snatches such as Artistotle's mention that children do not dream before the age of four (!) or Locke's reminder that supposedly innate truths are not known to children in advance of experience. In the eighteenth century Smellie recognized the need for the systematic study of child behavior but he could not spare the time. Augustine aside, history provides scarcely any example of truly understanding observations of children's behavior before the 19th century.

2. *Biographical stage.* The second or biographical stage in the history of developmental psychology began during the second half of the seventeenth century and lasted, with some interruptions, until the end of the nineteenth century (Jaeger and Staeuble, 1978). The biographical or diary method, as Wright (1960) called it, emphasized the systematic, longitudinal observation of individual children and the publication of results in the form of baby biographies (Dennis 1946). The subjects of these investigations were usually the particular author's children. Dietrich Tiedemann (1748–1803), a German philosopher, published the first "baby biography" in 1787 (Murchison and Langner 1927, Tiedemann 1787, Ufer 1897). Even Itard's study of the *Wild Boy of Aveyron* (1801) clearly belongs to this genre of literature. After a period of relative neglect, the diary method became popular once more with the publication of an English translation of Hippolyte Taine's (1828–1893) study of language acquisition by his daughter (1876).

Darwin recorded his observations of the physical and mental development of his oldest child in 1840 but he published his notes almost four decades later after reading Taine's "very interesting account" (1877). Wundt, who entertained serious doubts about the scientific potential of developmental psychology, collected extensive diary information of his two oldest children during the late 1870s (Wundt 1900: 284–304). Preyer's classic, *Die Seele des Kindes* (1882), which summarized his own careful observation of the development of his son as well as the findings of many other investigators, may be viewed as the culmination of this period. Modern scholars in the field of developmental psychology are clearly aware of the shortcomings of the diary method but, nevertheless, fully acknowledge its continued value as a research tool (Kessen, Haith, and Salapatek 1970: 303):

> The (baby) biographies have the defects of their virtues: idiosyncratic selection makes comparison difficult, variation in observational procedures limits parametric analysis of variables, and the coherence of person that makes them convincing human documents often frustrates the student in search of an objective account. But, despite their weaknesses, the biographies are essential in our studies of language, emotional expression, problem solving, representation, and imitation in infants and they remain invaluable sources of observations and of leads toward better controlled observations on other matters of interest to the psychologist of infancy, particularly in the period between the newborn's hospital stay and the child's entrance into nursery school.

3. *Questionnaire stage.* The third or questionnaire stage was initiated by the pioneering investigation of Schwabe and Bartholomäi (1870) who collected extensive cross-sectional information in Berlin in the hope of finding out what children know when they begin school at the age of six. Their research inspired G.Stanley Hall (1844–1924) to conduct his pioneering study, *The Contents of Childrens' Minds,* in 1882 (Hall 1883). The early work of Binet, Stern, and Terman in the field of intelligence testing is a direct extension of this tradition!

4. *Experimental stage.* Finally, the fourth or experimental stage of child psychology began with the application of experimental methods by Wilhelm August Lay (1862–1926) to educational problems (1897, 1898, 1904) during the last decade of the nineteenth century. The introduction of laboratory procedures so dramatically intensified interest in the study of child behavior that Ernst Meumann (1862–1915), perhaps the most original of Wundt's early students, required three volumes just to summarize recent research in the still new field of experimental pedagogy a few years later (1907–1908).

Experimental procedures in modern psychology are generally considered the method of choice for demonstrating relationships among variables. Thus, one is tempted to view the developmental sequence, which I have just described, as lawful and to regard the earlier stages as necessary prerequisites in the evolutionary process. One unfortunate consequence of such an orientation is the prejudice that to be really excellent, all research should follow the experimental paradigm. A less obvious result is the belief that systematic research in experimental psychology did not exist prior to Taine and Darwin and that the experimental method was not valid in the field of developmental psychology before the late nineteenth or early twentieth century.

During our recent biographical researches on Wundt, however, it was discovered that refined experimental studies of child behavior were published nearly two decades before Darwin's *Biographical Sketch of an Infant Mind* (1877) and more than half a century before the publication of Meumann's *Vorlesungen zur Einführung in die experimentelle Pädagogik* (1907–1908). The noted German internist *Adolf Kussmaul* (1822–1902) conducted these experiments and published them in 1859 under the title: *Untersuchungen über das Seelenleben des neugeborenen Menschen* (Investigations of the mental life of the newborn child).

One can, of course, discover forerunners of almost any modern-day discovery in psychology and related fields, if one searches long and hard enough. Kussmaul's work is remarkable because it represents a far more sophisticated form of investigation than the more popular writings by Darwin (1877), Preyer (1882), or Hall (1883) in the same area.

Elaborate details about the life and intellectual career of Kussmaul are richly available in the two volumes of his autobiography, which are rightly counted among the very best medical autobiographies (Bringmann 1976; Kussmaul 1899, 1903). In addition, his encounters with scientific luminaries like Puchelt, Henle, Semmelweiss, Rokitansky, Virchow, Roller, Helmholtz, and many others are remarkably candid and enlightening.

Although he was about ten years older than Wundt, Kussmaul knew Wundt well. They both had graduated from the same high school, both had received the much coveted research award of the Heidelberg University Medical School and both had been among the founders of the Heidelberg Natural Science Association. Wundt had reviewed Kussmaul's book on speech pathology and Kussmaul in turn characterized Wundt in his autobiography as follows (1903:72):

> Despite his youth he was exceptionally well read. Although his critical comments were often poignant, he expressed them gently. Wundt was personally warm-hearted, and we spent a good deal of time together on our hikes through the beautiful Neckar valley.

Unlike Wundt, whose medical education was geared towards an academic and research career, Kussmaul, throughout his life, was very interested in clinical practice and was acclaimed as an outstanding physician.

Kussmaul wrote his book on the psychology of newborn children near the end of his association with Heidelberg University. He was supporting himself and his family as a public health physician. It is likely that the experiments with newborn children were made possible by this appointment. Kussmaul had demonstrated a special interest in pediatrics and obstetrics during his postgraduate studies at Vienna and Prague more than ten years before. Discussions on normal child development were also an essential part of his lectures on psychiatry during the Heidelberg period (1859:7):

> As a teacher of psychiatry, I began my lectures with a developmental history of the human mind, since I had observed that, in this manner, I was able to give my students the quickest and most vivid picture of the elements of mental events. . . .

Dissatisfaction with the existing literature on early childhood behavior led him to conduct his own experiments (1859: 8):

> I discovered the big gaps which the empirical study of the mind still had to fill in. It was primarily the earliest time of life about which I was able to tell my students little that was certain. This is the reason why I carried out several observations and experiments with newborn children.

Kussmaul's *Investigations* (1859) apparently served as his official *Habilitationsschrift* for Erlangen University. Although the book was reprinted in 1875 and 1896, it attracted much less attention among psychologists than his monograph on speech pathology, *Die Störungen der Sprache* (1877).

The mental life of the newborn

Kussmaul, like a good scholar, began his monograph by defining his subject matter as the psychological processes of "sensation, imagination, thought, and motivation" in the newborn child (1859: 3). It is clear that he fully appreciated the difficulties associated with studying these activities in young children (1859: 4):

Knowledge of our own mental activities is mediated directly by consciousness. It is more difficult to understand the mind of another organism, since we can only make indirect inferences from their movements. However, one and the same movement frequently can either have a psychic or merely a mechanical cause. It is not enough to simply conclude from the similarity and form of a given movement to another, that is commonly mediated by the mind, that the mind has caused a given movement. Rather, one must document that a given movement or a sequence of responses ... could not ordinarily have been the result of mechanical causes. ...

Although he relied on behavior as the major source of his data, Kussmaul differed radically from other early behaviorists. He insisted that mechanical causation of movements must be ruled out before behavior can be attributed to psychological processes. He avoided using "purposefulness of movement" as a dependable criterion of psychological causation because robots—or to use his term— *"automata"* (1859: 4) existed in his time, which were able to "write, draw, make music and swim in the most purposeful and deliberate manner" (pp.4–5). In fact, he took the remarkably modern point of view that (1859: 5):

... the making of errors in the choice of means can be considered as better evidence for the existence of mental abilities than the apparently superior purposefulness with which the most ingenious machine works.

Review of the literature

About one-fourth of his book (pp.8–22) is devoted to a scholarly review of classical and recent literature concerning the behavioral repertoire of the human neonate. Interestingly, he found the developmental position of Artistotle more compatible with his experimental findings than those of the British Associationists, like John Locke (1632–1704), who held that the mind of the newborn child is in effect a *tabula rasa.* With rare exceptions, Kussmaul saw little of value in the literature. He summarized his criticisms as follows (1859: 10–11):

A comprehensive and independent attempt to write a history of the human mind has not been made to my knowledge. The history of the child's mind has recently been given to us in the little work of Berthold Sigismund, which contains a valuable collection of his own observations and has been written in a warm-hearted style. However, one cannot completely agree with the interpretation of some of the facts by this author. As far as the mental activities of the newborn are concerned, many physicians and philosophers have devoted much attention to them, however, no one to my knowledge subjected these to careful study or used experimentation in the process. The assertions of the various authors are full of contradictions and, on closer examination, prove to a large extent to be incorrect.

The experiments

In the remaining half of the book (pp.22–47), Kussmaul describes his experiments to collect baseline information on the sensory repertoire of newborn children. He studied taste, touch, temperature sense, smell, vision, hearing, and the muscle sense. He addressed himself to the investigation of hunger and thirst, and he closed the book with a discussion of various responses, which were to him indicative of intelligence. Each set of experiments has been described by Kussmaul with the traditional information about the subjects of the investigation, the experimental equipment and materials, the testing procedures employed, and finally the results. Kussmaul also critically evaluated the results of each experiment and attempted to integrate his findings with the existing information in the field. Whenever his own results were unsatisfactory or incomplete, Kussmaul made use of other data which he thought were pertinent.

Experiments on taste

The subjects from Kussmaul's study of the sense of taste consisted of slightly more than twenty newborn children. Although we do not know the exact composition of the sample, he informs us that they included children (1859: 22–23):

> ... who had barely left the womb, and who had not yet taken in any milk ...
> full-term and strong babies of both sexes, as well as ... some children who had
> been born prematurely in the seventh or eighth month. ...

As experimental stimuli for his study of taste, Kussmaul used "sweet" and "bitter" liquids, which had first been warmed and which were applied to the mouth with a "fine camel hair brush." His rigorous concern with experimental control can be seen in the following direct quote (1859:22):

> These liquids consisted of a satiated sugar solution and a solution of 10 grams of
> sulphate of quinine in half an ounce of water. This substance had a very bitter
> taste and was used in this concentration in all experiments without exception.

The application of such precautions seemed indicated, in order to draw correct conclusions from comparative experiments with different individuals.

His major finding was (1859: 22):

> The sugar and quinine solutions produced the same muscular movements in the neonate, which are designated in adults as the facial expressions of sweet and bitter taste.

Kussmaul's graphic description of the children's reactions clearly demonstrates differential responses to sweet and bitter stimuli (1859: 23):

> When sugar was brought into the mouth, the children arched their lips like the snout of an animal, pressed the tongue between the lips and began to suck with pleasure and to swallow. In response to the quinine solution, the face was distorted. When small amount of quinine were applied, only the muscles controlling the nostrils and the upper lip contracted. The use of larger amounts of quinine caused the muscles, which control the wrinkling of eyebrows and the closure of the eyelids, to be activated. The eyelids were actually pinched together and kept closed for a period of time. The throat contracted spasmodically; the children choked, the mouth was opened wide and the tongue protruded as much as an inch; and the applied liquids were often partially expelled, together with a great amount of saliva. At times, the children actively shook their heads, like an adult might do, who is overcome by nausea.

From these and other observations, Kussmaul concluded that (1859: 26):

> ... the sense of taste among newborn children already functions in its major forms and that they do not merely experience taste in a completely vague manner as Bichat thought. . . .

Experiments on touch

Kussmaul's experiments of the sense of touch in newborn children were extensive, although they concentrated primarily on the facial area. He specifically explored the touch sensitivity of the tongue, the lips, the nasal membranes, and the eyelashes. We will look at his experiments concerned with the function of the eyelashes as sensory organs as an illustration of his innovative and painstaking methodology (1859: 32–33):

> The eyelashes are extremely sensitive to the slightest touch. If the waking child has opened his eyes, one can proceed with a thin glass rod almost to the cornea before the eye will be closed. However, as soon as a single eyelash is touched,

the eye closes at once. The touching of the eyelids is by no means as effective in producing a closure of the eye.

The extreme sensitivity of the eyelashes can be beautifully demonstrated by the following experiment. If one blows on the cheeks or the forehead of a newborn, it blinks with his eyes. At first, I had incorrectly explained this behavior as a response of the skin to changes in temperature. If one, however, directs air through a narrow paper tube alternatively to different parts of the face, one can observe that the child will blink only if the airstream touches one of the eyelashes. The eye on the stimulated side responds more intensively and quickly.

Kussmaul concluded that this reflexive response served to guard the eye against injury at a time when conscious experience could not yet control the closing of the eyelids. As a good physiologist, he also suggested that it might be worthwhile (1859: 33):

> ... to determine if fully formed endings of the nerves of touch exist at the roots of the eyelashes.

Kussmaul closed this section of his book with the observations that newborn children respond to tickling of their palms and the soles of their feet with a feather, although he wrote that he had not had an opportunity to make these observations with premature babies.

Temperature sensitivity

Kussmaul readily acknowledged that he did not collect systematic observation on temperature sensitivity in newborn children. However, he concluded from clinical experience that they "... possess a very intense sensitivity for cold and warmth" (p.34).

Experiments on smell

Research on the sense of smell in newborn children is not easy, as Kussmaul found out quickly. He was unable to record appropriate olfactory responses in 20 children, which he studied while they were awake. His main problem was, of course, the absence of specific response patterns similar to those found with taste. However, he concluded after experimentation with sleeping children, that newborn children "... already experience strong smells as unpleasant" (p.34). A major problem, however, even with sleeping children, was a tendency to adapt quickly to intense smells.

Visual experiments

By and large, Kussmaul's results on the sense of vision in newborn children, confirmed the established view that vision is very primitively developed at birth. However, he was able to demonstrate the ability of newborn children to accommodate pupil size to amount of light ("Weber's Experiment"). He also noted that 2–4 day old children pinched their eyelids together, gave a sudden start and woke up when the bright light of a candle was brought near their closed eyes. Kussmaul also made the interesting observation that (1859:36):

> ... a prematurely born male child was able to turn his head, which had been averted from the window, repeatedly toward the window and the light in the early evening of the second day of his life, even when his position was changed back after each attempt. He was undoubtedly seeking light. Thus, his visual organ not only functioned two months before the normal time of birth but soft light also seemed to produce a pleasurable sensation in the day old child, causing him to search for it.

According to Kussmaul, children do not learn to fixate objects until they are at least three weeks old. In the context of his research on vision, he concluded that (1859: 37–38):

> It would be extremely interesting to study the sequence of exercises by which man gradually acquires control of ocular movement and accommodation. Of course, experiments in this area will encounter serious obstacles. Yet, I believe that it is one of the most important and the most urgent tasks of physiological psychology to determine the way in which we arrive at the numerous judgments, which are such an integrated part of our sensations of light that we are later on unable to separate them. After so many thick books have been written about psychology, it is truly depressing to discover such great gaps in the cognitive development of the mind.

Auditory experiments

Kussmaul had little to say about the hearing of newborn children (1859: 38):

> Of all senses hearing slumbers the deepest. One can produce the loudest and most discordant noises before the ears of newborn children during the first days without their being affected. Many experiments, which I carried out in this direction were unsuccessful.

Nonetheless, a resident in obstetrics, Herr Feldbausch, assured Kussmaul that he had seen (1859:38):

sleeping children give a sudden start when he clapped his hands together under the cribs in a very quiet room. The youngest child with whom he made this experiment was three days old.

Since "Herr Feldbausch" was known to be a "cautious" observer, Kussmaul had to concede reluctantly "that the sense of hearing cannot be denied in all newborn children" (p.38).

Experiments on pain, muscle sensitivity, and air hunger

The sections on sensitivity to pain and on the muscle sense are purely anecdotal and contain no experimental results. Kussmaul's retiscence to experiment with pain is probably explainable by his personal gentleness and often-expressed concern with the happiness and well-being of his young patients. For example, he discontinued experimental trials with tartaric acid because the children seemed to experience considerable discomfort and were restless and cried in the night after that particular experiment. His discussion of kinesthetic sensitivity or the "muscular sense," as he preferred to call it, focused exclusively on fetal movements and was anecdotal in nature. The same restrictions apply to his comments about "air hunger."

Experiments on hunger and thirst

Kussmaul's research on hunger and thirst in the newborn was quite valuable. He suggested that children experience a combination of hunger and thirst during the first 6–24 hours of life. An experiment, which he performed with a "lively, pretty newborn girl" (p.45), provides considerable information on his experimental approach (1859: 45–46):

She was born around 7 a.m. and soon gave repeated signs of hunger but was not fed until noon. By that time, she had become very restless, moved her head back and forth as if searching for something and cried a lot. I stroked her left cheek softly with my index finger without touching the lip when she did not cry. Quickly she turned her head to the left side, grabbed my finger and began to suck. Next, I removed my finger and began stroking the right cheek. Just as quickly she turned to that side and once again took hold of my finger. Again I removed my finger and stroked the left cheek. It was quite a surprise how deftly the child turned back on the left side and again grasped the finger.

He continued the experiment alternating left and right cheeks until the child began to scream loudly and became upset. He then had the baby placed at her mother's breast without placing the nipple directly into her mouth (1859: 46):

> She again calmed down and moved her head back and forth in a searching manner but was unable to find and take hold of the nipple. The nipple had to be placed between her lips and jaws and then she began to suck. Thus, it is clear that the child was able to grasp the firm, long index finger at once but not the soft, small nipple.

He concluded that newborn children are able to make sucking movements but cannot nurse well without assistance. There are significant individual differences among children in acquiring this important skill, and some very clumsy children may never successfully learn to nurse.

Intelligence of neonates

In the last section of his book (pp. 47–57), Kussmaul attempted to integrate and interpret his earlier findings as evidence of intelligent functioning in the newborn. The final result is a hierarchy of child behavior based on the extent of mediation between stimulus and response (1859: 47–48):

> At the lowest level can be found the interplay of the pupil in light and dark. Self observation tells us that we cannot consciously perceive these changes. The stimulation of the retina results in movement of the iris but we are unaware of these movements. We are also unable to modify these responses by conscious control of the nerves of the iris ... Apart from the sensation of light and dark which accompanies this excitation, which cannot be separated from at least a mild degree of consciousness, no mental activity mediates between the original sensation and the resulting movement.

According to Kussmaul, a clearly higher level of intellectual functioning is involved (1859: 48):

> when the hand which is being tickled takes hold of the tickling object, when the lips suck at the finger or nipple, when the ingestion of the quinine solution results in facial expressions or, when the eyelids close against sudden light. ...

In all these examples movement occurred at first merely as a reflexive response to sensory stimulation. However, (1859: 48–49):

> ... soon the consciousness of sensation is coupled not only with the original sensation but also with the completed movement. Muscle sensations, pleasant

and unpleasant feelings and the desires, which arise from them, gradually grow into sensory concepts of the most basic type. Finally, the will learns to control these movements, to repress or intensify them, in brief, to regulate them in the interest of the individual.

Kussmaul ranked highest those movements which, regardless of their developmental origin, could no longer be elicited by mere sensory stimulation (1859: 29):

> When the thirsty child searches for nourishment, when it turns the head towards the side where his cheek is being stimulated, grabs the stroking finger and begins to suck on it, it is no longer possible to explain these phenomena merely as the result of sensory reflexes. Rather, we are forced to include in our explanations, ideas which mediate the actual movement. Obviously, we are concerned here with actions, whose origin must be sought in the child's intelligence. In other words, these are quite selective responses, which the individual carries out to satisfy an important need.

According to Kussmaul intelligent behavior in the child has its beginning even before the child is born (1859: 51):

> At the very moment when a human being leaves the womb, he already possesses a fully equipped sensory system, which enables him to find out through his external and internal senses what occurs in the world around him and in his own body. He also owns a well-equipped and rather complex motor-apparatus-machine whose mainsprings he only must learn to properly activate, in order to get them to function purposefully and independently. The newborn child, however, is not only equipped with excellent tools and able to learn their use, but he has already begun to utilize some of them in the womb and to gain some experience and skills, despite the inconvenience of his location. It is absolutely incorrect to claim that the life of the newborn resembles that of a plant, as well-known philosophers (Hegel) and scientists (Herboldt) have asserted.

Of course, conscious and intelligent behavior in the neonate differs clearly from the same states in the adult human (1859: 54):

> . . . we should not imagine that the newborn child can already carry out conscious actions or even solve syllogisms. Man acquires such abilities only with difficulty and very late in his development. . . . we are dealing here with instinct-like actions which result from the association of certain sensations or needs with simple, sensory representations. They are accompanied by a state of consciousness which is not much clearer than that of an adult who carries out some action in half-sleep.

Kussmaul's final conclusion about the intelligence of newborn children is very clear (1859: 55):

> At any event, the actions of the newborn give evidence of the existence of intelligence. Ideas play a part, even though they are not very distinct. Therefore, no

claim is more incorrect than the one by Karl Vogt, according to which newborn humans possess no trace of intelligence and ... exist consequently on an endlessly (!) lower level of ability than a dog or any other mammal.

Discussion and conclusion

Kussmaul's dissertation (1859) was partially replicated during the early 1870s by Alfred Genzmer, a doctoral candidate in "Medicine and Surgery" at Halle-Wittenberg University (1873, 1882). In contrast to Kussmaul, Genzmer did not summarize the relevant research literature in the intervening years. His study focused exclusively on "the sensory perception" of newborn children: touch (pp.6–11), temperature (pp.11–12), pain (pp.12–13), muscle sense (pp.13–14), taste (pp.14–17), air hunger (pp.17–18), hunger and thirst (pp.18–19), smell (pp.19–20), hearing (pp.20–21), and vision (pp.21–25).

Genzmer reported that he collected his data at a training school for midwives in Leipzig, It is, therefore, very likely that his infants came from the same lower middle class population as those examined by Kussmaul in Heidelberg. Although he claimed that he had studied the sensory behavior of 50 children (1873: 6), he did not record the same observations for each of these children. For example, his data on the sense of touch were derived from only 20 children but he tested for pain sensitivity in "almost 60 children" (p.12).

In general, Genzmer confirmed most of the empirical findings of Kussmaul. Minor differences were reported in only a few instances. Genzmer's subjects were most sensitive to touch at the tip of their noses and dit not readily close their eyes when their eyelashes were touched.

Kussmaul did not examine the sense of pain and the reactions of newborn children to oxygen deprivation empirically for quite obvious humanitarian reasons. Instead, his discussion of these topics was based on incidental rather than experimental observations. Genzmer, however, did collect his own data about infants' responsitivity to pain (1873: 12):

> The sense of pain is exceptionally poorly developed in the neonate ... During the first days (of their lives) I pricked premature infants with fine pins in the most sensitive parts (of their) noses, upper lips and hands so intensely that small drops of blood oozed from these openings. They gave no evidence of discomfort—not even a slight quivering.

He acknowledged that "the wetness of their eyes" increased when he pierced the children's faces with his needles but concluded that the children were only suffering from colds (!).

Genzmer also studied the effects of oxygen deprivation by pinching closed the noses of his newborn victims reporting the following consequences (1873:17–18):

> ...after about five seconds ...one observes a few attempts at swallowing. Soon afterwards the children become restless, toss their heads violently from side to side, wake up from sleep, and finally begin to scream and breathe through their mouths ...full-term babies tend to cry sooner, while premature infants bear the lack of air more than half a minute without a reaction.

He did not share the reactions of the mothers to his experiments with us, however! While Genzmer's findings are novel and may potentially have important implications, Kussmaul's caution and humane common sense are indubitably preferable.

A modern "successor" of Kussmaul

In recent years test procedures, which are strikingly similar to those applied by Kussmaul more than one hundred years ago (1859), have been standardized to provide objective information about the behavioral repertoire and developmental potential of newborn children (Self and Horowitz 1979). The basic research has been carried out by T.Berry Brazelton, M.D., the Director of the Child Development Unit of the Children's Hospital Medical Center in Boston (Brazelton 1973; Brazelton, Robey, and Collier 1969).

The *Brazelton Neonatal Behavior Assessment Scale* (BNBAS) consists of 20 neurological items (i.e. 1. Planta grasp, 2. Hand grasp ... 17–20 Passive movements of arms and legs) which are rated on a 4-point scale for intensity of response. In addition, 11 specific behaviors are observed or elicited with simple instruments (Quinn 1982) like:

> ...a red spice box with popcorn kernels, a small bell, a flashlight, an orange rubber ball one inch in diameter, a paper clip ... (p.25).

The following items on the behavior scale are highly reminiscent of Kussmaul's and Genzmer's techniques (Self and Horowitz, 1979:155):

(1) Response decrement to light
(2) Response decrement to rattle
(3) Response decrement to bell

(4) Response decrement to pinprick
(5) Focusing and following an object
(6) Reaction to an auditory stimulus.

The eleven behavioral items are each rated on a 9-point scale. The midpoint of the scale denotes the expected performance of a normal, three-day-old infant.

The BNBAS has been found useful in the assessment of cross-cultural differences in newborn children (Freedman and Freedman, 1969) and to detect the impact of socioeconomic differences in infant behavior (Justice, Self and Gutrecht 1976). The Brazelton scale has also been employed to detect the effect of maternal drug taking on neonates (Aleksandrowicz and Aleksandrowicz 1974) and it appears to have promise in predicting physical and mental development during a child's first year of life (Scarr-Salapatek and Williams 1973).

Kussmaul and Psychology

An English summary of Kussmaul's results was published in the *Cornhill Magazine* in 1863, and Kussmaul and Genzmer were included among the list of authors whom Preyer quoted most frequently in his classic, *Die Seele des Kindes* (The Mind of the Child, 1882). Preyer seems to have regarded both authors primarily as convenient providers of normative information and to have disregarded the experimental source of their data.

Specific findings from Kussmaul's dissertation (1859) have found their place in major reference works in developmental psychology from Murchison's *Handbook of Child Psychology* (1930) to Mussen's third edition of *Carmichael's Manual of Child Psychology* (1970). A quick examination of these handbooks (Carmichael, 1946, 1954; Murchison 1930, 1933; Mussen 1960, 1970) reveals that Kussmaul is mentioned an average of 15 times in each volume. The comparative figures for Genzmer, G.S. Hall, Preyer, and Tiedemann are 10, 4, 12, and 33 times, respectively. Unfortunately, references to Kussmaul and Genzmer seldom exceed a few words, while Hall, Preyer and Tiedemann attract substantially more attention and discussion. Recent research handbooks in infant and child psychology (Osofsky 1979, Reese and Lipsitt 1970) generally give the impression that little significant research in this field existed before our own time. Consequently, they contain no references to Kussmaul and Genzmer or other types of historical information.

172   Bringmann, Bringmann & Balance

Among standard histories of psychology and developmental psychology listed in Watson's bibliographical guide (1978), only a single one included relevant information about Kussmaul's infant research. Hehlmann's *Geschichte der Psychologie* (1963, 1967) mentions briefly on page 153 that Kussmaul published his "... investigation of the mental life of newborn children (1859) in the same year in which Darwin's *On the Origin of Species* (1859) appeared." Consequently, he placed the name of Kussmaul at the very beginning of this chronology of "Child and Adolescent Psychology" (1967: 435). A facsimile copy of Kussmaul's dissertation, which has recently been reprinted in the United States (Bringmann 1976), and an English translation of the entire work, will hopefully introduce this pioneering study to modern historians of psychology.

References

Aleksandrowicz, M. and Aleksandrowicz, D. (1974) Obstetrical pain-relieving-drugs as predictors of infant behavior variability. *Child Development* 45: 935–945.

Brazelton, T. (1973) *Neonatal behavioral assessment scale*. Philadelphia: Lippincott.

Brazelton, T., Tobey, J. and Collier, G. (1969) Infant Development in the Zincanteco Indians of Southern Mexico. *Pediatrics* 44: 274–293.

Brazelton T., Tronick, E., Adamson, L., Als, H. and Wise, S. (1975) Early mother-infant reciprocity. In *Parent-Infant Interaction* (CIBA Foundation Symposium 33). Amsterdam: North-Holland.

Brazelton, T., Tronick, E., Lechtig, A. and Lasky, R. (1977) The behavior of nutritionally deprived Guatemalan infants. *Developmental Medicine and Child Neurology* 19: 364.

Bringmann, W. (Ed.) (1976) *The origins of psychology*. (vol.3). New York: Liss.

Carmichael, L. (Ed.) (1946) *Manual of child psychology*. New York: Wiley.

—(1954) *Manual of child psychology* (2nd ed.). New York: Wiley.

Darwin, C. (1845) *On the origin of species by means of natural selection, or the preservation of favoured races in the struggle of life*. London: Murray.

—(1877) A biographical sketch of an infant. *Mind* 2: 285–294.

Dennis, W. (1949). Historical beginnings of child psychology. *Psychological Bulletin* 46: 224–235.

Diamond, S. (Ed.) (1974) *The roots of psychology*. New York: Basic Books.

Ebbinghaus, H. (1911) *Grundzüge der Psychologie* (3rd ed.) (2 vols.) Leipzig: Veit, 1913.

Freedmann, D. and Freedman, N. (1969) Behavioral differences between Chinese American and European American newborns. *Nature* 24: 1227.

Genzmer, A. (1873) *Untersuchungen über die Sinneswahrnehmungen des neugeborenen Menschen*. Halle: Plötzsche Buchhandlung, 1882.

Hall, G.S. (1883) The contents of children's minds. *Princeton Review* 11: 249–272.

Hehlmann, K. (1963, 1967). *Geschichte der Psychologie*. Stuttgart: Kröner.

Hehlmann, W. (1963) *Geschichte der Psychologie*. Stuttgart: Kröner, 1967.

Itard, J.M. (1932) *The wild boy of Aveyron*. New York: Century. Originally published in 1801.

Jaeger, J. and Staeuble, I. (1978) *Die gesellschaftliche Genese der Psychologie.* Frankfurt/New York: Campus Verlag.

Justice, L., Self, P., and Gutrecht, N. (1976) Socio-economic status and scores on the Brazelton Neonatal Behavioral Assessment Scale. Paper presented at the Southeastern Conference on Human Development, Nashville, Tennessee.

Kessen, W., Haith, M. and Salapatek, P. (1970) Infancy. In Paul H. Mussen (Ed.) *Carmichael's manual of child psychology.* (3rd ed.) New York: Wiley.

Kussmaul, A. (1859) *Untersuchungen über das Seelenleben des neugeborenen Menschen.* Heidelberg: Winter.

—(1877) *Die Störungen der Sprache.* Leipzig: Vogel.

—(1899) *Jugenderinnerungen eines alten Arztes.* Stuttgart: Bonz.

—(1903) *Aus meiner Dozentenzeit.* Stuttgart: Bonz.

Lay, W. (1897) *Grundfehler im ersten Sprachunterricht.* Karlsruhe.

—(1898) Mental imagery, experimentally and subjectively considered. *Ps. R. 5, Mng. Suppl. 7.*

—(1904) *Führer durch den Rechtschreibunterricht.* (3rd. ed.).

Meumann, E. (1907–1908) *Vorlesungen zur Einführung in die experimentelle Pädagogik und ihre psychologischen Grundlagen.* Leipzig: Engelmann.

Murchison, C. and Langner, S. (1927) Tiedemann's observations on the development of the mental faculties of children. *Journal of Genetic Psychology* 34: 205–230.

Murchison, C. (Ed.) (1931) *A handbook of child psychology.* Worcester, Mass.: Clark University Press.

—(1933) *A handbook of child psychology* (2nd ed.). Worcester, Mass.: Clark University Press.

Mussen, P. (Ed.) (1970) *Handbook of research methods in child development.* New York, Wiley, 1960.

—(1970) *Carmichael's manual of child psychology* (3rd ed.). New York: Wiley.

Osofsky, J. (1979) *Handbook of infant development.* New York: Wiley.

Preyer, W. (1882) *Die Seele des Kindes.* Leipzig: Grieben.

Quinn, S. (1982) Your baby is smarter then you think. *Families,* 24–28.

Reese, H. and Lipsitt, L. (1970) *Experimental child psychology.* New York: Academic Press.

Scarr, M., Salapatek, S. and Williams, M. (1973) The effects of early stimulation of low birth weight infants. *Child Development* 44: 94–101.

Schwabe, H. and Bartholomäi, F. (1870) Über Inhalt und Methode einer Berliner Schulstatistik. *Berliner Städtisches Jahrbuch* 4: 1–77.

Self, P. and Horowitz, F. (1979) The behavioral assessment of the neonate: an overview. In J. Osofsky (Ed.), *Handbook of infant development.* New York: Wiley.

Taine, H. (1876) Note sur l'acquisition de langage chez les enfants et dans l'espèce humaine. *Revue Philosophique* 1: 3–23. Trans. in *Mind* 2: 252–257.

Tiedemann, D. (1787) Beobachtungen über die Entwicklung der Seelenfähigkeiten bei Kindern. *Hessische Beiträge zur Gelehrsamkeit und Kunst* 2: 313–315; 3: 486–488.

Ufer, C. (Ed.) (1897) *Dietrich Tiedemann's Beobachtungen über die Entwicklung der Seelenfähigkeiten bei Kindern.* Altenburg: Bonde.

Watson, R. (1978) *The history of psychology and the behavioral sciences.* New York: Springer.

Wright, H. (1960) Observational child study. In Paul H. Mussen (Ed.), *Handbook of research methods in child development.* New York: Wiley.

Wundt, W. (1900) *Die Sprache.* (vol. 1). Leipzig: Engelmann.

Part II

William T. Preyer—His Time, His Work, and His Influence

Preyer's Road to Child Psychology

by Georg Eckardt

It came somewhat as a suprise to note during the preparations for the recent centennial of the establishment of the Leipzig Psychological Institute that historians of psychology from many different countries rarely view Wilhelm Wundt (1832–1920) as the "father" or "founder" of modern psychology. There was, however, considerable agreement that Wundt played a predominant role among the scholars who, in a manner of speaking, surrounded the cradle of the infant science. In the same vein, one realizes that William T. Preyer (1841–1897) has also rarely been considered as the "founder" or scientific "father" of child and developmental psychology (Pongratz 1967). The French historian of child psychology, Debesse, in fact, stated emphatically that Preyer was "no pioneer." Still, his *magnum opus, "Die Seele des Kindes"* (The Mind of the Child, 1882), is widely acknowledged as a seminal contribution to the field. According to Höhn (1959), one can view Preyer's work as a "threshold from which begins a period of systematic research on developmental questions in psychology." Jarosevsky (1976) also believed that "a new period in the investigation of the mental development of the child" was ushered in by Preyer.

Preyer was not the only scholar of his time who was interested in the behavior of children. Many empirical observations of child development were being published, and in fact an interesting feature of this literature is its international character. There was work from England (Darwin 1877, Sully 1881), France (Taine 1876, Perez 1878), Germany (Strümpell 1880), Italy (Ferri 1879) and Russia (Kapterev 1877). Comparison with these writings was not always favorable to Preyer. For example, Bühler (1918), who generally placed a high value on Preyer's contributions, was of the opinion that *The Mind of the Child* "lacked ideas," and Reinert (1976) concluded that the volume by Perez contained more original ideas than did Preyer's. Perhaps the most severe criticism of Preyer can be found in Wundt's *Philosophische Studien* (Philosophical Studies), where Eber (1896) evaluated Preyer's publication as merely "a 'physiological' pilot study for 'an exact psychological investigation of the beginnings of human consciousness'." He bluntly labeled the book "a disappointing mixture of logic and psychology" and was especially critical of Preyer's use of "the vulgar reflex psychology" to interpret psychological data.

In view of these critical comments, the question remains as to why Preyer's monograph—and not an earlier similar publication of another contemporary scholar—became the "initial chapter" or "basic handbook" of modern child psychology. How did Preyer's perspectives give impetus to an actual child study "movement"? There are, of course, no easy answers. Perhaps certain needs and interests within society were the root cause, which in turn, were perhaps the expression of the concrete historical situation. Reinert has noted that the psychological *Zeitgeist* "was receptive for psycho-physiological matters" and favored "precise and clear methodologies" (Reinert 1976: 880).

It is our view that Preyer distinguished himself from his contemporaries by the ability to identify and transfer methods and perspectives, which had originated in diverse disciplines and theories, and to integrate them with his new subject matter—the psychological development or "psychogenesis" of the child. No contemporary even approached Preyer in this unique talent.

Before we address ourselves to the sources of Preyer's fame and accomplishments in the new field of empirical child psychology, we need to talk briefly about an intellectual force which has left almost no imprint on Preyer's design for a developmental psychology—Wilhelm Wundt's *"Grundzüge der physiologischen Psychologie"* (Principles of Physiological Psychology, 1873, 1874). Preyer reviewed both parts of the first edition in the *Jenaer Literaturzeitung* (Preyer 1874b), and his sharp comments reveal that he either did not understand or value the basic goals which Wundt had set for the new psychology. Full autonomy from speculative-metaphysical philosophy and from experimental physiology was Wundt's rallying cry. Preyer minced no words in his blunt review (1874b:71):

> Any reader, who is also a researcher, will gain the impression that the author (Wundt, G.E.) merely wanted to finish his book quickly. Although he begins with the facts of outer and inner experience, he did not find an organic whole, which could subsume both methods of approach, but a multitude of big and small parts from basic anatomy, embryology, elementary nerve physiology and pure psychophysics. . . .

Then, in his review of the second part of Wundt's *Principles* (1874b), Preyer tried to finish off Wundt's psychology in even blunter terms. The "riveting and gluing" of unrelated parts, according to Preyer, would not create a "physiological psychology which is able to live." Although he recognized the *Principles* as a physiological text, he totally dismissed their psychological contributions (1874b: 551):

> As soon as the author leaves the firm land of physiology . . . and reaches the high sea of philosophy, his hand loses the rudder and all critical faculties. . . . We put the book aside not without regret that such a meritorious and comprehensive physiological work has been distorted by serious and consequential errors and a lack of comprehensibility.

This scathing review reveals to us that Preyer saw only two alternatives for dealing with psychological matters. One could make statements about psychic processes by investigating their material basis. In other words, to be a psychologist, one had to be a physiologist! Or, he acknowledged, there was the possibility of approaching the subject matter of psychology through philosophical speculation. Wundt's recognition that psychology constitutes an original field of investigation which must defend its independence against both philosophy and physiology, was alien to Preyer in 1874. Thus, one cannot be surprised that he has been accused of not sharing in the scientific developments of this classical period of experimental psychology. For example, it was said that he relied on the outdated models of faculty psychology and the "vulgarisms" of reflexology for the interpretation of his behaviour observations of children. Preyer's child psychology, thus, existed largely outside the mainstream of experimental psychology, which otherwise dominated the period. Child psychology originated alongside physiological psychology. It did not evolve out of its traditions.

Three major sources for Preyer's ideas and methods of child psychology can be distinguished: (1) physiology, (2) psychophysics, and (3) evolutionary theory.

(1) Physiology

Although Preyer did not fully perceive the possibilities of a psychology which would exist independently from philosophy and physiology, he did not believe that psychological questions could and should be reduced to physiological problems. We read in the "Preface" to the *Mind of the Child* (1882): "the vital phenomena of man during the period of his independent existence are . . . so complicated and diverse (p.v)" that the "mental and physical development" of newborn children and infants "must be studied separately" (p.v). It is important to remember that Preyer refused to restrict his investigations to the assessment of the physiological functions of children. Although, he liked to speak of his baby diary (1882) as a companion volume for his "Special Physiology of the Embryo," it must not be concluded that he thought that psychological matters were only physiological epiphenoma. Preyer disdained philosophical speculations. He labeled "the most intelligent speculations about the interaction of body and soul" as "irrelevant" (1880b: 201ff.). He believed that comparisons of human and animal behavior and "... observations in the nursery" were far more productive (1880b: 201.) According to Preyer, physiology should "provide the foundation of empirical psychology" (Preyer 1880b: 202). This statement suggests that physiology is not the same as psychology and can neither replace or become part of it.

The fields of neuro- and sensory physiology and physiological embryology were Preyer's favorite specialties in physiology. The latter had become the "dominant field of investigation (in biology, G.E.), and the new microtome technology played an essential role" (Krausse 1982: 141) in its development. Embryology was well suited for the application of the genetic approach. In retrospect, we can understand how Preyer may have been encouraged to transfer these new methods to his child research.

(2) Psychophysics

As a physiologist, acknowledging a need for an "empirical psychology," Preyer's interest in the field of psychophysics followed quite logically. He lectured on the subject during the winter semester of 1871–1872, and in 1873, he initiated an ten—year long scientific correspondance with Gustav Theodor Fechner (1801–1887). In 1874, he even attempted to formulate a "myophysical law" similar to Fechner's psychophysical principles. Although his new "law" was quickly shown to be invalid, Preyer remained convinced that such rules existed. He also seems to have transferred the major achievement of psychophysics—the discovery of an invariable relationship between stimulus and experience—to his study of child development (1897: 84):

> What matters is the collection of natural facts and the determination of how these ... phenomena are related ... We must identify the type of relationship or ... function.

Preyer cautioned his audience, however, against interpreting such functional dependencies as cause-effect relationships.

Before we can fully understand such functional connections, it is necessary to recognize the "objective symptoms of mental events" which he defined in the following manner (1897:84):

> I know nothing but muscular movements—impulsive, reflexive, instinctive, mimical, gesticulatory, deliberate movements . . . nothing else, unless one wishes to count certain secretions like the sweat of fear or tears. However, these are never found without their concomitant and characteristic muscular movements. Psychodiagnosis must rely always on them.

Although these phrases resemble a behavioristic program, Preyer was neither a behaviorist nor a predecessor of this orientation in modern psychology. He was only interested in showing that dependable, functional relationships can and must be identified.

(3) Evolution theory

It is well known that Preyer was one of the most fervent followers of Darwin in Germany, that he wrote the first Darwinian dissertation in Germany, that he carried on an extensive correspondance with Darwin, wrote a popular biography of his idol, and generally propagandized his theories. He also explicitly identified his child psychology as an application of Darwin's evolutionary thinking (1896: 165). Such an application of evolution to psychology was suggested by Darwin himself in the *Origin of Species*. We read in the final section (1859:488):

> Psychology will be based on a new foundation, that of the necessary acquirement of each mental power and capacity by gradation. Light will be thrown on the origin of man and his history.

Darwin personally moved in this direction with the *Biographical Sketch of an Infant*, composed in 1840 and published in 1877. His biological approach was seemingly more attractive to Preyer than the mechanistic physiology of the time, which placed ahistorical stress on chemical and physical variables rather than biological ones (1886).

The application of evolutionary principles to the new field of empirical child psychology led to the extensive use of the comparative method. Darwin's monograph on the *Expression of Emotions in Man and Animals* (1872) virtually served as the model. Inspired by Darwin, Preyer demonstrated the utility of the new comparative technique in his *Mind of the Child* on the following levels (1882):

(a) Comparison of repeated observations for the same individual: Preyer recorded a psychological observation of his son "almost daily" (p.vi).

(b) Observations of different children: Preyer urged mothers, educators, physicians, teacher, philosophers, physiologists, and psychologists to collect "child diaries" in the hope of eventually obtaining a range of representative materials.

(c) Comparison of animal and human behavior: In the fourth edition of the *Mind of the Child*, one reads that "observations and experiments with very young animals are highly desirable to gain recognition for comparative and genetic psychology as a science" (Preyer 1895: xi).

(d) Anthropological comparisons: Preyer suggested that explorers should carry out "comparisons of small children among uncivilized nations with (child behavior) in Germany."

(e) Comparison of normal and abnormal development: Several editions of *The Mind of the Child* contain discussions of how microcephalic children learn to walk, how deaf children acquire concepts, and how children who are born blind learn to see.

In summary, Preyer, like Darwin, moved from an interest in genetic questions to the systematic application of the comparative method. Still, comparative psychology, for him, was only a program of research rather than a fully developed branch of modern psychology.

Preyer's evolutionary orientation was not free from false conclusions, inappropriate generalizations, or naive applications of Darwin's theories. Three such problem areas include:

(a) Biogenetic law. At the time Preyer published his book on *The Mind of the Child* (1882), scientific circles were hotly debating Haeckel's (1866) biogentic law and its implications for the mental development of children. Haeckel's view that "Ontogenesis is the abbreviated and speedy recapitulation of phylogenesis" (1866, I: 300) has been called "recapitulation theory." The biogenetic law was accepted as a major theoretical focus by the "evolutionary psychobiology" subdivision of psychology (Woodward 1982: 169, 174). Its impact on the "new" Wundtian psychology can be documented as well. Actually, Haeckel's original "law" contains only a statement about parallels in the sequence of phylogenetic and ontogenetic histories of organisms. Ontogeny and phylogeny approach estimated level of 70 to 80 percent in agreement. Unfortunately, the observed "correlations" were popularly interpreted as causal relationships, probably encouraged by Haeckel himself, who characterized "phylogenesis (as) the mechanical cause of ontogenesis" (Jahn 1982: 407).

Preyer's close personal and professional contact with Haeckel at Jena suggests that he might have borrowed the recapitulation theory not only for biological explanations but also for his interpretations of psychological development. His *magnum opus* (1882), however, is remarkably free from recapitulationistic thinking! Only in some of his later works is it possible to find evidence of Preyer's generalization of the biogenetic law to psychic processes. For example, during an invited address to the plenary session of the Third International Congress of Psychology in Munich, he made these comments (1897:93):

> The concept of development always includes general and individual development. That the latter is an abbreviated repetition of phylogenesis . . . is no longer questioned as far as the formation of organisms is concerned. As far as the psyche is concerned, it is no less true for children and young animals . . . the mental development of all of mankind can be found in the child in an abbreviated form.

As Tweney (1982) has shown, Preyer did not apply the biogenetic law to his empirical child observations. A specific example of his refusal to adopt the recapitulation theory for his empirical research in child psychology can be found in his scientific controversy with the philosopher and educator F.Schulze around 1880. They were debating whether the so-called "principle of least effort," which has been validated in the history of linguistics, also applied to the acquisition of speech by the individual. Preyer opposed the concept, categorically stating that "many facts contradict this law" (1882: 348). He then concluded:

> There is no generally valid and temporal sequence of sounds in the language of children, because each language possesses another sequence of sounds based on their frequency (in the respective language). *Heredity* must be without *influence* because each healthy child, who hears a language from birth on, which was unknown to his ancestors, will still learn to speak this language perfectly. What is hereditary is the great *plasticity* of the entire speech apparatus . . . (p.349, emphasis, G.E.).

It appears that we are dealing with a situation, common during the second half of the nineteenth century, where theoretical statements were diametrically opposed to empirical results. As a "theoretician" Preyer was inclined to broad generalizations (i.e. the expansion of the biogenetic law to the problem of psychogenesis) but as an empirical researcher he accepted only facts (i.e. irrelevance of the biogenetic law to actual language development). In the same manner, Wundt, theoretically had favored psychological parallelism, although his empirical research techniques were based on the premise of psychophysical interactionism. Preyer's tragic dilemma was the incommensurability of this theories and his empirical data. We must respect that his basic empirical outlook overcame his penchant for speculation in the debate with Schulze.

(b) Struggle of survival. The missapplication of evolutionary ideas is exemplified in Preyer's interpretation of Darwin's concept of the "struggle of life," which Preyer translated as the "principle of competition" his *Prinzip der Konkurrenz*. He subsequently redefined the "principle" as a natural and necessary regulator of societal relations and supplemented it with crude polemics against social-democratic demands for the abolishment of social injustice. Thus, we read in his published lecture *Competition in Nature* (1880a : 93):

> Everything (his principle of competition, G.E.) applies to relations among people. The abolishment of free competition, accompanied by the socialist delusion of equality and equal rights, would immediately turn the healthy organism of our state into a decaying cadaver.

To fully comprehend the implications of such an extreme position, it must be mentioned that Preyer gave this speech on December 3, 1879—only 6 weeks after repressive "Anti-Socialist Legislation" became effective in Germany.

(c) Extension of evolutionary viewpoint. Preyer believed that Darwin's theory of evolution should not be restricted to biological organisms but should include the entire organic and inorganic realm of nature. For Preyer "all inorganic matter" was "the product of secretion, rigidification, decay, refrigeraton of living bodies" (1880a: 52). Elsewhere, he was even more explicit in his view "What is alive came first; what is dead (inorganic) is still being formed by the same processes of life by which it was previously formed" (1880a: 319). His assumption that organic matter historically preceded the inorganic was derived from Fechner's 1873 publication, *Some Ideas on the History of Creation and Development*.

We have tried to show Preyer's road to child psychology by describing in considerable detail three intellectual traditions which influenced his empirical and theoretical work in developmental psychology. Let us pause and look for a moment at the communalities between these three sources (physiology, psychophysics, and evolutionary theory).

(a) Physiology, psychophysics and evolutionary theory all share an empirical methodology and claim to disdain speculation. Only what can be studied and recorded by objective methods is scientifically valid.

Consequently, the new child psychology valued the collection of exact, replicable data.

(b) Physiology, psychophysics and evolutionary theory are almost exlusively concerned with man as a biological organism. Man's social nature was largely overlooked. Consequently, developmental aspects, in which man's social characteristics are obvious, were explained largely by physiological principles. For example, Preyer believed that "the development of the sens-of-ego" could be described by the connections among the various senses (1882:369):

> Connections in the central nervous system were made only by the association of disparate sensory experiences—taste-touch, sight-taste, sight-hearing, sight-smell, taste-smell, hearing-touch. The different centers for ideas or images of the ego (then) produce a unitary ego which is a complete abstraction.

Preyer failed to realize that we must include social parameters if we wish to describe and explain the development of self-consciousness in the young child adequately. Preyer's belief that one could restrict the study of individual development in children to objective procedures adapted from experimental biology, reflected the ideological situation in Wilhelminian Germany. It was not acceptable to study man's social life by scientific methods. Marxism and Social Democracy were perceived as sufficient dangers. Preyer was no revolutionary. He was a devoted subject of the emperor and a disciple of Bismarck! I hope that I have shown the potential of Preyer's approach without neglecting the concrete-historical limitations of his type of psychology.

References

Bühler, K. (1918). *Die geistige Entwicklung des Kindes.* Jena.
Darwin, C. (1877). Biographical sketch of an infant. *Mind, 2,* 285–294.
—(1872). *The expression of the emotions in man and animal.* London: J. Murray.
—(1859). *The origin of species.* London: Murray, 1859.
—(1980). *Die Entstehung der Arten durch natürliche Zuchtwahl.* Leipzig.
Debesse, G. (1970). L'Enfance dans l'Histoire de la Psychologie. In H.Gratiot-Alphandéry, & R. Zazzo (Eds.), *Traité de Psychologie de l'Enfant* (Vol.1.). Paris.
Eber, H. (1896). Zur Kritik der Kinderpsychologie, mit Rücksicht auf neuere Arbeiten. *Philosophische Studien,* 12.
Fechner, G. (1873). *Einige Ideen zur Schöpfungs- und Entwicklungslehre.* Leipzig.
Haeckel, E. (1866). *Generelle Morphologie der Organismen.* Berlin: Reimer.
Höhn, E. (1959). Geschichte der Entwicklungspsychologie und ihrer wesentlichsten Ansätze. In *Handbuch der Psychologie* (Vol.3). Göttingen.

186 Eckardt

Jahn, I. (1982). *Charles Darwin.* Leipzig: Urnia.

Jaroševsky, P. (1976). *Istorija psichologgi* (2nd ed.). Moskva.

Kapterev, P. (1877). *Pedagogičeskaja psichologija dlja narodnych učitelej, vospitatelej i vospitatel'niz.* St. Petersburg. (1982).

Krausse, E. Zur Geschichte der Biologie im 19. Jahrhundert. In: *Beiträge zur Wissenschaftsgeschichte: Die Zeit der industriellen Revolution.*

Perez, B. (1878). *La psychologie de l'enfant. Les trois premières Années de l'enfant.* Paris.

Pongratz, L. (1967). *Problemgeschichte der Psychologie.* Bern and München.

Preyer, W. (1874a). *Das myophysische Gesetz.* Jena.

—(1874b). Review of W. Wundt "Grundzüge der physiologischen Psychologie." *Jenaer Literaturzeitung, 5, & 36.*

—(1880a). Die Concurrenz in der Natur. In: *Naturwissenschaftliche Thatsachen und Probleme.* Berlin.

—(1880b). Psychogenesis. In *Naturwissenschaftliche Thatsachen und Probleme.* Berlin.

—(1880c). Die Hypothesen über den Ursprung des Lebens. In: *Naturwissenschaftliche Thatsachen und Probleme.* Berlin.

—(1880d). Der Lebensbegriff. In: *Naturwissenschaftliche Thatsachen und Probleme.* Berlin.

—(1882). *Die Seele des Kindes.* Leipzig: Grieben.

—(1889). Physiologie und Entwicklungslehre. In: *Biologische Zeitfragen.* Berlin.

—(1896). *Darwin.* Berlin.

—(1897). Die Psychologie des Kindes. In: *Dritter Internationaler Kongress für Psychologie in München vom 4. bis 7. August 1896.* München.

Reinert, G. (1976). Grundzüge einer Geschichte der Human-Entwicklungspsychologie. In: H. Balmer (Ed.), *Die Psychologie des 20. Jahrhunderts,* (Vol. 1). Zürich.

Stern, W. (1914). *Psychologie der frühen Kindheit.* Leipzig.

Tweney, R. Linguistics in nineteenth century German science. Paper read at International William T. Preyer Symposium, Jena, GDR, September, 1982.

Woodward, W. (1982). Wundt's program for the new psychology: vicissitudes of experiment, theory, and system. In W. Woodward, M. Ash (Eds.), *The problematic science: psychology in nineteenth century thought* (pp. 167–197). New York: Praeger.

Wundt, W. (1873). *Grundzüge der physiologischen Psychologie.* (Part I). Leipzig: Engelmann.

—(1874). *Grundzüge der physiologischen Psychologie.* (Part II). Leipzig: Engelmann.

Cognitive Developmental Psychology Before Preyer: Biographical and Educational Records

by John C. Cavanaugh

Introduction

> ... great as is the number of occasional observations in regard to many children, I do not thus far know of diaries regularly kept concerning the mental development of individual children. ... It is hard to discern and decipher the mysterious writing on the mind of the child.
>
> (Preyer 1882/1888: x, xv)[1]

This quote, taken from the preface of his landmark book *Die Seele des Kindes*, shows that William Preyer believed that he was exploring new territory when he set out to describe the mental development of the child. That he was up to the task is self-evident; several papers in this volume document his success (e.g. Eckardt, Fritsche and Ortmann, Jaeger, Sprung and Sprung). In this regard, whether or not one enumerates Preyer's factual inaccuracies or theoretical biases, one important fact remains—Preyer perfected the observational method of child study which is still being used by many researchers today in investigating cognitive development. Since other chapters in this volume discuss Preyer's substantive contributions and his role as a catalyst in the young field of scientific research on children, they will not be considered here. Rather, the purpose of this chapter is to consider some of the work on children's mental development that predates Preyer's own.

Overview

Although Preyer's book was by contemporary accounts (e.g. Sully 1882, 1889) the most comprehensive report to that point, he was not the first person to ponder the mysteries of children's mental development, nor the first to publish his results. However, much of this earlier work was fragmentary (as Preyer noted), published in a piecemeal fashion, and often appeared in unlikely places. Progress was slow, naturally, but by the time *Die Seele des Kindes* appeared two data sets were accumulating. The first, and arguably the model for Preyer, was the information provided by the so-called "baby biographers" and other diaristis. This literature was also the more empirical of the two, although it was clearly influenced by the strongly held biases of the observer which often led to considerable overinterpretation of the data.

The second data set came from educational writers who were less interested in careful observation of children than they were in formulating pedagogical theory. Yet, contained in their often detailed accounts of teaching methods were observational data on cognitive development. Additionally, some of the diary data had its origins either in classrooms or homes of prominent (and even of not so famous) educators. Thus, the two data sources are more conceptually, rather than methodologically, distinct.

Although both of these sources will be discussed, limits in coverage need to be made clear. Most important, this review will be limited primarily to work conducted in Great Britain or the United States during the eighteenth and nineteenth centuries. However, from time to time individuals in other countries will be considered providing that their work eventually appeared in English. Likewise, it is not exhaustive; rather, studies that are representative of particular trends or ideas were selected for inclusion. Moreover, the purpose here is not to provide a detailed summary of the data, but rather to provide a sense of the kind of information that was collected and was available by 1882. These coverage limitations should be kept in mind as we explore the early literature on the mental development of the child.

Biographical data

Any examination of early data on the mental development of children must begin with biographical sources. Numerous parents (typically) kept more or less detailed records of their children's development; a few of these were published. Most accounts of this early work (e.g. Dennis, 1949) only include the formally published diaries; thus, the observations of Tiedemann, Darwin, and others (as we shall see) are well known and are generally thought to be the only sources of information. However, these accounts are certainly not the only ones that exist from this period, and are unique largely because they were formally published, not necessarily because of their content. Moreover, it is doubtful given the publication time-lag involved in many cases that the diarists initially intended these records for the public domain. To give one well-known example, Darwin's notes were published separately almost 40 years after they were made.

Consideration of biographical records will begin with those from the eighteenth century, since it is from this period that the "scientific" study of children is usually dated.

Eighteenth-century records

The available information concerning the mental development of children dating from the eighteenth century is quite fragmentary, mostly being contained in personal diaries and correspondence of parents. This information appears not to have been kept mainly as a record of the child, but rather as just another aspect of the recorder's life. Almost none of these records were formally published.

For the most part, information about mental growth is limited to commentary relating to the two topics of child rearing and morality. Advice on child rearing had a long history even by the eighteenth century (e.g. Mulcaster 1581), so that a small corpus of observational data had been accumulated. Among the topics discussed in these manuals were feeding, toilet training, the importance of early education, discipline, and emotions. In many of these writings, there was an overt recognition that children's mental capacities are not only quite different from and less advanced than adults, but also that they varied from child to child. So, for example, Cotton Mather argued that teaching had to be adjusted to the abilities of children, "even as nurses cut small bits for little children" (1702: 28), and books intended for young readers appeared more frequently.

It is in the area of moral development, however, that the best information is available. Events such as talking and obedience were of great concern because of their relationship to future moral training (e.g. Barnard 1737). It was commonly believed that infants' "first glimmerings of reason and understanding" were apparent "while they are scarce weaned from the milk or drawn from the Breast" (Barnard 1737: 22). "Willfulness" of children was of major concern. Infants were thought to be naturally "wild," and not yet full-fledged human beings. Once beyond infancy, children were considered as highly impressionable rather than as inherently evil, although slipping into wickedness was always a danger if parents did not remain constantly vigilant (cf. Barnard 1737).

Perhaps the most difficult task in examining eighteenth century literature is in obtaining a feeling for the history and development of topics that were to become of major importance later. For example, little direct information is available concerning children's fears except from secondary sources (e.g. Janeway 1749).

It was against this background of scattered information that Tiedemann began his work, which was first published in Germany in 1787. In his introduction and again in the concluding paragraph, Tiedemann makes two points that separate him from other mere diarists: he considered previous work to be much too disconnected and unsystematic, and he called for others to continue the work of mapping the developmental course of children's minds. He seems to have been aware of other records of mental growth ("There is among men a great deal of information which is therefore not disseminated"); unfortunately, we are not so privileged since they were not published and he provided no clues about his sources. That Tiedemann was not the first to record mental milestones is clear from our previous discussion; however, his contribution is important because he may have been the first to recognize the need for *published* accounts of systematically obtained developmental data. Unfortunately, Tiedemann's call for additional published work went mainly unheeded; it would take another 90 years until the idea finally caught on for good.

Before jumping to the next century, however, one final comment of historical interest concerning Tiedemann is in order. Preyer apparently thought little of Tiedemann's work. Preyer (1882/1889: 260) referenced Perez's abridged version of Tiedemann's data rather than the original, and commented, "But it is merely an account of its historical interest that the book is mentioned here, as the scanty (and by no means objective) notes of the diary were made a hundred years ago" (Preyer 1882/1889: 260). Did Preyer mean to imply that Tiedemann's work is not valid *primarily* because it was old?

Nineteenth-century records

As indicated earlier, it was not until the last quarter of the nineteenth century that Tiedemann's wish for systematic observational records was finally granted. This second coming of the biographical method seems to have been spurred by three developments in the middle of the century: Darwin's work in evolution, interest in the origin of language, and research on sensory processes. Since all these topics are discussed in detail in other chapters in this volume, only this brief mention of them will be made here. The important point for the present discussion is that together they set the stage for more detailed observations by providing a theoretical framework and rationale for pursuing research on infants, and by providing interesting research questions. Rather than dwelling on this issue, however, the highlights of the rebirth of infant observations will be discussed.

Work before Taine. In examining the nineteenth century literature, one is struck by two things. First, very little substantive information devoted to infant development appeared during the first three-fourths of the century. However, after 1877 there was a veritable flood of articles by comparison. The interesting question, obviously, is what happened in 1877 that was so momentous for this field? Most commentators in this area, of course, would say that Darwin's biographical study, published in that year, was an important event. Although Darwin's paper was important, for reasons that will become clearer later, I feel that the key event was really the publication of Taine's report on the acquisition of language in *Mind* that was the turning point. Therefore, Taine's paper will serve as the point of separation between "early" and "late" work in the pre-1882 period.

Biographical records from the early- and midnineteenth century represent a transition from the personal diary approach typical of the eighteenth century and the data-based reports typical of later works. Specifically, writers still tended to focus mainly on their own feelings and reactions to the infants, but also included more observations in their reports than did earlier authors. For example, Briggs' article was inspired by her curiosity as to what young people are thinking. She argued that "we give less credit to children for their intelligence than they deserve" (1849: 98); unfortunately, she did not provide enough detail in her several observational examples to document her case adequately. One of the best examples of the transitional reports was one by Mrs. Emma Willard, which appeared as an appendix to the English translation of Madame Necker de Saussure's *Progressive Education* (1835). In it, she carefully (and at length) noted her philosophical and emotional reactions to her child; the observational data also are presented more completely than was typical in other contemporary accounts. Milestones in the infant's physical, emotional, linguistic, and moral development were described and interpreted in terms of the major orientations of the time.

The bulk of the developmental literature in English prior to Taine's paper concerned language development. Though typically only portions of the complete data were reported, the question of how quickly and extensively language develops in children appears to have been on the minds of several individuals. For example, Holden (1877) and Hun (1868) described the vocabulary development of children ranging in age from two to four and one-half years. Holden was sensitive to the generalization problems of single-subject research; his paper is a comparative study of three two-year old children complete with statistical analysis. Holden also speculated that these studies of vocabulary development provided more information than just grist for statistical mills: "the [vocabulary] tables here given seem to me to have more than a merely statistical value, as rightly studied they throw much light upon the mental processes of the child, and give us a clue as to the desires, impulses, and thoughts which continually seek and find expression" (1877: 62). Although not always acknowledged so objectively, later researchers would think so too.

Another line of investigation was much closer to the kind of research that became the predominant method of child inquiry—experimental manipulation. One of the first to attempt experiments on babies was Kussmaul (1859), whose findings were summarized in the *Cornhill Magazine* in 1863. This particular paper is enlightening on at least two counts. Obviously, it summarizes Kussmaul's investigations of the sensory abilities of twenty male and female newborn infants. In this regard it provided scientific evidence that the author hoped would go far in settling debates between female caretakers and male scientists about the newborn's abilities. But perhaps even more interesting and important than the summary of Kussmaul's research is the long discussion about the belief that the infant's mind is *not* a *tabula rasa* (Locke notwithstanding), a belief that, it was argued, had long been held by mothers and nurses, but which needed scientific verification before men (i.e. scientists) would be convinced. Indeed, the whole point of this article seems to be that while infants may not be quite on the intellectual plane of adults, they are clearly not operating with a blank mind at birth either:

Reviewing these evidences, we cannot escape the conclusion that, from the first, a baby manifests the special sensibilities which are, as it were, the *pabulum* of the mind, and through which it gains its knowledge of the external world ... the advance of psychology, founded on physiology, has made it pretty certain that if not furnished with readymade truths, if not enriched with innate ideas, the mind is from the first furnished with hereditary tendencies and aptitudes, even in directions purely intellectual (p.655–656).

Taine. The invocation of "hereditary tendencies" in this last quotation provides our bridge from the "early" work to Taine. When placed in the context of evolution, and espacially evolution with recapitulatory overtones, the study of infant development became important in a way Tiedemann never dreamed. Taine is a key figure in this transition who is often overlooked, even though he provided the impetus for Darwin to reconsider and publish his own biographical sketch, which in turn led to the proliferation of such work. The author of a book on intellectual development (Taine 1870/1889) but remembered primarily for describing a longitudinal study of language development (Taine 1877), Taine invoked recapitulation as a theoretical way of describing the child's mental development in the easily overlooked concluding paragraph of this latter article. Whether it was the description of linguistic development or fitting it into a hereditary framework that got Darwin to reexamine his diary is not clear in Darwin's paper. That Taine provided his source of inspiration, however, is clear in Darwin's opening sentences.

From Darwin to Preyer. The period from 1877 to 1882 saw a dramatic increase in the number of published biographical studies of children's development. For the most part, the first round of publications were inspired by Darwin's (1877) account, which seems to have served as an acknowledgment that research on infants was appropriate. So, for example, Pollack (1878) and Champneys (1881) published brief reports about language development to add to Taine's and Darwin's records. But not all of the authors from this period invoked Darwin. Humphreys (1880), for instance, continued in the tradition of linguistic research described earlier by continuing the debate over how to determine the actual size of a child's vocabulary. In any case, the majority of biographical studies published immediately after Darwin's concerned language development almost exclusively.

Perhaps the three most important developments that occurred in the years between Darwin's article and Preyer's book were: (a) an increase in the scope of research; (2) a movement toward more scientific rigor; and (3) the push for infant research to be conducted by every concerned parent. In terms of scope, the period from 1877 to 1882 saw attempts at more complete longitudinal descriptions of children than the fragments offered earlier. A notable example of this work is Perez's (1878/1888) book concerning development during the first three years of life. Besides the obligatory discussions of sensation/perception and language, Perez's book explored such topics as emotions, intellect, will, attention, memory, ideation, esthetics, and morality. Although this breadth helped expand the field of inquiry in infant *psychology*, many of the topics already had been debated and discussed extensively in the *pedagogical* literature of the time, as will be discussed later. Since Perez was concerned with education, it is not surprising that he was one of the first to consider many of these issues in a developmental-psychological context.

Despite these insights, Perez had little discernable impact on the biographers immediately following him even though he used an evolutionary framework. Perhaps this is partly because it was largely an abstract of his linguistic work that was widely translated rather than his entire book (which did not appear in English until Preyer had become well-known). Additionally, the fact that Preyer (1882/1889: 260) himself dismissed the book is noteworthy. Still, in his introduction to the English edition of Perez's book, Sully (1889: xxii) cautiously praised it as "a rich mine of facts" if one bears in mind Perez's failure in some instances to differentiate the exceptional case from the typical course of development. Nevertheless, it is still a noteworthy fact that Perez's work, originally published in French four years before Preyer's *Die Seele des Kindes,* is often overlooked as a major early attempt at describing infant development.

The last group of articles in this section have ties to the year 1881, a curious one in several respects. This was the year that Preyer's (1880/1881) article on psychogenesis appeared widely in English (although a summary by Sully [1880] was published the year before), and the year in which it became clear that infant development was to become a major field of study. Representing a combination of important observational data with the common tendency at the time to overinterpret the findings was a paper by Wyma (1881). This article is interesting in that it contains references to informal observations of depth perception, classification, and the growth of knowledge; it also reflects the spirit of the times by including a lengthy discussion on the acquired trait of a child's preference for certain dolls.

A second paper appearing in 1881 was Sully's "Babies and Science." Sully tackled several interesting issues: a justification of babies' existence, an evolutionary approach to understanding infants' and mothers' behavior, the *tabula rasa* debate, research methodology, and emotional development. The major thrust of his paper differed from most of the others that we have considered. Whereas earlier writers were usually content with only descriptions, Sully pushed for theoretical explanations that served to tie different observations together. Most often, his accounts were cast in a recapitulatory framework, the typical approach at the time despite von Baer's (1828) criticims. Overall, Sully's paper represents one of the best early attempts at blending theory and data in a short paper meant for both scientific and nonscientific readers.

We come now to the year in which Preyer's *Die Seele des Kindes* appeared. Two other publications appeared in 1882 that exemplify the seriousness with which people were by this time taking systematic research on infants' "mental development." In the published account of the United States Department of Education meeting held in 1881 (Talbot 1882), the strongest emphasis was on the need for more data. Early that year, the Department had distributed a circular asking parents to record several developmental milestones and to report their findings to the Department. The published account included six case-study examples, as well as letters on the subject from Charles Darwin and Bronson Alcott. A second call for data to be gathered in 1882 was also included, as were reprints of several biographical studies. This approach reflects the widely held belief that all that was needed in order to understand mental development in children was a large data base. Once that was obtained, the developmental progressions would "emerge" and the problem would be solved.

The second publication of note was a small book, *The Mother's Record* (1882). Influenced directly by Preyer, the author (apparently Arthur Gilman, although the credit is to "A Mother") describes the book as follows:

> In an essay on "Psychogenesis, or Development of the Soul," Doctor Preyer, Professor of Physiology in the University of Jena, says, "Each one should keep as exact a journal as possible concerning his child from its very birth".... It is the object of this little book to encourage parents to keep such a record (from Introduction).

The most interesting feature of the book is its format—it is nothing more than a structured diary with blank spaces where parental observations are to be recorded. Tiedemann's call for systematicity had finally been answered in a curiously modern way—providing parents with a ready-to-use book with topics for observation already determined in order to make infant research easier to do and more reliable across observers.

Summary

Movement toward systematic biographical-observational studies of infants was slow and sputtering during the eighteenth and nineteenth centuries. From its beginning as merely an element of adults' personal diaries, the biographical approach eventually moved to focus more on the infant. Calls for the collection of observations by parents and scientists appeared long before 1882, but few individuals took up the challenge. Those who did varied considerably in the scope of their efforts. For the most part, narrowly-defined areas of development (e.g. language) were the approach of choice. A few (e.g. Perez) did attempt broader coverage. It was suggested that these broader-based efforts took their lead from educational literature, to which we now turn.

Educational data

It remains a basic truism that if one wants to educate children, then one must have some ideas about how to do it. Furthermore, for educational procedures to be effective, one needs some insight and some data about how children learn and think. Upon first examination, the educational writings of the eighteenth and nineteenth centuries seem long on method and theory, and very short on data. But closer consideration reveals a good deal more description of children's mental growth than most commentators generally acknowledge. In fact, the desire for systematic observational data on infants and children was more consistent and stronger in this field than in the traditional biographical literature reviewed above. This very point provided the basis for the argument made in the nineteenth century that there was no existing science of education. For example, consider the following point made by Gregory (1881:386–387):

> Our conclusion against the present existence of a true science of education will seem clearer if we note more fully the fields of observation to be visited, and

visited not with the careless and cursory attention heretofore given, but with the keen and steady scrutiny which the chemist gives to his experiments, which Huxley gives to biological phenomena, and Helmholtz gives to physics.

Childhood is still an unread riddle, almost an unknown land. . . . We need facts such as only the parents and primary teachers can observe,—facts gathered daily, hourly almost, through the stretch of childish years, with an observation of scientific keenness, and recorded with scientific correctness and completeness. This must be repeated by the same observer in as many cases as possible, and the observers must be multiplied widely and their observations trained upon the same classes of phenomena till we have the means to determine what is constant and what is variable in these phenomena, and what are the causes, range, and exact character of the variations. . . . As hundreds of telescopes nightly sweep the skies to gain astronomic truth, let thousands of eager searchers direct their gaze upon the phenomena of childish life. Thus and only thus will the possible science of education become an actual science.

Gregory was not alone. He was also not the first. Nearly half a century earlier, Madame Necker de Saussure, a prominent European educator, bemoaned the lack of data with which to test educational theories (1835: 117, 119, 123, 124):

It seems to me astonishing that, while the science of Astronomy has been cultivated with a perseverance so admirable, mankind have never studied infancy methodically. The most important of all problems, is perhaps that which has been least regarded with constant and rigorous attention. . . . It is undoubtedly necessary to beware of precipitate conclusions, and we can prove nothing from solitary examples. But as everybody knows, that in multiplying observations abundantly, accidental differences become obliterated; and that the peculiar qualities of the individual disappear before the attributes of the species. . . . It is necessary to make our observations systematically: we should have, in the immense multitude that we know, that which would furnish most valuable data. . . . To succeed in fullfilling it, I earnestly exhort young mothers to keep an exact journal of the development of their children. . . . I would have an accurate journal, where the gradual progress is noted down, as well as all the vicissitudes of physical and moral health, and where we might find, by regular dates, the advancement of a child in all its faculties. The words, ideas, percep-tions, feelings—all that is acquired or developed, should be noted in this jour-nal—we should then discover the first trace either of virtues or defects, and could thus be able to judge of their origin.

Gregory and de Saussure have been quoted at length to illustrate several points. First, both writers argued that there was far too little systemati-cally obtained information about children's development. Without such data, they felt that educational theorizing was essentially an inter-esting intellectual exercise, but one that held little hope for success. Second, Gregory and de Saussure argued that haphazardly obtained observations would not do. Rather, scientific principles needed to be applied if child development was to be understood. Third, their suggestions for the collection of the data had two interesting aspects—it was to be done by parents (mainly) or by primary teachers, and it was to be longitudinal. Note that there was no hint that persons who had formal training in observation (i.e. training in how to conduct research) should be taking the data; this view did not appear until much later. Nor was it believed that short-term projects could uncover the secrets to development; indeed, similar calls for longitudinal studies based on the same rationale are still made today. Finally, the fact that nearly fifty years separated these two similar exhortations points out another similarity, namely, a largely unresponsive readership.

Clearly, educational writers and commentators saw the need for carefully obtained observational data many years prior to 1882. Moreover, the kinds of observations they felt were needed were broad-based, since it was believed that only by collecting large amounts of data on many issues from many children would child development begin to be understood. Unfortunately, these and similar calls for scientific observations of children went largely unheeded. However, a few educational theorists did incorporate personal observations into their thinking. It is to two types of these exceptions that we now turn.

Educational records

In order to examine the observations made by educators, it is not necessary to consider their theories in detail. However, it is helpful to understand the general orientation of education during the eighteenth and nineteenth centuries. At the risk of oversimplification, two tendencies should especially be noted in the present context. One major concern stemmed from the influence of Rousseau and his critics concerning the best way to impart knowledge (i.e. by letting children develop "naturally" or by structuring the environment). The second major concern that is important for the present discussion was the emphasis of educators on moral and ethical development. In this regard, consideration of how to shape the child's will, emotions, and morals was based on "traditional" Christian ethics.

Observations by theoreticians. These two concerns are reflected in the commentaries that accompany many of the educators' discussions of children's mental development. For the most part, these writers unfortunately did not provide extensive descriptions of infant and child development; rather, they typically provided such information only to illustrate a point or to document the basis or origin of their particular educational theory. Finally, many of the observational reports (including the two to be discussed here) were usually not widely available, a serious problem that will be considered in more detail later.

Two reports that are representative of the ecucational tradition are those of Pestalozzi and Alcott. Both were prominent leaders in education, Pestalozzi in Europe during the late eighteenth and early nineteenth centuries, Alcott in the United States in the nineteenth century. Each made observations of his children during their infancy.

Pestalozzi kept a journal[2] in which he wrote some observations of his son Jacob (referred to in the journal as Jacobli) during 1774. At the time, Pestalozzi intended to apply Rousseau's ideas to the education of his son, and the observational notes document some of these attempts. The published journal entries (begun when his son was three years old) reveal the gradual development of some of Pestalozzi's educational principles as a result of his observations of and experiments on his son.

Examination of the available published fragments from the journal show that the type of information recorded differs considerably from that noted by the baby biographers. For example, Pestalozzi rarely commented on physical development. Rather, the record contains reports of teaching exercises, third party confirmation of Pestalozzi's conclusions, and his own evaluation of his son's progress and performance. Overall, the journal entries give more insight into the presumed cognitive abilities of young children than into the general development of the child. In this regard, the fact that Pestalozzi believed he could teach a three and one-half year old the meaning of numbers, Latin, and how to read is informative.

Bronson Alcott (1882) also made occasional notes about the first seventy-eight days of his eldest daughter's development following her birth in March, 1831. The published record is scant; Alcott transcribed a few of his notes in a letter to Professor W.T. Harris at the United States Department of Education, and apparently never published the remainder. Nevertheless, his observations are noteworthy on two counts. First, they are more objective than Pestalozzi's; the urge to confound observation and interpretation was largely avoided in the report. In fact, Alcott seems downright conservative when compared with other early (and even late) nineteenth-century diarists. On more than one occasion, he noted that he was unable to know for certain whether a particular developmental milestone had been reached. But one must be cautious in making too much of this objectivity, which brings us to the second point. The published notes were clearly the result of a careful selection process. Alcott himself implied that his own reflections may have been edited from the diary in order to publish an objective account. Thus, although the record shows that Alcott could separate behavior from inference, it is unclear whether this resulted from critical thinking (by separate entries) in 1831 or careful editing during his writing of the letter in 1881.

Perhaps not surprisingly, Alcott's notes bear a striking resemblance to others published in the 1870s. His focus was an sensorimotor development, emotional and social behavior, and attention. Thus, he also took a fairly broad approach in his observations that led him to record developmental progressions along several dimensions. Although it is difficult to draw explicit comparisons between his notes and his educational theories, the fact that he closely observed children's abilities did influence his teaching method (Peabody 1874).

Other educational-developmental work. The major educational theoreticians of the eighteenth and nineteenth centuries were not the only individuals concerned with pedagogy who made observations of children's cognitive development. One popular type of study involved documenting various teaching methods. Many of these reports were nothing more than testimonials written to support (typically) or to criticize (rarely) a particular method or theory of education. Since these really did not supply systematic data, they will not be considered here.

One of the earliest and most complete of the remaining more objective documentaries was compiled by Elizabeth Peabody (Alcott and Peabody 1835, 1836, 1837; Peabody 1874), who published detailed accounts of the proceedings of Bronson Alcott's school in Boston. Alcott's technique involved getting students to participate through modified Socratic dialogues, or "conversations" as he termed them. Peabody claimed that her records of many of these conversations were recorded as nearly verbatim as possible. Even viewed cautiously, the published accounts provide a detailed compendium of children's reasoning in Alcott's classroom about moral, intellectual, and spiritual-religious topics.

A second type of educational study is more well-known. This approach focused not on teaching methods, but rather on what children know. Investigations of the contents of children's minds provided the basis for two important methodological changes that would prove to be important in developmental research—an emphasis on group averages or trends, and the use of interviews in studying children.

Although Stoy, at Jena, conducted some of the first studies in this area, the first published large-scale investigation of the contents of children's minds was conducted in Berlin in 1869, reported by Bartholomäi the following year (1870/1901). Regular classroom teachers examined children entering school by testing two general categories of knowledge: which common objects (e.g. pond, squirrel, etc.) they had experienced and their level of language comprehension. A total of 75 items were included. The results surprised many, since they revealed that first graders were apparently ignorant of many simple phenomena.

Three other similar projects were undertaken prior to 1882. Lange (1879) conducted as smaller version of the Berlin investigation at Plauen; he noted considerable gender differences in the number of concepts understood, with boys being superior. Additionally, both Hartman (at Annaberg) and G. Stanley Hall began their series of investigations in 1880.

Finally, a third approach was nothing more than careful diary-keeping, identical in all formal respects to the observational records considered earlier. The best example of observational research inspired directly by an educator was Mrs. Willard's (1835) report. As described earlier, her notes were published as an appendix to the English translation of de Saussure's book, and it served as a model for future efforts.

Most educational writing in the eighteenth and nineteenth centuries was philosophically rather than empirically based. However, a few of the major figures did keep records of their children's development. For some, like Pestalozzi, the notes document that pedagogical theories originated in their observations and experiments. Overall, however, the record is scanty if one considers only the originators of educational practices.

The picture brightens somewhat when work by disciples and other interested persons is included. The documentation of children's cognitive abilities (especially reasoning) in Peabody's work, combined with the studies in the late 1860s through 1882 on the contents of children's minds, provide a more complete view of early child development.

These latter studies foreshadowed the methodological approach taken by many other late-nineteenth and early-twentieth century researchers, namely group studies and interviews.

Discussion

It should be clear at this point that consideration of children's cognitive development had a reasonably long history by 1882. Recognition of the need for many published accounts of development during infancy and childhood was demonstrated by many people from at least the time of Tiedemann. Several attempts were made during the eighteenth and nineteenth centuries to produce these accounts; many of them were noted in this chapter.

In considering the literature on children's cognitive development published before Preyer's book on the topic, several themes emerge which help put these writings into perspective. Four of these themes will be discussed in the following sections: the range of topics, style of reporting, similarities and differences in the two literatures, and the availability of the records.

Range of Topics

Perhaps the first thing that strikes a reader of the early work on children's mental development is the broad range of topics that were included in the reports. Most authors believed that mental development was a complex topic involving more than simply the growth of high-level logical thinking removed from environmental constraints and contexts. Typically, they believed that mental development was the result of many converging influences: sensory and perceptual processes, attention, emotions, language, intention or "will," and motor development. Thus, virtually every topic that could be charted developmentally and involved psychological functioning was considered a mental phenomenon appropriate for study.

This almost encyclopedic inclusiveness had both benefits and costs. Clearly, it led to many interesting observations of infant and child behavior. Moreover, nearly every major concern of modern child psychology has historical, if not conceptual, roots in this literature. Taking a broad view also helped the early writers appreciate more fully the enormous complexity of child development, since they were faced with the seemingly overwhelming task of describing intricate interactions of progressions in many domains. But everything has its price. In this area, it eventually became clear that careful, detailed descriptions of all aspects of development was an impossible task even if attempted in a serious fashion. This point is apparent in most of the writings reviewed here; even the most detailed descriptions of development proved insufficient when it came to making inferences about the *process* of development. Thus, the broad conception of mental development espoused by most eighteenth and nineteenth century writers did not last; cognitive development ultimately became a fractionated discipline.

Style of reporting

Another characteristic of the early writings on cognitive development concerns the style in which the observations were presented. Specifically, most of the work of this period contains an interweaving of observation, interpretation, and commentary that cannot always be differentiated. It is very rare to find a work in which the author did not go well beyond the data in making inferences or drawing conclusions. The big problem, though, is that frequently these inferences and conclusions are presented as "fact" rather than "interpretation," making it difficult to evalute the "observations" as data.

Others who have examined portions of this literature have also pointed out this problem but use it to question the validity of the data (e.g. Kessen 1965). To the extent that this criticism is aimed at writers who offered little evidence to support armchair speculation, it may be valid. However, unbiased observation of behavior remains unlikely (if not impossible) today (e.g. Buss 1979; Kahneman, Slovic, and Tversky 1982; Riegel 1979). Eighteenth and nineteenth century observers were following the models and theories of their day, and by those standards were probably no more guilty of confirmation bias or jumping to conclusions than we are by contemporary standards. Nevertheless, a certain level of skepticism is always a good idea.

Once it is acknowledged that these works are not neatly divided into separate "results" and "discussion" sections, however, their content can be considered on their own merits. On this score, the records contain many provocative observations (especially concerning language and emotions) and many thought-provoking discussions about the nature of children. When the literature is examined in this manner, one cannot help being impressed with the number of issues noted in biographical sources.

Similarities and differences

Altough the early literature on children's mental growth can be seen as representing the two orientations described earlier, they did not represent two mutually exclusive traditions. As noted at several points, particular works (e.g. Perez, 1878/1889) represent a merger of orientations. Therefore, one would suspect that several similarities exist between the biographical and the educational literatures.

Such speculation is easily confirmed. Most obvious is the arbitrariness with which some of the works have been classified here (e.g. Alcott's and Willard's records could really be classified either way). Specific points of agreement cluster mainly in three areas: particular categories of observations, research methods, and pleas for more data. On the first point, both literatures include the wide variety of topics described earlier. For example, de Saussure (1835) was just as concerned with sensorimotor and emotional development as Wyma (1881).

The major data collection technique of writers in both literatures was identical—naturalistic observation. All of the information in biographical and educational reports about children's mental development came from the notes (written and mental) made by parents, relatives, teachers, and interested others. A few attempted to perform simple environmental manipulations and then watch for alterations of behavior, but for the most part these individuals were content to observe the "natural" course of development.

After reading the many calls for further efforts in the field, one gets a sense of the enormous and difficult task that these early writers had created. The kinds of observations that they wanted were not easily obtainable, in that they took hours of careful watching each day for several years. Thus, on the one hand, it is easy to understand why it took so long for the idea to catch on. Yet, one also sees a similarity on another side. Very few of the writers who called for more research cited others' efforts or attempted to collate and integrate them with their own. (The next section considers this problem in detail.)

Differences are also apparent when the two literatures are compared. Perhaps the key point in this regard is the general lack of work on language development in the educational tradition. Relatively few of these writers went to the lengths that some biographers (e.g. Holden 1877) did in documenting linguistic development, although there is some evidence that the issue at least was recognized as important by educators (e.g. Talbot 1882). Additionally, there seems to be more overt discussion of philosophical issues, such as Locke's notion of *tabula rasa*, in the biographical literature. The major exceptions to this general trend, of course, involve philosophical issues or ideas pertaining specifically to education, such as Rousseau's. Overall, however, there was a stronger push in the biographical literature to use existing theory (e.g. recapitulation) to interpret data, whereas educators tended to use the data to create new theories.

Availability of records

From time to time in this chapter, it was pointed out that the literature on children appeared in piecemeal fashion. An important question to consider, therefore, is whether the various writers knew what had been done by their predecessors. Examinination of the evidence reveals that they usually did not. It was not until the late 1870s that works by earlier authors were routinely cited. Prior to that time it appears that writers largely worked in a vacuum. So, for example, de Saussure (1835) expressed surprise that no father had ever made notes on his child's development, despite Tiedemann's and Pestalozzi's existing accounts. Even though Preyer himself was not completely informed, as he admits in the first appendix to *Die Seele des Kindes,* although he did know some work had been done (even if he did dismiss it as inadequate).

So, it would seem that the majority of the early writers on cognitive development were simply unaware of studies conducted before their own. Upon reflection, this problem puts a new perspective on an issue noted earlier, specifically, the continued call for more reports. If the biographers and educators who pioneered cognitive developmental research truly did not know that others had tried before, then it is no wonder that almost every major work prior to 1882 contained a call for research. It is as if each of these individuals saw himself or herself as a "lone researcher," blazing new trails, mapping new territory. But these scientists needed company, and observations needed corroboration, so each writer asked for help that many believed never came. The unfortunate part is that it *was* there; they simply did not know it.

Conclusions

In conclusion, Preyer was not the first to tackle the issue of children's mental development. Indeed, the biographical and educational records published in English before Preyer provide a wealth of information on the subject. The major difficulty, it seems, is that these sources have not been examined sufficiently by developmentalists interested in the history of their field, so they are as unknown today as they were to writers at the time. More careful scrutiny of them is needed if we are to come to a better understanding and appreciation of the contributions they made and still may make to the study of child development.

References

Alcott, B. (1882). Mr. Alcott's Letter. *American Journal of Social Science* 15: 8–10.
Alcott B. and Peabody, E.P. (1835). *Record of a school.* Boston: James Munroe.
—(1836). *Conversations with children on the gospels* (vol.1). Boston: James Munroe.
—(1837). *Conversations with children on the gospels* (vol.2). Boston: James Munroe.
Baer, K.E. von (1828). *Entwicklungsgeschichte der Thiere: Beobachtung und Reflexion.* Königsberg: Bornträger.
Barnard, J. (1737). *A call to parents and children.* Boston: T.Fleet.
Bartholomäi, F. (1870). Vorstellungskreis der Berliner Kinder beim Eintritt in die Schule. *Städtisches Jahrbuch, Berlin und Seine Entwicklung* 4: 59–77. (Trans. as: The contents of children's minds on entering school at the age of 6 years. *Report of the United States Commissioner of Education for year 1901* 1: 709–729.)
Briggs, C.A. (1849). Intellect of children. *Mother's Assistant* 9: 97–101.
Buss, A.R. (1979). *A dialectical psychology.* New York: Irvington.
Champneys, F.H. (1881). Notes on an infant. *Mind* 6: 104–107.
Darwin, C. (1877). A biographical sketch of an infant. *Mind* 2: 285–294.
Dennis, W. (1949). Historical beginnings of child psychology. *Psychological Bulletin* 46: 224–235.
Gilman, A. (1882). *The mother's record.* Boston: D.Lothrop.
Gregory, J.M. (1881). Is there a science of education? *Education* 1: 384–387.
Guimps, R. de (1904). *Pestalozzi, his life and work.* (Trans. from 2nd French ed. by J.Russell.) New York: Appleton.
Holden, E.S. (1877). On the vocabularies of children under two years of age. *Transactions of the American Philological Association* 8: 58–68.
Humphreys, M.W. (1880). A contribution to infantile linguistic. *Transactions of the American Philological Association* 11: 2–17.
Hun, E.R. (1868). Singular development of language in a child. *Quarterly Journal of Psychological Medicine* 2: 525–528.
Janeway, J. (1749). *A token for children.* Philadelphia: B.Franklin and D.Hall.
Kahnemann, D., Slovic, P., and Tversky, A. (1982). *Judgment under uncertainty: Heuristics and biases.* New York: Cambridge University Press.

Kessen, W. (1965). *The child.* New York: Wiley.

Kussmaul, A. (1859). *Untersuchungen über das Seelenleben des neugeborenen Menschen.* Heidelberg and Leipzig: C.F. Winter. (A trans. summary appeared in the article: The mental conditions of babies. *Cornhill Magazine* (1863) 7: 649–656.)

Lange, K. (1879). Der Vorstellungskreis unserer sechsjährigen Kleinen. *Allgemeine Schul-Zeitung* 56: 327–329.

Mather, C. (1702). *Cares about the nurseries.* Boston: T.Green.

Mulcaster, R. (1581). *The training up of children.* London: Thomas Vautrollier.

Niederer, J. (1828). *Notes on Pestalozzi:* Aix-la-Chapelle. (Cited in R. de Guimps, *Pestalozzi, his life and work.* New York: Appleton, 1904.)

Peabody, E.P. (1874). *Record of Mr. Alcott's school* (3d ed.). Boston: Roberts Brothers.

Perez, B. (1878). *La psychologie de l'enfant: les trois premières années.* Paris: Alcan. (Trans. as: *The first three years of childhood.* New York: E.L. Kellogg, 1888.)

Pollack, F. (1878). An infant's progress in language. *Mind* 3: 392–401.

Preyer, W. Psychogenesis. (1880) *Deutsche Rundschau* 23: 198–221. (Trans. in: *Journal of Speculative Philosophy* (1881) 15: 159–188.)

—(1882). *Die Seele des Kindes.* Leipzig: T.Grieben. (Trans. as: *The mind of the child* (2 vols.). New York: Appleton, 1888–1889.)

Riegel, K.F. (1979). *Foundations of dialectical psychology.* New York: Academic Press.

Saussure, M.N. de (1835). *Progressive education.* (Trans. by Mrs. E.Willard and Mrs.Phelps). Boston: Ticknor.

Sully, J. (1880). Mental development in children. *Mind* 5: 385–386.

—(1881). Babies and science. *Cornhill Magazine* 43: 539–554.

—(1888). Introduction. In B.Perez, *The first three years of childhood.* New York: E.L. Kellogg.

Taine, H. (1879). *De l'intélligence* (2 vols.). Paris. (Trans. as: *On intelligence* (2 vols.). New York: Holt and Williams, 1889.)

—(1876). Note sur l'acquisition de langage chez les enfants et dans l'espèce humaine. *Revue Philosophique* 1: 3–23. (Trans. in: *Mind* 1877, 2, 252–257.)

Talbot, E. (1882). Infant development: Report of the secretary of the department. *American Journal of Social Science* 15: 5–52.

Tiedemann, D. (1787). Beobachtungen über die Entwicklung der Seelenfähigkeiten bei Kindern. *Hessische Beiträge zur Gelehrsamkeit und Kunst* 2: 313–315 and 3: 486–488. (Trans. as: Tiedemann's observations on the development of the mental faculties of children. *Pedagogical Seminary* (1927) 34: 205–230.)

Willard, E. (1835). Observations upon an infant, during its first year. By a mother. Appendix in Saussure, M.N. *Progressive education.* (Trans. by Mrs. E.Willard and Mrs. Phelps). Boston: Ticknor, 1835.)

Wyma (1881). The mental development of the infant today. *Journal of Psychological Medicine and Mental Pathology* 7: 62–69.

Notes

1 Page citations for all quotations refer to the English translation editions.

2 Unfortunately, Pestalozzi's entire journal was not published. Portions of it appeared in de Guimps' (1904) biography of Pestalozzi, who in turn got them from Niederer's (1828) book.

The Relationship Between Preyer's Concept of Psychogenesis and his Views of Darwin's Theory of Evolution

by Ethel Tobach

The study of development after the appearance of Darwin's *Origin of Species* may be said to have two main goals: the understanding of descent and the relationship among species; and, the understanding of natural selection as it is revealed in the relationship between heredity and environment. The two are interdependent, although the work of a particular investigator does not necessarily reflect this dependence. Gould (1977: 135) discussed the interdependence in regard to heterochrony and selection processes, as it is expressed in the pervasive influence of the recapitulation theory in such complex societal concerns as child psychology and education. As expressed by Gould (1977: 135): "Recapitulation supplied an obvious general answer (to what evolutionary history had to say about the nature of children, E.T.): we understand children only when we recognize that their behavior replays a phyletic past." On p. 147 he cited a passage from G. Stanley Hall, one of the founders of child psychology in the United States (Hall 1904, vol. 2: 221–222):

> Children thus in their incomplete stage of development are nearer the animals in some respects than they are to adults, and there is in this direction a rich but undiscovered silo of educational possibilities which heredity has stored up like the coal-measures, which when explored and utilized to its full extent will reveal pedagogic possibilities now undreamed of.

As Gould pointed out, one of the effects of the influence of recapitulation theory led to a child-centered education. The approach emphasized the necessity of an environment in which the inherited endowments of the individual child would be permitted to unfold. Such an extreme statement of the hereditarian position (Tobach 1973) was modified by its proponents in the face of practical concerns to propose a program in which the educators would tame the ancestral, animal-like tendencies of the inheritance. Further, the program needed to be based on the legacy of the past which determined differences among various populations of people and between women and men (Hall 1904). Gould briefly cited Preyer's book on the child as part of Preyer's general "evolutionary study of infancy" (Gould 1977: 136), and a factor in the development of interest in children as a consequence of Darwin's influence. Hall's metaphor is an interesting echo of Preyer's own (see below) when he discusses the relationship between heredity and environment within the context of natural selection. However, Preyer's program differed significantly from that of Hall who, in true hereditarian fashion, sought an idealist norm of development. Preyer interpreted Darwinian theory as leading to an appreciation of the individual differences among children, thus requiring individual evaluation and training.

Preyer's influence persisted beyond the methodological because of the substantive contributions of his studies in the embryogeny of behavior. This was in great part the result of the activities of one of the most productive developmental psychologists, Leonard Carmichael. He was responsible for bringing Preyer's work on the embryogeny of behavior to a new generation of scientists in the English-reading countries (Carmichael 1973). In his chapter "On the onset and early development of behavior" in the *Manual of Child Psychology*, which he edited in 1946, he set forth Preyer's work in great detail. In that chapter he also gave some history of the study of early developmental stages. It is evident that the earliest scientific investigators in biology were interested in the development of a variety of species and the intellectual curiosity and motivation for such work reflected the general status of the philosophy of science of the time. By the time Carmichael wrote his chapter, he reflected the dominant view of U.S. psychology since World War I: the "knowledge of behavior in prenatal life throws light upon many traditional psychological problems" and "much more is known in certain respects concerning the early development of life in ... animals ... and much of this information has direct bearing upon an understanding of human development" (1946: 43).

Ruth Cruikshank in the same *Manual* discussed the inherently comparative aspect of developmental studies and cited passages from the writing of John Fiske (1883), Mills (1898) and Small (1899). The statement by Small which she reproduced is most explicit. "It may never be possible to reconstruct a complete psychic organism from the evidence of a single trait ... an ideal borrowed from morphology ... but something surely may be accomplished towards a *comparative embryology* of the soul. What Preyer and others have done for the human infant, needs to be done also for the baby-animal of every species" (Cruikshank 1946:189).

Although she considered Preyer a "pioneer in the experimental study of the psychological aspects of infancy considered in the broad comparative sense," she characterized him primarily as someone whose "studies ... do not fall into the error of considering it (behavioral development, E.T.) as a strictly postnatal phenomenon" (1946:168).

In general, it may be said that in the conceptualization of Carmichael and others in the *Manual* the study of the development of embryonic and behavioral development was primarily of interest in the light it shed on such issues as the relationship between the early and later stages of development, and the relationship between morphological and behavioral stages of development; comparative studies related to issues of descent and relationship among species were of small moment.

In Preyer's own development of interest and work in the earliest stages of growth and development, the relationship between a possible concern with phylogeny and the evident concern with ontogeny as an expression of the heredity of the organism is not clear. Schmidt and Becker point out that here are three sources of Preyer's commitment to developmental studies: his physiological-psychological studies on the early stages of many organisms, his Darwinian interests, and his interest in educational reform (1981: 252–252). As Preyer stated in his autobiographical sketch (Schmidt and Becker 1981), he would always remain a physiologist. The basis for this commitment warrants investigation.

Although it is thought (Holmes, personal communication)[1] that Darwinism was not brought to the fore by Preyer's experience in Claude Bernard's laboratory (Geus 1975, Fischer 1962), Schiller (1967) points out that there were a number of characteristics of Bernard's scientific philosophy which resembled Darwin's[2]: (1) Neither of them used mathematics to any degree in the development of their studies. (2) Another problem of common interest was heredity, which they envisaged in different perspectives, the common trait being their ignorance of the work of Mendel. Darwin approached the problem of heredity in a direct fashion. He proceeded from experiments with plants ... but the significance of the obtained Mendelian proportions escaped him (1967:143).

Schiller goes on to say that Claude Bernard viewed heredity as a problem of general physiology which was not studied experimentally; however, the existence of heredity could not be ignored. (1967: 144)

Claude Bernard thought the laws and conditions of consistency and variability of species could be studied experimentally and that physiology would find the basis of those laws. Although Bernard saw limitations to the theory of evolution, he was an outspoken subscriber to it. He was not indifferent to the problems posed by the natural sciences—morphology, taxonomy, heredity—but experienced difficulty experimentally and conceptually with the problem of heredity. "All the morphological generalizations . . . which serve as the basis for naturalists (in regard to heredity, E.T.) are too superficial and as such insufficient for the needs of the physiologist" (1967:146). Schiller points out that Bernard thought one could scientifically produce new species by experimentally manipulating the internal nutritional milieu of the egg. In this way, Bernard lead to a new discipline, biochemical embryology.

It may have been Bernard's combination of interest in embryology and commitment to physiology which influenced Preyer more than might have been suggested. Although his developmental studies appeared some twenty years after his experience in Bernard's laboratory, the significance of that experience is not to be discounted. Whether he had accepted Bernard's concept that physiology was the only way to approach descent and relationship among species is not known. Whether he embarked on the physiological and psychological characteristics of developing embryos, because he would someday bring out relationships among species, is possible (Preyer and Zirkel 1862, Preyer 1866). It is likely that if he had been interested in phylogeny, he would not have approached this topic morphologically because of his avowed commitment to physiology. It is also most likely that he would have taken the path of Haeckel, his friend and colleague.

In trying to understand the role of such past experiences and their effects on one's choice of research problem, it becomes clear that one must deal with the fact that the individual is changing not only in regard to the amount and type of information available but also in regard to the demands and situation in which he works. Preyer was clearly a productive scientist and teacher. That the earlier interests would persist is probably true; the form and emphasis they would receive in later writing would probably be somewhat different. It would appear that he did not primarily undertake the study of the embryogeny of sensory function because of an interest in phylogeny as such. It was likely that there was another aspect to his interest in the study of embryos.

What might be the other interest and how is it related to the Darwinian interest? For this one must look at the writings on he subject of evolutionary thinking: *Der Kampf um das Dasein* (1868); and his book on Darwin (1896).[3]

For example, in his popular biography of Darwin (1896), Preyer lists the special contributions that Darwin made. Despite the fact that there had been the stirrings of ideas about evolution before Darwin, there was "no one explanation for organic forms; no one translated artificial selective breeding into natural; no one understood the mechanical necessity for the unknown development of adaptation; no one understood variation and heredity as the explanatory basis for biological teleology; no one understood the descent of people from animals as a scientific resolution to such problems with a newly discovered insight and method. All this Darwin did" (1896: 74). "... The development of Darwinism led to the genetic and comparative studies which showed themselves in his embryonic and developmental phases. These methods of his will outlast his hypotheses. With these he created the new science which carried the old name of "Biology." By posing questions about phenomena and their history he made it clear that what exists today was not always so; did not always appear as it does today" (1896:75).[4]

This may be seen as relevant to his earlier emphasis in *Der Kampf um das Dasein* (1868) on development (his psychogenesis). In both books, his interest in Darwinian concepts of development are formulated in terms of environment and heredity.

The small popularly written book on the struggle for survival was undertaken while he was probably preparing his thesis for publication, and during that time he also published his work on hemoglobin and prussic acid. Towards the end of that book he discussed the significance of differences among children and the consequences for their education. Some children are born more gifted and with more richly endowed natural talents than others. Further, the inborn tendencies of a child are like diamonds in the earth: until they are polished by hard work and education, one does not know they are there (1868: 34). "Each one forges personal success; but what avails the forge without iron? The iron is that which one's ancestors provide. Indeed, the iron is malleable, warm and pliable, when one is young" (1868: 35).[5] He points out that education is worthwhile at early stages of development and when the raw material is fundamentally good. Ultimately, however, human beings, like other animals and plants, are in competition with each other; but, competition is progressive (1868: 37), for the human weapons in the struggle are morality, human love, and justice (1868: 38).

As Schmidt and Becker (1981) pointed out in their article on Preyer, the motivation for Preyer's interest in child psychology is not clear. There are no obvious links with other psychologists (Stumpf or Ebbinghaus) (see Boring 1952). But, Preyer was interested in educational reforms, and this may well have been a strong impetus to his studies. It is possible also that his interest in educational reform stemmed from his understanding of Darwinian evolution. Given his very clear statements about heredity and environment in the preface to *The Mind of the Child* (Dennis 1948, see citation below), it is likely that this aspect of evolutionary theory was an early and primary interest. His interest in the physiology of the fetus and infant may have been based on his concern with development in relation to heredity.

In 1880, W.H. Larrabee translated an article "Psychogenesis in the Human Infant" by Professor W.Preyer of Jena, which was printed in the *Popular Science Monthly.* The article gives us another look at Preyer's understanding of the relationship between heredity and the postnatal experience of the individual (1860:625–626):

> Schoolmasters and tutors can give but little help in the investigation, (of the growth of the human mind, E.T.) for the development of the faculties begins long before they are called in to assist it.
> The study of the earliest mental growth is useful in its bearing upon the future training of the child. Only certain faculties are innate in every man. A true method of instruction should proceed from the given inherited faculties; should take account of their diversities; should not measure all children with the same measure; and should not train them after the same model."

At the end of the article, we get still another view of his fundamental conceptualization of the value of studying child development (1880:625):

> If we compare the defects of childish speech with the lapses of grown persons after their faculties have been disturbed by sickness, we shall discover parallels of uncommon interest and astonishing completeness. All the faults of speech caused by sickness have their miniature counterpart in the child. From illness, the matured man is no longer in a condition; in childhood, the unmatured man is not yet in a condition, to speak correctly. In the former case, existing powers are disturbed; in the latter the powers of articulation and phrase-making have not been perfected. One condition helps us to understand the other. The parallel can not, however, be pursued here, for the material for illustrating it is rich and will not admit of abridgment. My present purpose has simply been to sketch the fundamental conditions of the earliest development of the infant mind independently of the theories of the day, and to set forth the extraordinary significance of the study.

In the Preface to his work, *Der Kampf ums Dasein* (1869), Preyer was even more explicit:

> If the infant brings into the world a set of organs which begin to be active only after a long time, and are absolutely useless up to that time—as, e.g., the lungs were before birth—then the question, To what causes do such organs and functions owe their existence? can have but one answer—heredity.
>
> *This, to be sure, explains nothing;* (E.T. emphasis) but dim as the notion is, much is gained toward our understanding of the matter, in the fact that some functions are inherited while others are not.
>
> What is acquired by experience is only a part. The question whether a function of the brain, on which everything depends in the development of the child's mind, is inherited or acquired, must be answered in each individual case, if we would not go astray in the labyrinth of appearances and hypotheses.
>
> Above all, we must be clear on this point, that the fundamental acitivities of mind, which are manifested only after birth, do not originate after birth.
>
> The mind of the new-born child, then, does not resemble a *tabula rasa*, upon which the senses first write their impressions, so that out of these the sum-total of our mental life arises through manifold reciprocal action, but the tablet is already written upon before birth, with many illegible, nay unrecognizable and invisible, marks, the traces of the imprint of countless sensuous impressions of long-gone generations. So blurred and indistinct are these remains, that we might, indeed, suppose the tablet to be blank, so long as we did not examine the changes it undergoes in earliest youth. But the more attentively the child is observed, the more easily legible becomes the writing, not at first to be understood, that he brings with him into the world. Then we perceive what a capital each individual has inherited from his ancestors—how much there is that is not produced by sense-impressions, and how false is the supposition that man learns to feel, to will, and to think, only through his senses. Heredity is just as important as individual activity in the genesis of mind. No man is in this matter a mere upstart, who is to achieve the development of his mind (psyche) through his individual experience alone; rather must each one, by means of his experience fill out and animate anew his inherited endowments, the remains of the experiences and activities of his ancestors.
>
> It is hard to discern and to decipher the mysterious writing on the mind of the child. It is just that which constitutes a chief problem of this book.

The commitment to the developmental study of physiological and psychological processes would seem to be directly related to Preyer's analysis of the most noteworthy aspect of Darwin's work. In his life of Darwin, in the chapter on Darwin's work, he speaks of the most characteristic aspect of that work: the genetic method. "Before Darwin, attempts to order our understanding of nature were descriptive. Darwinists ask: which process had to occur to make it possible for natural phenomena to result as we see them today? Darwin proceeded from the proposition that that which exists was not always the way it appears today. In the course of its growth, everything changes. One needs to seek the traces of what went before. And this leads to one answer: the genetic method emerges from the facts of development. Darwin's discovery of the metamorphosis and conservation of species, in short, his general principle or law of development, affected history, politics, society, linguistics, history of literature and culture" (1896:75–76).[6]

Preyer's interest in the physiology of the fetus and embryo and in the psychology of the child, might well be based on an underlying commitment to evolutionary theory and the concept of heredity as it was understood then by many adherents of Darwinism.

Bibliography

Boring, E.G. (1950) *A history of experimental psychology.* New York: Appleton-Century-Crofts.

Carmichael, L. (1973) William Preyer and the prenatal development of behavior. *Perspectives in Biology and Medicine* 16:411–417.

—(Ed.) (1946) *Manual of child psychology.* New York: Wiley.

Cruikshank, R.M. (1946) Animal infancy. In *Manual of child psychology,* L.Carmichael, Ed. New York: Wiley, pp.167–189.

Dennis, W. (1948) *Readings in the history of psychology.* New York: Appleton-Century-Crofts.

Fischer, I. (1962) Wilhelm Thierry Preyer, *Biographisches Lexikon.* Munich: Urban & Schwarzenberg, p.1246.

Geus, A. (1975) William Thierry Preyer. *Dictionary of Scientific Biography.* New York: Scribner's, pp.135–136.

Gould, S.J. (1977) *Ontogeny and phylogeny.* Cambridge, Mass.: The Belknap Press of Harvard University Press.

Hall, G.S. (1904) *Adolescence: Its psychology and its relations to physiology, anthropology, sociology, sex, crime, religion, and education.* (2 vols.) New York: Appleton.

Holmes, F.L. (1982) Letter to E.Tobach, March 25.

Preyer, W. (1866) Über die Bewegung des Seesternes. *Mitt. Zool. Sta. Neapel.* 7: 27–127; 8: 191–233.

—(1869) *Der Kampf um das Dasein.* Bonn: Eduard Weber's Buchhandlung.

—(1880) Psychogenesis in the human infant. Translated by W.H. Larrabee. *Popular Science Monthly,* (May–Oct), pp.625–635.

—(1896) *Darwin: Sein Leben und Wirken.* Berlin: Ernst Hofman.

Preyer, W. and Zirkel, F. (1862) *Reise nach Island.* Leipzig: F.A. Brockhaus.

Schiller, J. (1967) *Claude Bernard et les problèmes scientifiques des sons temps.* Paris: Les Editions du Cèdre.

Schmidt, H.D. and Becker, K.H. (1981) Dokumente über Wilhelm Preyer's Beziehungen zur Berliner Universität. *Zeitschrift für Psychologie* 189: 247–254.

Tobach, E. (1984) Social Darwinism rides again. In *The four horsemen: Racism, sexism, militarism and social Darwinism.* E.Tobach, Ed. New York: Behavioral Publications, pp.97–123. (Introduction pp.3–19).

Notes

[1] I wish to thank Edie Stahlberger for her assistance in library research. I also owe a special thanks to RUTH NEWMAN who translated much of the German material for me. I alone am responsible for all translations cited.

[2] "I would be surprising if BERNARD was sufficiently concerned with Darwinian theory to influence Preyer in this direction . . ." I am obliged to Dr. Holmes for the Schiller reference.

[3] Unfortunately, I only had two of his original works available to me. My comments must be severely circumscribed by lack of information.

[4] Free translation.

[5] c.f. Hall above.

[6] Free Translation.

Preyer as a Pragmatic Methodologist

by Helga Sprung and Lothar Sprung

It is not uncommon in the history of modern science that significant breakthroughs are accomplished not by recognized experts in a given field, but are the work of scholars from a related discipline. For example, psychology began to become an autonomous science around the middle of the nineteenth century through the efforts of sensory physiologists and empirical neuroscientists (Wertheimer 1979; Bringmann and Tweney 1980; Lander 1980; Sprung and Sprung 1981; Woodward and Ash 1982; Eckardt and Sprung 1983). Philosophers, theologians, and educators with traditional interests in psychological matters played a relatively minor role in this development.

Similarly, the field of empirical child psychology adopted its radical evolutionary orientation from leading experimental physiologists like Karl Vierodt (1818–1884) and William Preyer (1841–1897). Even the few studies in which empirical data were actually collected through direct, behavioral observations of children were conducted by practicing physicians (Sigismund 1856, Kussmaul 1859) and not by experimental psychologists like Fechner, Wundt, and Ebbinghaus.

It is not at all easy, of course, for experts to depart from the beaten path of thought and to follow a new road to scientific discovery. Perhaps originality and creativity require, among other aptitudes, the courage to abandon traditional methods and to experiment with radically different alternatives.

Preyer seems to have possessed this ability when he observed the first three years of his son's life through the "spectacles" of a natural scientist. Actually, he did not invent anything new. He only transferred the habits of cautious and methodical study, which he had acquired duxing his biological field and laboratory training, to a novel situation. Still, we must agree with Bühler that Preyer's *Mind of the Child* (1882) "is a remarkable book, full of interesting and conscientious observations but lacking in originality" (1925). Even his somewhat derogatory label for Preyer's approach *Kinderstubenpsychologie* (nursery psychology) is not completely unjustified (Bühler 1925:30).

Preyer's original and revolutionary contributions to modern psychology consisted of the transference of the highly successful methods of empirical, scientific research to the analysis of child development (Sprung and Sprung 1983, a, b, c; 1984 a, b). Preyer made his discoveries by the exact observations and precise recording of the seeming "trivialities" of the nursery. However, he became successful and famous in this novel field of research, because he was willing to popularize and even to propagandize his findings. As one of the leading Darwinians in Germany, he fully shared the positive as well as the negative traits of the famous *Gründerzeit* (Wilhelminian Epoch) in recent German history (Goetz 1930; Hamann and Hermann 1965, Meyer 1910, Ziegler 1899). His active involvement in the school reform movement of his day, which he supported with physiological and psychological arguments from his developmental researches, at least made an indirect contribution to the establishment of German psychology as an independent discipline. Unfortunately, Preyer's importance for general psychology has largely been overlooked in the historical literature in favour of his undeniable impact on child and developmental psychology (Eckardt 1979; Sprung 1979; Wertheimer 1979; Bringmann and Tweney 1980; Brozek and Pongratz 1980; Danziger 1980; Lander 1980; Meischner and Metge 1980; Sprung and Sprung 1980, 1981; Jaeger 1982; Woodward and Ash 1982; Sprung and Sprung 1984b; Sprung, Jahnke, Sprung and Bringmann 1984; Sprung, Sprung, and Kernchen 1984).

Preyer's work over a relatively short academic career—he died at the age of 56—is extensive and exceptionally varied. First, we find a significant number of individual research studies dealing with relatively restricted topics from embryology to muscular, respiratory and sensory physiology (vision and hearing). Next, must be mentioned important scientific investigations which extended over longer periods of time like his investigation of the effects of *Hydrocyanic Acid* (1868–1870), his work on *Blood Crystals* (1871) and his persistent research on the *Myophysical Law* (1894) and others. Preyer had a special talent for popularizing scientific findings for educated laymen. Of particular interest in this context are his publications on *The Causes of Sleep* (1877), *Explanation of Mind-Reading* (1886), *Contemporary Biological Questions* (1889), *Hypotism* (1890) and his Darwin biography (1896). Finally, Preyer worked diligently to improve the level of natural science instruction in public schools (1887) and, generally, to increase the scientific interest and understanding of young adults (1880, 1885) through his educational writings.

Preyer, who was personally acquainted with some of the leading scholars of his time, merits special credit for his efforts as editor of the correspondence between the physicist Robert Mayer (1874–1878) and the neurologist Wilhelm Griesinger (1817–1868), from 1842–1845 (Preyer 1889). In 1890 he published his own exchange of scientific letters with Gustav Theodor Fechner (1801–1887), which has become a classic.

The Mind of the Child, published in 1882, has been regarded by some as the culmination of Preyer's lifework. The book became a bestseller eventually reaching its twelfth edition (Preyer 1912). It was followed in 1893 by a briefer volume on *The Mental Development in Early Childhood,* which was written in a more popular style and which included a special section of instructions for parents to carry out psychological observations of their own children (Schmidt 1970, 1977; Schmidt and Becker 1981; Jaeger 1982).

The question of which specific concepts and methods were responsible for Preyer's success with the establishment of empirical child psychology needs to be considered and will be our major consideration. By way of introduction, we shall attempt to sketch the scientific context in which he carried out his physiological researches.

Preyer's methodological approach was the direct result of advances in experimental physiology during the first half of the nineteenth century. The traditions of Johannes Müller (1801–1858) can be identified, as well as the stronger influence of Claude Bernard (1813–1878). Consequently, one recognizes important distinctions between naturalistic observation and formal experimentation in his work (Bernard 1865; Preyer 1867).

The impact of Charles Darwin (1809–1882) and his work (Darwin 1923, 1980, 1982; Jahn, Lother and Senglaub 1982; Richards 1982) must not be underestimated. Preyer became a Darwinian early in his career and remained an advocate of evolutionary thinking throughout his life.

William Preyer specifically acknowledged his indebtedness to his older contemporary Hermann Helmholtz (1821–1894) for his methodological orientation. In The Task of Science he described the views of Helmholtz with obvious approval (1876:248):

> He regarded the search for laws by which individual, natural events can be reduced to general laws . . . as the first task of the physical sciences. These [laws] can be discovered through experimentation and are only generic notions by which all related phenomena are classified.

Finally, Preyer's close association with the psychophysical tradition in experimental psychology of Ernst Heinrich Weber (1795–1878) and Fechner cannot be overlooked. Evidence for this relationship can be found in Preyer's persistent search for a "myophysical law" which would be analogous to Fechner's "psychophysical law" (Fechner 1860; Preyer 1874; Marshall 1969, 1982; Sprung and Sprung 1981, 1983a). Preyer corresponded with Fechner for ten years about myophysical and psychophysical questions (Preyer 1890). However, during this period he appears to have realized that muscle contractions do not follow the laws of psychophysics and that his famous law was invalid (Preyer 1890).

We shall present the specific theoretical and methodological views found in the scientific and popular writings of Preyer in some detail. The following comments about the differential functions of naturalistic observations and experiments are taken from a popular lecture (1867: 99):

> Observations inform us about the structure of our body . . . the experiment teaches us the [pertinent] laws.

In the tradition of nineteenth century physiology, Preyer listed the chief characteristics of the experiment as "the artificial production of conditions" (1867: 99), "the isolation of phenomena" (1876: 259), and the "replicability of facts" (1876: 269). Yet, as a Darwinian and ardent proponent of evolutionary perspectives, he quickly cautioned his readers against adhering too rigidly to absolute standards (1876: 242):

> During the second half of [this] century the diffusion of general concepts and the consequent departure from traditional principles, which were previously regarded as secure foundations, was the outstanding characteristic of scientific research. Now it becomes increasingly apparent that it is more productive to adopt *variability* as a principle and to take it into consideration everywhere than to [search] for rigid norms.

At the same time Preyer seemed to fear that the widespread use of the "principle of variability" and the "principle of development" might inadvertently encourage metaphysical speculations in science (1876: 241–242):

> Like a businessman, who has acquired a fortune after many years of hard work . . . the scientist can easily be tempted by the example of metaphysicians to incur obligations beyond his ability to pay. The capital, of which metaphysics can dispose, is minute in comparison to that of the sciences, but metaphysics speculates all the more daringly. However, some of the debentures have been acquired by science and what the educated public was accustomed to expect from philosophers and metaphysicians, it demands now from scientists. This is the reason

why science, instead of first checking carefully whether it is at all obligated to give answers, becomes on occasion involved in irresponsible speculations and thus significantly damages its own credit. There is only one solid speculation, which will not harm the initial investment and it demands scientists never to leave the solid ground of facts.

The idea of a "developmental principle" soon became a cornerstone of Preyer's methodological thinking. It is also expressed in the synonyms "genetic method" or "comparative approach," which he contrasted with the inductive method, introduced by Bacon, Galileo, and Newton to modern science. The genetic method was something new for Preyer. He was fully aware of its future potential, as he showed in his biography of Darwin, which he published shortly before his death (1896:75–76):

> The genetic method differs from other approaches to the study of nature and mankind primarily by the questions it poses. Before Darwin all mental powers were used to describe objects and events and to classify them according to space and time. The Darwinians essentially want to know how the highest and most purposeful phenomena of nature evolved, how they function now, and, which processes had to occur for them to function as they do.
> Darwin assumed that everything has not always been what it appears to be at the present time. With all means of comparison, speculation and fantasy, the traces of earlier transformations must be identified in the bodies and events which we know today. The genetic method, therefore, derived from the fact of evolution.

Preyer, however, did not just collect facts or resign himself to obtuse speculations about theoretical models. He was convinced that all empirical, scientific research in physiology and psychology must be guided by theories, as he showed in his popular lecture on "The Limits of Sensory Perception" (1876:123):

> It is neither the sheer increase of knowledge by many, great discoveries nor the accumulation of empirical data alone that characterizes splendid periods of science, but rather new insights into the nature of man and total involvement in the new method of research.

Somewhat later in the same essay he stated even more explicitly what he regarded as the core of science (1876: 123):

> The greatest accomplishment of Galileo consists neither in his discoveries of the laws of falling stones and swinging pendulums . . . nor in his famous retort "it does move!" but in his *method*. He was the first to directly observe phenomena through experiments using . . . common sense to create the science of mechanics.

Preyer's views of the nature of scientific laws and rules and their mathematical formulation leads us to the difficult question of his episte-mology. Information for this section was found again in his lectures and essays and, most importantly, in his experimental researches. Although he wrote much, contradicted himself often and was at times a master of ambiguity, it must be conceded that he never realy strayed far from the position of an experimental scientist. Objective reality truly existed for Preyer, although he did not always view it as the primary source of human experience.

In general, Preyer believed that philosophy could provide an important methodological basis for science (1872:32):

> As long as we don't accept philosophy as the science which deals with principles in the same way as mathematics, progress, however fast, will not be sufficiently secured.

At one time, his arguments in defense of philosophy were almost materialistic, although his idealistic premises were soon revealed (1876: 274):

> Foremost with us all are our feelings, which reason converts into perceptions by giving them a cause and by assigning them to a period of time and a location. After this objectivation as phenomena, they are placed in functional relationship with each other. Thus, the nature of our world depends on us . . . we cannot have another world but our own.

And he concluded a few pages later (1876: 276):

> In the final analysis, all physical laws are acutally physiological and psychological and, hence, logical principles of explanation.

Preyer's particular epistemological position fully merits a more extensive analysis than will be possible in these pages (Engels 1948; Lenin 1949, 1957; Erpenbeck 1980; Erpenbeck and Hörz 1977; Hörz and Wessel 1983 a, b; Wessel 1983 a, b, c; Pester 1984). One has the impression that the contradictions in Preyer's thinking reflect nineteenth century neo-Kantianism and the naive materialism of his era. The influence of Kant is most evident in his sharp distinction between "pure" laws and rules (1880c: 275):

> The intellect does not create its laws [a priori] from nature, but dictates them to nature.

Rules or empirical laws, on the other hand, are only approximately true and cannot be defined mathematically (1880c: 275):

> All knowledge of things by pure intellect or by pure reason is nothing but an illusion. The truth lies in experience alone.

Today the discussion of pure and empirical laws is identified as the "principle or problem of repesentation" (Sprung and Sprung 1983 a, b, c, 1984a).

As we have previously mentioned, Preyer was never a person of narrow interests. In fact, he had a special talent for transgressing the borders between related disciplines. Thus, he was constantly attracted to new research questions, including the field of psychology (1880a: 99):

> Today science is often accused of occupying itself with matters which are really none of its business . . . [as with] the theory of the mental activities of man. Whereas it was believed in the past that such problems could be answered and solved only by quiet meditation before one's desk, it has now been only realized that something more is needed—namely *observations* and *experiment.*

In retrospect, it appears that Preyer's life before the publication of his *magnum opus* was only the preparation for his work in empirical child and developmental psychology. He was, of course, not the first to address himself to this problem—we only need to recall Tiedemann (1787), Sigismund (1856) or Kussmaul (1859). Still, Preyer seems to have been the best qualified person for the task by means of his academic training, his extensive research experience and his generalist *Weltanschauung.* His publications ushered in a new era of child study in the USA, France, England, Russia, Bulgaria, and eventually even in Germany (Stern 1923).

In his last major work—the Darwin biography—Preyer has given us perhaps his most emphatic justification of the importance of the genetic approach in biology and psychology (1896):

> Embryology, in particular, is necessary to discover our first ancestors (p.177). [The investigation] of ontogeny or individual development of each organism before and after birth is the most important tool in discovering the relationships of an animal to all others, and its natural place within the system of [evolution] . . . (p.117).

Even the mental development of young children can be understood better from phylogenetic comparisons, according to Preyer (1893: viii):

> I have found the observation of untrained young animals and their comparison with young children very useful in helping me understand the nature of young children. It is hoped that the establishment of a comparative psychology on a phylogenetic basis will be more successful than the adherence to speculative psychologies of the past.

Preyer was fully aware of the immense theoretical and practical importance of scientific researches on the "mind of the child," as can be seen from this excerpt from his lecture on the problem of *Psychogenesis* (1880f:204):

> It would be desirable if several men with a good education in physiology could carefully observe a larger number of newborn children and infants and then compare their results. Fathers, who know each other could exchange observations about their own children and thus control and critically examine them. A solitary father is too prone to overgeneralize what is true only for his children.

In the late fall of 1882 Preyer published his empirical observations about the development of his own child. When Preyer experimented beyond his own specialty, he put modern child and developmental psychology on the map. For this we owe him unstinted gratitude.

References

Ash, M. (1980). Experimental psychology in Germany before 1914: aspects of an academic identity problem. *Psychological Research*, 42, pp.75–86.

Bacon, F. (1962). *Das neue Organon*. Berlin: Akademie.

Bernard, C. (1961). Einführung in das Studium der experimentellen Medizin. *Sudhoffs Klassiker der Medizin*, 35, (1865).

Bringmann, W. and Tweney, R. (Eds.) (1980). *Wundt Studies*. Toronto: Hogrefe.

Brozek, J., and Pongratz, L. (Eds.) (1980). *Historiography of modern psychology*. Toronto: Hogrefe.

Büchner, L. (1902). *Kraft und Stoff oder Grundzüge der natürlichen Weltordnung. Nebst einer darauf gebauten Sittenlehre.* (20th ed.). Leipzig: Thomas.

Bühler, C., and Hetzer, H. (1929). Zur Geschichte der Kinderpsychologie. In: E. Brunswick et al. (Eds.), *Beiträge zur Problemgeschichte der Psychologie*, pp.204–224. Jena: Fischer.

Bühler, K. (1925). *Abriß der geistigen Entwicklung des Kindes* (2nd ed.). Leipzig: Quelle & Meyer.

Copernikus, N. (1959). *Über die Kreisbewegung der Fremdkörper*. Berlin: Akademie.

Danziger, K. (1980). Wundt's psychological experiment in the light of his philosophy of science. *Psychological Research*, 42, pp.109–122.

Darwin, C. (1923). *Die Abstammung des Menschen*. Leipzig: Kröner.

—(1980). *Die Entstehung der Arten durch natürliche Zuchtwahl*. Leipzig: Reclam.

—(1982). *Erinnerungen an die Entwicklung meines Geistes und Charakters (Autobiographie) 1876-1881. Tagebuch des Lebens und Schaffens (Journal) 1838-1881*. Francis Darwin. Erinnerungen aus meines Vaters täglichem Leben 1887. Leipzig: Urania

Eckardt, G. (Ed.) (1979). *Zur Geschichte der Psychologie*. Berlin: Deutscher Verlag der Wissenschaften.

Eckardt, G., and Sprung, L. (Eds.) (1983). *Advances in histography of psychology*. Berlin: Deutscher Verlag der Wissenschaften.

Engels, F. (1975). Dialektik der Natur. In *Marx-Engels-Werke* (Vol.20). Berlin: Dietz.

Erpenbeck, J. (1980). *Psychologie und Erkenntnistheorie*. Berlin: Akademie.

Erpenbeck, J., and Hörz, H. (1977). *Philosophie contra Naturwissenschaft.* Berlin: Akademie.

Fechner, G. (1860). *Elemente der Psychophysik* (2vols.) Leipzig: Breitkopf & Härtel.

Fischer, J. (Ed.) (1933). *Biographisches Lexikon der hervorragenden Ärzte der letzten fünfzig Jahre.* Berlin: Urban & Schwarzenberg.

Goetz, D. (1966). *Hermann von Helmholtz über sich selbst.* Leipzig: Teubner.

Goetz, W. (1930). Die geistige Bewegung im 19. Jahrhundert. In: W.Goetz (Ed.), *Propyläen-Weltgeschichte* (Vol.8.). Berlin: Propyläen.

Haeckel, E. (1960). *Die Welträtsel.* Berlin: Akademie.

Hamann, R., and Hermann, J. (1965). *Gründerzeit.* Berlin: Akademie.

Helmholtz, H.v. (1971). *Philosophische Vorträge und Aufsätze.* Berlin: Akademie.

Hörz, H., and Wessel, K. (1983a). Der Dialog zwischen Naturwissenschaftlern und Philosophen—eine ständige Herausforderung. *Wissenschaftliche Zeitschrift der Humboldt-Universität zu Berlin. (Mathematisch-Naturwissenschaftliche Reihe, 32).*

—(Eds.) (1983b). *Philosophische Entwicklungstheorie—Weltanschauliche, erkenntnistheoretische und methodologische Probleme der Naturwissenschaften.* Berlin: Akademie.

Jaeger, S. (1982). Origins of child psychology: William Preyer. In: W.Woodward, & M.Ash (Eds.), *The problematic science. Psychology in nineteenth-century thought.* New York: Praeger.

Jahn, I. (1982). *Charles Darwin.* Leipzig: Urania.

Jahn, R., Löther, R., and Senglaub, K. (Eds.) (1982). *Geschichte der Biologie.* Jena: Fischer.

Jaroschewski, M. (1975). *Psychologie im 20. Jahrhundert.* Berlin: Volk und Wissen.

Klix, F. (1979). Hermann von Helmholtz, Beitrag zur Theorie der Wahrnehmung. In: G.Eckardt (Ed.), *Zur Geschichte der Psychologie,* pp.45–59. Berlin: Deutscher Verlag der Wissenschaften.

Kraft, F., and Meyer-Abich, A. (Eds.) (1970). *Grosse Naturwissenschaftler.* Frankfurt: Fischer.

Kussmaul, A. (1859). *Untersuchungen über das Seelenleben des neugeborenen Menschen.* Heidelberg: Winter.

—(1919). *Jugenderinnerungen eines alten Arztes.* Stuttgart: Bonz & Comp.

Lander, H. (1980). Hauptentwicklungslinien in der Entwicklungsgeschichte der wissenschaftliche Psychologie. In: Meischner, W., & Metge, A. (eds.), *Wilhelm Wundt-Progressives Erbe, Wissenschaftsentwicklung und Gegenwart.* Leipzig: Karl-Marx-Universität.

Lenin, W. (1949). *Aus dem philosophischen Nachlass.* Berlin: Dietz.

—(1957). *Materialismus und Empiriokritizismus.* Berlin: Dietz.

Löbisch, J. (1951). *Entwicklungsgeschichte der Seele des Kindes.* Berlin: Haas.

Marshall, M. (1969). G.Fechner, Dr. Mises, and the comparative anatomy of angels. *Journal of the History of the Behavioral Sciences,* 5, pp.39–58.

—(1982). Physics, metaphysics, and Fechner's psychophysics. In: Woodward, W.&M. Ash (Eds.). *The problematic science. Psychology in nineteenth-century thought.* pp.65–87. New York: Praeger.

Meischner, W., and Eschler, E. (1979). *Wilhelm Wundt.* Leipzig: Urania.

Meischner, W., & Metge, A. (1980). *Wilhelm Wundt. Progressives Erbe, Wissenschaftsentwicklung und Gegenwart.* Leipzig: Karl Marx-Universität.

Metge, A. (1979). Zur Methodenlehre Wilhelm Wundt's zu frühen experimental-psychologischen Arbeiten im Leipziger Institut für experimentelle Psychologie. *Wissenschaftliche Zeitschrift der Karl-Marx-Universität Leipzig. Gesellschafts- und Sprachwissenschaftliche Reihe,* 28, pp.181–186.

228   Sprung and Sprung

Meyer, R. (1910). *Die deutsche Literatur des Neunzehnten Jahrhunderts* (2 Vols.). Berlin: Bondi.

Pagel, J. (Ed.) (1901). *Biographisches Lexikon hervorragender Ärzte des neunzehnten Jahrhunderts.* Berlin: Urban & Schwarzenberg.

Pester, R. (1984). Zur Stellung von Hermann Lotze in der Geschichte der Naturwissenschaften. In: Wessel, K. (Ed.), *Philosphie und Naturwissenschaften in Vergangenheit und Gegenwart.* Berlin: Humboldt-Universität (In Press).

Preyer, W. (1874). *Das myophysische Gesetz.* Jena: Fischer.

—(1877). *Über die Ursache des Schlafes.* Stuttgart: Enke.

—(1879). Akustische Untersuchungen. In: W.Preyer (Ed.), *Sammlung physiologischer Abhandlungen.* Jena: Fischer.

—(1880a). Die Aufgabe der Naturwissenschaft. In: W.Preyer (Ed.) *Naturwissenschaftliche Thatsachen und Probleme.* pp.239–277. Berlin: Paetel.

—(1880b). Die Grenzen der sinnlichen Wahrnehmung. In: W.Preyer (Ed.) *Naturwissenschaftliche Thatsachen und Probleme.* pp.121–152. Berlin: Paetel.

—(1880c). Die Concurrenz in der Natur. In: W.Preyer (Ed.), *Naturwissenschaftliche Thatsachen und Probleme.* pp.65–96. Berlin: Paetel.

—(1880d). Psychogenesis. In: W.Preyer (Ed.) *Naturwissenschaftliche Thatsachen und Probleme.* pp.199–237. Berlin: Paetel.

—(1880e). Empfindungs- und Bewegungs-Nerven. In: W.Preyer (Ed.), *Naturwissenschaftliche Thatsachen und Probleme.* pp.97–119. Berlin: Paetel.

—(1880f). Über die allgemeinen Lebensbedingungen. In: W.Preyer (Ed.), *Naturwissenschaftliche Thatsachen und Probleme.* pp.1–32. Berlin: Paetel.

—(1882). *Die Seele des Kindes.* Leipzig: Grieben.

—(1885). Aus Natur- und Menschenleben (2nd Ed.) *Allgemeiner Verein für Deutsche Literatur,* Berlin.

—(1886). *Die Erklärung des Gedankenlesens, nebst neuen Verfahrens zum Nachweis unwillkürlicher Bewegungen.* Leipzig.

—(1887). *Naturforschung und Schule.* Stuttgart: Spemann.

—(1889). *Biologische Zeitfragen. Schulreform—Lebensforschung—Darwin—Hypnotismus* (2nd Ed.), Allgemeiner Verein für deutsche Literatur, Berlin.

—(1890a). *Wissenschaftliche Briefe von G.T. Fechner und W.Preyer.* Hamburg: Voss.

—(1890b). *Der Hypnotismus.* Wien: Urban & Schwarzenberg.

—(1893). *Die geistige Entwicklung in der ersten Kindheit, nebst Anweisungen für Eltern, dieselbe zu beobachten.* Leipzig.

—(1896). *Darwin. Sein Leben und Wirken.* Berlin: Hofmann.

Richards, R. (1982). Darwin and the biologizing of moral behavior. In: W.Woodward and M.Ash (Eds.), *The problematic science, psychology in nineteenth-century thought.* New York: Praeger.

Rothschuh, K. (1953). *Geschichte der Physiologie.* Berlin: Springer.

Ruff, P. (1981). *Emil du Bois-Reymond.* Leipzig: Teubner.

Schmidt, H.D. (1970). *Allgemeine Entwicklungspsychologie.* Berlin: Deutscher Verlag der Wissenschaften.

Schmidt, H.D., and K.H. Becker (1981). Dokumente über Wilhelm Preyers Beziehungen zur Berliner Universität. *Zeitschrift für Psychologie* 189, pp.147–254.

Schmutzer, E., and W.Schütz (1975). *Galileo Galilei.* Leipzig: Teubner.

Sigismund, R. (1856). *Kind und Welt. Vattern, Muttern und Kinderfreunden gewidmet.* Braunschweig: Vieweg.

Sprung, L. (1974). Kant i psychologia. *Czowiek i Swiatopoglad II*, pp.68–81.

Sprung, L., and Sprung, H. (1980). Zur Geschichte der Psychologie—Aspekte des progressiven Erbes für die Entwicklung der Psychologie in der DDR. In: F.Klix, A.Kossakowski & W.Mäder (Eds.) *Psychologie in der DDR.* (2nd Ed.), pp.22–34. Berlin: Deutscher Verlag der Wissenschaften.

—(1981). Wilhelm Maximilian Wundt—Ancestor or model? *Zeitschrift für Psychologie*, 189, pp.237–246.

—(1983a). G.T. Fechner y el surgimiento de la psicologica experimental. *Revista Latinoamericana de Psicologica*, 15, pp.349–368.

—(1983b). Problem und Methode in der Psychologie—disziplinäre und interdisziplinäre Aspekte einer Entwicklungsgeschichte. In: H.Parthey und K.Schreiber (Eds.) *Interdisziplinarität in der Forschung*, Berlin: Akademie.

—(1983c). The communication-theoretical approach: historical developments and new foundation of a theory of psychological methods. In: G.Eckardt and L.Sprung (Eds.), *Advances in Historiography of Psychology.* Berlin: Deutscher Verlag der Wissenschaften (In Press).

—(1984a). *Grundlagen der Methodologie und Methodik der Psychologie—Eine Einführung in die Forschungs- und Diagnosemethodik für empirisch arbeitende Humanwissenschaftler.* Berlin: Deutscher Verlag der Wissenschaften (In Press).

—(1984b). Rudolph Hermann Lotze als Psychologe—Ein (Berliner) Rückblick aus experimentalpsychologischer Sicht im Jahre 1981. In: K.F. Wessel (Ed.) *Philosophie und Naturwissenschaften in Vergangenheit und Gegenwart.* Berlin: Humboldt-Universität.

Sprung, L., Jahnke, U., Sprung, H., and Bringmann, W. (1984c). Early history of scientific psychology at the University of Berlin (1850–1894). *Storia e Critica della Psicologia* (In Press).

Sprung, L., Sprung, H., and Kernchen, S. (1984d). Carl Stumpf and the origin and development of psychology as a new science at the university of Berlin. *Revista de Historia de la Psicologia* (In Press).

Stefan, S. (Ed.) (1899). *Hundert Jahre in Wort und Bild. Eine Kulturgeschichte des XIX. Jahrhunderts.* Berlin: Pallas.

Stern, W. (1923). *Psychologie der frühen Kindheit bis zum sechsten Lebensjahr, mit Benutzung ungedruckter Tagebücher von Clara Stern* (3rd Ed.). Leipzig: Quelle & Meyer.

Tiedemann, D. (1897). Beobachtungen über die Entwicklung der Seelenfähigkeiten bei Kindern. *Hessische Beiträge zur Gelehrsamkeit und Kunst.* (Vol.2.)

Turner, R.S. (1982). Helmholtz, sensory physiology, and the disciplinary development of German psychology. In: W.Woodward and M.G. Ash (Eds.), *The problematic science. Psychology in nineteenth-century thought.* pp.147–166. New York: Praeger.

Tutzke, C. (Ed.) (1980). *Geschichte der Medizin.* Berlin: Volk und Gesundheit.

Vierodt, K.v. (1977). *Physiologie des Kindesalters.* Tübingen: Laupp.

Wertheimer, M. (1979). *A brief history of psychology* (Revised Edition). New York: Holt, Rinehart & Winston.

Wessel, K.F. (1983a). Zum Verhältnis von Philosophie und Psychologie. *Wissenschaftliche Zeitschrift der Humboldt-Universität zu Berlin, Mathematisch-Naturwissenschaftliche Reihe 32*, pp.334–338.

—(1983b). Einige Bemerkungen zur Geschichte der Psychologie. *Wissenschaftliche Zeitschrift der Humboldt-Universität zu Berlin, Mathematisch-Naturwissenschaftliche Reihe, 32*, pp.339–343.

230 Sprung and Sprung

—(1983c). Das Entwicklungsprinzip und die Psychologie. *Wissenschaftliche Zeitschrift der Humboldt-Universität zu Berlin, Mathematisch-Naturwissenschaftliche Reihe, 32,* pp.345–351.

Woodward, W.R. (1980). Toward a critical historiography of psychology. In: J.Brozek and L.J. Pongratz (Eds.) *Contemporary historiography of psychology,* pp.29–67. Toronto:Hogrefe.

Woodward, W.R. and M.G. Ash (Eds.) (1982). *The problematic science. Psychology in nineteenth-century thought.* New York:Praeger.

Wundt, W. (1863). Vorlesungen über die Menschen und Thierseele. Leipzig: Voss.

—(1874). *Grundzüge der Physiologischen Psychologie.* Leipzig: Engelmann.

Wussing, H. (1877). *Isaak Newton.* Leipzig: Teubner.

Ziegler, T. (1899). Die geistigen und sozialen Strömungen des neunzehnten Jahrhunderts. In: P.Schlenther (Ed.) *Das neunzehnte Jahrhundert in Deutschlands Entwicklung.* Berlin: Bondi.

Preyer and the German School Reform Movement

by Siegfried Jaeger

One of the lesser known aspects of William Thierry Preyer's work is his contribution to educational and school reform. Preyer's articles on this subject, scattered in various newspapers, periodicals and essay collections, make up an essential part of the publications of the last decade of his life. These publications may be used as a case study of the problems of scientists in this period, who quite often used relatively undeveloped theories of evolution to criticize social conditions and develop alternatives. The results were often social models which appeared to be scientifically derived, but were not.

In this paper I attempt to determine the place of Preyer's practical and theoretical activities in the German school reform movement, and to decide how the logic and goals of his pedagogical reform models relate to his physiological and psychological theories.

After all democratic and liberal plans for education reform failed along with the bourgeois revolution, the school reform movement developed again only gradually, reaching a first peak in about 1890. Discussions about the internal and external organization of the school system and about curricula and pedagogical theory made their way effortfully through the ups and downs of halfhearted state reforms and restaurative regulations. Until the 1860s, transformations of the school system that corresponded to economic and technical developments and social change could hardly be expected from a ministerial bureaucracy that emphasized Christian ideology more than education and science. The school system continued to be dominated by elementary schools with very limited financial and pedagogical means and humanistic *Gymnasien* (higher schools of the classical type), which had hardly changed since the beginning of the century, except for the award of the monopoly of preparation for the university in 1834. Within this educational landscape a variety of state and local professional and science-oriented higher schools[1] grew up, reflecting a differentiation in the educational needs of the middle classes.[2] After the mid-1860s state efforts to improve schools according to the "educational needs of the period" expanded, and in the following decades there was growing public debate about the form and content of a unified school system and the improvement of teacher training.

This debate centered upon the question of *Gymnasium* reform, as the educational interests of the rising bourgeoisie articulated most strongly. In addition to the controversies on the "social question," the problem of schooling became a "national question," the solution of which was regarded as an essential means of securing internal peace and economic and political strength. The emergence of the school reform issue is indicated by the increasing number of pedagogical periodicals (250 in 1890), by the 345 reform models presented to the Prussian Ministry of Education between 1882 and 1888, and by the growing activities of teachers' associations.[3] There was also an increase of citizens' initiatives advocating the inclusion of special subjects in the curriculum, such as drawing or handicrafts,[4] or engaging in preschool or supplementary education.[5] The popularization of the school question was secured by upper-middle-class periodicals[6] such as *Die Gartenlaube, Schorer's Familienblatt,* and the *Deutsche Rundschau.*

The main issue in the *Gymnasium* reform debate was the *Überbürdungsfrage* ("overload" question), raised in 1836 by the physician Lorinser. The controversy on this issue continued for nearly a century and comprised far more than the standardization of the relation of mental and manual training and overall demands for schooling related to the capacity of children of different ages. The concept of "overload" became a battle-cry in controversies on classical versus scientific education, the distribution of educational chances, the planning of curricula, the regulation of breaks between study periods and of school architecture, the constitution of school boards and the participation of parents in education. Pedagogues, politicians, physicians, psychiatrists, psychologists, philologists, and natural scientists used the concept of "overload" in order to legitimize their quite divergent ends, until by the turn of the century the concept dissolved into special aspects of fatigue research, hygiene, child psychiatry, and experimental pedagogy and psychology.[7] The concept of overload functioned as a battle-cry because it legitimized a far-reaching criticism of the school system, attributing guilt with a medico-scientific argumentation of health damage that made reform seem inevitable. It did not matter if the cause of overload was seen in the school, in parents, students, or teachers; actually the concept was often used by opposing groups.

We may say, however, that there was a marked turn "from a pathology of the school to a pathology of the student,"[8] coinciding with the popularization of theories of giftedness and degeneration.

When Preyer began his intervention in the debate on *Gymnasium* reform, he already had famous scientific predecessors, including Helm-holtz (1862), Du Bois-Reymond (1877), Brücke (1879), Mach (1886) and Haeckel (1877, 1887). Du Bois-Reymond is important here because of the arguments he used to legitimize the claims of science. Using the theory of history, which posited a discontinuity between the "technico-inductive age" and the past, he identified modern science as a decisive bearer of culture. For Du Bois-Reymond contemporary culture was mainly threatened by "Americanization," i.e. the orientation to immediate goals and material interests. He developed his ideas about preventing the "superficiality of youth" into a widely read criticism of the *Gymnasium*, for which he prescribed the reform of nonscientific curricula in order to combat "Americanization."

Preyer quite consciously put himself in this tradition when he pre-sented his talk "Science and the School" to the Association of German Scientists and Physicians in 1887.[9] In this talk he emphasized the claim that science, which was becoming dominant in nearly every other part of society, should finally achieve more influence in the schools.[10] At the same time he argued that the continuity of education, idealism, and culture had long since been broken, thus opposing the philosophy of history and the corresponding plea for the classical *Gymnasium* predom-inant among philologists. "Our education is based on the emancipation from ancient and feudal limits of thinking brought about by Copernicus, Galilei and Luther" (Preyer 1887a: 47).

This claim and a scientific concept of education were the cornerstones of Preyer's criticism of the *Gymnasium* and of his alternative models. Somewhat later he described the contrast in terms of the "earlier encyclopaedic, cosmopolitan and ancient classical education" (Preyer 1889c: 82). He thus indicated his desire to establish a meritocracy among the sons of the bourgeoisie, whose nationalism would guarantee their loyalty to the state.

According to Preyer's criticism, nearly all higher schools and, espe-cially, the *Gymnasium* violate the laws of physical and mental development by overtaxing the students mentally and by using inap-propriate learning materials and methods of teaching, which reverse the natural order of learning how to think. Thus the *Gymnasium* cannot achieve its aims; its human capital bears low interest (1887a: 19).

He substantiated his criticism with statistical material from educa-tional and army offices, trying to prove the fact of overload in the schools and to show its damaging consequences, such as weakness, shortsightedness, paleness, nervousness, school migraine, lack of body growth, and other physical misdevelopments. He offered information that the *Gymnasium* was to be only marginally efficient and that its students were only marginally fit for the army.[11] The bulletin of the Ministry of Education rejected his statistically based criticism at first. Yet Preyer, resuming the controversy in 1890, was able to assert that his data were correct (Preyer 1889e: 497).

There is a peculiar interlacing of Preyer's criticism of curricula and teaching methods. Instead of proceeding from the natural interests of students in the visible, real and present to the abstract, philologists reverse the sequence. Thus, years of drilling vocabularies, grammatical rules, and formal translations result only in weak performance, and counteract the aim of preparation for a scientific profession. The majority of students, who finished *Gymnasium* were unwilling to learn, unable to use their senses, unable to observe, showed no skills in the discovery of causal and functional relationships, and could not distinguish the essential from the unessential.

Preyer also gave his massive criticism of the *Gymnasium* a political turn: "The rapid growth of cosmopolitan, social democratic, even nihilistic party activities, opposed to tradition and the established order, the incessant debates on issues of secondary importance . . . all this is due to an unphysiological treatment of the young mind, the unproportional cult of words and letters and the neglect of the real and its causes in the *Gymnasien*"(Preyer 1887a: 21).

He supplemented his criticism of the *Gymnasium* with an attack against the educational policy of the state. The state favored the classical *Gymnasium* for untenable reasons. Neither the aim of a general formal education nor that of an ideal philosophy of life levelling social class differences was achieved; "social class differences remain like individualities, and differences of education remain as well" (Preyer 1887a: 27).

In addition Preyer, again arguing statistically, showed that in the universities the mathematical, scientific, and medical disciplines developed more rapidly than the others, in terms of student numbers, staff, and content. The state should therefore have the greatest interest in abolishing compulsory *Gymnasium* attendance, as a requirement for university entrance.

Preyer's first demand, the abolition of the *Gymnasium's* monopoly on university preparation, aimed at achieving equal status for the classical *Gymnasium*, the *Realgymnasium* and the *Oberrealschule* with regard to admittance to the university and public service. The state's fear of producing an academic proletariat by opening up educational chances was unjustified, for longer periods of study at the university and the high demands of state examinations would prevent this effect. The best defense against a rapid increase of misfits, however, would be learning for life rather than philological half-education (Preyer 1889a: 414).

Preyer did not demand the abolition of the classical *Gymnasium,* but expected its transformation or disappearance in the face of sound competition from other types of high school.

Preyer's second demand was the total transformation of the school system on the basis of a physiological pedagogy still to be developed. However in his contributions to the school reform debate there is no systematic discussion of the "natural, physiological pedagogy" he refers to. One must therefore look at his physiological and psychological works, since for Preyer "true pedagogy is applied physiology and applied empirical psychology." More precisely, his concern was the application of "elementary laws of morphological development and physiological working conditions," or the "generally valid physiological laws of development and education" (Preyer 1889c: 79–80).

For Preyer the competition of individuals of the same species in the struggle for life raises needs which form organs. The need to improve some particular activity determines the final form of the organ, which is then inherited and, as a disposition, precedes the function. It is generally true, he claimed, that the ontogenetic development of the organs of physical and mental functions is primarily dependent on functional activity, which in turn interacts with external conditions (Preyer 1879, 1886). One-sided overexertion of an organ may result in damage to an inheritable function and thus of the whole organism, as organs are interlinked by inheritance and require balanced development. "How the brain and the soul develop, whether one-sidedly or balanced depends on the nature of sense impressions in youth and on inheritable dispositions" (Preyer 1887a: 7).

True pedagogy, therefore, must proceed from inheritance and its differences. People cannot all be drilled according to the same model (Preyer 1880a: 203); their individuality is to be taken into account. By systematic selection of sense impressions education must regulate movements and actions, and develop fully and harmoniously the dispositions for the individual and society while checking the detrimental or dangerous ones. Thus, the development of body, reason, and will can be canalized and secured. This process must be supplemented by keeping out bad influences, providing mentally and physically sound personal models and opportunities to develop a strong will in competition with the will of others.

These are, briefly sketched, Preyer's basic ideas for a physiological pedagogy, which he summarized in the slogan "First nature without drill, then culture" (Preyer 1895: x) and which he subsequently tried to realize in the schools.

First steps in this direction should be the control of hygiene by school physicians and the training of students and teachers in physiology and psychology. This would provide physiologically suitable working conditions and cultivate a level of physical development that would secure the advantages of the Germanic race[12] and prepare students for military training (Preyer 1889c: 79, and 1889d: 353). The main emphasis was to be on new curricula and methods of teaching, and the formation of character and physical fitness was the aim. Students "are to enter life not as premature critics, but rather as patriots with firm ethical principles and prepared for scientific and other higher professions" (Preyer 1887a: 41).

The formation of character is accomplished primarily, in German language and literature, by ethics courses and by history courses including local history and by "asserting the advantages of the monarchy" (1887a: 41). Equally important is instruction in science beginning with instruction in the proper use of the senses. Preyer's concept of instruction in science was based on the idea that different sense impressions, are the elements of all experience, knowledge, and skill. They need to be developed in sequence, proceeding from the concrete and tangible to the abstract.

Spontaneous discriminative capacity should be supported with special training in spatial perception using drawing and model-building. Instruction in plane and solid geometry would then proceed to analytical geometry, which would cultivate logico-mathematical thinking.

The training of thought was completed, according to Preyer, by "temporology," i.e. a new science, which proceeds from arithmetic and algebra to physics and chemistry linking experimental observations, and logical exercises, thus controlling the coherence of thought. The keystone in Preyer's curricular outline is instruction in elementary physiology, which is to provide "knowledge of man, the world and the necessary conditions of life" (1887a: 44).

The essential thing, however, was not the subjects offered—these may be reduced to the typical and factual—but rather the methods of training and the establishment of a unified and comprehensive worldview.[13] This, along with physical training, would guarantee firm character formation. In Preyer's argument, then, the content and the structure of instruction were derived, apparently naturally, from physiological theories and developmental psychology.

His rapidly popularized talk, "Science and the School," had five editions within a year. It lent decisive support to the Schenckendorff Petition of 1887, which demanded that the Prussian Ministry of Education reform the higher school system and received 22,400 signatures.

The "school battle" escalated, as shown by the foundation of many special periodicals and associations for and against a reform of schools.[14]

In the following years Preyer, now head of the "General German Association for School Reform," which he founded in 1889 together with the pedagogue Hugo Göring, tried to meet the criticism triggered by his talk on "Science and the Schools." He went on to spread his ideas of "a perfectly new German school for the sons[15] of the upper classes" (Preyer 1889e: 498) and pressed for the unification of the school reform movement and the realization of Göring's outlines for a model school.

In the often heated and polemical controversy, Preyer was accused of lacking historical understanding and of having a one-sided concept of education. He also had to counter arguments that the *Gymnasium* was the only natural educational institution, because it treated the educational history of the individual as a recapitulation of cultural history (Vaihinger 1889). Preyer was hardly convincing when he argued that this analogy is superficial and misleading. He used it elsewhere himself to describe language development, while simultaneously pointing out the different concepts of continuity in the natural and cultural sciences. With regard to history instruction he kept on a pragmatic level. He acknowledged that it is not possible to cover everything, and argued that the history of one's own country is most useful, while ancient history with its republican virtues might even be detrimental to the cultivation of monarchical feelings.

On May 1, 1889, the Emperor decreed that schools were to combat socialist and communist ideas. He demanded a reform of instruction in religion and history along ethical and patriotic lines. And at the beginning of 1890, became law a reform in the training of the cadet corps. Preyer and Göring felt supported in their ideas and hoped for the same sort of change in the public school system. The seemed justified, for the decree of 1890 made it "the aim of all education and especially, of military education, to form character by equal and balanced physical, scientific, and moral training," demanded the simplification of the curriculum "by eliminating all superfluous details," and made "German language and culture the center of instruction" in order to enable cadets to "display their moral and intellectual influence in the army or to take their appropriate place in any other profession" (cf. *Die Neue Deutsche Schule* 1 (1889/90: 539–541). Preyer agreed "not only in general, but in detail" (Preyer 1889e: 501) with Göring's New German School (cf. Burnham 1891), a program that reads like an over-zealous effort at realizing the Emperor's intentions. Some citations from this program convey an idea of why Göring and Preyer regarded the Emperor as the born protector of the New German School:

> As a state institution the new German school will be an important factor in the social reform process, which is the primary task of our time. . . . It offers the following advantages to the state:
>
> 1. It removes the basis for Social Democracy or any other revolutionary ideas by raising all labour to honour, by cultivating the joy of work and by introducing youth to knowledge of the historically developed contemporary state, weeding out any interest or faith in utopian state fantasies.
> 2. It brings youth in military discipline and thus supports the development of our state into a military state worth striving for.
> 3. It preserves for the state a rich capital of capable men and makes the people fit for military service. It trains hardened and muscular youths with sharp senses and dexterous hands, and educates them to be men of character, knowledgable and capable.
> 4. It allows retired officers and other civil servants to offer their teaching talents in the service of the 'German School'. . . .
> 5. It no longer authorizes windy half-education, but rather true performance, and leads every man to the profession for which he is suited. . . . It must cultivate from youth onward the military spirit which made Germany great. From the earliest childhood years it must fill people with the idea that they live not for themselves but for the whole. . . . [It] must cure those family diseases which turn so many sons into degenerate weaklings and reckless egoists. It must eradicate that Americanism, which . . . is beginning to threaten even German circles. . . . For the time being, it will only be able to accomplish these aims as a private institution, shutting out the morbid phenomena of our cultural life as much as possible and leading its charges back to healthy simplicity (Göring 1890: 174ff.).

This boarding school was to accomplish the formation of strong will and individuality mainly by military training; school gardens and workshops were to convey elementary scientific and craft knowledge, the works of Jordan, Freitag, and Dahn were to introduce German literature; and the works of Du Bois-Reymond, Henle, Czermak, and Preyer were to introduce science.

There also was criticism of this proposal, with regard to its radical break with educational tradition, its danger to family life, its early introduction of children to the industrial world, and the conditions of political life. It was also believed that an education for all social classes might produce discontent and thus nurture Social Democracy (cf. Unger 1891).

At the great School Conference in December 1890, a number of reform demands were met, but yet the unification of the upper level schools was not accomplished. The *Gymnasium's* monopoly on university preparation was not abolished for another decade. Reform enthusiasm grew weaker. A vague hope remained that the overcrowding of the *Gymnasium* would force further compromises by the school bureaucracy. When the December Conference rejected Göring's reform ideas and proposals, he and Preyer withdrew their efforts to reform the *Gymnasium*. Preyer had no contribution to the debate in the last volume of the association's periodical. His last discussion of the issue, "The Emperor and School Reform," was published posthumously in 1900. Göring's proposal to unite with the Association for School Reform ended this chapter in the history of the Wilhelminian school reform movement.[16]

An evaluation of Preyer's contribution to the school reform movement may begin with the observation that Preyer lent a seemingly scientific legitimation to reform ideas which actually articulated the interests only of a particular faction of the bourgeoisie, the national liberals. While new scientific theories may coincide more or less with the interests of this or that social group, the crucial question remains whether and to what extent scientific theories can legitimize social reform.

Preyer's criticism of the school system was justified in many respects, and some of his reform proposals may sound progressive even today. Yet he went quite beyond the realm of scientific legitimation. What appears to be the application of scientific principles and discoveries is mostly a biased selection and interpretation.

This should not be read as a plea for separating pure and applied science, or for an ivory-tower mentality, because social and scientific problems are intertwined so closely. Persistent efforts are needed to recognize the limits of science without dismissing its social context. Studies in history of science and psychology can, I think, make important contributions here.

Notes

1   The middle level schools were named *Real-, Latein-, Stadt-, Gewerbe-, Bürger-, Vor-* and *Mittelschule,* the upper level schools *Oberrealschule, Provinzial-Gewerbe-schule, höhere Bürgerschule, Realgymnasium, Progymnasium* and *Prorealgymnasium.*
2   To my knowledge the 1870 study by Schwabe and Bartholomäi, commissioned by the city of Berlin, is the first quantitative-empirical approach to the question of "how the educational needs of the population or its various groups relate to the existing schools and their efficiency." In this context, their survey on the "contents of children's minds on entering school in Berlin" gives an outline of the preconditions of primary schooling.
3   The most important association was the "Association for Scientific Pedagogy," founded in 1869 by T.Ziller. It was comprised mainly of Herbartians.
4   I would like to mention primarily the "German Association for Boys' Manual Work," organized on a national scale in 1886 by the middle-class politician Schenckendorff. Like the handicrafts museums, this association aimed to prepare the production of high quality goods which could stand international competition. Family life was also to be supported by cooperative work. Manual and intellectual labor were to be reconciled.
5   Like the institutions for physically and mentally disabled children, these associations generally had the status of private welfare institutions. They aimed to compensate for the specific living conditions in the cities by advocating the institutionalization of kindergartens, child care centers, playgrounds, schoolyards, school workshops, and supplementary education for youth.
6   To bring the school reform question "to the forefront of public debate" was the declared concern of *Schorer's Familienblatt,* which from 1886 to 1890 published a series of declarations by known personalities under the title "Be Mindful of your Children", and offered information about domestic and foreign school reform efforts. Its editor also suggested the formation of free associations for school reform and the organization of an international congress.
7   Cf. the works of E.Kraepelin (1894), L.Burgerstein (1891), J.Trüper (1893), H.Emminghaus (1887), L.Stein (1895) and H.Ebbinghaus (1897), which depart from the question of overload and proved significant for further developments.
8   This is the title of an unpublished M.A. Thesis at the Psychological Institute of the Free University of Berlin (1982). The author, Petra Hagemeier, analyses the formation of child psychiatry and remedial pedagogy and its relation to the debate on the overload question.
9   In the beginning of 1887, the last volume of *Kosmos,* the organ of the German Darwinians, was published. Preyer was also a contributing editor to *Kosmos.* In the last volume the editor stated that Darwinian principles have generally become established in science, but not in public consciousness (*Kosmos* 19: 38ff. and 482). Preyer justified his publications in nonscientific journals in similar terms.

[10] Ten years earlier at the fiftieth meeting, in 1877, Haeckel had already proposed to use evolutionary theory as the comprehensive principle of education in schools. For him the application of the "genetic method" could facilitate inevitable school reforms. Virchow felt so provoked by this proposal that, instead of giving his prepared talk, he warned at length against emphasizing so much descendency theory which—he felt—was not yet sufficiently substantiated.

[11] Preyer tried to demonstrate in detail that very few students qualified for the *Abitur* certificate (3.3 percent of all pupils) completed their school career (14 percent of all starting in a higher level school), achieved the *Abitur* at the proper time (31.2 percent), obtained authorization to serve as one-year volunteers (5.3 percent) or, as one-year officers, be judged fully fit for army service (32 percent)—cf. Preyer 1888b.

[12] An explicitly racist elaboration is found in Ammon (1892); with reference to Darwin, Galton, Preyer, and the anthropologist Lapouge, Ammon sought to provide a theoretical foundation for the practical aims of the school reform movement.

[13] Preyer and Göring used the terms "worldview," "ideology," and "unified consciousness" synonymously.

[14] Apart from the professional General German Association of *Realschule* Men, which had demanded the unlimited access of *Oberrealschule* students to the university since 1875, these were: the General German Association for School Reform, founded in 1889 by Preyer and Göring which advocated the most comprehensive reform program (its organ from 1889 on was *Die Neue Deutsche Schule);* the Association for School Reform, led by the editor of the newspaper *Tägliche Rundschau,* Lange, and the General Secretary of the Association of German Engineers, Peters (founded in 1889, with its organ, *Zeitschrift für die Reform der höheren Schule)* and demanding a unified middle school of six years; the German Association for a Unified School, led by Hornemann, Frick, and Schiller (founded in 1887, its publication was called *Schriften des Deutschen Einheitsschulvereins),* which sought the preservation of the *Gymnasium* monopoly by giving more room to modern subjects; the not very significant Association for the Promotion of a School System without Latin, and the Association of *Gymnasia,* which fought against the efforts to establish a unified school system and the weakening of classical education. Besides these new foundations, which focused on university-preparatory education, a special organ for the reform of the elementary school was established called *Neue Bahnen,* which was a monthly calling for an up-to-date education of youth (edited from 1889 on by J.Meyer); finally, there was the *Zeitschrift für Schulgesundheitspflege,* which centered on problems of school hygiene (edited from 1889 on by L.Kotelmann). For the history of the foundation of Preyer's association cf. Göring, 1889.

[15] Preyer was not interested in the reform of girls' schools; it should be mentioned, however, that at the time this reform was already widely discussed.

[16] I cannot say whether this amalgamation actually took place.

References

Ammon, O. (1892). Die Mittelschule als Werkzeug der natürlichen Auslese. *Zeitschrift für die Reform der höheren Schule,* 4, 45–51.

Brücke, E.v. (1879). *Über die Notwendigkeit der Gymnasialbildung für die Ärzte.* Wien: Braunmüller.

242   Jaeger

Burgerstein, L. (1891). *Die Arbeitskurve einer Schulstunde.* Hamburg: Voss.

Burnham, W. (1891). The German school. *The Pedagogical Seminary, 1,* 13–18.

Du Bois-Reymond, E. (1877). Kulturgeschichte und Naturwissenschaft. *Deutsche Rundschau,* 13, 214–250.

Ebbinghaus, H. (1897). Über eine neue Methode zur Prüfung geistiger Fähigkeiten und ihre Anwendung bei Schulkindern. *Zeitschrift für Psychologie,* 13, 401–459.

Emminghaus, H. (1887). *Die psychischen Störungen im Kindesalter.* Tübingen.

Göring, H. (ed.) (1889–1891). *Die Neue Deutsche Schule.* Hamburg: Verlagsanstalt und Druckerei.

—(1889). Die Entstehung des Allgemeinen Deutschen Vereins für Schulreform. *Neue Deutsche Schule,* 1, 65–72.

—(1890). *Die neue deutsche Schule.* Leipzig: Voigtländer.

Häckel, E. (1877). Über die heutige Entwicklungslehre im Verhältnis zur Gesammtwissenschaft. Paper read at Annual Convention Deutscher Naturforscher und Ärzte, Munich.

—(1887). Real-Gymnasium und Formal-Gymnasien. *Tägliche Rundschau* (7–3).

Helmholtz, H.v. (1862). Über das Verhältnis der Naturwissenschaften zur Gesamtheit der Wissenschaften. Prorektoratsrede. Heidelberg.

Kraepelin, E. (1894). *Über geistige Arbeit.* Fischer: Jena.

Lorinser, F. (1836). Zum Schutz der Gesundheit in den Schulen. *Medizinische Zeitung,* 5, 1–4.

Mach, E. (1896). *Der relative Bildungswert der philologischen und der mathematisch-naturwissenschaftlichen Unterrichtsfächer der höheren Schule.* Prag.

Preyer, W. (1879). Die Konkurrenz in der Natur. *Nord und Süd,* 8, 191–212.

—(1880a). *Naturwissenschaftliche Tatsachen und Probleme.* Berlin: Paetel.

—(1880b). Psychogenesis. *Deutsche Rundschau,* 23, 198–221.

—(1886). Über die wahre Aufgabe der Physiologie. *Deutsche Rundschau,* 49, 38–51.

—(1887a). *Naturforschung und Schule.* Stuttgart: Spemann.

—(1887b). Zur Schulstatistik. Beilage zur *Münchner Allgemeinen Zeitung* (12–30).

—(1887c). Der erste Unterricht im Lateinischen und die Forderungen der Gegenwart. In *Biologische Zeitfragen.* Berlin: Allgemeiner Verein für Deutsche Literatur.

—(1888a). Zur Schulstatistik II. *Pädagogisches Archiv,* 30, 551–559.

—(1888b). Zahlen beweisen! In *Biologische Zeitfragen.* Berlin: Allgemeiner Verein für Deutsche Literatur.

—(1888c). Aphorismen zur Schulreform. In *Biologische Zeitfragen.* Berlin: Allgemeiner Verein für Deutsche Literatur.

—(1889a). *Biologische Zeitfragen. Schulreform—Lebensforschung—Darwin—Hypnotismus.* Berlin: Allgemeiner Verein für Deutsche Literatur.

—(1889b). Naturforschung und Schule. *Neue Deutsche Schule,* 1, 25–30.

—(1889c). Stand und Ziele der Schulreformbewegung. *Neue Deutsche Schule,* 1, 73–85.

—(1889d). Die Zukunft der Schulen in Deutschland. *Deutschland,* 1, 6–7.

—(1889e). Die Neue Deutsche Schule. *Neue Deutsche Schule,* 1, 491–501.

—(1889f). Meine Gegner in der Schulreformfrage. *Neue Deutsche Schule,* 1, 524–533.

—(1890). Eine neue deutsche Schule nach Hugo Göring. In Wilhelm Meyer-Markau (Ed.). *Sammlung pädagogischer Vorträge* (Vol.3.). Bielefeld: Helmich.

—(1890b). Meine Gegner in der Schulreformfrage. (Dr. Oskar Jäger). *Neue Deutsche Schule,* 2, 215–220.

—(1890c). Meine Gegner in der Schulreformfrage. (Dr. Wilhelm Schrader). *Neue Deutsche Schule,* 2, 270–273.

—(1890d). Hypnotismus und Erziehung. *Neue Deutsche Schule,* 2, 177–186.

—(1891). Die Betäubungsmittel und die Selbsterziehung. *Neue Deutsche Schule,* 3, 419–424.

—(1895). *Die Seele des Kindes.* Leipzig: Grieben.

—(1900). Unser Kaiser und die Schulreform. In: *Zur Pädagogik der Gegenwart.* Dresden: Bleyl & Kämmerer.

Schwabe, H., and Batholomäi, F. (1870). Inhalt und Methode einer Berliner Schulstatistik. Berlin und seine Entwicklung— *Städtisches Jahrbuch for Volkswirtschaft und Statistik,* 4, 1–77.

Stein, L. Experimentelle Pädagogik. *Deutsche Rundschau,* 83, 240–250.

Trüper, J. (1893). *Psychopathische Minderwertigkeiten im Kindesalter.* Gütersloh.

Unger, J. von (1891). Dr. Hugo Görings Deutsche Schule. *Neue Deutsche Schule* 2: 2–20.

Vaihinger, H. (1888). *Naturforschung und Schule.* Köln: Ahn.

Darwinism and the Emergence of Developmental Psychology

by Roger A. Dixon and Richard M. Lerner

It has been remarked that the present age is the most historically minded of all ages.[1] Ever more frequently, historians and historiographers of science have emerged to cultivate and advance what is perhaps a fundamental principle of historical inquiry: viz., to fully understand the present moment in a given science one must learn something of the processes or events that preceded it.[2] It is evident that this mission of historical self-understanding has been similarly pursued in the many intellectual arenas of the social and behavioral sciences. Recently, as evinced by this volume, participants in that explicitly historical social science—developmental psychology—have also taken to this method in their efforts to promote self-understanding and to achieve disciplinary integrity.[3] The historical vision of many of these early investigations has been justifiably confined to the terrain of the present century. To the extent that the bulk of developmental theorizing and research has occurred in the last several decades such a restriction is legitimate.

Nevertheless, in keeping with the historical mission (which, on another level of analysis, is analogous to the developmental mission), the primal frontiers of developmental psychology are being ever more avidly explored. Some authors have scanned the panorama of recent centuries for snatches of developmental prototheories, while others have focused more closely upon specific segments, movements, or figures. The present chapter adopts the latter strategy. The prevailing natural science ideology of the middle years of the nineteenth century—Darwinism—is examined for its influence on the emergence of developmental psychology. Other recent inquiries[4] have either explicitly identified or simply alluded to Darwinism as a necessary but not sufficient precursor to the developmental approach to human study. However, there has been little elaboration of this historical connection. The central thesis of this paper is that for developmental psychology to have emerged at all, the intellectual scenery of the nineteenth century has to be furnished (if not infused) with a thorough sense of history and temporality. Darwinism, which served as an exemplar of historicity in nineteenth-century letters, contributed to the propagation of the historical approach in realms of intellectual activity ranging from biology to sociology and from psychology to epistemology.[5] In examining both the context for the emergence of Darwinism and the subsequent influence of Darwinism in the emergence of developmental psychology, this paper sets the stage for numerous recent reviews of post-Darwinian developmental theory.[6]

Writing in 1888, in patently excessive intonations, Grant Allen expressed enthusiasm for the intellectual good that the Darwinian revolution has wrought:

> There is no department of human thought or human action which evolutionism leaves exactly where it stood before the advent of the Darwinian conception. In nothing is the fact more conspicuously seen than in the immediate obsolescence (so to speak) of all the statical pre-Darwinian philosophies which ignored development, as soon as ever the new progressive evolutionary theories had fairly burst upon an astonished world.[7]

In the present chapter the question of whether the Darwinian hypothesis constituted a *bona fide* revolution in the history of science is not of direct concern. Falling short of asserting that time or history was "discovered" in the nineteenth century, the present authors restrict themselves to a descriptive account of the encounter with history in this period. As will become evident on several occasions throughout this chapter, the complexity and gradual nature of the ascendancy of evolutionism is as unquestionable as is the observation that it reached its climax with the Darwinian proposals.[8]

The encounter with history in the nineteenth century

To propose that Charles Darwin is salient amont the originative figures of developmental psychology is certainly not a novel idea.[9] For instance, White[10] has argued that:

> Within 50 years after the publication of Darwin's *The Origins of Species* in 1859, the theory of evolution has crystallized its influence upon developmental psychology not once but several times. As happens with a broad and powerful ideology, different people took different messages from evolutionism and occasionally those messages could come into conflict.

Indeed, it has been argued that, today, there are at least five major models of developmental psychology (organicism, psychoanalysis, mechanism, contextualism, and dialecticism), and that these models share Darwinism as a point of common historical heritage.[11]

It should be noted at the outset, however, that nowhere in these pages is Darwin identified as the singular or even the most influential of originative figures. Rather, a more modest claim is advanced; viz., the intellectual climate of historicity that both preceded Darwin and gained impetus from him—and which in some ways was epitomized by him—is one of the originative intellectual cores of contemporary developmental psychologies. It is also not proposed that all present versions of developmental psychology embrace a Darwinian evolutionism, for this is simply not the case. Indeed, some versions of contemporary developmental psychology may in fact reject major portions of Darwin's evolutionary theory, or the neo-Darwinian versions of contemporary biology. Nevertheless, the developmental tradition, propagated in part by Darwin, is still present in these systems, and their intellectual heritage may, at least indirectly, be traced to (or through) Darwin. Among early evolutionists, it is Darwin whose contributions have been both lasting and most finely tuned to be the concerns of the human sciences in general and the developmental human sciences in particular.

A general sociology of knowledge perspective

An abiding principle of a general sociology of knowledge is that in any society characterized by a succession of generations, social and intellectual change is effected by the fresh contact of new generations with the existing cultural milieu.[12] Intellectual discoveries influence the ideologies, ethics, and intellectual commitments of each generation commensurate to its duration in that system.[13] To understand the emergence of a new mode of thought (such as developmental psychology), or the intellectual shift of an extant one, the observer must attend to its sociohistorical and intellectual context.[14] Thus, prior to a consideration of the present state of developmental theory,[15] some characterization of the context of the emergence of the developmental approach to human psychological study in the nineteenth century is in order.

Pluralization of the social order is often accompanied by diversification in the extant world of thought; ideologies, the prevailing interpretations of the world, fragment and mingle. The assumption that a unity underlies the social and intellectual worlds is rendered problematic at best. Some social interpreters[16] have suggested that the resultant strain in the individual sector may be resolved through the creation of a psychological worldview. The unity of internal psychological man counteracts the amorphous plurality of the social and intellectual context. The wide variety of knowledge produced by individuals in such contexts reflects the pluralized nature of the knowledge-producing environment. Seldom is there immediately vived unity emerging from such diversity. Conflicting ideologies beget divergent methods of gathering knowledge and mutually exclusive criteria of what to admit as *bona fide* articles of knowledge.

Economic and social change occurring in the context of the industrial revolution provided for a rather sudden diversification of social classes and groups. In turn, the social system assumed a dynamic pace and a relatively objective, impersonal demeanor.[17] The existing unity (primarily religious in nature) between the social order and the world of thought, gradually unravelling since at least the Copernican revolution, was further fractured by the swift advance of science an technology. Further, "the medieval attitude—a striving for a universal synthesis and a monistic interpretation of life—was all but destroyed ... pluralism and pragmatism were to become the rule."[18] As Berger[19] notes, the macrolevel fragmentation resulted in a split between the private and the public on an individual level. It remains problematic whether this, as Berger seems to suggest, created a "psychological" need for psychology (as a replacement for, say, religion) or whether advances in psychological research (which, after all, had been proceeding since at least Descartes) created their own place in such a world, a place that happened to hold wind enough to fill the sails of certain intellectual entrepreneurs.

The psychology advancing in the wake of social dynamism and pluralization was an approach to the study of man; it was, at least in England and the United States, an historical approach, a temporal approach, a developmental approach. It brought to human study a particular view of humankind: viz., on the species level the human condition is the outcome of phylogenetic evolution and on the individual level it is the ever-unfinished product of ontogenetic development. Eiseley[20] sees in the emergence of evolutionary thought as a contrast to the "dour prophecies" of Christianity; the human condition was no longer destined to worsen. Rather, just as it had progressed from a benign organic soup to an aggressive and relatively successful hominid, it could continue to progress to unknown higher levels of the evolutionary scale. A predilection to consider the past, especially as it informed explanation of the present and augured the future, began to emerge in the intellectual climate.

Partly as a result of the publication of Darwin's *Origin of Species* in 1859, the notions of temporality, historicity, and open-ended development began spreading through nineteenth-century science and letters.[21] Overcoming the preexisting barrier of antagonism between science and history was as important a contribution of Darwin in this regard as was his evolution theory.[22] Prior to evolution theory the subject matter of science was essentially static, whereas the subject matter of history was essentially progressive. Following Darwin both areas of thought viewed their subject matter in terms of the genetic concept of evolution, a capitulation (Collingwood says) of the scientific perspective to the historical.[23] Scientific inquiry—indeed, most intellectual study—became infused with history. Even metaphysicians, such as Adam Sedgwick (1785–1873), and theoretically-inclined scientists, such as Louis Agassiz (1807–1873), felt obliged to produce progressionist theories, explicitly intending to reconcile scientific advance with Christian cosmology. In these efforts, development was admitted into the system, but in a human-centered, teleological way; change and emergence were not products of the natural process of evolution, but of miracle.

A thorough natural scientific rendering of the evolution of organic species was considered blasphemous and, as Sedgwick intoned, a brutalizing blow upon the social fabric. In the period immediately preceding and following the publication of Darwin's *Origin* restrictions on the openness with which scientists could address questions of evolution from a natural science perspective were quite apparent. Whereas Herbert Spencer (1820–1903) and Thomas H. Huxley (1825–1895) openly defended evolutionary theory, others such as Charles Lyell and Robert Chambers were far more discreet. The latter, for example, was discreet to the point of being invisible; Chamber's never publicly acknowledged that he was the author of *Vestiges of the Natural History of Creation* (which appeared in 1844), a well-known work applying the principle of increasing differentiation (from Karl Ernst von Baer) to the evolution of species.[24]

It would appear that in this period developmentalism assumed something of an ideological status. While the term evolution was only just coming into modern use[25] it became, perhaps, a "catchword which dominated human thought far beyond the limits of zoology and gave it [the latter half of the nineteenth century] a characteristic period flavour, just as the ideas of Providence and Order had done in earlier times."[26] Evolution was, in any case, an orienting feature of intellectual inquiry in the century and a necessary stimulus in the human sciences in general and the developmental approach in particular. In one sense, the replacement of the religious notions of growth with the scientific-historical notions of evolution and development may indeed be viewed as partially substitutional. In the jargon of Foucault, the special creation theory was the "episteme" of the moment, the historical *a priori* delimiting the field of knowledge, and the qualitatively different naturalistic theory of evolution succeeded it.[27] Religion (especially the creation cosmology) became discredited in the public world of thought through both biblical scholarship and scientific advance, thus contributing to the well-documented secularization of the nineteenth century.[28]

It is not accurate to suggest that evolutionism itself brought about the demise of teleological, religious accounts of the natural world. The demise of the notion of a deity as an active, controlling agent, as the disposer and cause of all, was actually accomplished as much from within the ranks of defenders of the faith, as from without. Such influential scientists as William Whewell (1794–1866), John Herschel (1792–1871), and John Stuart Mill (1806–1873) argued that the invariable laws of the diety governed only the origin of the universe and species; all other functions in the natural world operated according to natural laws.[29] Darwinism contributed to this growth in the realm of influence of natural science, and to the further expansion into the remaining domain of religious explanation (i.e. the question of origins), but it was not solely responsible for bringing it about.

Religion also served a private need and, in the face of anonymous technological progress and pluralization, this private need may have been reflected in an effort to rediscover personal and phylogenetic origins. In fact, on the personal level, and in terms of the emergence of developmental psychology, it may have been in part a reaffirmation of a unique origin or other personal myth of self. Inasmuch as developmental psychology was continuous with the scientific worldview and acquainted the individual with continuity between (personal) past and present—with, also, a myth or ideology of sorts—it grew in significance among scientific researchers and, through the intelligentsia, began spreading its influence through the social and educational systems. Increasingly, for incoming generations, it became part of the received view of science, especially geology and biology, and of human history.

In sum, the nineteenth century witnessed a discovery of developmental time, a discovery so pervasive and influential as to critically affect the regard held for other ideologies and cosmologies. The discovery set scientific disciplines such as geology, biology, and psychology upon a path which, to this day, in one variation or another, they continue to walk. In some ways it was, as Eiseley put it, Darwin's century. That Darwin was a young man was propitious indeed,[30] but more importantly his youth was fused with a cause and a passion for detail. From the perspective of general sociology of knowledge, however, it was Darwin's century only partly because of his salient contributions to science and philosophy; it also happened that the world was ripe for such contributions. After Darwin and his surrounding generations—after the novel, world-shattering views they inserted into the intellectual and social context—much of science and philosophy got on with its normal activity under the banner of a new developmental ideology. According to Eiseley:[31]

> It is not enough to say that man had come into possession of time, or even of eternity. These he had possessed before the other cultures, but never with this particular conception of on-goingness. To see an to re-create the past, to observe how it has come to mold the present, one must possess the knowledge that all things are new under the sun and that they are flowing in the direction of time's arrow, never to return upon their course—that time is noncyclic, unreturning, and creative.

This characterizes both the scientific and philosophical views of development and evolution that loom large in the nineteenth century heritage of developmental psychology. In the following section, some of the sources of the propitious developmental context which Darwin both benefitted from and advanced are examined.

Evolutionary theory and the concept of development

The conception of the on-goingness of time, of the enormous forward motion, of the continuous process, was, of course, not entirely novel. As early a writer as Lucretius (97?–54 B.C.) inserted elements of chance and boundless temporality into his account of the origin of the universe. Even the concept of natural selection was anticipated in Lucretius' *On the Nature of the Universe*.[32] Still it wasn't until much later that these notions became pervasive. Mandelbaum[33] observes:

It is generally agreed that one of the most distinctives features of nineteenth-century thought was the widespread interest evinced in history. The
manifestations of this interest are not only to be found in the growth and diversification of professional historical scholarship, but in the tendency to view all of
reality, and all of man's achievements, in terms of the category of the development.

The category of development implies the method of historicism. That
is, an adequate understanding of any phenomenon (biological or philosophical) requires that it be considered in terms of its position in the
present situation and its role in a continuous developmental or
historical process. As Mandelbaum describes it, the concern is not with
the "nature of the event itself, [but] . . . with its place in some process of
change."[34] Events have no autonomous existence (and, especially, no
independent meaning) outside the role they play in a stream of history.
In the human sciences where the events of concern are sociohistorical in
nature (e.g. wars and plagues) the province of general human history is
indicated; where the events are of an individual nature (e.g. onset of
logical thinking, puberty, or marriage), the province of individual
human history, or developmental psychology, is implied.

In general, during this period the concept of development received
attention on two fronts, both of which had some influence on the emergence of developmental psychology. As has been said, the thrust of the
interest in the idea of development (and individual development in
particular) was a continuing attempt by researchers in a variety of disciplines to understand humankind in a temporal and historical context.
On the philosophical front, this involved a dynamic, dialectical theory
of history, such as the idealist philosophy of G.W.F. Hegel
(1770–1831) and the materialist philosophy of Karl Marx
(1818–1883).[35] On the scientific front the interest in development was
manifested in two mutually influential areas of investigation. On the
one hand there were the notions of natural history informed by research
in geology; of particular note in this regard was the uniformitarian
method of Sir Charles Lyell (1797–1875). On the other hand, there
were the varieties of a biological theory of evolution, especially those of
Jean Baptise de Lamarck (1744–1829), Darwin (1809–1882), and
Herbert Spencer (1820–1903).[36]

While Darwin was perhaps the exemplary component of the emergence of historicism in the nineteenth century, he was not without intellectual antecedents. Although it is certainly difficult to disentangle his
multiple intellectual influences, for the sake of clarity they may be

portrayed as deriving from two interrelated strands. On the one hand, it has been shown that Darwin gathered from his own life history and early cultural context much of the intellectual disposition seemingly necessary to effect a massive scientific revolution and to effect the precise kind of revolution with which he was associated. Family influences are apparent from his nearly notebooks,[37] and generally these are thought to have influenced his aversion to theological castings of natural science.[38] It has been suggested[39] that perhaps there was a family *Weltanschauung* regarding the then precarious relationship between religion and science. His grandfather, the distinguished early evolutionist, Erasmus Darwin (1731–1802), certainly contributed to the climate of naturalism that apparently imbued Darwin's early life.[40] Nevertheless, the politically astute Darwin tread cautiously when briefly alluding to the creation cosmology in the *Origin.*

On the other hand, it is quite clear that Darwin possessed an identifiable intellectual lineage deriving from more formal or academic sources. It is by now well-known that Darwin, relatively originative with regard to the human sciences, owed (and acknowledged) a strong intellectual debt to geology, and in particular to the work of Charles Lyell. Lyell, in turn, extended the work of the Scottish geologist James Hutton (1726–1797), whose research in natural history led him to confirm the continuous, historical, biographical nature of geological phenomena. In addition, Lyell was influenced by the critical history of Karsten Niebuhr (1733–1815).[41] Lyell's extension of Hutton, as evidenced in his monumental *Principles of Geology* (published in 1830–1833), affirmed the latter's uniformitarianism. The competing faction of the geology of the time, progressive catastrophism, was represented by such luminaries as Baron Georges Cuvier (1769–1839), a vigorous opponent of evolutionism, and William Smith (1769–1839), the inventor of stratigraphy.[42] The special creation hypothesis allowed but several thousand years to the earth's past. Thus, based on the arguments of (for example) David Hartley (1705–1757), any process short of miracle was explicitly precluded. Later, in his *Époques de la Nature* (published in 1778), Georges Buffon (1707–1788) extended the earth's age to about 75,000 years, still not sufficient time for the gradual evolution of species. However, the work of Lyell, Hutton, and other geologists provided indefinite millions of years to the evolutionary equation.

Darwin, originally trained in catastrophist geology, took Lyell's *Principles* with him on his celebrated voyage on the *Beagle.* After his return as a confirmed uniformitarian, Darwin and Lyell began a continuing conversation that was both intellectual and personal.[43] Lyell's version of uniformitarianism (a) suggested a principle of incessant change, (b) rejected all notions of final cause (and, in so doing, much of Christian cosmology), including the limitations and directionality imposed upon time and history, (c) suggested a cumulative interpretation of natural history, and (d) began (with later volumes of his *Principles)* focusing attention on the problem of life. In contrast, the proponents of catastrophism allowed nonobservable, even supernatural, influences to enter into their historical analyses (and thus were not necessarily at odds with a creation cosmology).

It is perhaps coincidental that at about the same time as the advent of Lyell's *Principles,* which contained a section considering life forms from the uniformitarian perspective, the German chemist, Friedrich Wöhler (1800–1882), first synthesized (in 1828) an organic compound, urea, from inorganic materials. Further, at about the same time, the Swedish chemist, Baron Jöns Jakob Berzelius (1779–1848), demonstrated that the same quantitative laws applied to both inorganic and organic matter. The landscape, fossils, rocks, and other inorganic materials which served as the focus of investigation for geology were found to be subject to a continuous, cumulative, and creative historical change—in short, to evolution. At the same time, biological forms, living and formerly living things, were being more intimately linked to the same laws and processes as their nonbiological counterparts.

Lyell's early conception of the history of life forms was, however, somewhat influenced by Lamarck. It remained for Darwin to produce a creative synthesis: the continuous historicism of Lyell combined with the mechanisms of evolution absent, or incorrect, in Lamarck.[44] This mechanism, believed to have been adapted from Thomas Robert Malthus (1766–1834) and from Lyell's translation of Augustin de Condolle (1778–1841) was, in the first instance, the "struggle for existence," and in the second, the "war of nature." Much has been made of the extent to which Darwin adopted (or was directly influenced by) Malthus's *Essay on Population.*[45] Certainly, the connection, although sometimes extraordinarily indirect, is well established.[46] It appears, however, that Darwin critically reinterpreted what had been a univocal term, arriving at a historically unique multivocal metaphor.[47] While asserting no definite link, Riegel described a certain similarity between Darwin's emerging view and the social organizational philosophy of Thomas Hobbes (1588–1679), which was also strongly steeped in a struggle for survival metaphor.[48] In any case, Darwin seized these notions and gradually transmuted them into the natural selection hypothesis.[49]

In sum, the concept of development emerging from Darwinism was characterized by (a) continuity of historical change (as against the catastrophists), (b) multidirectionality of evolution (as against Lamarck in biology and Marx in social history), (c) an ongoing or progressive character (as against, to some extent, Lyell's view of cyclical time), and (d) creativity and emergence (as against much of prevailing cosmology). As change and development became the universal principles of biological study, they came to be applied to the study of human societies[50] and human individuals. It is to this latter development that the attention of this paper now turns.

The emergence of developmental psychology

In brief section of child psychology, Peters refers to two general categories of influence in the emergence of developmental psychology in the nineteenth century.[51] The first, a quite practical social influence, consisted of pressure applied by educational administrators and social planners concerned with the large-scale education of a growing population of children. Such a development served to focus institutional attention upon the practical issues of ontogenesis.[52] The second was the history of evolution, especially insofar as it focused some attention on the scientific analysis of progress and suggested a certain measure of continuity both between human and animal and (significantly for inchoate developmental psychology) between adult and child. In the first instance, the rapid rise of comparative psychology, which focused on the continuity between human and animal, may be linked to the study of behavioral ontogenesis. Numerous contemporary authors have suggested that the study of ontogenesis is both theoretically and methodologically associated with comparative psychology.[53] It is known that George J. Romanes (1848–1894), who was one of the very early comparative psychologists, constructed his theoretical edifice from a thoroughly Darwinian foundation.[54] In his *Mental Evolution in Man* (published in 1889), Romanes developed an evolutionbased, empirical approach to the study of ontogenesis. As had Darwin, Romanes argued that natural selection could, in effect, cooperate with animal intelligence (and habit) in the development of ever more adaptive behavior.[55] Numerous attempts to articulate the relationship between ontogeny and phylogeny were made, the most influential of which was proposed by Ernst Haeckel (1834–1919). His well-known and widely misunderstood "biogenetic law" described the character of the relationship in terms of recapitulation, i.e. ontogeny recapitulates phylogeny.[56] In the early twentieth century G.Stanley Hall employed this principle to develop what was perhaps the first genuine (although never widely accepted) theory of human psychological development.[57]

Thus, the logic moved as follows. If, as Darwin[58] and early comparative psychologists suggested, there was descriptive and explanatory continuity (i.e. homology) between human and animal at a given point in time, and if this continuity could be extended longitudinally through childhood, then the adult of the species was, at least in part, a product of the child (or, with regard to recapitulation theory, a product of the adult of ancestral species[59]). In this way, the early attempts at applying the concept of development to the study of individuals may be viewed as efforts to understand the child within the adult. Further, as contemporary observers have noted, this understanding was neither motivated from nor designed to remain in purely academic strata.[60] Rather, it was to be used to enhance the development of individuals (and, by implication, the species and society) by providing, for example, an optimal educational context.

Evolutionism was epoch-making in psychology inasmuch as it brought the study of mental activity firmly into the realm of the natural sciences. Mind or human behavior, als much as features of human anatomy and physiology, had evolved gradually and as a function of the environment to which the organism was adapted. The process of natural selection operated upon mental as well as physical qualities of organisms; that is, both mental and physical qualities served in the continuing struggle for survival.[61] Such a view led to the development of the functional approach to psychology, a subsidiary of turn-of-the-century American contextual pragmatism. Clearly indebted to Darwin, functionalists such as William James (1842–1910), John Dewey (1859–1952), and James Rowland Angell (1869–1949) focused explicit attention upon psychological processes (as against static elements or abstracted structures) as they functioned in the business of adaptation.[62]

The extent to which Darwin himself was instrumental in these developments should not be underestimated. His last book, published in

1881, reported a series of studies on the behavior and experiential intelligence of earthworms. The mental qualities of earthworms, viewed in terms of their functional relationship to the broader ecological demands, were portrayed as continuous with, and representing the origin of, higher mental abilities.[63] Especially with respect to his behavioral investigations of more complex animals, Darwin emphasized the importance, but not pervasiveness, of the functional or adaptive features of behavior. In his *Expression of Emotions in Man and Animals*, which was concerned with the genesis of emotional expressions, Darwin was quite clear in describing some such expressions that were evidently devoid of functional significance. Notably, some of these afunctional behavioral patterns in adult individuals of a given species have their ontogenetic parallel in infant behavior. This linking of infant and adult behavioral patterns bespeaks a fundamentally developmental approach.[64]

The nineteenth century may be reviewed as a formative period in the development of developmental psychology.[65] In support of this argument, three major advances may be notet: (1) the appearance of the first psychological diary of the growth of a young child by Dietrich Tiedemann (1748–1803); (2) Friedrich August Carus' (1770–1808) efforts to develop a "general age-oriented science"; and (3) Adolphe Quetelet's (1796–1874) influential cross-sectional attempts to discover the influences on the course of human development.[66] In the same vein, Cairns and Ornstein call the period 1880–1912 the "era of discovery" in developmental psychology.[67] Darwin's "Biographical Sketch of an Infant" was one of the earliest attempts at careful, observational ontogenetic study.[68] Although other such descriptive, ideographic investigations were being conducted,[69] it was Darwin's evolutionism and the associated genetic method which nourished the roots of the emerging discipline of developmental psychology. In addition to evolutionism, the concomitant pangenesis theory, as well as the empirical studies of Preyer, Galton, and Hall strengthened the foundation.[70]

As alluded to above, Peters notes that prior to Darwin emphasis was placed on differences between human and animal on the one hand, and adult and child on the other.[71] After Darwin's argument for continuity in the former case, emphasis in human study shifted to the detection and consideration of similarities between adult and child.

> And if, under the influence of theology, men had tended to say before Darwin: "What a piece work is man," they now tend to say, under the influence of biology: "How wonderful are children and the beasts of the field."[72]

Certainly there was ontogenetic thinking prior to Darwin. Jean Jacques Rousseau's (1712–1778) *Emile*, a study of a fictitious individual through young adulthood, is an example of this,[73] as is the work in Germany of Tiedemann, Carus, and Johan Nikolas Tetens (1736–1807). Nevertheless, this work was largely unsystematic and scattered across the continents and centuries. Although some thinkers (e.g. Tetens) developed relatively powerful programmatic outlooks, they failed to infuse the larger intellectual and sociological climate of science with developmental thinking; in short, the developmental science they preferred failed to proliferate.[74]

Darwin, in his work of 1874, *The Descent of Man*, argued that the predominant social value system of the nineteenth century was in need of significant reorganization. Not only should the social system reflect scientific advance, but it should itself advance, i.e. keep pace with the critical developments in the scientific sector. In a sense, a dialectical— certainly interactional—relationship between science and society was proposed. Especially in the latter half of the century it became clear that they were both of a dynamic character and intimately interrelated in their developmental trajectories. Specifically, Darwin urged that (a) since morally and spiritually animals exhibit behaviour continuous with that of humans, society should entertain fewer "illusions" about the absolute uniqueness of human beings, an (b) since the relationship between adult and child is also characterized more by similarity than dissimilarity the absolute, ahistorical view of adults is also called into question. Thus, not only is an interspecies comparative method advanced, but both intraspecies—historical and cultural—and intra-individual—developmental—approaches are suggested, particularly with respect to human study.

In part, the heritage of Darwin may, today, be epitomized by the placement of the study of ontogenetic development in a multidisciplinary framework which incorporates historical (evolutionary) and sociocultural influences on the individual. This contribution has had an impact on developmental psychology through, for example, the relatively recent interest in elaborating contextual views of development,[75] that is, perspectives which view person and context as reciprocally interactive across the history of the individual and the collective. Of course, this contribution may also be found in the work of leading biologists of the day, who similarly stress that an organism's ontogeny must be understood as involving reciprocal, dynamically interactive development in a changing (sociocultural) context. For instance, consider the view of the comparative and developmental psychologist Gollin,[76] who, in commenting about the relation between organism and environment, says that:

> The relationship between organisms and environments are not interactionist, as interaction implies that organism and environment are separate entities that come together at an interface. Organism and environment constitute a single life process ... For analytic convenience, we may treat various aspects of a living system and various external environmental and biological features as independently definable properties. Analytical excursions are an essential aspect of scientific inquiry, but they are hazardous if they are primarily reductive. An account of the *collective behavior* of the parts as an organized entity is a necessary complement to a reductive analytic program, and serves to restore the information content lost in the course of the reductive excursion.... In any event, the relationships that contain the sources of change are those between organized systems and environments, not between heredity and environment.

Furthermore, consider the position of the geneticist Lewontin[77] who, in discussing the character of the constraints genes impose on the context, notes that:

> The question is not whether the nature of the human genotype is relevant to social organization, but whether the former constrains the latter in a nontrivial way, or whether the two levels are *effectively* decoupled.
> ... [In] fact, constraints at one level may be destroyed by higher level activity. No humans can fly by flapping their arms because of anatomical and physiological constraints that reflect the human genome. But humans do fly, by using machines that are the product of social organization and that could not exist without very complex social interaction and evolution. As another example, the memory capacity of a single individual is limited, but social organization, through written records and the complex institutions associated with them, makes all knowledge recoverable for each individual. Far from being constrained by lower-level limitations, culture transcends them and feeds back to lower levels to relieve constraints. Social organization, and human culture in particular, are best understood as negating constraints rather than as being limited by them.

Conclusions

The present analysis suggests that Darwinism, steeped as it was in the sociohistorical context of the nineteenth century, supported, if not fostered, an interest in the study of behavioral ontogeny. As has been described by other observers, early developmental psychologists (e.g. James Mark Baldwin, Wilhelm Preyer, G. Stanley Hall) drew a measure of sustenance from evolutionism and then turned to face the fresh contact of their own social or intellectual milieu. In so doing, the contributions of Darwinism were selected and molded to fit unwonted social, cultural, historical, and intellectual contingencies, as well as personal and political motivations. Darwinism was sufficiently multifaceted and ambiguous to propagate developmental theories that very soon became mutually exclusive.

That is, perhaps one of the greatest contributions of Darwinism to the emergence of developmental psychology may derive from its accentuation of underlying general issues pertaining to ontogeny. Among these abiding problems are such now classical polarities as nature vs. nurture, continuity vs. discontinuity of development, and unidirectionality vs. non- or multidirectionality of temporal progression. To an extent that cannot be further elaborated here, Darwinism provided an intellectual basis for several distinct positions along each of those continua.[78] Thus, it is reasonable to assert that the structure of several developmental theories may cut across these salient issues in qualitatively different ways. In this way, contemporary developmental theories may share a certain intellectual lineage, embrace a generalized historical or developmental approach to human phenomena, and at the same time have relatively dichotomous theoretical positions.

- It would appear that, while contemporary developmental psychologies share to some extent a common antecedent, the early developmentalists exercised selective perception in their adaptation of both their immediate intellectual predecessors and the evolutionary model. The modulating factors in the apparent selectivity may very well be idiosyncratic; but their genetic nature may be identified with a rather high degree of confidence. Certainly if, as general sociologists of knowledge suggest, the psychologies produced by originative figures in the field are influenced by the historical (social, religious, intellectual) context, the selectivity exercised, the creative synthesis, may be similarly governed. The many interesting questions about how and why specific transitions occured in developmental theory and method are left to later investigations.[79]

Notes

1 Edward H.Carr, *What is History?* (New York: Vintage Books, 1961).
2 Arnold Thackray, "Making History", *Isis* 72 (1981): 7–10. See also R.G. Colling-wood, *The idea of History* (Oxford: Oxford University Press, 1956).
3 See also Paul B. Baltes, "Life-span Developmental Psychology: Some Converging Observations on History and Theory," in *Life-span Development and Behavior,* vol.2, ed. by Paul B. Baltes and Orville G.Brim, Jr. (New York: Academic Press, 1979), pp.256–279; Paul B. Baltes "Life-span developmental psychology: Observations on history and theory revisited," in *Developmental Psychology: Historical and Philosophical Perspectives,* ed. by Richard M. Lerner (Hillsdale, NJ: Lawrence Erlbaum, 1983); Robert B. Cairns and Peter A. Ornstein, "Developmental Psychology," in *The First Century of Experimental Psychology,* ed. by Eliot Hearst (Hillsdale, NJ: Lawrence Erlbaum, 1979); John C. Cavanaugh, "Early Developmental Theories: A Brief Review of Attempts of Organize Developmental Data Prior to 1925," *Journal of the History of the Behavioral Sciences* 17 (1981): 38–47; Karl J. Groffmann, "Life-span Developmental Psychology in Europe: Past and Present," in *Life-span Developmental Psychology: Research and Theory,* ed. by L.R. Goulet and Paul B.Baltes (New York: Academic Press, 1970), pp.54–68; Robert J.Havighurst, "History of Developmental Psychology: Socialization and Personality Development through the Life Span," in *Life-span Developmental Psychology: Personality and Socialization,* ed. by Paul B. Baltes and K.Warner Schaie (New York: Academic Press, 1973), pp.3–24; Richard M.Lerner, David F.Hultsch, and Roger A.Dixon, "Contextualism and the Character of Developmental Psychology in the 1970s," *Annals of the New York Academy of Sciences,* in press; Guenther Reinert, "Prolegomena to a History of Life-span Developmental Psychology," in *Life-span Developmental and Behavior,* vol.2, ed. by Paul B. Baltes and Orville G.Brim, Jr. (New York: Academic Press, 1979), pp.205–254; and Robert R. Sears, "Your Ancients Revisited: A History of Child Development," in *Review of Child Development Research,* vol.5, ed. by E.Mavis Hetherington (Chicago: University of Chicago Press, 1975).
4 See, e.g. Baltes and Reese, "History;" Cairns and Ornstein, "Developmental Psychology;" Cavanaugh, "Developmental Theories;" Roger A. Dixon and John R. Nesselroade, "Pluralism and Correlational Analysis in Developmental Psychology; Historical Commonalities," in Lerner, *Developmental Psychology;* Reinert, "Prolegomena;" and Joachim F.Wohlwill, *The Study of Behavioral Development* (New York: Academic Press, 1973).
5 Stephen Toulmin and June Goodfield, *The Discovery of Time* (Chicago: University of Chicago Press, 1965).
6 For example, Cavanaugh, "Developmental Theories;" Roger A. Dixon and Richard M.Lerner, "A History of Developmental Psychology," in *Developmental Psychology: An Advanced Textbook,* ed. by Michael E.Lamb and Marc H.Bornstein (Hillsdale, NJ: Lawrence Erlbaum, 1983, in press).
7 Front Grant Allen's *English Worthies* (1888), as quoted, with qualification, in John T.Merz, *A History of European Thought in the Nineteenth Century,* vol.2 (New York: Dover, 1965), pp.607–608.
8 Ernst Mayr, "The Nature of the Darwinian Revolution," *Science* 176 (1972): 981–989. See also Toulmin and Goodfield, *Discovery;* and Wolf Lepenies, *Das Ende*

der Naturgeschichte: Wandel kultureller Selbstverständlichkeit in den Wissenschaften des 18. und 19. Jahrhunderts (Baden-Baden: Suhrkamp, 1978).

9 See Henry Misiak and Virginia S.Sexton, *History of Psychology in Overview* (New York: Grune and Stratton, 1966); Wohlwill, *Behavioral Development;* and Cavanaugh, "Developmental Theories."

10 Sheldon H.White, "The Learning-maturation Controversy: Hall to Hull," *Merrill-Palmer-Quarterly* 14 (1968): 187–196; quotation is from p.187.

11 Dixon and Lerner, "History."

12 Karl Mannheim, *Ideology and Utopia* (New York: Harcourt, Brace & World, 1936); Karl Mannheim, "The Problem of Generations," in *Essays on the Sociology of Knowledge* (London: Routledge & Kegan Paul, 1952); Allan R. Buss, "The Emerging Field of the Sociology of Psychological Knowledge," *American Psychologist* 30 (1975): 988–1002. It should be noted that the method adopted in the present chapter is not a specifically Mannheimian sociology of knowledge, with which there are many well-known difficulties. Rather, the interest is to emphasize that multiple interdependent sources converged and informed the consequent interconnected programs of developmental psychology. This general approach has been recently described by Nico Stehr, "The Magic Triangle: In Defense of a General Sociology of Knowledge," *Philosophy of the Social Sciences* 11 (1981): 225–229.

13 Buss, "Emerging Field."

14 Ibid., See also *Psychology in Social Context,* ed. Allan R. Buss, (New York: Irvington, 1979).

15 See, e.g., Paul B. Baltes, Hayne W.Reese, and Lewis P.Lipsitt, "Life-span Developmental Psychology," *Annual Review of Psychology* 31 (1980): 65–110; Lerner, Hultsch, and Dixon, "Contextualism."

16 See Peter L.Berger, "Towards a Sociological Understanding of Psychoanalysis," *Social Research* 32 (1965): 26–41; Peter Berger, Brigitte Berger, and Hansfried Kellner, *The Homeless Mind: Modernization and Consciousness* (New York: Vintage Books, 1973).

17 Herbert E.Barnes, *An Intellectual and Cultural History of the Western World,* vol.3 (New York: Dover, 1965).

18 Barnes, *Intellectual History,* p.950; See also Dixon and Nesselroade, "Pluralism."

19 Berger, "Sociological Understanding."

20 Loren Eiseley, *Darwin's Century* (Garden City, NY: Doubleday, 1958).

21 Michael Ruse, *The Darwinian Revolution* (Chicago: University of Chicago Press, 1979).

22 Toulmin and Goodfield, *Discovery.*

23 Collingwood, *Idea.*

24 Chamber's book went through 12 anymous editions before his death, and the subsequent identification of him as the author, in 1884. See also Arthur O.Lovejoy, "The Argument for Organic Evolution before the *Origin of Species,* 1830–1858," in *Forerunners of Darwin 1745–1859,* ed. by Bentley Glass, Owsei Temkin, and William L.Straus, Jr. (Baltimore: The Johns Hopkins Press, 1968); Thomas H.Huxley, *Man's Place in Nature* (Ann Arbor: University of Michigan Press, 1959; first published in 1863).

25 P.J. Bowler, "The Changing Meaning of 'Evolution'," *Journal of the History of Ideas* 36 (1975): 95–114; Ruse, *Darwinian Revolution.*

26 Toulmin and Goodfield, *Discovery,* p.232. It may also have begun to assume the

character of what Robert A.Nisbet, *The Sociological Tradition* (New York: Basic Books, 1966), termed a unit idea.

27 Michel Foucault, *The Order of Things: An Archeology of the Human Sciences* (New York: Vintage Books, 1970); N.C. Gillespie, *Charles Darwin and the Problem of Creation* (Chicago: University of Chicago Press, 1979).

28 Gillespie, *Charles Darwin*. Among theologians, however, the reaction to Darwinism was hardly one of complete surrender. Indeed, J.R. Moore, *The Post-Darwinian Controversies: A Study of the Protestant Struggle to Come to Terms with Darwin in Great Britain and America* (Cambridge: Cambridge University Press, 1979), described the reaction as occurring in the form of three identifiable strands. These strands are: (a) the Christian anti-Darwinians rejected Darwinism primarily for scientific and philosophical reasons, eschewing the more theologically cast Biblical appeals of their twentieth century descendants; (b) the Christian Darwinists incorporated a non-Darwinian (usually neo-Larmarckian) theory of evolution into their theology; and (c) the Christian Darwinians paradoxically maintained that only an orthodox theology could embrace an orthodox Darwinism.

29 David L.Hull, "Charles Darwin and Nineteenth-Century Philosophies of Science," in *Foundations of Scientific Method: The Nineteenth Century*, ed. by Ronald N.Giere and Richard S.Westfall (Bloomington: Indiana University Press, 1973). It should be noted that Robert Nisbet, History of the Idea or Progress (New York: Basic Books, 1970), warns against exaggerating the number and intensity of Darwin's critics.

30 See Thomas S.Kuhn, *The Structure of Scientific Revolutions*, 2nd ed. (Chicago: University of Chicago Press, 1970); Mannheim, *Ideology*; and Ruse, *Darwinian Revolution*.

31 Eiseley, *Darwin's Century*, p.331.

32 Lucretius, *On the Nature of the Universe* (Baltimore, MD: Penguin Books, 1951). See also Nisbet, *History*.

33 Maurice Mandelbaum, *History, Man, and Reason* (Baltimore: The Johns Hopkins Press, 1971), p.41.

34 Ibid., p.43.

35 The *Naturphilosophie* of Johann Gottfried von Herder (1744–1803) and Friedrich W.J. von Schelling (1775–1854), as well as the *Entwicklungs* and *Bildungs* literature of such as Johann Wolfgang von Goethe (1749–1832), may have also been influential in this regard.

36 Also deserving note (*vide infra*) is the embryological recapitulation theory of J.F. Meckel (1781–1833), Karl Ernst von Baer (1792–1876), and Ernst Heinrich Haeckel (1834–1919).

37 Edward Manier, *The Young Darwin and his Cultural Circle* (Dordrecht, Holland: D.Reidel, 1978).

38 Gillespie, *Charles Darwin;* Howard E.Gruber, *Darwin on Man: A Psychological Study of Scientific Creativity* (New York: Dutton, 1974).

39 Gruber, *Darwin on Man.*

40 Erasmus Darwin's evolutionism bore resemblance to that of Lamarck.

41 Toulmin and Goodfield, *Discovery.*

42 Walter F.Cannon, "The Uniformitarian-Catastrophist Debate," *Isis* 51 (1960): 38–55; Charles Couston Gillespie, *Genesis and Geology* (Cambridge: Harvard University Press, 1951); Rachel Lauden, "The Role of Methodology in Lyell's Science," *Studies in the History and Philosophy of Science* 13 (1982): 215–249; William

Whewell, "Review of *Principles of Geology,* vol.2, by Charles Lyell," *Quarterly Review*47 (1832): 103–132.

43 Charles Darwin, *The Autobiography of Charles Darwin* (New York: W.W. Norton, 1958); Manier, *Young Darwin.*

44 See, e.g. Charles Coulston Gillispie, "Lamarck and Darwin in the History of Science," in *Forerunners of Darwin: 1745-1859,* ed. by Bentley Glass, Owsei Temkin, and William L.Straus, Jr. (Baltimore: The Johns Hopkins Press, 1968).

45 Malthus' essay, written in 1798, was read by Darwin in 1838.

46 P.J. Bowler, "Malthus, Darwin, and the Concept of Struggle," *Journal of the History of Ideas* 37 (1976): 631–650; Steven Jay Gould, "Darwin Vindicated," *New York Review of Books* 26 (13) (1979): 36–38; Ernst Mayr, "Evolution through Natural Selection: How Darwin Discovered this Highly Unconventional Theory," *American Scientist* 65 (1977): 321–328; S.S. Schweber, "The Origin of the *Origin* Revisited," *Journal of the History of Biology* 10 (1977): 229–316.

47 Manier, *Young Darwin.*

48 Klaus F.Riegel, "Influence of Economic and Political Ideologies on the Development of Developmental Psychology," *Psychological Bulletin* 78 (1972): 129–141.

49 The theory of natural selection has its own historical controversy. It is well known that Alfred Russel Wallace (1823–1913) independently developed the same principle (see his *Contributions to the Theory of Natural Selection,* which was published in 1870). The unexpected appearance of Wallace's idea in the late 1850s advanced Darwin's plans for publishing the *Origins.* A similar principle was described by Edward Blyth (1810–1873) even earlier (in the 1830s), although there is some dispute as to whether Blyth attempted to prove the fixity or evolution of species. It has also been suggested that Patrick Mathew developed at least the rudiments of the natural selection hypothesis in 1831. All of this intellectual convergence, of course, corroborates the notion that the theory of evolution by natural selection arose in nothing less than a fertile intellectual climate. As Robert K.Merton, "Resistance to the Systematic Study of Multiple Discoveries in Science," *European Journal of Sociology* 4 (1963): 237–282, would suggest, there were multiple, simultaneous discoveries exhibiting the same general features as the evolutionary theory of Darwin. For further discussions of the Darwin-Wallace controversy see A.C. Brackman, *A Delicate Arrangement: The Strange Case of Charles Darwin and Alfred Russell Wallace* (New York: Times Books, 1980); Loren C.Eiseley, *Darwin and the Mysterious Mr. X: New Light on the Evolutionists* (New York: Dutton, 1979); Stephen Jay Gould, *Ontogeny and Phylogeny* (Cambridge: Harvard University Press, 1977); Gould, "Darwin Vindicated;" and B.J. Loewenberg, *Darwin, Wallace, and the Theory of Natural Selection* (Cambridge:Arlington, 1957).

50 For example, it was Herbert Spencer, who had long espoused a total, albeit Lamarkian, evolutionism, who first used the phrase "survival of the fittest," and who proffered what he called the "developmental hypothesis." In his *The Principles of Psychology,* vol.1. 3d. ed., (New York: Appleton, 1886) Spencer explicitly asserts that in order to understand present mental organization one must trace the successive stages of organization.

51 R.S. Peters ed., *Brett's History of Psychology* (Cambridge: The M.I.T. Press, 1965).

52 Sears, "Ancients Revisited."

53 Baltes, "History;" Cairns and Ornstein, "Developmental Psychology;" Gilbert

Gottleib, "Comparative Psychology and Ethology," in Hearst, *First Century,* Richard M.Lerner, *Concepts and Theories of Human Development* (Reading, Mass.: Addison-Wesley, 1976); T.C. Schneirla, "The Concept of Development in Comparative Psychology," in *The Concept of Development,* ed. Dale B.Harris (Minneapolis: University of Minnesota Press, 1957); T.C. Schneirla, "Behavioral Development and Comparative Psychology," *Quarterly Review of Biology* 41 (1966): 283–302.

54 L.S. Hearnshaw, *A Short History of British Psychology 1840–1940* (New York: Barnes and Noble, 1964); Sheldon H.White, "The Idea of Development in Developmental Psychology," in Lerner, *Developmental Psychology.* Romanes was the protege to whom Darwin bequeathed much of his unpublished observations of animal characteristics and behavior.

55 George J.Romanes, *Mental Evolution in Animals* (New York: Appleton, 1884); George J.Romanes, *Mental Evolution in Man* (New York: Appleton, 1889); see also George J.Romanes, *Darwin, and After Darwin* (London: Longmans, Green, 1900).

56 Gould, *Ontogeny;* Arthur O.Lovejoy, "Recent Criticism of the Darwinian Theory of Recapitulation: Its Grounds and its Initiator," in Glass, Temkin, and Straus, eds., *Forerunners.*

57 G.Stanley Hall, *Adolescence* (New York: Appleton, 1904); see Edward Lee Thorndike, "The Newest Psychology," *Educational Review* 28 (1904): 217–227.

58 In his *Descent of Man,* published in 1871, and *Expression of Emotions in Man and Animals,* published in 1872.

59 Stephen Jay Gould, *Ontogeny and Phylogeny* (Cambridge: Harvard University Press, 1977).

60 Cairns and Ornstein, "Developmental Psychology;" Peters, *Brett's History;* Reinert, "Prolegomena;" Sears, "Ancients Revisited."

61 Hearnshaw, *Short History.*

62 John Rowland Angell, "The Province of Functional Psychology", *Psychological Review* 14 (1907): 61–91; John Dewey, "The Reflex Arc Concept in Psychology." *Psychological Review* 3 (1896); John Dewey, *The Influence of Darwin on Psychology* (New York: H.Holt, 1910), 357–370; Philip P.Wiener, *Evolution and the Founders of Pragmatism* (Cambridge: Harvard University Press, 1949).

63 Charles Darwin, *The Formation of Vegetable Mould Through the Action of Worms* (London: John Murray, 1881).

64 Michael T.Ghiselin, *The Triumph of the Darwinian Method* (Berkeley: University of California Press, 1969), remarks that the core of a concept of psychological regression is present in Darwin's *Expression.*

65 Reinert, "Prolegomena;" see also Groffman, "Life-span."

66 See, e.g. Dietrich Tiedemann, "Beobachtungen über die Entwickelung der Seelenfähigkeiten bei Kindern." *Hessische Beiträge zur Gelehrsamkeit und Kunst* 2 (2–3; whole No.6–7) (1787); Friedrich August Carus, *Psychologie: Zweiter Theil: Specialpsychologie* (Leipzig: Barth and Kummer (1808), or *Geschichte der Psychologie* (Leipzig: Barth and Kummer, 1808); Adolphe Quetelet, *Physique sociale ou essai sur l'homme et la développement de ses Facultés* (Paris: Bachelier, 1869).

67 Cairns and Ornstein, "Developmental Psychology."

68 Charles Darwin, "Biographical Sketch of an Infant," *Mind* 2 (1877): 285–294.

69 See W.Dennis ed., *Historical Readings in Developmental Psychology* (New York: Appleton-Century-Crofts, 1972).

70 Francis Galton, *Inquiries into Human Faculty and its Development* (London:

266   Dixon and Lerner

Macmillan, 1883); G.Stanley Hall, "The Contents of Children's Minds," *Princeton Review* 11 (1883): 249–272; Wilhelm Preyer, *Die Seele des Kindes* (Leipzig: Fernau, 1882); Wilhelm Preyer, *Mental Development in the Child* (New York: D.Appleton, 1893); see also Don C.Charles, "Historical Antecedents of Life-span Developmental Psychology," in Goulet and Baltes, eds., *Life-span.*

71   Peters, *Brett's History.* There were, however, some notable exceptions to this, e.g. Julien Offray de La Mettrie who argued in *L'homme Machine,* published in 1747, that, with appropriate education, apes could behave and communicate intelligently.

72   Peters, *Brett's History,* p.732.

73   Jean-Jacques Rousseau, *Émile ou de l'éducation* (Amsterdam: Néaulme, 1762).

74   Partly because of the somewhat more active pre-Darwinian developmental psychology in Germany, and the subsequently greater degree of pre- and post-Darwinian continuity, Reinert, *Prolegomena,* warns against overestimating the impact of Darwin on the origin of developmental psychology. More importantly, perhaps, because much of the German developmental psychology of this period had its roots in philosophy, evolutionary thinking was more slowly assimilated. It is not surprising, therefore, that when psychology is conceived as a subdiscipline of philosophy, predominantly biological principles would play only a minor role in its development. Ghiselin, *Triumph,* discusses this latter issue.

75   Richard M.Lerner, David F.Hultsch, and Roger A.Dixon, "Contextualism and the Character of Developmental Psychology in the 1970s," *Annals of the New York Academy of Sciences* (in press); See also Urie Bronfenbrenner, "Toward an Experimental Ecology of Human Development," *American Psychologist* 32 (1977): 513–531; Theodore R.Sarbin, "Contextualism: A World View for Modern Psychology," in *Nebraska Symposium on Motivation, 1976,* ed. by J.K. Cole (Lincoln: University of Nebraska Press, 1977).

76   Eugene S.Gollin, "Development and Plasticity," in *Developmental Plasticity: Behavioral and Biological Aspects of Variations in Development,* ed. by Eugene S.Gollin (New York: Academic Press, 1981), p.231–232.

77   Richard C.Lewontin, "On Constraints and Adaptation," *The Behavioral and Brain Sciences* 4 (1981): 244–245.

78   Dixon and Lerner, "History."

79   The interested reader is also referred to the earlier reviews cited in the foregoing.

Evolutionary Thought and the Doctrine of Ancestral Immanence

by Richard Lowry

Among the many famous names associated with the University of Jena is of course the name of Ernst Haeckel (1834–1919), whose book *Natürliche Schöpfungsgeschichte* (1868) was published just nine years after Darwin's *Origin of Species* (1859). In his own day Haeckel was widely known as a competent biologist, as an ardent spokesman for the new Darwinian worldview, and as a spirited expositor of his own version of "monistic philosphy." Nowadays we remember him chiefly for his promulgation of what he called "the fundamental biogenetic law," which held that ontogenesis, the development of the individual, is a "brief, accelerated repetition" of the phylogenesis of the species (Haeckel 1868: 276). Thus the familiar formula "ontogeny recapitulates phylogeny." Although the only firm empirical basis for this law was an assortment of embryological observations, Haeckel considered these facts to be of surpassing importance, because they showed in the clearest possible way the "inner causal connection between ontogeny and phylogeny" (p.651). He believed this connection to be so strong and deep as to extend throughout the whole range of ontogenetic phenomena, including even those pertaining to "that highest of all problems, the question of the place of Man in nature" (p.262).

Darwin, too, had been impressed by the facts of embryology, although he was apparently chary of elevating recapitulation to the level of a fundamental law (Darwin 1859: 439–450). Be that as it may, Haeckel's basic concept of an "inner causal" phylogenetic connection was entirely congenial with both the letter and the spirit of Darwinian theory. It was especially congenial with that portion of the theory that centered upon the assumptions of evolutionary gradualism and thoroughgoing phylogenetic continuity. One of the main watchwords of the new Darwinian worldview was the Latin dictum quoted by Darwin himself in *The Origin of Species, natura non facit saltum* (Darwin 1859: 194, 471). Its meaning, when applied to the evolutionary process, was that nature does not move by leaps and bounds, but rather by small steps and continuous gradations. The evolutionary changes that take place within a species from one generation to the next amount in every case to nothing more than minute modifications of already existing characteristics, in accordance with the laws of inheritance and natural selection. It is as though each characteristic of a species were a musical theme, which in the course of time comes to have increasingly complex variations played upon it. The eventual form of the theme might seem quite different from the original, but the basic, primordial motif is still there, and it can still be heard if one knows how to listen for it.

This is what I refer to in the title of this paper as the doctrine of ancestral immanence. It was a very prominent feature of late nineteenth-century evolutionary thought, and its appeal to the imagination of that period is certainly not difficult to understand. For it suggested that traces of a species' phyologenetic past might still be dwelling within it, and even on occasion visibly manifesting themselves. The appeal to the imagination was of course especially strong in reference to the human species. In evolving to its present stage, the human species had accumulated a great host of phylogenetic ancestors. The doctrine of ancestral immanence suggested that these primitive forebears, even now, might still be thumping within the human breast.

This compelling imagery captured the imagination of quite a number of intellectuals of that period, including some prominent figures in the history of psychology. But of course it was not just the imagery that captured the imagination. There was also a kind of implacable logic to the Darwinian evolutionary theory of that day. It went something like this: *If* evolutionary theory is true, *then* these further conclusions must also be true.

Thus we find William James (1842–1910) writing in his *Principles of Psychology* of 1890 of the "instinct" that must be supposed to underlie such human acitivities as hunting, fighting, violence, cruelty, and the like: "If evolution and the survival of the fittest be true at all, the destruction of prey and of human rivals *must* have been among the most important of man's primitive functions, the fighting and the chasing instincts *must* have become ⌊deeply⌋ ingrained.... It is just because human blood-thirstiness is such a primitive part of us that it is so hard to eradicate." (James, 1890, vol.2: 412). This passage presupposes something about the phylogenetic history of the human species that is still far from certain, namely, that we stem from blood-thirsty carnivorous stock. It presupposes some other things as well, which I will not take time here to examine. The main point I want to make is that James saw ancestral immanence as the direct logical consequence of the Darwinian theory of evolution.

Although the influence of evolutionary thought can be seen on almost every page of James' *Principles*, his involvement with the question of ancestral immanence appeared chiefly in his chapter on "Instinct," especially in the portion of that chapter that dealt with human instincts. And it is worth noting at this point that James introduced his section on human instincts with a reference to another famous *Gelehrter* of this University, William Thierry Preyer (1841–1897), in whose honor this conference is being held. Preyer had begun his own chapter on instinct in *Die Seele des Kindes* (1882), with a word of caution and restraint that could hardly have appealed to someone inspired, as James was, with grand, sweeping visions of primeval forebears still thumping within the human breast. Preyer had written: "Human instinctive motivations are few in number and (except for the sexual) difficult to recognize once earliest youth is past" (Preyer 1882: 174). James quoted the passage only to deny it, for to him the human species seemed shot through and through with instinctual impulsions. These included not only such specific behavioral instincts as Preyer was willing to recognize (grasping, sucking, sitting up, locomotion, etc.), but also such overarching instinctual impulsions as sympathy, jealousy, hoarding, curiosity, sociability, cleanliness, modesty, hunting and fighting, to name only a few. The discussion was heavily laced througout with references to comparable instincts in animals, with speculations about the utility of such instincts in the earlier evolutionary stages of the human species, and with inferences to the effect that these instinctual impulsions must still be with us as "primitive elements in our nature" (James 1890, vol.2: 428).

James described Preyer's *Die Seele des Kindes* as "a careful little work" (James 1890, vol.2: 403). I think it would be proper to describe his own chapter on instinct as an "un-careful little work." Certainly it was out of keeping with his accustomed tendency to grind every theoretical principle "in the teeth of irreducible and stubborn facts" (Perry 1936, vol.2: 40). In James' defense, however, it must be added that his rather uncritical acceptance of the imagery of "primitive elements in our nature" did not play a preeminent role in his overall psychology. This was because he saw these primitive elements as tempered by the effects of "habit," and as capable of being directed by "attention" and controlled by "will." I have examined these central conceptions of James' psychology at greater length elsewhere (Lowry 1982: 123–141), and one of the other participants in this conference will also be discussing them in his paper (Robert J.Richards, "William James'

Theory of Mental Evolution"). For present purposes it will suffice to say that James, despite his embracement of the logic and imagery of ancestral immanence, was able to avoid being completely carried away by it.

The same cannot be said of James' American contemporary, the developmental psychologist G.Stanley Hall (1844–1924), who wrote toward the end of his life that reflection upon the all-encompassing implications of evolutionary principles had given him "the deepest intellectual satisfaction" that he had ever known. In his autobiographical statement of 1924 Hall recounted how the evolutionary writings of Darwin, Spencer, and Haeckel, among others, had opened up large new vistas for him, leading him "to realize that everything within and without was hoary with age, so that in most experiences we are dealing only with the topmost branches of vast but deeply buried trees" (Hall 1924: 358–359). In his psychological writings this vision made its fullest appearance in his two-volume work of 1904, *Adolescence.* There is, he wrote, a "general psychonomic law" through which "we are influenced in our deeper, more temperamental dispositions by the life-habits and codes of conduct of we know not what unnumbered hosts of ancestors, [so] that our souls are echo-chambers in which their whispers reverberate" (Hall 1904, vol.2: 61).

As it happened, Hall's own soul was an echo-chamber not only for the general evolution notion of ancestral immanence, but also for the much more specific concept of recapitulation. Indeed, a large part of his interest in developmental psychology was impelled by his conviction that the psychological development of the child can be seen as "the great revealer of the [phylogenetic] past of the race" (Hall 1904, vol.2: 94). Thus, the evolutionary history of the human species must once have passed through a fish-like stage. Anatomically, this ancestry is recapitulated by the gill-like formations that appear in the development of the human embryo. Psychologically, it is recapitulated by such behavioral instances as the following: Newborn babies make "peculiar paddling or swimming movements;" these are clearly "vestiges of watery life." Young children often enjoy swaying from side to side or back and forth: "this suggests the slow oscillatory movements used by fish." And of course there is the fact that children "after the first shock and fright take the greatest delight in water;" this aquatic passion of childhood must surely have originated on that "shore where [life] forms first emerged [from the sea] and became amphibian." (vol.2: 192–195)

Indeed, there was very little about child development that Hall did not see as evidence of recapitulation. What shall we make, for example, of that quite un-fish-like "horror of water" that we sometimes find in children? Obviously it is a recapitulation of our more recent simian ancestry, as are the prehensile reflexes of infants, the young child's enjoyment of climbing, and his inveterate fear of thunder, lightning, and snakes. (vol.2:214ff.)

It would be an understatement to say that Hall's vision of ancestral immanence sometimes carried him to extremes. The more accurate statement would be that it often led him to proclaim veritable humbug. Here is one of my favorite examples, and a timely one at that. Apropos that fish-like state of our phylogenetic history, Hall noted that women more often than men choose drowning as a method of suicide. The reason for this is easy to see. It is that "woman's body and soul is phyleti-cally older and more primitive." Women are therefore closer than men to the primeval fish-like ancestors of the species, and thus more strongly attracted to the water's embrace. Indeed, some women "can hardly bathe without an almost imperative impulse to plunge in forever, as if to go back to an old love." Hall even cited Havelock Ellis to the effect that the increasing incidence of drowning suicides among women indicates that "women are becoming more womanly" (vol.2:194).

Although I do not wish to suggest that the doctrine of ancestral immanence led its psychological proponents to the espousal of humbug in every instance, it is true all the same that any thorough historical treatment of the topic would have to devote many pages to the recounting of such humbug. The present treatment is of course not a thorough one. For the sake of brevity I have presented only a very brief glance at the topic. William James and G.Stanley Hall, the two American psychologists whom I have mentioned, were certainly not the only psychological thinkers of their day to fall under the influence of the logic and imagery of ancestral immanence. Even today, among psychologists and others, the doctrine is far from dead, as is evidenced by those periodically resurfacing visions of man as "naked ape" and by the current vitality of that old-new movement lately known as "socio-biology." And although these newer versions are certainly far more sophisticated than some of the older ones, I think it is fair to say that even they are not always entirely free of humbug.

And yet, despite all the humbug, I think it must be acknowledged that the idea most deeply underlying the doctrine of ancestral immanence has on the whole broadened and enriched our understanding of human nature. It is that humankind has a very long history, and that the facts of that history cannot be entirely unrelated to the facts of the present. Any idea can lead to humbug, but that does not mean that it must be so necessarily. Even in the late nineteenth century there were some who took the evolutionary idea very seriously, but nonetheless kept their wits about them. Certainly one of the most level-headed of these was William Preyer. In his Foreword to the first edition of *Die Seele des Kindes* Preyer expressed his view that the tablet of the human mind is "even before birth inscribed with many marks," which are the traces of our long evolutionary history. But these tracemarks are by no means easy to read. One cannot simply look at them and say, here is the mark of a fish, here of an ape, and so on. For the most part these marks are "unreadable, even unrecognizable and invisible;" and even when they are visible, they are so "blurred and indistinct . . . that one could easily mistake the mind for a *tabula rasa.*" It is only in the earliest stages of childhood that these evolutionary tracemarks can be seen with any clarity at all. And even here they are but a "cryptograph [*Geheimschrift*], difficult to recognize and decipher" (Preyer 1882:vi–vii).

Preyer acknowledged that one of the main aims of his study of child development was to detect and decode these cryptic evolutionary tracemarks. It is to his credit that he pursued the task with intellectual discipline and restraint. William James called *Die Seele des Kindes* a "careful little work." I do not know why he called it "little"—but "careful" it most certainly was! Even today, a century after ist publication, *Die Seele des Kindes* stands out as a model of intellectual carefulness. It presents no gripping visions of naked apes, fish-like recapitulations, or anything of the sort. Its many systematic observations on the facts of child development are of course informed by theoretical considerations—but they are not squeezed into a theoretical mold. One could surely wish that there were much more of such intellectual carefulness in the past and present of our science!

References

Darwin, C. (1859). *On the origin of species.* London: John Murray.
Haeckel, E. (1868). *Natürliche Schöpfungsgeschichte.* Berlin: Georg Reimer.
Hall, G.S. (1904). *Adolescence* (2 vols.). New York: Appleton.
—(1924). *Life and confessions of a psychologist.* New York: Appleton.
James, W. (1890). *The principles of psychology* (2 vols.). New York: Henry Holt.

Lowry, R. (1982). *The evolution of psychological theory: A critical history of concepts and presuppositions* (2d ed.). New York: Aldine.

Perry, R.B. (1936). *The thought and character of William James* (2 vols.). Boston: Little, Brown.

Preyer, W. (1882). *Die Seele des Kindes*. Leipzig: Th. Grieben.

William Preyer's Contributions to the Scientific Study of Hypnosis in Germany

by Christina Fritsche and Frank Ortmann

The historical development of hypnosis is one of the most exciting and instructive chapters in the history of culture, and one which directly affects public welfare.

F.S. Völgyesi, 1955

The phenomenon of hypnosis has been known to man since time immemorial and this fascinating topic has been practiced and studied in many theoretical and ideological contexts. Perhaps the most fruitful period for scientific research in the field of hypnotism was the period from 1880–1890, which has been called the "decade of hypnotism" in German scientific literature. By the end of this period, Lehmann (1890) was actually convinced that the field had been "experimented to death." We may demur from this pronouncement with respect to publications. For example, a special journal for hypnotism was not started until 1892.

William T. Preyer (1841–1897) played to key role in this movement which is still to be assessed by historians of psychotherapy. Before we attempt to highlight his importance to the scientific study of hypnotism in Germany, a brief historical synopsis of theoretical explanations of hypnosis will be provided.

Despite official academic dismissal, the doctrine of "animal magnetism" and its associated phenomena attracted the attention of both educated laymen and physicians with a common interest in psychological matters. It was even more popular among individuals with mystical and spiritualistic inclinations. The field was not accepted by medical researchers, however, as an area of legitimate study, and the situation was not improved when hypnosis became a favorite form of treatment among all types of nontraditional healers who practiced outside established medicine. In fact, the use of hypnosis was considered a trademark of Charlatanism among the healing professions. Langen (1964) believes that the repeated disappearance of the topic of hypnosis from scientific discussion in the nineteenth century symbolizes the unresolved conflict about this issue in medicine. The adherence of older authors like Wohlfahrt, Kluge, Eschenmeyer,

Ennemoser, Kieser, and Carus, to Mesmer's speculations about the nature of hypnotic processes, must be considered as an additional barrier to the development of a scientific research tradition in the field. Braid and Liebeault represent an "interim period" in the history of hypnotism (Langen 1964), because they rejected the "fluidum theory," they paved the way for the "suggestion theory." Unfortunately, as Loewenfeld (1901) has shown, the theoretical advances of Braid and Liebeault had no impact on the medical acceptance of hypnosis. The first documented scientific researches in the nature of hypnotic phenomena in Germany were carried out in 1872 by Czermak, a noted physiologist, who used animals as his subjects. His interests in the "taboo topic" had been aroused by the performance of an amateur hypnotist. Czermak's experiments were the stimulus for Preyer's own research in this field. Preyer's major goal was to reexamine Czermak's results and, if possible, supplement them with his own findings (Preyer 1873). Czermak had explained that hypnotic phenomena in animals were the result of a state similar to sleep. Preyer, however, concluded that the animals were in a condition of shock which he called "cataplexy." By the use of detailed observational records of his experiments, Preyer conclusively demonstrated the difference between ordinary sleep and cataplexy. At the same time, he was also able to refute the claims of Heubel in Kiev, who had previously supported Czermak's conclusions. Preyer explained cataplexy in terms of hypothetical centers for the inhibition of reflexes in the brain and the spinal cord. Thus, it was a physiologist who took the first step in the abolishment of the "fluidum theory" of hypnotic phenomena. Unfortunately, the promising scientific discussion between Preyer and Czermak was curtailed by the latter's death in 1873.

In the following years other physiologists, including Heidenhain, Berger, and Grützner, devoted themselves to the topic of hypnosis, which they were able to introduce to the medical establishment by way of a physiological approach. Hypnosis made a breach in the deterministic views of the mind on the body without giving up the standards of the scientific model with regard to precision and control. Physiologists thus vouched for the scientific nature of hypnosis and extended belief in the validity of the scientific method by showing that isolated behavior in animals like cataplexic states could be explained under the model of causation.

The sucessful use of hypnosis by laymen was another challenge to established medicine to improve its understanding of hypnosis and to gain control of the field. Loewenfeld (1901) has noted that the hypnotic experiments with animals aroused scant attention among German scientists and Preyer has stressed that (1881:49):

> Charcot's observations [about hypnotism] caused enormous attention in Germany. Yet, scientists were not induced [by them] to conduct experiments with humans . . . until an adventurer, a Dane without scientific training, started to give hypnotic performances.

The new conceptualizations of hypnosis, which focused heavily on physical response patterns and which downplayed the importance of psychological variables, were reflected in the sequence in which the various medical specialties became interested in this topic. The physiologists (i.e. Berger, Preyer, Heidenhain), who had a headstart, were soon followed by the psychiatrists (i.e. Bleuler, Binswanger, Krafft-Ebing, Forel, Moll) and the occasional internist (Rosenbach), who now focused on the therapeutic benefits of hypnosis. Psychologists in academia did not become significantly involved in the field until their own experimental methods had lost their initial prestige and popularity (Lehmann 1890, Wundt 1892).

Preyer's methods, his results and the chronological order of his publications on hypnotic topics illustrate how the interaction between physiological and therapeutic perspectives led eventually to his psychological interpretations of hypnosis.

In the form of "suggestion theory," hypnosis was legitimized as an appropriate subject area for medical psychology. Research on hypnotic phenomena and its therapeutic applications soon became "fashionable" in Germany. According to Langen (1964) the "decade of hypnosis" began with only 14 publications on the subject. By 1884, there were 79 articles and Dessoir's bibliography, which appeared in 1888, lists the stupendous total of 812 titles.

Preoccupation with the problems of the therapeutic use of suggestion an hypnosis belong to the roots of modern medical psychology. In 1880 any type of psychotherapy was equated with hypnosis. Developments in the field of psychology since then either derived directly from hypnotherapy or were in direct conflict with it.

Preyer made the transition from animal hypnosis research to the investigation of similar phenomena in man by means of his physiological research on the nature of sleep. According to Preyer, human sleep was naturally related to hypnotic phenomena (Preyer 1877, 1878).

Table 1.

William T. Preyer's Publications on the Question of Hypnosis

Publication Date	Title
1873	Über eine Wirkung der Angst bei Thieren. Berlin.
1877	Über das Magnetisieren bei Thieren. Ein Beitrag zur Physiologie des Erschreckens. Berlin.
1878	Die Kataplexie und der thierische Hypnotismus. Jena.
1878	Der thierische Magnetismus und Mediumismus einst und jetzt. Berlin.
1880	Über den Hypnotismus. Jena.
1880	On sleep and hypnotism. Cambridge.
1880	Das „Magnetisieren" der Menschen und Thiere. Berlin, Vortrag, gehalten in Jena am 12. December 1877.
1880	Literarische Notizen zum animalischen Magnetismus. Berlin.
1881	Die Entdeckung des Hypnotismus. Berlin. Nebst einer ungedruckten Original-Abhandlung von Braid in deutscher Übersetzung.
1882	Der Hypnotismus. Ausgewählte Schriften von J. Braid. Deutsch herausgegeben von W. Preyer.
1882	Über die Wirkung wiederholter Hypnosen.
1887	Der Hypnotismus in physiologischer Hinsicht. Wien.
1887	Hypnotismus. In: Real-Encyclopädie der gesammten Heilkunde. Herausgegeben von A. Eulenburg, Bd. 10, 2. Aufl.
1890	Der Hypnotismus. Vorlesungen an der K. Friedrich-Wilhelms Universität zu Berlin. Wien und Leipzig.

In 1881 Preyer published a German translation of an article by Braid, which allegedly had appeared in 1871 under the title *The Discovery of Hypnosis.* "The article was later identified by Braid's son as on original manuscript. Preyer changed the original text by adding an introduction, a summary of Braid's theory with modifications and a synopsis of his own views. Although Charcot and Richet appear to have minimized Braid's contributions, Preyer identified him as the modern discoverer of hypnotism. He also claimed that Braid's theories had been consistently confirmed by later investigators.

In 1890 Preyer published a monograph on the subject of hypnotism, based on a series of public lectures in Berlin from the preceding year, in which he took the following position (1890: 130):

> The hypnotic state is induced by a strong, one-sided arousal of attention which favors uniform sense impressions. This external process is represented psychologically by an intensive imagination in an otherwise empty field of consciousness. While the somatic and psychic effects of the restriction of consciousness vary from individual to individual, they can be best understood and desbribed as symptomatic conditions of the hypnotic state. Their physiological explanation remains, however, open to discussion. Hypnosis could be caused by an accumulation of fatigue toxins in certain regions of the brain.

Preyer regarded suggestibility as a side-effect. He emphasized, nevertheless, that the direct connection between suggestion and the induction of fantasy was necessary for hypnosis. Preyer declared his allegiance to Liebeault's school of "verbal suggestion." Later authors regarded Preyer also as a supporter of the somatic school of Charcot (Maack 1888, Loewenfeld 1901, Forel 1921). Preyer's writings show that he was fully aware of the importance of suggestions for hypnosis (1890: i):

> The physician should not forget that some procedures used in hypnotizing—for example, suggestion—are also very effective in the treatment of sick people without hypnosis.

He also stressed that a competent physician must be responsible for the use of hypnosis as a treatment procedure in general medicine.

Acceptance of the "suggestion theory" occurred with the alliance of Bernheim and Liebeault. This was promoted by the efforts of psychiatrists like Moll and Forel in Germany. Schultz (1963) credits Oskar Vogt as the actual founder of scientific hypnotism.

In conclusion Preyer made Braid's manuscripts accessible to German researchers in the field of hypnosis, and his own empirical research helped prepare the way for the "suggestion theory" of hypnosis. Preyer's experimental and physiological studies on hypnosis in animals merit our attention beyond their mere historical importance.

References

Charcot, J.M. (1889). Persönliche Mitteilung an Guttmann. *Deutsche Medizinische Wochenschrift*, 15.

Czermak, J.N. (1872). Nachweis echter hypnotischer Erscheinungen bei Thieren. *Sitzungsbericht der kaiserlichen Akademie der Wissenschaften*, 66.

Dessoir, M. (1888). *Bibliographie des modernen Hypnotismus*. Berlin: Duncker.

Forel, A. (1921). *Der Hypnotismus oder die Suggestion und die Psychotherapie*. Stuttgart: Enke (11th Ed.).

Heidenhain, R. (1880). *Der sogenannte thierische Magnetismus*. (4th ed.). Leipzig.

Hoff, P. (1980). Der Einfluß des Mesmerismus auf die Entwicklung der Suggestionstheorie in Deutschland. Dissertation. Universität Mainz, FRG.

Katzenstein, A. (1978). *Suggestion und Hypnose in der psychotherapeutischen Arbeit*. Jena: Fischer.

Klumbies, G. (1980). *Psychotherapie in der inneren und Allgemeinmedizin* (3rd. ed.). Leipzig: Hirzel.

Korn, G. (1903). Neuropathologie. In M. Neuburgger & J. Pagel (Eds.), *Handbuch der Geschichte der Medizin* (Vol. 2., pp. 717–735). Jena: Fischer.

Langen, P. (1964). Die Entwicklung zur modernen Hypnotherapie. *Deutsche Medizinische Wochenschrift, 89*.

Lehmann, A. (1890). *Die Hypnose und damit verwandten normalen Zustände*. Leipzig: Reisland.

Loewenfeld, L. (1901). *Der Hypnotismus*. Wiesbaden: Bergmann.

Maack, F. (1888). *Zur Einführung in das Studium des Hypnotismus und thierischen Magnetismus*. Berlin: Heuser.

Moll, A. (1890). *Der Hypnotismus mit Einschluß der Psychotherapie* (2nd ed.). Berlin: Heuser.

Moll, A. (1892–1893). Literaturbericht. *Zeitschrift für Hypnotismus, 1*.

Neumann, R. (1980). Leben und Werk des Physiologen William Thierry Preyer. Dissertation. Friedrich Schiller University, Jena, GDR.

Schneider, J. (1952). *Die psychologische Ursache der hypnotischen Erscheinungen*. Leipzig: Abel.

Schultz, H. (1963). Die Begründung des wissenschaftlichen Hypnotismus in Deutschland durch Oskar Vogt. *Zeitschrift für Neurologie, Psychiatrie und medizinische Psychologie, 15*.

Völgyesi, F. (1955). Entwicklung der Hypnose-Psychotherapie gemäß der Entdeckungen J. Braids and der Lehre Pavlovs. *Zeitschrift für Neurologie, Psychiatrie und medizinische Psychologie, 7*.

—(1969). *Hypnose bei Mensch und Tier* (3rd. ed.). Leipzig: Hirzel.

Wundt, W. *Hypnotismus und Suggestion*. Leipzig: Engelmann.

Wetterstrand, O. (1891). *Der Hypnotismus*. Wien: Urban und Schwarzenberg.

Ziemssen, H.v. (1889). Die Gefahren des Hypnotismus. *Münchener Medizinische Wochenschrift, 5*.

Part III

Methodological and Theoretical Approaches to Child Development

Linguistics and Psychology in Nineteenth-Century German Science

by Ryan D.Tweney

The centennial of William Preyer's *Die Seele des Kindes* was justly honored in 1982 as a landmark in the history of development psychology. With a degree of scientific rigor never before attempted in this domain, Preyer characterized the cognitive and linguistic development of young children, seeking to understand mental growth as an orderly, lawful, developmental process, a reflection of the biological coherence of human experience. Because his analysis was based on precise, detailed, and fully reported observations, the book retains its value as a scientific monograph, even in light of the rapid progress of developmental psychology in recent decades.

Preyer's book seems to stand out when compared with most other theoretical and empirical work of its time, and for this reason we must be cautious. It is far too easy to make Preyer into a mythical figure, someone whose genius saw beyond the views of this contemporaries into a future containing only our own ideas. Such hero worship may comfort those who look to history for justification of their own inevitability, but it is of no use to those who seek to *understand* history. We must instead seek to place Preyer in the context of his times by looking carefully at that context. The main purpose of this paper is to do that with just one aspect of his intellectual milieu, the linguistic science of his day. In particular, I will try to enlarge our perspective on Preyer's contribution by examining the following issues: (1) the progress of linguistic science from the late eighteenth century to 1882; (2) the emergence of psycho-logically relevant generalizations from linguistic investigatons of the history of language, (3) the linguistic context at Jena and Leipzig and the role of psychology language studies during this period; (4) the possible relicance of Preyer of these developments in formulating his approach to child language research; and (5), the continuing interplay of linguistics and psychology in the period from 1882 to 1933. As we shall see, Preyer's book was published in a year that nearly coincides with the peak of one of the most important controversies in the history of linguistic science, the great *Lautgesetz* (sound-law) controversy, which, by highlighting the nature of the laws which linguistics could expect to discover, was of direct relevance to psychological studies of language in general, and Preyer's work in particular.

I

Naturalistic explanations of the phenomenon of human language were first seriously pursued in the late eighteenth century.[1] The relation between language and thought is, of course, one of the foundations of Locke's theory of knowledge (Locke 1690)[2], but it is present also in Cartesian philosophy, where it derives from Descartes' use of language as the differentiating feature between humans and animals (Descartes 1637)[3]. Both traditions created substantial interest throughout the eighteenth century in the natural laws that underlie language (what we would now call psycholinguistics). Aside from its role in purely philosophical accounts, however, other Enlightenment trends led to the same point: estheticians needed to know how poetic beauty was achieved (cf. Abrams 1953), social theorists needed to understand language as a vehicle of communication (e.g. Adam Smith 1761), and historians began to discuss the role of language in the progress and decline of nations (Stam 1976). That scientific studies of language were ripe for emergence in the years before 1800 was thus clearly "overdetermined."

Enough was known at this time about the derivation of modern European languages from Latin and Greek to lend a decidedly historical cast to most Enlightenment studies of language. Thus, Horne Tooke (1786/1805) sought to reconstruct the origins of English words using etymological derivations based on Lockean first principles. In this way, he hoped to clarify the true meaning behind political phrases and slogans. Herder (1771) explored the origin of language and concluded that naturalistic explanations were not possible. Instead, language was an *invention* of the human spirit, a point Herder supported with illustrations drawn from comparisons between languages, anecdotal observations of child language, and etymological observations. Herder's essay in turn inspired the extensive child language diary of Dietrich Tiedemann (1787), perhaps the first such day-by-day account. Much of the speculation during this period was sterile as a scientific starting point[4] (whatever its utility for philosophical analysis) and it might have remained so were it not for a discovery which is commonly regarded as launching modern linguistics: the discovery of the striking similarity between Sanskrit and Latin. Though his priority can be disputed[5], Sir William Jones is commonly credited with the discovery in 1786. By pointing to the remarkable number of cognates between Latin and Sanskrit, and the similarity of the verb inflections in the two languages, Jones first articulated the view that both had "sprung from some common source, which, perhaps, no longer exists" (Jones, 1788, as cited in Waterman 1963:16).

The discovery created a fertile grounded for the application of objective analyses. Friedrich von Schlegel (1808) carried out comparative studies by closely examining the parallels between Sanskrit, German, Greek, and Latin. He then used the results to classify all known languages into types. Following Schlegel, Franz Bopp (1816) sought to discover the origin of grammatical forms, reaching the important conclusion that the modern European languages could not have been derived from Sanskrit as it now existed; instead both form must have emerged from an earlier protolanguage, as Jones had first suggested. Rasmus Rask, at about the same time, enlarged the domain of discourse by showing that Icelandic was closely similar to the Slavonic languages, and speculated that perhaps the common link was to be found in the Indian languages, including Sanskrit (Diderichsen 1974).

By 1820, there was in existence a richly detailed basis for a taxonomic classification of languages, a situation very much like that which existed in the biological sciences (Salmon 1974). It is striking to note that the notion of language *evolution* became important earlier in linguistics than in biology. In the period from Jones to, say, the publication of August Schleicher's *Die Darwinische Theorie und die Sprachwissenschaft* in 1863, comparative linguistics led to historical linguistics, which in turn formed the basis of nearly all of the linguistic theorizing of the day. By 1867, with the publication of Curtius' *Zur Chronologie der indogermanische Sprachforschung*, the triumph of evolutionary ideas was complete in linguistics. In detailed reconstructions of what we now usually call "Proto-Indo-European," it even possessed a kind of paleontology. Much remained to be done, of course, but, by 1870, historical linguistics possessed most of the characteristics of a mature scientific paradigm.[6]

II

It is in this context that we can see how psychology began to loom large in linguistics. Psychological speculation had never been entirely absent from linguistic theorizing, but it was not until after the posthumous publication of Wilhelm von Humboldt's 1820 *Über die Kawisprache auf der Insel Jawa* in 1836–40 that such speculation acquired a meaningful empirical context.[7] Humboldt's great contribution was to regard language as a human activity, rather than as an abstract formal system, and to argue that its most characteristic features could only be understood if the psychological processes underlying its use were understood. By insisting that all human languages reflected human creativity, he largely undercut the focus upon questions of progress *vs.* decay in language history. His arguments rendered moot any ethnocentric attempt, like Schlegel's, which sought to characterize one language as "better" than another.

The importance of psychology for linguistics emerged also in the context of perhaps the greatest empirical tool discovered by linguists in the nineteenth century, namely, the sound laws *(Lautgesetze)* governing the shift, in historical time, of the sounds of a language.

Jakob Grimm (1822) was the first to develop a sound law, by noticing the great regularity with which voiced stops (like "d," "b," "g") became voiceless stops ("t," "p," "k"), which in turn became fricatives ("th," "f," "ch") which could finally become voiced stops again. This relationship, now known as "Grimm's Law," explains such shifts as that of German *dann* to English "then," or *Tag* to "day," and was a powerful tool for historical analysis. Similar relationships (and qualifications of those found by Grimm) were richly elaborated in German linguistics between 1822 and the 1870s, and constitute its greatest empirical achievement.[8]

The efforts to discover sound laws were so successful that it was perhaps inevitable that the status of the empirical sciences should tempt linguists. The notion that linguistics was more akin to the natural sciences (*Naturwissenschaften*) than to the social and historical sciences (*Geisteswissenschaften*) was not new. Schleicher is often credited with such views, because of his claim that language and nature were one, and because of his publication, in 1863, of the classic *Die Darwinische Theorie und die Sprachwissenschaft: Offenes Sendschreiben an Herrn Dr. Ernst Häckel.* Häckel was Schleicher's colleague at Jena, and first introduced him to Darwin's writings. But Schleicher was a Hegelian, and his true goal was to use sound laws to gradually reconstruct the ultimate protolanguage, uncorrupted by such worldly processes as phonetic change (Davies 1975, Jankowsky 1972). Whatever his goals, he clearly identified the sound laws a basic to empirical work in linguistics. Interestingly, Schleicher (1861–62) also published a brief but sophisticated analysis of phonetic development in his own children.

The decade of the 1860s marks a turning point, then. The sound laws had started as methodological tool for the comparative analysis of languages, but became in the next decade the regulating principle of linguistics as a natural science, and a rallying cry for a small, brilliant group of young linguists, the *Junggrammatiker,* or neogrammarians.[9] That sound-laws have no exceptions (the phrase is Leskien's *Die Ausnahmslosigkeit der Lautgesetze*[10] was the rallying cry, and it implied that all language change could be subsumed under the sound laws. The exceptions were only apparent ones—momentary deviations caused by psychological or social forces that could not obscure the underlying order. Linguistics was a natural science because it possessed an overriding natural law that governed sound change.

While the formulation seemed simple, the empirical realities were not. In particular, an enormous number of the discovered historic changes in language appeared to be governed by a process of analogy. For example, the original plural for English "cow" was "kine," but it became regularized to "cows," by analogy with "sow"—"sows." Similarly, the original past form for "help" was "holp," which became regularized to "helped," by analogy with the -ed past tense in other verbs. Historical changes which appeared to be due to analogy quite frequently fell outside the domain of any conceivable sound laws; "kine" to "cows" does not even remotely resemble an allowable phonetic shift. The neogrammarians were thus faced with a choice: admit that sound laws *had* exceptions, thus undercutting linguistics as *Naturwissenschaft,* or hand over the problem to psychology, while postulating the exceptionless character (*Ausnahmslosigkeit*) of the sound laws as a deeper, "more real," process than analogy. Clearly, a fertile ground for controversy!

III

The detailed development of the controversy in the 1880s need not concern us, because we can now turn to the fledgling discipline of psychology during this period. The neogrammarian movement centered in just two institutions; a larger group at Leipzig and a smaller one at Jena.[11] According to Wilbur, "The period 1875-1886 was the time of turnover when a crusading, dragon-killing spirit radiated from Leipzig and infected the younger members of the linguistic community throughout the world" (1977: lviii). Leipzig was a center for such work in part because of the magnetic attraction of the distinguished comparativist Georg Curtius (later one of the severest critics of the neogrammarians). Berthold Delbrück (one of the most prolific of the neogrammarians) provided a focus at Jena, accepting a chair there in 1870, two years after the death of Schleicher (who was also at Jena). That both univerisities were centers for the drive to make linguistics a natural science is not surprising, both having taken a lead in the 1870s in clarifying the range of application of scientific methods in the social scienes. Leipzig was especially strong in psychology during this period. When the neogrammarians relegated the problem of analogy to psychology, they may have felt they were placing it in good hands, in particular, in Wilhelm Wundt's at Leipzig.[12] The linguists were certainly aware of Wundt who, in fact, used the third volume of his *Philosophische Studien* as a forum for an important clarification of the sense in which sound laws could be considered exceptionless (Wundt 1886). Linguists may not have been fully aware of this significance of Preyer's work, since he was not cited in the linguistic works of the period. This may reflect the fact that Preyer, as Professor of Physiology at Jena, was outside the realm of controversy. Sound laws, however, were said to be *physiological*, not psychological. Thus, it is more likely that Preyer's work was ignored by the parties to the controversy because it was *developmental*. While occasional references were made to child language by the linguists directly engaged in the controversy, they were anecdotal remarks, and scholarly literature was rarely cited.

What was seen by linguists as the relevant psychology was primarily derived from one of three sources: Herbartian associationism, Wundt's writings, and Lotze's writings. In all three cases, appeal was made to the principles of memory and/or association for an explanation of analogical change. The role of the child as a causal agent in language change seems to have become important only after the neogrammarian controversy had quieted (in the late 1880s). The use made of psychology by linguists is exemplified in Hermann Paul's (1880) treatise, which took somewhat of a middle ground between the neogrammarians and the more traditional Indo-Germanic scholars like Curtius.

Paul discussed the psychological antecedents of both analogy and physiological (sound law) change. He derived his psychology from Lotze (1852), relying especially heavily on the importance of *Bewegungsgefühl* ("motory-sensation") in preserving traces of words long enough for the operation of memory and association (see Paul 1889/1886: 36-37). Child language played little role in language change for Paul. He did not cite Preyer.

Much of Paul's work addressed itself to a criticism of Wundt's views. We know that Wundt was very knowledgeable about linguistics even before coming to Leipzig 1875 (Wundt 1920: 260-263). Wundt's attempt to develop a *Sprachpsychologie* as part of *Völkerpsychologie* was opposed by Paul, whose sympathies did not lie with the Lazarus-Steinthal tradition (Steinthal 1850, 1860). Even so, Wundt's discussion of exactly what could be meant by an "exceptionless sound law" is a model of clarity (1886). He proceeded by first carefully distinguishing the various senses of the word "law;" the two important ones for the sound law controversy were (1) laws as normative principles governing all manifestations of phenomena, and (2) laws as empirical regularities which expressed what most phenomena in fact were. Both kinds of laws could potentially tolerate exceptions, but the role of exceptions differed. In the first sense, laws could admit of exceptions if the lawful manifestations were hidden by other factors. In the second sense, the laws were merely generalizations. Hence, whether or not an observation conformed to the law or constituted an exception was irrelevant to the status of the observation. In the second sense, exceptions were not something to be "explained away." For Wundt, the associative principles of psychology constituted the second sort of law; they were generalizations, not regulating principles. But linguists faced a mixed case. Whereas the sound laws could be construed as regulating principles, the observational domain was so richly overlain with associational processes that one could not dismiss their operation as a problem outside the domain of linguistics.[13] The controversy was thus in many ways more apparent than real, said Wundt. Proponents of exceptionless sound laws should not dismiss apparent exceptions so lightly, but opponents should admit that sound laws were, in essence, regulating principles.

Toward the end of the century, linguists began to utilize the techniques of the new experimental psychology to resolve some of these issues. The most ambitious effort was made by Albert Thumb, a pupil of Brugmann's, and Karl Marbe, who worked in Wundt's laboratory with Wundt, Külpe, and Meumann (Esper 1973:64). Thumb and Marbe (1901) attempted experiments in which word-associations were classified by grammatical class, and related to reaction times. Since most of the associations recorded experimentally were in the same categories that presumably had changed historically via analogy, they concluded that the explanation of analogic change via psychological associations was confirmed.[14] Wundt (1901), rather predictably, criticized the study on the grounds that the artificiality of laboratory studies is too great to allow generalization to processes of language change in history. For Wundt, *Sprachpsychologie* belonged to *Völkerpsychologie*, and was concerned with process which could not be investigated experimentally.

It thus appears that, while many bases for an interaction between psychology and linguistics arose from the sound-law controversy, none appeared to be specifically developmental. We may speculate about one further reason for this situation, one based on the nature of neogrammarian linguistics. In reacting against their predecessors, the neogrammarians argued that the prime source of observational data had to be living languages. While they did not oppose the attempt to reconstruct the history of language, nor deny the evolutionary postulate, they did seek to redirect attention to currently existing languages. For the neogrammarians, synchronic comparisons (e.g. among dialects) were more important than diachronic comparisons (e.g. across time). Thus, for the neogrammarians, diachronic studies of child language, while they certainly dealt with living language, may have seemed to be entirely outside the realm of linguistics.

IV

If the neogrammarians generally slighted the value of Preyer's work, can we detect, in *Die Seele des Kindes* (1882), the reciprocal influence? Did Preyer rely on linguistic analysis as the basis for his observations?[15]

A superficial glance at his text suggests that the answer is no. He gives no references to the work of linguists, and mentions only Steinthal (negatively) among those psychologists who made language a principal concern of their research. References to earlier works on language development, on the other hand, are frequent, and those he is most favorable toward (e.g. Sigismund and Strumpell) are analyzed in great detail. His frequent citations of neurological and physiological work are also in accord with expectations. But no linguistics.

It is possible, of course, that Preyer was unaware of the ferment of ideas in linguistic science, though it seems unlikely. His was not the sort of mind that avoided difficult scholarship, nor was he prone to slight the achievements of others, nor can we see him as an isolated, unworldly figure. It seems easiest to assume that he knew of the soundlaw controversy, and the attempts to include linguistics among the *Naturwissenschaften*, but rejected them as irrelevant to his purposes.

Such a judgment would have been consistent with his general viewpoint, as we learn from internal evidence in his book. At the outset, he rejected the "labyrinth of appearances and hypotheses" (1882/1890: xii) that can lead one astray in the investigation of complex phenomena. He was, in fact, opposed even to the simplest hypotheses about the causes of the observed sequence of phonetic development in children. Thus, he opposed the notion advanced by Schulze (1880) that children acquired the easiest consonants and vowels first, adding others in the order of relative difficulty. Preyer's objections to the claim were based on his observations: his own child did not follow such a sequence, nor did those of other diarists. Further, within the first eight months of life, every observed infant was seen to have made all of the sounds of the adult language, and many more besides.

Preyer's approach to such question was decidedly, almost aggressively, empirical. We see, in fact, a kind of *Naturwissenschaft* on foundations very different from those of the neogrammarians. For Preyer, the issue, whether or not rule-like laws applied in the study of child language, was an empirical one. He was firmly convinced that nothing useful could be learned until after good diary studies were available, and he was equally certain that too few such studies were available to do more than reject certain obviously inappropriate laws. In contrast to the neogrammarians, Preyer did not begin with the assumption that he would find regulating principles in the sequence of sound changes observed in children. His "laws" were statistical generalizations, not invariant principles.

Preyer was not, of course, a positivist. He openly used theories and results from another domain to structure his inquiry, but the domain was neurolinguistics, not linguistics as such. His indebtedness to Kussmaul and Broca was freely admitted, and his neurological theory of the bases of language acquisition was taken as a given (not as a hypothesis to be tested). In this connection, it is important to note that, at least with regard to language acquistion, Preyer was *not* an evolutionist, much less a recapitulationist along the lines of Ernst Häckel. This is a frequently misunderstood point, based no doubt on the assumption that, since he was an embryologist (Preyer 1885), he must also have subscribed to embryological analogies in his theory of language. Had he embraced recapitulation, he might well have found the neogrammarian sound laws a fertile arena for speculation,[16] but he in fact accepted neither.

Preyer's use of the term "law" is interestingly revealed in what he regarded as one of his major findings: the fact that the rate and sequence of development of the sounds and grammatical categories of language vary temendously from child to child. Presenting comparative tables of distorted pronunciations and commonly used words by three different children at age 25 months, and of narrations of a simple story by two children (1880/1890: 234-239), Preyer noted that the errors were unlike, that different words were used, that there was extreme variation in what sounds were omitted, what sounds were transposed, and what sounds were substituted for each other. Across time, such variations were evident even in a single child. He took the evidence as clear disproof of the "law of least effort," and concluded that there cannot be "any chronological order of succession of sounds that holds good universally in the language of the child" (1880/1890: 241-242). Preyer thus rejected the universality of sound laws, and a neogrammarian perspective on child language as well.

Preyer did see language acquisition in an biological context, but it is equally true that he regarded thought as prior to language. It is an important point because, in our day, biological approaches to language acquisition have come to be associated with the view that the innermost structures of language are innate. Preyer saw no difficulty in asserting that, while the capacity to learn languagee was undoubtedly hereditary, *all* of the specific structures of language emerged out of the interaction betweeen the child's environment and his or her own activity. Language emerges in the first place because of the need to understand and to express ideas, but, for Preyer, there was nothing inherent in the forms it took. In this sense, the child could be said to *discover* language, but not to *invent* it (1880/1890: 215). Furthermore, the discovered forms of language were outside the child, in the social surroundings, not within. In no sense did this lead him to a passive, associative, view of language acquisition. In fact, he frequently noted the child's own creative activity in the formation of novel combinations of words, concepts, and pronunciations. In all such cases, Preyer saw the invented forms as generalizations, as extensions of previously learned forms.

V

In the years following 1882, both linguistics and psychology began to expand and to diversify in the problems considered. Paul's great work of 1880 went through many editions, and became one of the "bibles" of pre-Saussurean linguistics. Wundt went on to write his monumental ten-volume *Völkerpsychologie* (1900/1920; see also Wundt 1916), the first two volumes of which were devoted to language. Preyer revised *Die Seele* in 1884, and lived to see it hailed as the greatest contribution of its time to the study of child language, though he no doubt would have been amused (or angry) to see how quickly it reached the status of a "great book:" frequently cited but rarely read.

Linguists did eventually turn to language acquistition for insight into the general laws of language. In 1921, Otto Jespersen (himself a contributor to the sound-law controversy in the 1880s—see Wilbur 1977) wrote what may be the first general treatise on language to identify child speech as a major source of the forces that impel language change. Jespersen's book, following an historical introduction, in fact began with an account of language acquistition. Based primarily on his own observations, the book did not cite Preyer. Jespersen formulated a group of "sound laws" (e.g. "children in all countries tend to substitute [t] for [k]," 1921: 107), but most of his examples are not exceptionless, and the data base was far too casual to support the claims made. Little use was made of formal results from psychology—the book being far more naive than Preyer's in this respect—but there was at least recognition that psychological processes interact with purely physiological processes.

Experimental work in phonology began in earnest as one of the natural consequences of the neogrammarian movement (Kohler 1981). Such work rapidly became isolated from general descriptive and historical linguistics, however. In spite of the efforts of such men as E. W. Scripture (1902) to use experimental techniques to investigate the sound laws, there was remarkably little work directed at such issues until much later.[17]

Developmental psycholinguistics enjoyed continous interest from psychologists from Preyer's time down to the present day. The care with which Preyer investigated language development was not manifest in all of the work, however. Observational studies of very questionable methodology continued to be generated for decades (cf. Cavanaugh, this volume). Linguistic science did not begin to be used in a thoroughgoing fashion in developmental studies of language until after the work of Grégoire (1937). Why it took so long for psychologists to recognize the importance of linguistic methodologies is an interesting, but unresolved question, one that requires further investigation. Though a speculation (rather than a documentable historical fact), it is my view that the separate strands of research on language that almost converged in the 1880s, only to diverge again, were not brought together until the epochal work of Roman Jakobson on child language. Showing first that analysis of the speech stream using the concept of the distinctive feature could result in true laws, whereas such laws do not emerge from phonemic analyses, Jakobson then demonstrated that the concept of *Lautgesetze* could, in fact, take on broad meaning for language acquisition, phonetics, and historical linguistics (Jakobson 1941, Jakobson and Halle 1956). The impact of this demonstration led by a direct route to a new scientific account of the generativity of language. We can safely assume that, in the future as today, the value of both linguistic and psychological work for the understanding of child language will continue to be recognized, that the traditions will not again diverge.

Notes

[1] To be sure, there were many precursors in earlier years, language being perhaps the first category of human behavior to be subjected to systematic scrutiny. General accounts of the history of linguistics can be found in Robins (1979), Pedersen (1931/ 1924), and Parret (1976). More specific accounts can be located in the excellent bibliography by Koerner (1972). Koerner is also the editor of what is now the principal source of scholarly articles on the history of linguistics, *Historiographia Linguistica*, published by John Benjamin's in Amsterdam. The successive volumes of this journal include a number of specialized bibliographies.

[2] Cf. Aarsleff (1967), Fischer (1975), Kretzmann (1968), Nathanson (1973), and the earlier account by Stewart (1810).

[3] On Descartes and language, see Stam (1976). Cordemoy (1668) was the first to elaborate Descartes' rather cursory statement into a complete theory of human language. Chomsky's (1966) attempt to revivify "Cartesian linguistics" is a presentist history, and is of little value to the historian—cf. Aarsleff (1970) and Hymes and Fought (1975).

[4] Stam (1976) has a thorough account of the response to Herder's essay. See also Aarsleff (1976), the critical comments of Jespersen (1921), and the review of Stam's book by Hewes (1978).

[5] See Jespersen (1921), Salmon (1974), and Jankowsky (1972). Jones' paper was first delivered before the Asiatick Society of Bengal in Calcutta in 1786, and first published in 1788.

6   Wilbur (1977), following Hymes (1974), has argued that linguistics was not truly a paradigmatic science in the Kuhnian sense, because successive advances were based, not on the incorporation of older views by newer ones, but on their outright rejection. The statement seems accurate when applied to theoretical *explanations* of linguistic change, but is not so clear when applied to empirical *findings*. Since at least the time of Grimm, there has been no serious attempt to deny the comparative affinities among the Indo-European languages, nor, since the time of Schleicher, has there been any denial of the basic outlines of the evolutionary account of the development of the Indo-European family.

7   On Humboldt, see Jespersen (1921), Jankowsky (1972), Heeschen (1977), and Picardi (1977).

8   Whitney (1875) is still one of the best introductions to these phenomena; see especially ch.4 through7, and 10. Langacker (1973) provides and introduction based primarily on non-Indo-European languages. Jankowsky (1972: 71) notes that Rasmus Rask may have been the source of Grimm's own observations. See also Benware (1974) and Davies (1975).

9   On the neogrammarians, see Jankowsky (1972), Davies (1975), Davis (1973), and Wilbur (1977). Waterman (1963) has a brief, cogent introduction. Esper (1968, 1973) is the only recent psychologist to have dealt seriously with the issues raised.

10   See Waterman 1963: 50; the statement was first used in 1876.

11   My account of the institutional basis of the controversy is based on Wilbur's (1977) excellent account. The introduction to his book contains a masterful blending of "internalist" and "externalist" approaches to an understanding of the controversy. The bulk of the book contains reprints of key publications that appeared in the years 1885-1887 by Curtius, Delbrück, Brugmann, Schuchardt, Collitz, Osthoff, and Jespersen.

12   Wundt went to Leipzig from Zurich in 1875 (Bringmann, Bringmann, and Ungerer 1980). Preyer went to Jena in 1869 from Bonn (Gottlieb 1973). Blumenthal (1974: 1106) stated that Wundt was brought to Leipzig by the neogrammarians, but he does not cite a source for the claim, and I have been unable to verify it. Wundt's own account (1920) does not support such an interpretation.

13   Esper (1973) and Porsch (1980) discussed the dispute between Paul and Wundt but failed to mention the 1886 paper under discussion, and hence failed to see that many of the bases that led to the later reconciliation of linguistics and psychology were established by Wundt. The position taken by Wundt derived from his philosophical views on the nature of science—cf. Danziger (1980).

14   Subsequent studies of this sort were also carried out—cf. Esper (1973). Thumb (1907/08; 1911) argued for a working relationship between linguistics and experimental psychology, but such relationships have tended to be short-lived. I have dealt with some of the issues in my 1979 article. Esper tried to continue the approach advocated by Thumb; my 1974 review of Esper's book discusses his work.

15   Little has been written about Preyer's life and ideas. See Gottlieb (1973), Bühler (1934), and the papers in this volume.

16   Unlike Preyer, others did try to base developmental psychology on recapitulation, e.g. G.S.Hall (1904) and F.Tracy (1894). See Ross (1972).

17   On Scripture, see Hardcastle (1981), Sokal (1980), and Scripture (1936). Scripture's work in linguistics will be dealt with in a forth-coming paper by Stephen Siviy and myself.

References

Aarsleff,H. (1967) *The study of language in England, 1780-1860.* Princeton, NJ: Princeton University Press.
—(1970) The history of linguistics and Professor Chomsky. *Language* 46: 570–584.
—(1976) An outline of language-origins theory since the Renaissance. *Annals of the New York Academy of Sciences* 280: 4–17.
Abrams,M.H. (1953) *The mirror and the lamp: Romantic theory and the critical tradition.* London: Oxford University Press.
Benware,W.A. (1974) *The study of Indo-European vocalism in the 19th century from the beginnings to Whitney and Scherer: A critical-historical account.* Amsterdam: Benjamin.
Blumenthal,A.L. (1974) An historical view of psycholinguistics. In T.A.Sebeok (Ed.), *Current trends in linguistics* 12. The Hague: Mouton, pp. 1105–1134.
Bopp,F. (1816) *Über das Conjugationsystem der Sanskritsprache.* Frankfurt am Main.
Bringmann,W.G., Bringmann,N.J. and Ungerer,G.A. (1980) The establishment of Wundt's laboratory: An archival and documentary study. In W.G.Bringmann and R.D.Tweney (Eds.), *Wundt studies: A centennial collection.* Toronto: C.J.Hogrefe, pp. 123–157.
Bühler,C. (1934) Preyer, Wilhelm Thierry. In Seligman, E.R.A. and Johnson,A. (Eds.), *Encyclopedia of the Socal Sciences* 12. New York: MacMillan, pp. 349–350.
Chomsky,N. (1966) *Cartesian linguistics: A chapter in the history of rationalist thought.* New York: Harper and Row.
Cordemoy,G.de (1972) *A philosophical discourse concerning speech, conformable to the Cartesian principles.* London: John Martin, 1668 (First published in French 1668. Reprinted Delmar, NY: Scholar's Facsimiles and Reprints, 1972, with an introduction by B.Ross.).
Curtius,G. (1867) *Zur Chronologie der indogermanischen Sprachforschung.* Leipzig: S.Hirzel.
Danziger,K. (1980) Wundt's psychological experiment in the light of his philosophy of science. *Psychological Research* 42: 109–122.
Davies,A.M. (1975) Language classification in the nineteenth century. In T.A.Sebeok (Ed.), *Current trends in linguistics* 13. The Hague: Mouton, pp. 607–716.
Davis,B.H. (1973) Review of K.R.Jankowsky, *The neogrammarians.* In *Historiographia Linguistica* 1: 95–110.
Descartes,R. (1952) *Discourse on the method of rightly conducting the reason and seeking for truth in the sciences.* Chicago: Encyclopedia Britannica, 1952. "Great Books of the Western World, Vol. 31." Trans. by E.S.Haldane and G.R.T.Ross. (First published 1637.)
Diderichsen,P. (1974) The foundation of comparative linguistics: Revolution or continuation? In D.Hymes (Ed.), *Studies in the history of linguistics: Traditions and paradigms.* Bloomington, IN: Indiana University Press.
Esper,E.A. (1968) *Mentalism and objectivism in liguistics: The sources of Leonard Bloomfield's psychology of language.* New York: American Elsevier.
—(1973) *Analogy and association in linguistics and psychology.* Athens, GA: University of Georgia Press.
Fischer,K.P. (1975) John Locke in the German Enlightenment: An interpretation. *Journal of the History of Ideas* 36: 431–446.
Gottlieb,G. (1973) Dedication to W.Preyer (1841–1897). In Gottlieb,G. (Ed.), *Behavioral embryology* (vol.1). New York: Academic Press.
Grégoire,A. (1937) L'apprentissage du langage; les deux premieres années. Liège.

Grimm,J. (1848) *Geschichte der deutschen Sprache.* Leipzig. (First published 1819, 2d ed. 1822).

Hall, G.S. (1904) *Adolescence: Its psychology and its relations to physiology, anthropology, sociology, sex, crime, religion, and eduction* (2 vols.) New York: Appleton.

Hardcastle, W.J. (1981) Experimental studies in lingual coarticulation. In R.E.Asher and E.J.A.Henderson (Eds.), *Towards a history of phonetics.* Edinburgh: Edinburgh University Press.

Heeschen, Volker. (1977) Weltansicht—Reflexionen über einen Begriff Wilhelm von Humboldts. *Historiographia Linguistica* 4: 159–190.

Herder,J.G. (1966) *Essay on the origin of language.* New York: Frederick Ungar. Trans. by A.Gode (First published 1771).

Hewes, G.W. (1978) Reviwe of J.H.Stam, *Inquiries into the origin of language: The fate of a question* (1976). In *Historiographia Linguistica* 5: 174–189.

Horne Tooke, John. (1786, 1806) *Epea Ptereonta, Diversions of Purley,* Parts 1 and 2. London: for J.Johnson.

Humboldt, W. von. (1963) Über das vergleichende Sprachstudium in Beziehung auf die verschiedenen Epochen der Sprachentwicklung. In *Werke in 5 Bänden,* vol.3. Stuttgart, pp. 1–25. (First published 1836–40, written in 1820.)

Hymes, D. (Ed.) (1974) *Studies in the history of linguistics: Traditions and paradigms.* Bloomington, IN: Indiana University Press.

Hymes, D. and Fought,J. (1975) American structuralism. In R.A.Sebeok (Ed.), *Current trends in linguistics* 13: *Historiography of linguistics.* The Hague: Mouton, pp. 903–1176.

Jakobson, R. (1968) *Child language, aphasia, and phonological universals.* The Hague: Mouton (First published 1941).

Jakobson, R. and Halle, M. (1956) *Fundamentals of language.* The Hague: Mouton.

Jankowsky, K.R. (1972) *The neogrammarians: A re-evaluation of their place in the development of linguistic science.* The Hague: Mouton.

Jesperson, O. (1964) *Language: Its nature, development, and origin.* New York: W.W.Norton (First published 1921).

Jones, Sir W. (1788) A dissertation on the orthography of Asiatick words in Roman letters. *Asiatick Researcher* 1.

Koerner, E.F.K. (1972) *Bibliographia Saussureana, 1870-1970.* Methuen, NJ: Scarecrow Press.

Kohler, K. (1981) Three trends in phonetics: The development of the discipline in Germany since the nineteenth century. In R.E.Asher and E.J.A.Henderson (Eds.), *Towards a history of phonetics.* Edinburgh: Edinburgh University Press.

Kretzmann, N. (1968) The main thesis of Locke's semantic theory. *Philosophical Review* 77: 175–196.

Langacker, R.W. (1973) *Language and its structure: Some fundamental linguistic concepts* (2 ed.). New York: Harcourt Brace Jovanovich.

Locke, J. (1975) *An essay concerning human understanding.* Ed. by P.H.Nidditch. Oxford: Oxford University Press (First published 1690).

Lotze, H. (1852) *Medicinische Psychologie, oder Psychologie der Seele.* Leipzig: Weidmann.

Nathanson, S.L. (1973) Locke's theory of ideas. *Journal of the History of Philosophy* 11: 29–42.

Parret, H. (Ed.) (1976) *History of linguistic thought and contemporary linguistics.* Berlin: de Gruyter.

Paul, H. (1889) *Principles of the history of language* (trans. by H.A.Strong from the 2d ed. of 1886). London: Sonnenschein, 1889 (first published 1880).

Pedersen, H. (1931) *The discovery of language: Linguistic science in the nineteenth century.*

298 Tweney

Trans. by J.W.Spargo. Cambridge, MA: Harvard University Press (First published in Danish in 1924).

Picardi, E. (1977) Some problems of classification in linguistics and biology, 1800–1830. *Historiographia Linguistica* 4: 31–57.

Porsch, P. (1980) Linguistische Positionen Wilhelm Wundts. In W.Meischner and A.Metge (Eds.), *Wilhelm Wundt—progressives Erbe, Wissenschaftsentwicklung und Gegenwart.* Leipzig: Karl-Marx-Universität, pp. 350–358.

Preyer, W.T. (1882) *Die Seele des Kindes. Beobachtungen über die geistige Entwicklung des Menschen in den ersten Lebensjahren.* Leipzig: T.Grieben.

—(1885) *Spezielle Physiologie des Embryo. Untersuchungen über die Lebenserscheinungen vor der Geburt.* Leipzig: Grieben.

Robins, R.H. (1979) *A short history of linguistics* (2d ed.). London: Longman (First published 1968).

Ross, Dorothy. (1972). *G.Stanley Hall; The psychologist as prophet.* Chicago: University of Chicago Press.

Salmon, P.B. (1974) The beginnings of morphology: Linguistic botanizing in the 18th century. *Historiographia Linguistica* 1: 313–339.

Schlegel, F. von (1808) *Über die Sprache und Weisheit der Indier. Ein Beitrag zur Begründung der Altertumskunde, nebst metrischen Übersetzungen indischer Gedichte.* Heidelberg: Mohr and Zimmer.

Schleicher, A. (1971) Some observations made on children. In A. Bar-Adon and W.F.Leopold (Eds.), *Child language: A book of readings.* Englewood Cliffs, NJ: Prentice-Hall (First published 1861–62).

—(1863) *Die Darwinische Theorie und die Sprachwissenschaft. Offenes Sendschreiben an Herrn Dr. Häckel.* Weimar: H.Bohlau.

Schulze, F. (1880) *Die Sprache des Kindes; eine Anregung zur Erforschung des Gegenstandes.* Leipzig: Günter.

Scripture, E.W. (1902) *The elements of experimental phonetics.* New York: Scribner's.

—(1936) Autobiography in C.Murchison (Ed.), *History of psychology in autobiography,* vol. 3. Worcester, MA: Clark University Press.

Smith, A (1853) *Considerations concerning the first genius of original and compounded languages.* In Adam Smith, *The theory of moral sentiments,* New Edition. London: Henry G.Bohn (First published 1761).

Sokal, M.M. (1980) The psychological career of Edward Wheeler Scripture. In J. Brozek and L.J.Pongratz (Eds.), *Historiography of modern psychology: Aims, resources, approaches.* Toronto: C.J.Hogrefe.

Stam, J.H. (1976) *Inquiries into the origin of language: The fate of a question.* New York: Harper and Row.

Steinthal, H. (1850) *Die Classifikation der Sprachen, dargestellt als die Entwicklung der Sprachidee.* Berlin.

—(1860) Assimilation und Attraction, psychologisch betrachtet. *Zeitschrift für Völkerpsychologie und Sprachwissenschaft* 1: 93–179.

Stewart, D. (1810) *Philosophical Essays.* Edinburgh: George Ramsay.

Thumb, A. (1907/08) Psychologische Studien über die sprachlichen Analogiebildungen. *Indogermanische Forschungen* 22: 1–54.

—(1911) Experimentelle Psychologie und Sprachwissenschaft. Parts 1 and 2. Ein Beitrag zur Methodenlehre der Philologie. *Germanisch-Romanische Monatsschrift* 3: 1–15, 65–74.

Thumb, A. and Marbe, K. (1901) *Experimentelle Untersuchungen über die psychologischen Grundlagen der sprachlichen Analogiebildung.* Leipzig: Wm. Engelmann.

Tiedemann, D. (1927) Über die Entwicklung der Seelenfähigkeiten bei Kindern. *Hessische Beiträge zur Gelehrsamkeit und Kunst,* 1787. (Transl. in C. Murchison and S. K. Langer, Tiedemann's observation on the development of the mental faculties of children. *Pedagogical Seminary and Journal of Genetic Psychology* 34: 205–230.)

Tracy, F. (1894) *The psychology of childhood.* Boston: D. C. Heath.

Tweney, R. D. (1974) Review article of *Analogy and association in linguistics and psychology,* by E. A. Esper. *Historiographia Linguistica* 1: 385–398.

—(1979) Reflections on the history of the behavioral theories of language. *Bahaviorism* 7: 91–103.

Waterman, J. T. (1963) *Perspectives in linguistics.* Chicago: University of Chicago Press.

Whitney, W. D. (1875) *The life and growth of language: An outline of linguistic science.* New York: Appleton.

Wilbur, T. H. (Ed.) (1977) *The Lautgesetz-controversy: A documentation.* (New ed.) Amsterdam: J. Benjamins.

Wundt, W. (1886) Über den Begriff des Gesetzes, mit Rücksicht auf die Frage der Ausnahmlosigkeit der Lautgesetze. *Philosophische Studien* 3. 195–215.

—(1900–1920) *Völkerpsychologie. Eine Untersuchung der Entwicklungsgesetze von Sprache, Mythos und Sitte* (10 vols.). Leipzig: W. Engelmann and A. Kröner.

—(1901) Review of A. Thumb and K. Marbe, *Experimentelle Untersuchungen . . . 1901.* In *Indogermanische Forschungen* 12 *(Anzeiger)*: 17–20.

—(1916) *Elements of folk psychology: Outline of a psychological history of the development of mankind.* London: George Allen and Unwin. (Transl. by Edward Leroy Schaub).

—(1921) *Erlebtes und Erkanntes* (2d ed.). Stuttgart: Alfred Kröner (First published, 1920).

William James' Theory of Mental Evolution: The Religious and Moral Foundations of a Psychological Science

by Robert J. Richards

At the famous Oxford meeting of the British Association for the Advancement of Science in 1860, a few months after the publication of *Darwin's Origin of Species,* Bishop Samuel Wilberforce attacked the theory of evolution. He inquired of Thomas Huxley, Darwin's champion, whether it was on his father's side or his mother's that he claimed his descent from a monkey (Huxley 1900, vol. 1: 197–199). Today conservative religious opponents of Darwinian theory usually unload arguments that have the same scientific persuasiveness as that of Wilberforce. Serious religious thinkers of the nineteenth century, however, particularly those having scientific tranining themselves, began almost immediately to accomodate their religious views to the rising theory of Darwin. They had to. The strength of Darwin's demonstration of the fundamental fact of evolutionary change was so great that by 1882, the year of Darwin's death, the journal *Presbyterian Observer,* when challenged, could find only one naturalist willing to deny evolution in print. The accommodation made was usually to reemphasize that the Bible was not a scientific treatise, but a religious and moral guide. God's plan, they urged, could have been executed through the evolutionary process. As Darwin himself suggested, it would bespeak greater powe of the Creator to have established those natural laws that govern the evolution of life than to have fashioned each creature individually and, as it were, by hand (Darwin, 1859: 488).

Contemporary religious thinkers recognize the coercive claims of modern biology, yet have reservations when it comes to acquiescing in an evolutionary construction of man's distinctive traits of rational mind, moral judgment, and religious conviction. And even steely hearted scientists quake a bit at Edward Wilson's assertions, in his book *Sociobiology,* that our specific conceptual abilities, moral behaviors, and religious sentiments, can be translated into an evolutionary currency that would establish their true value (Wilson 1975: 547–75). But an evolutionary reconstruction of these human qualities need not have the significance that Wilson proclaims and most of his critics assume. I would like here to examine William James' psychological, moral, and religious uses of Darwinian ideas in order to suggest a different way of estimating the implications of evolution theory for our understanding of what seems distinctively human.

It was Darwin's theory, I believe, that provided the essential structure and objective justification for James' scientific and philosophical conceptions about the nature of mind, the acquistion of knowledge, and the possibility of moral action and religious hope. To comprehend fully James' achievement—and what it portends for us—demands, then, that we follow the careful construction of his psychology against the framework or Darwinian theory. But we must view his use of that theory, or so I will argue, principally in light of the spiritual crisis he suffered after he had returned from a sojourn in Germany.

James' depressive period, 1867–1878
Education and stay in Germany

James' educational and early professional pursuits were a continual *cursus interruptus*. Against the wishes of his father, Henry James Sr., he studied painting, till he finally admitted his talent was insufficient. He then entered the Lawrence Scientific School at Harvard to study chemistry, the sort of endeavor the elder James hoped might supply the rational and empirical equipment for his son to defend the father's Swedenborgian religious beliefs. But William was only a fair chemist; he quickly perceived that a lack of both mathematics and desire recommended a switch to comparative anatomy, a choice congenial to the artist's interest, but also one with a more practical consequence—it laid a path to medical school. James enrolled in the Harvard Medical School in 1864, though not from any secure vision of himself in clinical practice. In spring of 1867, he interrupted his studies and set out for Germany. He believed the travel necessary to preserve his health; it would also give him an opportunity to work up his German and perhaps to study somy physiology. But in Germany his health deteriorated, his mood turned black, and he found himself unprepared to follow the physiology lectures he audited in Berlin. He poured out his frustration in a letter to his friend, Tom Ward:

> My habits of thought have been so bad that I feel as if the greater part of the last ten years had been worse than wasted, and now have so little surplus of physical vigor as to shrink from trying to retrieve them. Too late! Too late! If I had been

drilled further in mathematics, physics, chemistry, logic, and the history of metaphysics. (H. James 1926, vol. 1:119)

Two months later, in January 1868, James attempted to console a despondent Ward with the confession of his own thoughts of suicide:

> I fancy you have always given me credit for less sympathy with you and understanding of your feelings than I really have had. All last winter, for instance, when I was on the continual verge of suicide, it used to amuse me to hear you chaff my animal contentment. (H. James 1926, vol. 1:129)

During his eighteen months in Germany, James' spirits ebbed and flowed. One episode of melancholy is of particular interest. It exuded mists of a faint hypothesis that eventually would become a more firm biopsychological theory. This occurred while listening to the piano-playing of Katherine Havens, an American he met in Germany and a pretty woman toward whom he felt a strong attraction. In his *Diary* for May 22, 1868, he wrote:

> Tonight while listening to Miss H's magic playing & the Dr. and the Italian lady sing, my feelings came to a sort of crisis. The intuition of something here in a measure absolute gave me such an unspeakable disgust from the dead drifting of my own life for some time past . . .—a horror of wasted life since life can be *such*—and oh god! an end to the idle, idiotic sinking into Vorstellung disproportionate to the object. Every good experience ought to be interpreted in practice. (James 1868–1873: MS p. 55)

James' feelings for Miss Havens went unrequited, since he could not put his *Vorstellung* into action. This experience was repeated with many women whom he knew before he finnally married Alice Gibbens in 1878. In the passage just quoted from his *Diary*, James resolved not to dwell on conceptions that he could not act upon. Later, he made this resolve a biopsychological principle. He came to argue that the function of cognition—its evolutionary purpose—was to produce action, to allow the will to be effective in the world.

James' mental collapse

James returned from Germany in November, 1868, and took up residence again in his father's house. In June of the next year he received his medical degree, but harbored no intention of practicing medicine. He passed the next four years in activities not calculated to secure him a livelihood. In the middle of this period, on February 1, 1870, he seems to have completely broken down. He suffered the event, as characteristic of the James family, with pen in hand.

> Feb. 1. A great dorsal collapse about the 10th or 12th of last month has lasted with a slight interruption till now, carrying with it a moral one. Today, I about touched botton. (James, 1868–1873)

James' spiritual crisis had three major components—professional, interpersonal, and psychometaphysical. Its gradual remission during the decade of the 1870s required specific but related therapies. James had despaired over his professional prospects, feeling that his education left him ill equipped for serious scientific work and that he had wasted his years in descultory study. In 1872, however, President Eliot of Harvard inquired of his neighbor whether he would be interested in filling a vacancy in the physiology department. Thus began James' teaching career at Harvard, a career that carried him from an appointment in physiology to one in psychology and finally to a professorship in philosophy, from which he retired in 1907.

During his early adulthood, James appears not to have been able to act on his feelings toward women. But in 1876, he was introduced to Alice Howe Gibbens, who pulled him back from his frustrations and bachelorhood. Alice supplied James that emotional elixir which sparked his sense of self-possibility and infused him with a zest for life. But perhaps even more than this. Schwehn has forcefully argued that Alice redeemed James, for in her he found a living embodiment of that religion which he had earlier rejected when his father preached it in dreamy Swedenborgian periods (Schwehn, in press).

The third dimension of James' spiritual crisis was psychometaphysical. During the 1860s, James became convinced that advanced science, particularly physiology, left no room for a free and independent mind. He expressed this conviction in a letter to Tom Ward in 1869:

> I'm swamped in an empirical philosophy. I feel that we are Nature through and through, that we are wholly conditioned, that not a wiggle of our will happens save as the result of physical laws. (H. James 1926, vol. 1: 152–53)

James' own lack of purpose, his inability to reduce *Vorstellung* to action, his "palsied" will (as he described it in his *Diary,* 1868–1873) could all be understood and even justified if mind were a puppet to nature's laws. The "task," then, as he concluded in his *Diary* in late 1869, would be "to act without hope." But the task, it appears was beyond him. In February of the following year he "about touched bottom."

Reading Renouvier

A few months after sinking into the depths, James chanced to read a book by the French Kantian Charles Renouvier, and this gave him his first great lift out of despondency. On April 30th, 1870, he recorded the decisive experience in his *Diary:*

> I think that yesterday was a crisis in my life. I finished the first part of *Renouvier's* 2nd Essay, and saw no reason why his definition of free will—the sustaining of a thought because I choose to when I might have other thoughts—need be the definition of an illusion. At any rate I will assume for the present—until next year—that it is no illusion. My first act of free will shall be to believe in free will. For the remainder of the year, I will abstain from the mere speculation & contemplative *Grübelei* which my nature taken most delight. (James 1868–1873)

In the chapters of the *Traite psychologie rationnelle* (1912) that captured James' attention (chs. 13 and 14), *Renouvier* analyzed two opposing doctrines of will, that of determinism and that of the liberty of indifference. He found both unacceptable. Determinism implied that authentic moral behavior, which assumed the agent could have done otherwise, was a delusion. Determinism thus undermined our primitive experience that men did make valid moral judgments. Moreover, if all men were determined, then their philosophical assertions would likewise be: each of their decisions, including the acceptance of determinism, had to result from coercive causal processes. In practice, then, truth and falsity would have to merge in a system that permitted no judgments freely executed for good reasons. Yet the position of those advocating the liberty of indifference stood no more securely. They endowed man with a pure will, indifferent to and uninfluenced by motives, intellectual convictions, or passions. But freedom in this sense became identical with chance.

Renouvier's own theory accorded man a will enmeshed in the thicket of judgment and motives, a will that did not simply react to pressing needs and passions, but one that antecedently reflected on plans that led to alternative motives for behavior. Will actively selected interests as well as responding to them. On this footing James erected his own theory of human liberty. He would come to define the free agent as one who chose what interests to pursue, who actively examined plans of action in order to evoke new motives within himself for behavior. Mind was preeminently a "fighter for ends" (James 1890, vol. 1:141).

But some might still insist on the doctrine of causal necessity, claiming with John Stuart Mill that induction proved it. To them Renouvier simply responded that the inductive method actually assumed causal regularity in order to demonstrate it: induction would fail were nature not constant and our perceptions not stable and reliable. But if an ultimate postulation of a first principle must occur without demonstration—as it must to avoid circular reasoning—then why not the principle that forms an inevitable part of our conception of human acts, one that makes sense of the epistemology of truth and error and that makes moral behavior meaningful—the principle of liberty (Renouvier 1912, vol. 1:321–28;vol. 2:97–8).

James adopted the approach of Renouvier in his first major essays, published in the late 1870s. He urged that we were right to confirm a theory which met with our natural preferences, because all ultimate foundations for philosophical or scientific theories rested, not on ineluctable reason—since first principles cannot be demonstrated—but on belief and conviction. If our taste ran to determinism, we had to recognize that such a choice nullified significant aspects of apparently valid experience. But if we decided for freedom, then we at least insured that moral action would not wither, but could be vigorously tested (James 1876).

The philosophical cure Renouvier offered seemed to have a real impact on James' emotional life. His father noticed the difference in attitude and asked him about it. In 1873, the father wrote to his other son Henry about William's recovery.

> He came in here the other afternoon when I was sitting alone, and after walking the floor in an animated way for a moment, explained "Dear me! What a difference there is between me now and me last spring this time: then so hypochondriacal . . . and now feeling my mind so cleared up and restored to sanity. It is the difference between death and life." He had a great effusion. I was afraid of interfering with it, or possibly checking it, but I ventured to ask what specially in his opionion had promoted the change. He said several things: the reading of Renouvier (specially his vindication of the freedom of will) and Wordsworth, whom he has been feeding upon now for a good while; but especially his having given up the notion that all mental disorder required to have a physical basis. This had become perfectly untrue to him. He saw that the mind did act irrespectively of material coercion, and could be dealt with therefore at first-hand, and this was health to his bones. (Perry 1935, vol. 1:339–40)

The elder James' letter suggests another important aspect of the cure Renouvier wrought, though not, I think, without the help of Darwin, as we will see. The doctrine of freedom meant that mind was not identical with brain, nor its slave. Hence any mental or emotional disturbances, any signs of insanity, which James appears to have noticed in himself, need not be attributed to an incurable organic disorder. Direct spiritual therapy could be effective. And James administered that to himself with strong doses of Renouvier, and, it would seem, with an anodyne that J.S.Mill also found effective, the poetry of Wordsworth.

James' protracted spiritual crisis climaxed in the early 1870s, and probably really only subsided after his marriage. The emotional consolation of a wife and the security of a teaching position helped considerably. But the remedy of Renouvier, taken alone was not potent enough for a lasting cure. The French Kantian demonstrated that the determinist position was not more logically persuasive than the libertarian; yet he failed to counter the full force of Vitorian science, which seemed to support determinism. James required some objective evidence to compound with his subjective preference for freedom. And this he found in Darwin. To understand, however, exactly what Darwin offered, we must first consider James' intellectual relation to that other great nineteenth-century evolutionist, Herbert Spencer.

The psychological uses of Darwinism
Spencerian evolutionism

Spencer, like Darwin, believed that the variety of extant species descended from simpler, more primitive forms over long periods of time. But unlike Darwin, Spencer retained an essentially Lamarckian device as his chief engine for species alteration: the acquisition of habit in response to environmentally produced needs, such that habit would eventually transform simpler organsims into more complex ones by molding their structures against external environmental relations. Spencer held that anatomical patterns mirrored their environmental causes.

Spencer's theory, then, declared that the chief mechanism of evolution was the internalizing of external relations most frequently encountered and that this mechanism progressively drove anatomical forms and conjoint mental structures from more generalized adaptive states to more definite correspondences with the environment, from simpler, more homogeneous patterns to more complex and heterogeneous configurations (Spencer 1886, vol. 1: 407–26). Or, as James liked to rephrase Spencer's law of evolution for his students: "Evolution is a change from a no-howish untalkaboutable all-alikeness to a somehowish and in general talkaboutable not-all-alikeness by continuous sticktogetherations and somethingelseifications' (Perry 1935, vol. 1 : 482).

Darwin pitted against Spencer

James constantly yielded to the allure of Spencer's philosophical science, though the temper of his considerations changed dramatically from his adolescence to early manhood. He recalled that as a youth he was "carried away with enthusiasm by the intellectual perspectives which [Spencer's book *First Principles*] seemed to open" (James, 1904: 104). His ardor for Spencer's evolutionism was, however, dashed in the cooler reflections of his friend Charles Sanders Pierce, who surgically exposed what he took as Spencer's vagueness, vacuity, and pretension. Nonetheless, James never lost his fascination for—almost an intellectually sadistic pleasure in—dismembering Spencer's speculations.

James' ideas about evolution theory gradually worked their way into the courses he offered as a lecturer in the anatomy department at Harvard, something his medical school-bound students complained about. His surviving lecture notes and marginal annotations in books he used for class indicate the depth and considerable breadth of his objections to Spencer. But most of his criticisms were variations on a single theme: Spencer's construction of mind as passive and fixed by natural forces—it is a theme, incidentally, that most people see characterizing Edward Wilson's approach to human evolution. It was this sort of conception that had plagued James during his spiritual crisis and that now could be scientifically assuaged only by a very different sort of evolutionary hypothesis, the Darwinian.

James introduced a new course into the curriculum of the anatomy department in 1876. This was physiological psychology, and Spencer's *Principles of Psychology* served as the text. In a class lecture entitled "Spencer's Law of Intelligence," James argued that Spencerian psychology "repeats the defects of Darwin's predecessors in biology" (James 1879b: MS 5). That is, the pre-Darwinians supposed anatomical adaptations to be the direct response to environmental relations, whereas Darwin showed them to have two different sources: spontaneous variations which do not mirror their causes; and a selection by external circumstances of fit variations, which if so retained would indicate a kind of correspondence with the environment.

In applying the Darwinian perspective to the mental realm, James did not wish to deny that ideas were often impressed upon us by immediate experience. He simply did not want to swallow Spencer whole, bones and all. He argued that the categories of thought acquired over our long evolutionary history and the novel ideas produced by men of genius—and ourselves on occasion—were not due to direct adaptations, to immediate environmental coercion. He proposed that new ways of thought and conceptual innovations sprang up in the mind as spontaneous mental variations, and that we would come to accept them as representations of the environment only if they continued to meet the test of survival. James, of course, recognized that Darwinian natural selection theory was ultimately deterministic; as usually interpreted, spontaneous variatons had their causes. He intimated, however, that our inability to give adequate scientific account of these causes kept open the possibility that mental variations might freely erupt. At least the strenght of the Darwinian analysis did not depend on specifying the causes of variations.

The Darwinian argument for the independence of mind

In February 1878, the year of his marriage and in other ways also very productive, James was invited to John Hopkins to give a series of ten lectures in the hopes he could be lured into the psychology department there. In these lectures he elaborated an extremely powerful evolutionary argument that would objectively ground his subjective need for an active and independent mind.

In the first five of his Hopkins lectures, he sought to demonstrate his control of brain physiology. He recounted the latest experiments from Germany and wove them into a coherent view. In the sixth lecture, however, he finally confronted the question of the relation between mind and brain, taking as his point of departure essays by William Clifford (1874) and Thomas Huxley (1874). Both British scientists advanced an extreme form of the passive view of mind— epiphenomenalism. The brain, they claimed, received stimulation from the environment and issued motor acts as a result; the engine of the central nervous system simply transformed one kind of energy into another, without consciousness playing any mediating role at all. Rather, conscious mind hovered over brain activity like mists of steam coughed up from the dynamo actually doing the work. In his remaining lectures

James indicted this materialistic theory with an argument as powerful as it was elegant. It is an argument that must be regarded as demonstrating the independence of mind from brain.

The argument has an *a priori* part and an *a posteriori* part. The *a priori* part can be reconstructed by the following sorites. Consciousness is a manifest trait of higher organisms, most perspicuously of man; like all such traits it must have evolved; yet it could have evolved only if it were naturally selected; but if naturally selected, it must have a use; and if it has a use, then it cannot be causally inert. Mind, therefore, must be more than an excretion of brain; it must (at least in some respects) be an independently effective process. Here then, as he put it in his lectures, was "objective evidence" for our "aesthetic demands" (James 1878a).

In the remaining lectures and more fully in the article based on them, "Are We Automata?" (1879a), and in the *Principles of Psychology* (1890), James laid out the empirical evidence for the efficacy of consciousness in the natural world. He noted, for instance, its role in the recovery of brain-damaged people, and the obvious uses of subjective feelings of pain and pleasure in preserving organisms. But of the many useful functions conscious mind seemed to perform, its most important was in establishing goals and selecting interests. Man and higher organisms clearly reveal purpose in their behavior; and they become fascinated by certain interests—from seeking food to seeking beauty. This cannot result from a passive accommodation to the occurrent environment, since goals and ideals are precisely those things beckoning from the future, and interests often transcend the common-place and the present-time. In James' view, goals, ideals, and interests can only be understood as spontaneous mental variations that, in the life of higher creatures, have been selected to steer them through their natural and social terrain. "Consciousness," in James' pugnacious metaphor, "is a fighter for ends" (1890, vol. 1:141).

James thus buttressed his *a priori* argument with empirical evidence for the uses consciousness might have, and the conclusion: mind must exist, in some of its acitivties at least, independently of brain. The Darwinian analysis vindicates the strongest urgings of our inmost selves—and James' preferred moral conception of the universe.

The reach of James' Darwinian psychology

The argument of James' Hopkins lectures and ensuing article formed the central nerve radiating out into the many other papers he composed during 1878 and the years following. Finally, after some ten years, he began systematically to incorporate most of these essays into the chapters and sections of his *Principles of Psycholgy,* which Henry Holt, with great relief published in 1890—with great relief, since James delivered his manuscript a decade after the time for which he had originally promised it. The Darwinian analyses of the selective capacities of consciousness and its spontaneously generated interests provided the framework for those several chapters that developed James' principal theses in epistemology, metaphysics and religion, psychology of the self, and ethics. Very briefly, let me indicate the ways in which Darwin came to James' aid in resolving central problems in just two of these areas.

Metaphysics and religion. The spontaneous and selective aspects of consciousness explain our postulation of a world of natural objects. Out of the booming-buzzing confusion that aboriginal experience presents, we must carve out a real, and well-structured world. What we decide to be real, James contended (1890, vol. 2, ch. 21), will depend on the nature of the intellectual environment that selects spontaneous mental variations that can organize our experience. Fundamentally we regard objects as real that can be tested against our sensations. Our ancestors who chanced to test their conceptions in the same way were able to avoid the saber-tooth tiger lurking in their paths; and we have inherited their mental penchant. As for those proto-men who fancied other criteria for real objects, well their lines have not prospered.

During his young manhood, James felt the sting of religious demands from several quarters. His father unleashed upon him baroque missiles of Swedenborgism, from which he defended himself with logical objection and retaliatory skepticism. Yet the father's feeling for religion, his profound conviction that an ideal reality hovered just above the horizons of human life, that there would be a "final evolution *of human nature itself* into permanent harmony with God's spiritual perfection" (James, 1885: 457)—these sentiments penetrated the son's defenses. James became a champion himself, not of orthodox theology, nor even of heterodox faith, but of the warm and energizing feeling of divinity. He marshalled this hopeful energy against the scientific materialism of his friends Chauncy Wright and Oliver Wendell Holmes.

James utilized Darwinian theory to provide scientific support for religion principally in three ways. First, he proposed that religious faith could be regarded as a spontaneously generated set of beliefs not yet rejected by the winnowing hand of reality. "We know so little about the ultimate nature of things, or of ourselves," he warned, "that it would be sheer folly dogmatically to say that an ideal rational order may not be real. The only objective criterion of reality is coerciveness, in the long run, over thought" (1878b: 17). Religious belief might yet be confirmed, as James liked to put it, *ambulando,* in the great by and by. Second, the reality that religion postulated might require our continued acquiescence in order to evolve. Divinity itself might well be, as his father held, an organic reality fed on our constant belief in it (1897:61). Lastly, though James regarded the spiritual world as something ultimately verifiable only when we passed beyond, he harbored no doubt about the effective reality of religious belief itself. Religion as purely a belief system gave natural advantage to those who possessed it. He thus cautioned that a nation which succeeded in suffocating the religious sentiments of its citizens, replacing them, for instance, with sterile doctrines of empirical science, "that nation, that race, will just as surely go to ruin, and fall prey to their more richly constituted neighbors, as the beasts of the field, as a whole, have fallen prey to man" (1897:132).

The moral will. In several early essays and in various chapters of the *Principles* (especially ch. 26), James poured the scientific foundations for moral choice. His construction was in two parts: first, an account of the evolutionary source of moral interests, and, second, an explanation of the way the will operated so as to make free choice possible. In tackling the first part, James' strategy was, of course, to argue that moral interests, like other ideal standards, were spontaneous mental variations that had been selected. Like Darwin, he conceived these interests, in his early essays and lectures, as instincts having survival value, and thus selectively perpetuated in intelligent organisms. But also like Darwin, he encountered a basic objection, that altruistic behavior, promoted by moral inclination, often appeared not to benefit the individual exercising it. James' solution to this conundrum was not so happy as Darwin's, though. Early tribal communities, he argued, had an interest in promoting the hero, the martyr, the gallant warrior, since, as he macabrely put it, "it is death to you, but fun for us" (1878: 9). That is, individual altruistic action would advance the welfare of the whole community, which then would become the selecting force for those organisms manifesting such behavior. Unlike Darwin, who saw altruistic behavior resulting from the selection of the whole tribe in competition with other tribes not having altruistic individuals, James seems to have conceived such behavior as a consequence of selfish individuals being selectively eliminated by their own communities. (This explanation, of course, presupposed an already existing community of moral individuals. James offered no account of the evolutionary origins of their altruistic behavior—nor, I think, could he have. He really did not fully understand something that Darwin saw straight through to the bottom, that to explain altruistic behavior the unit of selection cannot be the individual, since moral acts usually offer him no advantage. The unit of selection must be the whole tribe or community [Richards 1982].)

The second part of James' analysis, his account of the operation of the will, required accpetance of a particular evolutionary construction of ideas. Concepts, ideas, James supposed, originally evolved to facilitate action. "It is far too little recognized," he observed (1897: 65–6), "how entirely the intellect is built up of practical interests. The theory of Evolution is beginning to do very good service by its reduction of all mentality to the type of reflex action ... Cognition, in short, is incomplete until discharged in act." This theory of the motor function of ideas, which I believe had a motive in James' spiritual crisis, served to make free choice a scientific possibility for him. In deciding what to do in a situation, the mind, he believed, becomes the playground of competing plans of action. When one idea finally dominates our attention to the exclusion of rivals, action follows automatically. In a moral decision, selfish, pleasure-preserving proposals vie with altruistic intentions. A free act would, in James' estimation, simply consist in the mind selectively attending to one idea over the others, becoming interested in it, while letting the others fade. Such attention, the active entertaining of the moral idea, for instance, would put a thumb on the scale. With the moral intention the most weighty, moral action would follow as a matter of course. Natural selection within the social environment of the primitive tribe may have outfitted modern man with moral ideas, but his behavior will merit moral approbation only if he pursues those ideas freely.

James admitted that psychological introspection could never really decide whether the interest invested in an idea were merely a function of the idea's own attractive force or a mental varitation spontaneously bestowed on it (James, 1890, vol. 2: 569–74). Empirical investigation and sound theory—that is, Jamesean evolutionary psychology—proved to him that determinism, at least, was not a mandate of modern science.

But what science alone could not demonstrate, the subjective method of Renouvier allowed him to postulate: as a first principle we could choose freedom.

Conclusion

The subjective method of Renouvier served to boost James' declining spirits during his mental crisis. Yet it did not really alleviate the weight of modern science, which seemed to press toward determinism as a necessary conclusion. James needed an objective counter-balance to give the subjective method real force. He found this in Darwinian evolutionary theory, which in its application to cognition and behavior seemed to require a mind independent of the machinery of brain and one thus capable of free choice. The Darwinian approach extended far into the workings of James' scientific psychology, and supplied the unity of conception and power of explanation that made it a significant influence on the course of early modern psychology in America.

Good history should have those qualities, I believe, that Horace attributed to good poetry. It should be *dulcis et utilis.* Even a moderately faithful representation of James' intellectual development could not be less than sweetly fascinating, since an extraordinary mind, a lively wit, and a deeply emotional personality danced on virtually every page of his essays and books. The history of James' development is also usefully instructive. He formulated four different arguments that for me, and several others, are still intellectually coercive. These arguments demonstrate clearly, I think, that evolutionary considerations are not inimical to a moral or even a religious conception of man—the protestations of religious critics, Marxists, and hard-headed sociobiologists notwithstanding. Let me conclude by simply pointing out these arguments.

The first is the elegantly simple argument for the efficacy of a mind at least partly independent of brain machinery: if conscious mind is an evolved trait, which it certainly seems to be, then it could have been naturally selected for only if it added some utility to the material of the brain, that is, to that organ as it is usually described in physiology textbooks. Karl Popper, for one, has employed this argument, though apparently without recognizing its originator (Popper 1978).

The second contribution is a bit more complex, but equally persuasive. This is James' proposal that ideas be regarded as comparable to chance variations. Their truth value—in a correspondence sense—becomes then a function of their survival value in the various intellectual environments into which they are plunged. This epistemological hypothesis is grounded in a compelling argument adumbrated by James: if novel ideas are not innate, and not simply logically induced from observation, then only a kind of blind or unjustified variation could first introduce them; and they will be retained only if they are adapted to the intellectual problem-conditions to which they are applied. There are now several epistemologists about for whom this evolutionary theory of knowledge has struck home (Campbell 1960, 1974; Hull 1978; Richards 1977; Popper 1972; Toulmin 1972). The theory also has, I believe, important consequences for the historian of science; since it suggests an historiographic model far superior to others for the guidance of the historian in his craft (Richards 1981).

Third is James' approach to moral judgment, particularly his recognition of the instinctual base for other-regarding virtues. He thought that man, as an evolved animal, could not shed his biology upon being civilized. Rather, those instincts that constitute the possibility of society, such as parental affection and altruism, he took to be evolved traits, selected over our long evolutionary history. James did not blush to admit, nor I believe should we, that our moral character is as much an hereditary product as our ability to use language and think great thoughts.

Finally, there is the subjective method itself. Here again, the argument is disarmingly simple. No system of thought can demonstrate its own first principles, something Aristotle long ago recognized. Foundational principles must ultimately result from custom, preference, or personality. This conclusion has, for me, two important lessons, one philosophical, the other historiographical. First, if the postulation of freedom and a spiritual world enrich life and competitively exclude no more important considerations, then why should we hesitate to endorse their reality? Second, the historian of science must attempt to reconstitute the actual intellectual environment that spawned scientific ideas, and not rest satisfied with some rationally sanitized reconstruction of that environment. Those advocating what is usually called the "strong program" in sociology of science have perceived this (Barnes 1977, Bloor 1976). And while the historian, if he is really to portray the selecting environment, cannot be as antilogistic as are some enthusiasts for the strong program, it is clear he can no longer pursue that kind of history of science in which ideas inexorably unfold, bound together only by internal logical chains. This is neo-Spencerianism. The historian, rather, must give due weight to social influences, and, as James' own history powerfully shows, the psychology of individual personality.

Acknowledgment

While examining the James Papers, I received the kind and gracious aid of the staff of Houghton Library, Harvard University. This essay is an abridged and differently oriented version of "The Personal Equation in Science: William James's Psychological and Moral Uses of Darwinian Theory," *Harvard Lib. Bull.*, 30 (October, 1982): 387–425; portions of this latter essay have been used with permission. This research was supported by N.I.H. grant PHS 5 S07 RR-07029-12 and a grant from the National Science Foundations.

References

Barnes, B. (1977) *Interests and the growth of knowledge.* London: Routledge and Kegan Paul.

Bloor, D. (1976) *Knowledge and social imagery.* London: Routledge and Kegan Paul.

Campbell, D. (1960) Blind variation and selective retention in creative thought. *Psychol. Rev.* 67: 380–400.

—(1974) Evolutionary epistemology. In P. Schilpp (Ed.), *The philosophy of Karl Popper* (3 vols.) Lasalle, Ill.: Open Court.

Clifford, W. (1874) Body and mind. *Fortnightly Rev.* 22: 714–36.

Darwin, C. (1859) *On the Origin of Species.* London: Murray.

Huxley, L. (1900) *Life and letters of Thomas H. Huxley.* (2 vols.) New York: Appleton.

Huxley, T. (1874) On the hypothesis that animals are automata and its history. *Fortnightly Rev.* 22: 555–89.

James, H. (Ed.). (1926) *Letters of William James* (2 vols. 2d ed.). Boston: Little, Brown.

James, W. (1868–1873) *Diary.* Papers of William James. Houghton Library, Harvard University.

—(1876) Bain and Renouvier. *Nation* 22: 367–69.

—(1878a.) Ten Lectures (untitled) The Papers of William James. Houghton Library, Harvard University.

—(1878b) Remarks on Spencer's definition of mind as correspondence. *J. Speculative Phil.* 12: 1–18.

—(1879a) Are we automata? *Mind* 4: 1–22.

—(1879b) Spencer's law of intelligence. The Papers of William James. Houghton Library, Harvard University.

—(1885) *The literary remains of the late Henry James.* Boston: Osgood.

—(1890) *The Principles of psychology* (2 vols.) New York: Holt.

—(1904) Herbert Spencer. *Atlantic Monthly* 94: 99–108.

—(1897) *The will to believe.* London: Longmans, Green.

Perry, R. (1935) *The thought and character of William James* (2 vols.) Boston: Little, Brown.

Popper, K. (1972) *Objective knowledge: An evolutionary approach.* Oxford: Oxford University Press.

—(1978) Natural selection and the emergence of mind. *Dialectica* 32: 339–55.

Renouvier, C. (1912) *Essais de critique générale, Deuxième essai: Traite de psychologie rationnelle* (2 vols.). Paris: Colin. (This is a reprint of the 2d ed. of 1875, which James read.)

Richards, R. (1981) Natural selection and other models in the historiography of science. In M. Brewer and B. Collins (Eds.), *Scientific inquiry and the social scienes.* San Francisco: Jossey-Bass.

—(1982) Darwin and the biologizing of moral behavior. In W. Woodward and M. Ash (Eds.), *The problematic science: Psychology in nineteenth-century thought.* New York: Praeger.

Schwehn, M. (in press) Science and sensibility: William James and the life of the mind. *Harvard Lib. Bull.*

Spencer, H. (1886) *Principles of psychology* (2 vols. 3d ed.) New York: Appleton. (The 3d edition does not differ essentially from the 2d, which James read.)

Toulmin, S. (1972) *Human understanding.* Oxford: Oxford University Press.

Wilson, E. (1975) *Sociobiology.* Cambridge, Mass.

The Problem of Imitation and Explanatory Models in Early Developmental Psychology

by Kurt Danziger

While child psychology, in its early years, was notable more for its concern with practice and with the amassing of observations, a certain theoretical interest was present from the beginning. What was the source of this theoretical interest? Certainly not the nascent experimental psychology of the period. The questions and methods of early experimental psychology overlapped very little with the questions of early child psychology. Many of the most respected representatives of the new experimental psychology were openly sceptical about the real value of child study, and some of the key figures in the foundation of developmental psychology, like Baldwin and Hall, were men who had become impatient and disillusioned with the progress to be expected from the experimental psychology of the laboratory. Developmental psychology had its own theoretical concerns, and its rapprochement with experimental psychology was a long and difficult process marked by many ups and downs.

The first major incursion of child psychology into the realm of theory took the form of the recapitulationist doctrine that ontogeny repeats phylogeny. In theoretical intent this doctrine is recognizable as a secularized version of natural theology. The human order that is to be explained, in this case childhood, is seen as the manifestation of a fixed natural order that runs its inevitable course, uncreated by man, but following a superior wisdom of its own.[2] In practice this schema has the effect of allowing the theorist to bestow the blessing of supramundane providence on any aspect of human behavior he wishes to sanctify, for the analogical mode of reasoning, characteristic of this approach, is not constrained by the discipline of real world distinctions. In the context of developmental psychology recapitulation theory soon collapsed under the weight of its many absurdities, leaving the field clear for other approaches which were more in tune with prevailing theoretical imperatives.

Those imperatives were clearly generated by the success of the Darwinian theory of natural selection. That theory had demonstrated the power of a relatively simple model for explaining a natural genetic sequence. Was it possible that a similar model might be as serviceable in the explanation of ontogenetic development as natural selection had been in the explanation of phylogenetic development? But what would constitute a similar model, given the material difference between the development of human individuals and the development of biological species? One thing was clear. The theory of natural selection had demonstrated that the key to the explanation of the genetic sequence must be looked for in the relationship between individuals and the medium which supported them. Developmental psychology thus found itself faced with a theoretical challenge of no mean significance—the explanation of ontogenetic regularities in terms of individual-environment relationships.

But there were a number of fundamental difficulties to be faced in transferring the natural selection model from the phylogenetic to the ontogenetic level. Though many of these difficulties were not clearly grasped at the time, they determined the course of theoretical discourse all the same. In the first place, phylogenetic and psychological development take place in a different medium, nature in the one case and human society in the other. Was the nature of the medium irrelevant to the form of the process, and if not, what special forms of individual-environment relationship might be imposed by the social medium? Secondly, there was the problem of defining the individuals whose fate and development was decided by their relationship to the medium. In principle, the units involved in the developmental process could be defined as movements, as organized actions or as human individuals. Thirdly, the developmental sequence of childhood has a natural outcome, namely adulthood, while phylogenetic development was not dominated by a single end state. This meant that accounts of ontogenetic development were necessarily and fundamentally influenced by the manner in which its outcome was conceived, a factor which was in principle irrelevant on the level of phylogenetic development.

It was the topic of imitation which provided the ground on which early developmental psychology was forced to confront these theoretical problems in the most direct manner. The undeniable phenomenon of imitation clearly provided an instance of individual-environment relationship that was characteristic of childhood and that seemed to be relevant in a developmental context. Moreover, it clearly took place in a social medium, so that the explanation on imitation generally provided the key to the way in which different developmental theories came to terms with the fact that human development involves a social process.

The first generation of developmental theorists in psychology did not come to their task without some conceptual preparation. A problematic of mental development had already been defined within two philosophical traditions that were entirely alien to one another. One was represented by the philosophy of Hegel, which, though not concerned with the development of individuals, had introduced a dialectical perspective into the discussion of mental development in general. The other was the philosophy of British empiricism which generated a vigorous tradition of applying mechanistic models to the explanation of individual development. This tradition can be traced to the mid-eighteenth century founder of systematic associationism, David Hartley, whose work contains many references to learning in children.[3] In fact, it is a central concern of Hartley's to show how the association of sensations, ideas, and movements must necessarily generate a developmental sequence which results in a hierarchy of behavioral tendencies that promotes social order. A century later we find a closely related model in the work of Alexander Bain who also uses child behavior to illustrate how a mechanical process of association among elements generates behavior sequences that are regarded as voluntary.[4]

There is no indication that either Hartley or Bain made systematic observations of the actual behavior of infants or children. Yet they developed quite an elaborate mechanistic model to account for certain developmental sequences in the behavior of young human beings. Historically, therefore, the systematic construction of theory preceded the systematic collection of data. Moreover, these older theories were quite well known to those modern psychologists who made the first attempts at providing a theoretical explanation of the data on children's behavior that were beginning to become available at the end of the nineteenth and the beginning of the twentieth century. Bain's work was then still going into new editions, and Hartley's theory, though no longer studied directly, was known through the medium of his nineteenth interpreter, James Mill.[5]

The main explanatory category bequeathed to developmental psychology by empiricist philosophy was constituted by the concept of habit. Individual development was seen in terms of the accumulation of habitual associations among discrete psychological elements, sensations, ideas, and specific movements. These associations were purely external and contingent, that is to say, the meaning of psychological processes had no causal role in generating new acquisitions. Subsequently, Herbert Spencer assimilated the concept of instinct to this explanatory scheme, regarding instinctive reactions as bases on habitual reactions that had become inherited in the course of biological evolution. Thus when the first generation of developmental psychologists began to be interested in going beyond purely descriptive observations they had available to them at least one simple and comprehensive explanatory scheme. This was the scheme of habit and instinct, according to which the behavior of individuals in the course of development was to be explained in terms of the formation of new associative connections or the activation of connections previously formed, either by himself or by his ancestors.

How did the phenomenon of imitation fit into this scheme? For the classical mechanistic account learning by imitation introduced no new principles and was entirely reducible to either habit or instinct. It was either an unlearned response to certain stimuli, based on inherited ancestral learning, or it was simply a matter of forming contingent associative connections by the individual. Only those empiricist philosophers who did not completely accept psychological mechanism, notably members of the Scottish school, like Dugald Stewart, insisted on the nonreducible status of imitative learning. But these philosophers were very much out of favor by the end of the nineteenth century.

Among the first generation of modern psychologists who began to theorize about child development it was Thorndike who stuck most closely to the traditional mechanistic scheme. For him, imitation involves either specific innate tendencies to reproduce particular movements or it involves imitative learning. But the latter is entirely reducible to the formation of contingent connections between situation elements and response elements as described in the laws of exercise and effect. Social learning, and hence social development, had no special status and involved no principles that were not already at work in learning about the physical world. "The enunciation or gesture of another man, acting as a model, forms one's habits of speech or manners in just the same way that the physical properties of trees form one's habits of climbing."[6] In other words, there is a complete reduction of the relationship of persons and persons to the relationship of persons and things. Or to put it yet another way, the persons in the child's environment have theoretically the same status as things. But as human individuals, from this viewpoint, are essentially represented by an aggregate of movements, social learning is simply a process whereby certain things in the environment come to produce certain movements. The process by which movements are selected is very similar in Bain's model and in Thorndike's model. The organism offers a supply of movements to the environment, and only those survive which establish a "satisfying" relationship between individual and environment. This model obviously has some analogy to the model of natural selection on the phylogenetic level where the selective survivial of successful variants leads to changes in the pool of individuals rather than in the pool of movements.

There was only one significant respect in which Thorndike deviated from the learning model of Mill and Bain. But this deviation was in the direction of improving the purely mechanical nature of the model. In the older accounts there had been a certain ambiguity about the nature of the connection between the idea of an action and the action itself. That connection was often presented as a "necessary" one, as in the doctrine of ideomotor action. Thus, perceiving or thinking of an action was thought to entail an automatic tendency to produce the action, a connection that would obviously result in imitative movements. But Thorndike recognized that "necessary" connections, based on inherent resemblance between an action and its mental representation, could have no place in a consistently mechanistic account. Only external, purely contingent connection between causes and effects were allowable. Hence he argued very strongly that mental representations of movements and the movements they represent are not inherently connected but become associated by a process of learning, obeying the same laws as all other instances of learning.[7] This means that the child has to learn to imitate the actions of others. Thus imitation is not fundamentally a vehicle of learning but a product of learning. Essentially the same position was to be taken by Thorndike's mid-twentieth century heirs in the field of learning theory.[8]

One of the first to recognize that imitation could not be fitted into the traditional framework of habit and instinct was Karl Groos. He began by regarding imitation as a general instint, but subsequently modified his view and accepted the "necessary connection" between a movement and the concept of the movement as a condition of imitation which resulted in "a psychophysical adjustment, not in the ordinary sense instinctive."[9] Such a connection might then be made use of by specific social instincts but the general effect of imitative "adjustments" was to support the development of intelligent behavior, not to strengthen instinctive behavior.

In the development of these views Groos had been influenced by the ideas of James Mark Baldwin, a figure in whom early developmental psychology possessed a theoretical talent of the first rank. He quickly spotted some of the questionable implicit assumptions of the Bain-Spencer model of adaptive behavior, even before Thorndike gave this model its twentieth century reincarnation. The model, as Baldwin pointed out, involved the assumption that the environment remained remarkably constant. Without this assumption the selection of adaptive movement by the gradual growth of specific associations simply would not work. But such an assumption, while it might have some plausibility in the context of broad physical features of the environment, broke down in the context of the child's social environment. Thorndike and his heirs subsequently coped with this difficulty in two ways: First, by simply denying that there was any fundamental difference between relating to the human environment and relating to inanimate objects; second, by creating an artificial environment of experimental situations that were specially constructed to exclude the troublesome lack of constancy in the real environment. In this way the mechanistic model of development was saved, but the cost was considerable.

Baldwin followed a different path. He attempted to construct an alternative theoretical model of the processes that produced psychological development in the real world. He referred to his model as a "dialectic of personal growth." The use of the term "dialectic" was not merely a verbal flourish but was the product of a serious interest in dialectical philosophy which was quite unique among developmental psychologists. This interest gave a cast to his theorizing which sufficed to make it totally incomprehensible to virtually all psychologists in his own country. Historically, Baldwin's influence was limited to Europe, where Jean Piaget, in particular, was able to use some of his insights productively.

In elaborating his theory of the developmental process Baldwin based himself on the recognition that the regularity, which the child's social environment could not guarantee, was, in a measure, the product of the child's own activity.[10] This is where imitation plays its fundamental role, for it involves a circular process in which the child's action is not simply the response to a stimulus but a directed attempt to reproduce an impression. The fundamental element in the individual-environment relationship does not take the stimulus-response form but the form of a copy-producing action, that is to say, an attempt at producing a subjective reflection of the objective. Because such attempts normally do not succeed at once in producing a perfect copy of the model, they are the source of a continous stream of novel actions and novel impressions in the development of the child.[11] They are also the source of novel structures because of the tendency for the new approximations produced by the child to become assimilated to previously established models.[12] For Baldwin imitation is not primarily a reproductive but a productive action. The reduction of imitation to the reproduction of models, which is still a popular approach in present-day developmental psychology, assimilates the concept of imitation to the concept of habit in order to preserve a mechanistic model of the developmental process. Such an approach has more in common with the philosophy of Thorndike than with that of Baldwin.

As an account of the fundamental processes steering individual development, Baldwin's model of imitation corrected the deficiencies of the traditional mechanistic model in a number of important respects. Only some of these can be dealt with here. One fundamental aspect concerns the interrelationship of the basic terms that constitute the paradigmatic model of the individual-environment relation. In the traditional mechanistic model, the three terms of situation or stimulus, response, and reinforcement or pleasure or satisfaction have a purely external, contingent, relationship to each other and their connection is arbitrary. In Baldwin's model the connection between model, imitative action, and copy is intrinsic, and the effectiveness of the copy in investigating further action depends directly on its qualitative resemblance to the model. This introduces a source of developmental dynamics which has nothing to do with the narrowly conceived utilitarian doctrine of the traditional view. Indeed, as Baldwin pointed out, the imitation of models may directly oppose the operation of the pleasure principle in specific situations.[13] This insight has far-reaching consequences for the explanation of the cognitive and social development of the child.

It is in the area of social development that the consequences of Baldwin's approach were most obvious. The genesis of imitative action depends on a prior distinction of persons and things. That is to say, the infant comes to differentiate between those impressions that are to be acted upon and those that are to be imitated. The former belong mostly to things, the latter mostly to persons. At this stage the child constructs what Baldwin calls "personal projects," schemas of objects distinguished by the characteristic of "agency," which as yet involves only a primitive apprehension of a special unpredictability in their behavior.[14] But at this stage the child does not yet distinguish between himself and his own actions. It is his attempts at imitating these personal projects that lead to the discovery of his own agency, and only after that is a similar agency attributed to the model in a process which Baldwin calls "ejection." In his attempts at imitation the child builds up a conception of himself and of his social world. He begins by not distinguishing between himself and his actions nor between his own self and that of others. As Baldwin puts it, the individual person is not a social unit but a social outcome.[15] The fundamental questions of human development are questions of social development, and learning about things is embedded in a process of learning about his social world and his own social self.

The majority of developmental psychologists ignored Baldwin's insights and continued to assume that the individual-environment relationship on the social-psychological level could be analysed in terms of models taken from the world of physical objects and their spatial relationships. On this basis the problem of imitation lost its fundamental significance. In western psychology the major exceptions to this trend included: Freud, G.H.Mead, and Piaget. The last two were directly influenced by Baldwin, whereas Freud forms part of a very different line of historical development. I shall restrict myself to brief comments on the striking divergence between the contributions of Mead and Piaget. While the tendency of Baldwin's analysis had been to show the common basis of social and cognitive development, these two aspects are split in the work of his successors, Mead exploring the basic processes of social development and Piaget those of cognitive development. This had unfortunate consequences for the adequacy of their theories of human development and for the fields they influenced, leading to a troublesome gap between theories of cognitive development and theories of socialization.

Mead used the theories of Baldwin and of Wundt as a starting point, but he used the insights he had gained from Baldwin to criticize Wundt and the insights he had gained from Wundt to criticize Baldwin. Against Wundt's account of the origin of language in gesture he advanced the consideration that the self-conscious individual is himself a product of social interaction and cannot be quietly presupposed as Wundt had done.[16] Mead had early accepted Baldwin's conception of the self as a product of social development. But he rejected Baldwin's assimiliation of all forms of self-developing social interaction to the concept of imitation.[17] Here he showed a preference for Wundt's broader concept of a language of gestures based on expressive movements. On this basis Mead supplies a dimension that had been missing in Baldwin's account, the dimension of the symbolic. It is those imitative gestures that take on a symbolic function which play the crucial role in the social development of the individual. But they assume this symbolic function because of the way they are used by other individuals in interaction with the developing individual. A basis of social interaction in expressive gestures is necessary before the imitative gesture can be recognized as producing the same effect in oneself as in others and so produce a self as object, or social self.[18]

While Piaget, like Mead, also supplements Baldwin's account of imitation by reference to the genesis of a level of symbolic activity, their conceptions of this genesis could hardly be more opposed. Where Mead had found the source of symbolic activity in the child's social world, Piaget regards it as the achievement of the single individual. Its source is traced to deferred imitation, a development defined by physical rather than social parameters.[19] Thus, while Piaget leans much more closely than Mead on Baldwin's original model of imitative action, he develops it in the direction of an explanatory scheme for a purely cognitive kind of development that no longer has anything in common with Baldwin's conception of a "dialectic of personal growth." The seeds of this direction of thought were however sown by Baldwin himself when he failed to recognize that the distinction between "personal projects" and the inanimate part of the child's environment entailed a similar distinction on the level of the child's actions, that is to say, a distinction between manipulative and gestural acts.

On balance, the early theoretical concern with the role and nature of imitative action did lead to certain valuable gains for explanatory developmental psychology. It produced the concept of a mechanism, the circular reaction, which was far better able to do justice to elementary individual-environment relationships than the crude transfer of the model of natural selection to the level of individual development. It also established the importance of imitative action for the development of symbolic behavior. But it failed to come to terms with the crucial question posed by the phenomenon of imitation, namely, the question of the relationship between the child's interaction with things and its interaction with persons. Instead, it led to the development of two areas of research—in socialization and in cognitive development—which it has not been easy to bring together again. The suggestion that the secret of the relationship between the biological and the social in individual development is locked up in the phenomenon of imitation remained as a challenge to later generations of developmental psychologists.

Notes

1   Grinder,R.E. (1967) (Ed.) *A History of Genetic Psychology, the First Science of Human Development.* New York: Wiley.
2   Gould,S.J. (1977) *Ontogeny and Phylogeny,* ch.5. Cambridge, Mass.: Harvard University Press.
3   Hartley,D. (1966/67) *Observations on Man, His Frame, His Duty, and His Expectations.* London: 1749. (Reprinted by Scholars' Facsimiles and Reprints, Gainesville, Fla., and by Georg Olms Verlagsbuchhandlung, Hildesheim).
4   Bain,A. (1872) *The Senses and the Intellect,* 3d ed. New York: Appleton. (1st ed., 1866).
5   Mill,J. (1869) *Analysis of the Phenomena of the Human Mind,* 2d ed. London: Longmans etc. (1st ed., 1829).
6   Thorndike,E.L. (1913) *Educational Psychology,* vol.I: *The Original Nature of Man,* p. 175. New York: Columbia University.
7   Thorndike, *op. cit.,* pp. 176–185.
8   Miller,N.E. and Dollard,J. (1941) *Social Learning and Imitation.* New Haven: Yale University Press.
9   Groos,K. (1901) *The Play of Man,* p. 285. New York: Appleton. (German original published 1898).
10 Baldwin,J.M. (1925) *Mental Development in the Child and the Race,* 3d ed., p. 191. New York: Macmillan. (1st ed., 1894).
11 —(1897). *Social and Ethical Interpretations in Mental Development,* ch. 3. New York: Macmillan.
12 —(1925). *op. cit.* p. 360.
13 Ibid., p. 283.
14 Ibid., pp. 118–120.
15 —(1897). *op. cit.,* p. 87.
16 Mead,G.H. (1934) *Mind, Self, and Society.* University of Chicago Press.
17 —(1909). Social psychology as counterpart of physiological psychology. *Psychol. Bull.* 6: 401–408.
18 —(1922). A behavioristic account of the significant symbol. *J.Philos.* 19: 157–163.
19 Piaget,J. (1951) *Play, Dreams and Imitation in Childhood.* London: Heinemann.

The Application of Pavlovian Conditioning Procedures in Child and Developmental Psychology

by Peter J. Behrens

A neglected area of documentation in the history of child and developmental psychology is the contribution of Pavlovian conditioning procedures. For the most part, American textbooks of child psychology casually cite John Watson's experiments with Little Albert as the first demonstration of Pavlovian conditioning applied to children in America (Craig 1979, Brophy and Willis 1981), and then leap approximately twenty years to the successful application of Pavlovian conditioning to the treatment of a childhood behavior disorder, enuresis, by the Mowrers in 1938 (Johnson and Madinnus 1974). The Mowrers' procedure has stood the test of time and efficacy, but Watson's work has recently been critically examined and found wanting in theoretical and methodological sophistication (Harris 1979, Samelson 1980), producing something of a void in the historical record. This paper accepts the view that Watson's laboratory erred in representing the Pavlovian paradigm, and will attempt to trace the experimental research which follows the Pavlovian model of behavior applied to child and developmental psychology in America. In this process, three topics will be given consideration. First, mention will be made of the *Zeitgeist* which met the introduction of the conditioned reflex to American psychology. Second, the use of the conditioned reflex with infants and children will be reviewed in terms of methodological and programmatic considerations. Finally, some current areas of application of the conditioned reflex to child and developmental psychology in America will be reviewed.

The status of child and developmental psychology in America at the time of Pavlov's initial work on the conditioned salivary reflex—about 1900—was, for the most part, a view to consider child behavior as either a developmentally inferior level in the emergence of the adult personality after Freud's psychodynamic theory, or as the object for identification and application of pedagogical methods for the improvement of education in particular, and citizenship in general. Thus, Freud's report of the case of Little Hans in 1909 was taken as clinical verification of the Oedipal stage of personality development, as well as validation of psychoanalytic psychotherapy. At the same time, others in the field of education were strongly influenced by the genetic method of Darwinian biology as it could be applied to child study. G.Stanley Hall, James Cattell, and William James, among others, established the foundation for the genetic study of behavior in America through questionnaires, mental testing techniques, and systematic measurement of children. In these approaches, however, the distinction between behavioristic, objective study and introspection was blurred, even though the distinction was prominent in general psychology (Murchison 1931).

Nor did research in child and developmental psychology emanate from the laboratories of the "new" experimental psychology in the great German universities, or in the newly-founded American universities. Indeed, the tone of the "new" psychology was set decidedly against experimental child study by, among other forces, the influence of Wundtian psychology. In his *Gründzüge*, Wundt remarked on the minor role for child study in psychology:

> ... Thierpsychologie und die Psychologie des Kindes [sind] von relativ geringerem Werthe..., in Vergleich mit den physiologischen Disciplinen der menschlichen und der vergleichenden Entwicklungsgeschichte (1905: page 6).

According to Hall (1912), Wundt's psychology, by definition, could not accommodate child study as a major research emphasis, because of its dependence upon self-observation. The developmentally inferior nervous system of the child (to say nothing of infants) made the study of memory, sense discrimination, perception, and apperception misleading and erroneous for an understanding of adult processes, which, after all, Wundt was addressing.

The term *conditioned reflex* (CR) was first introduced by I.P.Pavlov about 1898 to describe an acquired reaction of the organism to a previously neutral stimulus, *conditioned stimulus* (CS), as a result of pairings with a psychologically potent stimulus, *unconditoned stimulus* (US). The peculiar property of the US, and the basis for the CR, is that it regularly elicits without training either an appetitive or an aversive *unconditioned reflex* (UR). Pavlov's program centered on the study of the acquired salivary reflex in dogs, which was a convenient, and, more importantly, a quantifiable appetitive reaction. His students, however, very early extended Pavlov's procedures, and one, N.I.Krasnogorski, was the first to demonstrate conditoned reflexes in children. His results appeared in 1909 in the *Jahrbuch für Kinderheilkunde* in an article titled

"*Über die Bedingungsreflexe im Kinderalter.*" Krasnogorski's experiments have an added significance for American psychology because his published accounts served as the model for the first American experiments on conditioned reflexes in children conducted at Clark University by Florence Mateer in 1914–1916, under the direction of William Burnham. Mateer's experiments (which constituted her doctoral dissertation) preceded Watson's conditioning of Little Albert at Johns Hopkins University by about two years, but followed Krasnogorski's original experiments by about 10 years.

The Krasnogorski-Mateer arrangement employed the swallowing reflex (UR) elicited by the sight and taste of food (US), associated with various neutral stimuli. Krasnogorski used the sound of a bell or tone as the CS (Krasnogorski 1925); Mateer used the application of a bandage over the eyes as the CS, which she thought was an improvement in the basic experimental design (Mateer 1918). Mateer measured swallowing reflexes in accordance with procedures first developed in Pavlov's laboratory, which included the Maley tambour and kymograph. Such precision measurement was unusual for this period of American child study, but reflected the Pavlovian concern with objective and quantifiable measurement. Mateer was able to demonstrate the conditioned swallowing reflex in two groups, one mentally defective, one normal, whose subjects ranged from 12 months to 73 months of age. In addition, other conditioning phenomena, such as conditioned inhibition (extinction) and conditioned disinhibition (spontaneous recovery) were demonstrated.

Although John Watson adopted Pavlov's conditioning terminology in his work, several important distinctions exist between the Krasnogorski-Mateer arrangement and the conditioning experiments conducted by Watson and his students (Watson and Rayner 1920, Jones 1924). First, a distinction between appetitive and aversive conditioning was made, which was of considerable importance for Pavlov (Babkin 1949). Appetitive, as opposed to aversive, reflexes have the advantage of being more easily quantifiable, and avoid both preparatory responses and escape and avoidance behaviors. Watson chose aversive procedures in his experiments with Albert, a questionable application of the Pavlovian paradigm. A second distinction pertains to response measurement: Krasnogorski and Mateer used physiological indices of the UR and CR, while Watson has been criticized elsewhere for failing to standardize and report Albert's behavior (Samelson 1980). A third distinction relates to control procedures for the CR. Withdrawal and reinstatement of the US provide within-subject control for conditioning. Dissipation of the CR with removal of the US and subsequent reappearance of the CR with a rest interval are used to confirm conditioning. Again, Samelson has observed that Watson's work failed to provide adequate control for the existence of a CR or to replicate the initial findings in any way. These considerations of basic experimental design suggest, at the very least, that Watson's procedure was not Pavlovian, but similar to those of Bekhterev and his school of "objective psychology," which emphasized the association between responses and their behavioral consequences, (instrumental conditioning, Kimble 1961, Reese and Lipsitt 1970). Thus, Mateer's experiments, and not Watson's, legitimately qualify as the first experiments employing Pavlovian techniques in America in the area of child and developmental psychology.

Mateer's work on the conditioned salivary reflex was the exclusive report in America on Pavlovian conditioning applied to children through 1930. Although the concept of the conditioned reflex was widely adopted and popularized (Burnham 1921, 1924, Watson 1924), the work of Pavlov and his students was largely inaccessible to American psychologists, except for those who could follow the original Russian, or German translation. Even in those instances in which Pavlov's program came to the attention of American psychologists (Yerkes and Morgulis 1909), reports about designs and procedures lacked in detail necessary for replication or extension. By 1933, a comprehensive review by Razran of conditioning research on children could cite only 11 American studies out of a total of 84 (Razran 1933). Even Krasnogorski's research program did not appear in English until 1925 (Krasnogorski 1925).

Therefore, it is not surprising that the major translation of Pavlov's work into English by Anrep was of considerable interest to American experimental psychology (Pavlov 1928). This interest clearly extended to child and developmental psychology, because the period 1930–1940 produced more research in America on the conditioned reflex in children than had the previous 20 years.

The expansion of research on the application of the conditioned reflex to child and developmental psychology was not without difficulty, however. Methodological problems seriously hampered research. Unlike Pavlov's work which was noted for its precision and meticulous attention to detail, American investigators tended to ignore or confuse subtleties in conditioning methodology (Marquis 1931,

Bregman 1934). Thus, aversive USs, such as loud noises, produced emotional reactions and responses of escape and avoidance as well. Habituation, in which the US loses effectiveness with repeated presentation, and sensitization, in which the CS produces a physiological reaction without training, assumed more importance in research with infants and children than in research with animals, because of the greater sophistication of the human brain and sensory systems and the wider range of response capability. This early period of experimentation, therefore, was characterized by inconsistent and contradictory interpretations of results. Figure 1 presents the Pavlovian conditioning procedures and controls typical of early experimental designs with infants and children (Rescorla 1967). A 1934 experiment by E.O. Bregman will serve to illustrate some design and control problems of the early period of study.

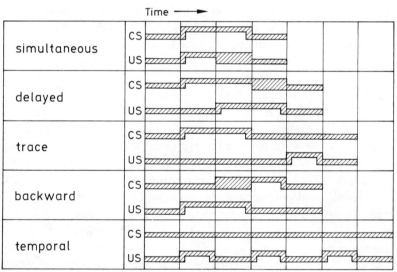

Time ⟶

▨▨▨ areas represent alternative procedures

The Bregman experiment attempted unsuccessfuly to condition negative and positive emotional responses in 15 infants. Subjects were trained with six objects (wooden blocks, rings, cloth curtains) as CSs. Half of these were paired with loud noise (US), and half were paired with a rattle sound and music from a music box. A one-second US presentation was interspersed four times during each 90 seconds CS presentation. Three-hundred-sixty conditioning trials took place over three training days. One test day presented each CS alone for 90 seconds.

Results were equivocal for the CSs paired with the US or with the rattle sound and music. Positive CRs were just about as frequent as negative CRs, regardless of training condition. The methodological flaws which likely contributed to the results were: (a) a loss of effectiveness of the US during training (habituation); (b) the subjective measurement of CRs in terms of gross body movements (negative, positive, or indifferent); and (c) CS periods not clearly defined in relation to non-CS periods.

Two areas of research emerged in the 1930s for American psychologists applying Pavlovian techniques to children. One was the relation between the conditioned reflex and level of nervous system development. Marquis first reported in 1931 the conditioned sucking reflex in infants (24 hours to 10 days old). The CS was a buzzer presented for 5 sec before the bottle was given at feeding. Marquis observed: "For every infant the most frequent reactions to the buzzer were increased general activity and increased head-movement" (1931: 488). Although this study was not free from methodological problems of the sort previously mentioned, it established the prototype for infant conditioning experiments.

Studies by Wickens and Wickens (1940) and Morgan and Morgan (1944) also helped to further establish the developmental significance of the CR. For example, Wickens and Wickens used a foot shock as an aversive US and a muffled buzzer as a CS to show that infants can be highly sensitive to so-called neutral stimuli, and that CRs, in infants less than one week old, are relatively long-lasting. The Morgans, who used an eyeblink conditioning task, demonstrated the ineffectiveness of a light bulb as the CS in infants less than 50 days old, and interpreted their results as establishing a casual relation between nervous system development and the CR.

Even before the developmental significance of the conditioned reflex was understood, some Americans foresaw the importance of the CR for another area of child psychology—the field of mental health. As early as 1924, the champion of the conditioned reflex concept in America, William Burnham, remarked: "The most important contribution of psychology to mental hygiene, providing a method of unlimited application, is probably the modern study of the conditioned reflex by the Russian school of Pavlov and his followers" (1924: 14). For approximately 15 years, Burnham, Professor of Pedagogy at Clark University and co-editor with G.Stanley Hall of the *Pedagogical Seminary*, wrote on the application of the conditioned reflex to the training of children and to the treatment of childhood disorders (Burnham 1932). Burnham's writings, however, were speculative and generally without experimental support. Burnham's practical but speculative child psychology contrasted sharply with vigorous laboratory programs and ambitious theories developed by experimental psychologists at Columbia (Thorndike and Woodworth), Yale (Hull), Chicago (Carr), and Berkeley (Tholman).

The programs for the application of the conditioned reflex to childhood disorders were far less extensive in America in the 1930s than the programs established in the Soviet Union. Only a few, isolated reports were published. The most important of these was by Mowrer and Mowrer on a procedure for the treatment of enuresis (Mowrer and Mowrer 1938). In this procedure, a bell (US) which produced bladder constriction and awakening (UR) was paired with the internal stimulus of bladder distension (CS) through an electrical circuit. The cure for enuresis occurred when the waking response became conditioned to bladder distension in advance of the onset of urination. The importance of this procedures was to place the conditioned reflex firmly within the therapeutic appliction of learning theory (Kazdin 1978). It was still ten years, however, before publication of Andrew Salter's *Conditioned Reflex Therapy* (1949); and another ten years before J. Wolpe's *Psychotherapy by Reciprocal Inhibition* (1958), which described a therapeutic program. These texts connected the conditioned reflex to a variety of behavior disorders in children and adults: anxiety neuroses, phobias, and personality disorders. Beginning in the late 1950s, "behavior therapy," finally was considered a serious alternative to traditional Freudian psychotherapy. Wolpe's procedure, for example, which he termed "desensitization," used a positive CR, relaxation, in association with a stimulus which aroused anxiety to decondition inappropriate emotional reactions.

The dissemination of theory and research on child and developmental psychology attained significant proportions in America in the period 1959 to 1969, during which a large number of journals began publication. Experimental research and therapeutic strategies, came to be published in journals which reflected a variety of theoretical orientations. The *Journal of Experimental Child Psychology*, for example, begun in 1964, has published articles which reflect a broad range of experimental designs on perceptual, social, emotional, and intellectual variables. The *Journal of Applied Behavioral Analysis*, on the other hand, since its inception in 1968, has published experimental research involving applications of Skinnerian conditioning in school, institutional, family, and other socially significant environments.

The founding in 1966 by W.H.Gantt and others of *Conditional Reflex*, a journal for experimental research employing traditional methods and modern variations on the Pavlovian model of behavior, was significant for the present paper. The title of the journal was changed in 1974 to *Pavlovian Journal of Biological Science.*

These journals cited above, as well as others, since about 1959 have published a wide range of research investigations in child and developmental psychology, including the use of Pavlovian techniques. Three problem areas will be discussed as representative of this "modern" use of the Pavlovian conditioning paradigm.

Pavlov's distinction between the first and second signalling system was a distinction between conditioned motor reflexes and speech (Babkin 1949). Today, laboratories investigate covert behavior of the first signalling system which accompanies language acquisition in children. Measurement of covert behavior includes the use of the electromyograph (EMG), electroencephalograph (EEG), galvanic skin response (GSR), and cardiac and respiratory processes. J.J.McGuigan and his students have used these techniques to follow muscular and glandular activity during vocal conditioning tasks (McGuigan 1978). In one experiment, covert behavior measured by the EMG was greater for a group of children which received a task involving oral mediation than for two other groups of children, which received a task involving non-oral mediation, and no mediation. Garrity (1979) has shown that there are sex and age differences in subvocal speech for the recall of items from short-term memory. Preschool boys depend more than preschool girls on subvocal speech for recall. Such research on covert behavior exemplifies current expansion of interest to Sechenov's theory of language.

The developmental importance of the CS has remained a topic for theory and experimental research. Early studies (Marquis 1931, Morgan and Morgan 1944) often focused on age in relation to the presence or absence of conditioned reflexes, overlooking the interdependence of CS, US, and methodology. With refinement in experimental procedures and measurement techniques, recent investigations have turned to CS effectiveness in relation to central and autonomic nervous system development. Infants (mean age 4.5 months) were used in a trace conditioning (see Fig. 1) experiment by Turco and Stamps (1980) to study heart-rate acceleration and deceleration with a visual CS. The US was a tone; the CS was a three-second pattern of blinking lights. Twenty CS-US pairings were separated by a three-minute interstimulus interval. A control group received randomized CS-US pairings. Male subjects showed a conditioned deceleration of heart rate and controls an acceleration, suggesting to the investigators that the CR is an augmentation of the spontaneous orienting response which prepares the organism for the US. Brackbill and his associates (Lintz, Fitzgerald, and Brackbill 1967; Fitzgerald and Brackbill, 1971), on the other hand, question the dependence of infant conditioning on the CS. Their research has shown differential effectiveness of temporal and auditory CSs for autonomically-mediated CRs. This means that the relationship between stimulus modality and response in infant conditioning may be too complex to be explained solely in developmental terms. The maturation of the cerebral structures which serve the reflex must be considered.

A final current area of experimental research is the relation between Pavlovian conditioning and behavior disorders in children. Mateer (1918) was the first American investigator to compare the conditioned reflex of normal and mentally defective children. The seven mental defectives differed from normals only in the rate of unlearning the conditioned reflex (inhibitory process). Recently, major programs have been established in America for the study of a wide range of learning, behavior, and personality disorders (Wortis et al. 1973). One example of this research is the application of Pavlov's concept of nervous-system sensitivity to children with attentional and hyperkinetic disorders. First defined in dogs, "strong" nervous systems were characterized as either well-balanced between excitatory and inhibitory processes, or dominated by one or the other in conditioning. Weak nervous system were characterized as predominantly inhibitory, because animals displayed weak CRs, even with increased stimulus intensity (Pavlov 1941).

Applied to human behavior, the distinction is the capacity of the nervous system to endure prolonged or frequently repeated excitations without reaching a threshold of inhibition or protection, called *transmarginal inhibition*. Individuals with strong nervous systems are able to endure greater stimulus intensities (Teplov 1972). Because hyperactive children are easily distracted and highly sensitive to stimulation, the hypothesis has been proposed that these children have weak nervous systems. Ackerman, et al. (1982) confirmed this prediction in a study of elementary school children referred to a Child Study Center. Tested on press-release reaction time tasks with varying intensities of tones (soft to loud), hyperactive children responded slower to more intense tones than those diagnosed as not-hyperactive.

Differences in performance between groups have not always been observed on conditioning indices. Wortis and his associates failed to show differences between normal and schizophrenic children in motor reflex conditioning (Wortis et al. 1974). Their procedure was to train positive and negative reflexes. Light signals were paired with the command "press" (positive) or "don't press" (negative) and reaction times measured under acquisition, extinction, reestablishment, and reversal procedures. No significant differences were obtained in reaction times, even though previous research had found consistent differences in motor conditioning between normal and behavior-disordered adults (Wortis et al. 1973).

The preceding discussion points to a single, clear difference between early studies and modern research. Current experimentation is more concerned with the objective tests of Pavlovian theory, and less with a strict adherence to a traditional conditioning methodology (Gray 1979). This trend has produced a greater breadth of research in recent years and has contributed to a new appreciation for the rich inheritance that Pavlov has left to child and developmental psychology.

The application of the Pavlovian paradigm to child and developmental psychology in America occurred slowly and with difficulty. Before 1920 the major research technique for child behavior involved controlled observation (i.e. case histories, clinical, and mental assessment, and naturalistic observation). Florence Mateer's doctoral dissertation stands out as the single exception until Pavlov's work became more accessible to American psychology about 1930. The developmental significane of the conditioned reflex and the application of the conditioned reflex applied to behavior disorders became the focus of attention for experimentation through about 1950. Modern research reflects efforts to test the Pavlovian theory of behavior to the traditional conditioning paradigm in such areas as the diagnosis and treatment of childhood disorders, the analysis of covert behavior accompanying speech, and the learning of voluntary and autonomically-mediated conditioned responses.

References

Ackerman,P.T., Holcomb,P.J., McGray,D.S. and Dykman,R.A. (1982) Studies of nervous system sensitivity in children with learning and attention disorders. *Pavl. J. Biol. Sci.* 17:30–41.

Babkin,B.P. (1949) *Pavlov: A biography.* Chicago: University of Chicago Press.

Boring,E.G. (1950) *A history of experimental psychology.* New York: Appleton-Century-Crofts.

Bregman,E.O. (1934) An attempt to modify the emotional attitudes of infants by the conditioned response technique. *J. Genet. Psychol.* 45:169–198.

Brophy,J.E. and Willis,S.L. (1981) *Human development and behavior.* New York: St.Martin's Press.

Burnham,W.H. (1921) The significance of the conditioned reflex in mental hygiene. *Men. Hyg.* 5: 673–706.

—(1924) *The normal mind.* New York: Appleton.

—(1932) *The wholesome personality.* New York: Appleton.

Craig,G.J. (1979) *Child development.* Englewood Cliffs, N.J.: Prentice-Hall.

Fitzgerald,H.E. and Brackbill,Y. (1971) Tactile conditioning of an autonomic and somatic response in young infants. *Condit. Reflex* 6:41–51.

Gantt,W.H. (1974) From "Conditional Reflex" to "Pavlovian Journal of Biological Science." *Pavl. J. Biol. Sci.* 9: 63–64.

Garrity,L. (1979) Sex differences in the relationship of recall to subvocal speech in preschool children. *Pavl. J. Biol. Sci.* 14:186–190.

Gray,J.A. (1979) *Ivan Pavlov.* New York: Viking Press.

Hall,G.S. (1912) *Founders of modern psychology.* New York: Appleton.

Harris,B. (1979) Whatever happened to little Albert? *Amer. Psychol.* 34: 151–160.

Johnson,R.C. and Medinnus,G.R. (1974) *Child psychology* (3d ed.) New York: Wiley.

Jones,M.C. (1924) A laboratory study of fear: The case of Peter. *Pedag. Sem.* 31:308–315.

Kazdin,A. (1978) *History of behavior modification.* Baltimore: University Park Press.

Kimble,G.A. (1961) *Hilgard and Marquis' conditioning and learning.* New York: Appleton-Century-Crofts.

Krasnogorski,N.I. (1925) The conditioned reflexes and children's neuroses. *Amer. J. Dis. Child.* 30: 753–768.

Lintz,L.M., Fitzgerald,H.E. and Brackbill,Y. (1967) Conditioning the eyelid response to sound in infants. *Psychon. Sci.* 7: 405–406.

Marquis,D.P. (1931) Can conditioned responses be established in the newborn infant? *J. Genet. Psychol.* 39: 479–492.

Mateer,F. (1918) *Child behavior.* Boston: Richard G.Badger.

McGuigan,F.J. (1978) *Cognitive psychophysiology.* Englewood Cliffs, N.J.: Prentice-Hall.

Morgan,J.J.B. and Morgan,S.S. (1944) Infant learning as a developmental index. *J. Genet. Psychol.* 65: 281–289.

Mowrer,O.H. and Mowrer,W.M. Enuresis—a method for its study and treatment. *Amer. J. Orthopsychiat.* 8: 436–459.

Murchison,C. (Ed.) (1931) *A handbook of child psychology.* Worcester, Mass.: Clark University Press.

Pavlov,I.P. (1928) [*Conditioned reflexes.*] (G.V.Anrep, ed. and trans.). London: Oxford University Press.

340   Behrens

—(1941) [*Lectures on conditioned reflexes,* vol. 2] (W.H.Gantt, ed. and trans.). New York: International Publishers.

Razran, G.H. (1933) Conditioned responses in children. *Arch. Psychol.* 23: (whole no. 148).

Reese, H.W. and Lipsitt, L.P. (1970) *Experimental child psychology.* New York: Academic Press.

Rescorla, R.A. (1967) Pavlovian conditioning and its proper control procedures. *Psychol. Rev.* 74: 71–80.

Salter, A. (1949) *Conditioned reflex therapy.* New York: Creative Age Press.

Samelson, F.J.B. (1980) Watson's little Albert, Cyril Burt's twins, and the need for a critical science. *Amer. Psychol.* 35: 619–625.

Teplov, B.M. (1972) The problem of types of human higher nervous activity and methods of determining them. In V.C.Nebylitsyn and J.A.Gray (eds.), *Biological basis of behavior.* New York: Academic Press.

Turco, T.L. and Stamps, L.E. (1980) Heart rate conditioning in young infants using a visual conditioned stimulus. *J. Exp. Child Psychol.* 29: 117–125.

Watson, J.B. (1924) *Behaviorism.* Chicago: University of Chicago Press.

Watson, J.B. and Rayner, R. (1920) Conditioned emotional reactions. *J. Exp. Psychol.* 3: 1–14.

Wickens, D.D. and Wickens, C. (1940) A study of conditioning in the neonate. *J. Exp. Psychol.* 26: 94–102.

Wolpe, J. (1958) *Psychotherapy by reciprocal inhibition.* Stanford, California: Stanford University Press.

Wortis, J., Floistad, T., Sersen, E.A. and Astrup, C. (1973) Childhood and adult behavior disorders: Some experimental comparisons. *Condit. Reflex* 8: 88–97.

Wortis, J., Sersen, E.A., Floistad, T., and Astrup, C. (1974) Childhood and adult schizophrenia: Some critical and experimental comparisons. *Pavl. J. Biol. Sci.* 9: 149–159.

Wundt, W. (1905) *Grundzüge der physiologischen Psychologie.* (5th ed.) Leipzig: Engelmann.

Yerkes, R.M. and Morgulis, S. (1909) The method of Pavlov in animal psychology. *Psychol. Bull.* 6: 257–273.

The Role of Developmental Concepts in the History of Gestalt Theory: The Work of Kurt Koffka

by Mitchell G. Ash

Conventional accounts of the history of psychology draw a straight line running from Darwinian evolutionary theory via functionalism to behaviorism and learning theory. They thus suggest, at least implicitly, that empiricist epistemology, evolutionary theory, and the progress of psychology are inextricably intertwined. However, developments such as the broad reception of the work of Piaget, Lorenz, and others have helped scholars realize that maturational lines of thought have also been compatible with both evolutionary theory and the progress of psychology. The purpose of this paper is to indicate the various roots of one maturatonal conception of psychological development, that of Gestalt theory. For reasons of space, the treatment will be limited primarily to the early work of the Gestalt theorist who addressed himself directly to the problem of development, Kurt Koffka, and to his single systematic work on the subject, "The Foundation of Psychical Development" (*Die Grundlagen der psychischen Entwicklung*), known in English as *The Growth of the Mind*. As I will try to show, Koffka did more than merely apply an already complete entity called Gestalt theory to an as yet nonexistent specialty called "developmental psychology." Rather, he attempted to synthesize concepts from other sources in addition to Gestalt theory into a consistent theory of psychical development. I will concentrate upon two of these sources in addition to Gestalt theory itself: (1) the "developmental history" proposed by the Frankfurt neuroanatomist Ludwig Edinger; and (2) the conception of "primitive mentality" presented by the Paris philosopher Lucien Lévy-Bruhl. After presenting the roots, the essential thrust and Koffka's initial reception of each of these conceptions, I will describe the uses Koffka made of them in his work.

The concept of developmental history

In contrast to the situation in the Anglo-Saxon world, in German-speaking lands the problem of growth and form was an important focus of opposition to Darwinian evolutionary theory at the end of the nineteenth century. In England and the United States, morphologists and evolutionists resolved their conflicts by splitting into subdisciplines (Allen 1978). In German-speaking culture, however, the idea of a "general biology" with philosophical implications remained compelling. Prominent opponents of Darwinism, including Wilhelm Blüntschli, Jakob von Uexküll and, of course, Hans Driesch maintained that Darwinian chance was insufficient to account for the particular formal characteristics of organisms, the variety of forms in nature, the coordinated adaptation of these forms to their environments, or the teleological character of growth and development (Cassirer 1969).

In this context, Ludwig Edinger's conception of "developmental history" (*Entwicklungsgeschichte*) was a pendant to Wilhelm Roux's notion of "developmental mechanics," against which Driesch had set his vitalism. Both Roux's notion and Driesch's response had been confined, at least initially, to embryonic development. Edinger's concept referred to a developmental sequence of species. He attempted to establish a mechanistic, evolutionary model at this level while retaining a place for the category of form. Edinger's schema linked anatomical to behavioral forms in a sequence corresponding to their evolutionary history. The central distinction, for which Edinger is remembered today, was that between the so-called "old brain" *(Paleoencephalon)* and the "new brain" *(Neoencephalon)*. The former, including everything from the head end of the spinal cord to the olfactory centers, he described as the seat of the reflexes and most instinctive movements. To the subsequently evolved "new brain" he ascribed the functions of "gnosis"—connection of signals from the sensory receptors—"praxis"—noninstinctive movements—and simple and complex associatons. In these functions, particularly in the construction of "memory images from many components," Edinger saw the dividing line between lower and higher animals (Edinger 1908b: 13; cf. Edinger 1908a: 443–44).

Because they lack this ability, the behavior of "old brain" animals is exclusively determined by preformed anatomical schemata. The same, "biologically adequate" stimuli always induce the same instinctive reations, while other, for us more impressive stimuli which the animals certainly receive, produce no reaction. Lizards, for example, listen closely to the sound of an insect crawling in the grass, but do not react to the sound of a stone struck loudly above their heads. The concept of "adequate" stimulation covers both internal and external states. Given properly chosen bait and appropriate weather conditions, a fish will still snap only when it is hungry; but if it is hungry and the other conditions have been fulfilled, then it must snap (e.g. Edinger 1911: 506–507). The anatomy of "new brain" creatures permits considerably greater flexibility of behavior. The areas lying between and in front of the sensory centers "*clearly increase in size as the animal increases its capacity to guide its observation and activity by intelligence*"*(1911: 523)*.

Edinger's schema has entered the relevant textbooks in many fields. Its potential applications to psychology, though only implicit in his presentation, were evidently considered important; he presented an outline of the model to a plenary session of the German "Society for Experimental Psychology" in 1908 (Edinger 1908a). As a response to the criticism of Darwinian evolutionary theory mentioned above, however, Edinger's model was limited at best. It offered, e.g. only a partial explanation for either the rich variety of animal forms or the fit of those forms to their environments. Its applicability to human behavior was equally limited; for Edinger said nothing about either the role of culture and society or the status of consciousness.

Kurt Koffka concentrated upon the latter point in an extensive review of Edinger's work published in 1912. As he pointed out, Edinger's model reached its limits when the achievements involved are no longer those of over behavior, instinctive or otherwise, but of reflected experience. Such views made it possible for "the psychologist of consciousness" to relegate instincts and reflexes to physology; for they are not experienced, but proceed "like processes in a dynamo machine. The investigaton of the old brain and its achievements is thus excluded from psychology; it is merely an affair of physiology. This boundary regulation is a gain for psychology" (Koffka 1912: 271). Still, Koffka had no intention of separating the two disciplines completely; for he found the distinction between "gnosis" and the other "new brain" functions useful. The physiological adjustments necessary for color constancy, for example, must take place in the "new brain," yet they are not experienced. Progress might thus be made by studying the relation of such "gnostic" functions to conscious processes like attention. "If we attribute to gnosis what it deserves," Koffka wrote, "we will arrive more quickly at correct results than by trying to invoke unconscious conclusions and errors of judgment" 1912: 278). This last point was an implicit criticism of David Katz's 1911 work on color perception, in which Katz had proposed a psychological, rather than a pysiological explanation for color constancy.

At this time Koffka was obviously more interested in the implications of Edinger's model for the "psychology of consciousness" than in its significance as a theory of development. Koffka's continued allegiance to conscious experience as the subject matter of psychology, at a time when comparative psychology was gaining adherents, is doubtlessly interesting. Perhaps more important, however, was the fact that Koffka offered no substitute of Edinger's associationistic conception of "gnosis" and the other "new brain" operations. This is surprising; for his critique was submitted to the *Zeitschrift für Psychologie* one month after Max Wertheimer offered his famous paper on motion perception to the same journal, and was printed immediately following that paper in the same issue. Instead, Koffka concluded his review by reminding psychologists that behind the apparent inconstancy of consciousness "a machine operates uninterruptedly," with effects that become evident only later (Koffka 1912: 278). Clearly, Koffka still equated physiological with mechanical processes. As we shall see, he did not continue to hold these views for long.

The concept of "primitive" mentality

Koffka had pointed out that Edinger's model of "developmental history" had no place in it for reflected experience. It also failed to apply evolutionary theory to culture or society. By 1914, Koffka had apparently found such a principle in the work of Lucien Lévy-Bruhl. That work reflected the growing realization in France that neither positivism nor neo-Kantianism could offer a sufficient basis for an empirically adequate social theory. The school around Émile Durkheim turned this realization into the foundation of a new "moral science;" Lévy-Bruhl attempted the required conceptual reform within the accepted disciplinary framework.

Against the widely held view that "primitive" thought was merely an inadequate copy of Western thinking, Lévy-Bruhl maintained that the consciousness of the simplest societies that we know is fundamentally different from our own, because it is determined by the group, not the individual thinker. The core of this argument is the concept of "collective representations" *(représentations collectives)*, explicated most fully in Lévy-Bruhl's book, *Les fonctions mentales dans les sociétés inférieures,* known in English as *The Mind of Primitive Man* (Lévy-Bruhl 1912). The term has often been mistranslated into German as *kollektive*

Vorstellungen and into English as "collective ideas." Such translations cover only half of Lévy-Bruhl's meaning. The "representations" are "collective," but they are not, or not only, ideas. According to Lévy-Bruhl, rigid distinctions between intellect and affect, the individual and the group, man and nature, or even the living and the dead do not exist in primitive consciousness. While the men of the village hunt, for example, the women at home perform rituals required to assure the hunt's success. However, they do this not in order to help the men in any Western sense of that word, but because the social rite would be incomplete, thus unsuccessful, if carried out by the men alone. To account for the ontological coherence of this world, Lévy-Bruhl invoked what he called the "law of participation." The existence of such complex unities, he maintained, cannot be explained by claiming, as ethnologists often did, that primitive peoples animistically project themselves or features of themselves onto the environment. Reality is more "full" in primitive consciousness, because abstraction hardly exists.

Even this sketch should make it clear that Lévy-Bruhl's intentions were primarily philosophical, not sociological or ethnological. He drew his picture of "primitive" mentality so starkly in order to impress his Western readers with its radical otherness. For this implicit critique of Enlightenment universalism he was duly criticized by Durkheim and others (Vogt 1976). However, he did not apply the concept to all primitive cultures in the same way: he presented it as what Max Weber would soon call an ideal type, thus implying the possibility of variations within it. Nor did he draw a continuous, evolutionary line between "primitive" and abstractly thinking, "civilized" man. However, by calling the thinking of primitive societies "prelogical," and by giving examples of societies located, conceptually at least, between the most primitive and our own, he made the idea of an evolutionary sequence plausible (Cazeneuve 1973).

In 1914 Koffka reviewed Lévy-Bruhl's work in the first and only number of the *Zeitschrift für Religionspsychologie* (Journal of the Psychology of Religion), which he founded with Wilhelm Stählin, a pastor who had been a subject in experiments Koffka conducted in Würzburg five years before. The review itself was little more than a thorough and sympathetic summary of the book just mentioned. But in their introduction to the new journal, Koffka and Stählin brought out the evolutionary implications of Lévy-Bruhl's thinking, and related it to current disputes in Germany. The psychology of religion, they wrote, must be rooted not in theological propositions or in speculations about

the "essence" of religion, but in "biological" and historical research
(Koffka and Stählin 1914: 2). This was a bold position to take,
especially for a minister of the established church in Prussia. Specifying
the sort of "biological" thinking they meant, they then alluded to the
"original lack of differentiation" of human thought. If this is so, they
argued, then it is false to speak of "primitive religion," since the true
beginning of religion is the separation of the sacred and the profane,
something that would not occur to the mind of primitive man. Thus
both Lévy-Bruhl's research and "the progress of psychology" showed
that "everywhere the parts were not present before the whole—that
therefore psychical like all biological development does not proceed
along the road of combination, but rather that of differentiation"
(Koffka and Stählin 1914:6).

  With this argument, Koffka and Stählin had apparently taken a
Spencerian view of cultural evolution; for it was Spencer who wrote that
all development proceeds "from an undifferentiated, incoherent
homogeneity to a more differentiated, coherent heterogeneity"
(Spencer 1867: 369). With respect to the general direction of
development their position was indeed Spencerian. For Koffka and
Stählin, as for Lévy-Bruhl, however, the original state from which development proceeds may be "undifferentiated;" but it is "incoherent"
only from a Western point of view. The reason at least for Koffka's
acceptance of that position will become blear only after an exposition of
what he and Stählin meant by "the progress of psychology."

Gestalt theory

Koffka and Stählin did not say precisely what they meant when they
invoked "the progress of psychology" to support their position. Judging
by the date, however, it seems clear that they were talking about Gestalt
theory, fundamental principles of which had been presented by Max
Wertheimer in 1912. Most relevant to the problem of development was
not Wertheimer's famous paper on apparent movement, but another
article entitled "On the Thinking of Primitive Peoples I: Numbers and
Number Concepts" (Wertheimer 1912a). There Wertheimer took a
methodological position similar to that for which Koffka and Stählin
had cited Lévy-Bruhl: "It is insufficient to ask what numbers and operations of our mathematics the peoples of other cultures have. The
question must be: what units of thought do they have in this field? What

tasks for thinking? How does their thinking approach them?" (Wertheimer 1912a:323).

Given this approach, it was not surprising that Wertheimer soon discovered number concepts different from those of Western arithmetic. Examples of the difference could be very simple: one horse plus one horse equals two horses; one person plus one person equals two people; but one horse plus one person may equal a rider. However, as Wertheimer pointed out, the difference was not always a matter of applying arithmetic in different ways. A builder goes to find pieces of wood for a house. "One can count them. Or, one can go with an image of a house in one's head and get the pieces of wood that are needed. One has a group image *(Gruppengebilde)* of the posts, which is quite concretely related to the form of the house" (1912a: 324–325). Wertheimer claimed that this kind of concrete, functional thinking, characterized by "the preponderance of form," often determines the handling of quantities, not only for so-called "primitives," but for "naturally thinking people" in "civilized" society as well.

With this claim Wertheimer made it clear that he was not taking a strong relativist position, as Lévy-Bruhl had done. Instead he was searching for phenomena that could become the basis for general laws of thought, thus preserving a commitment to Enlightenment universalism while opposing one of its central tenets—the primacy of abstract thought. Though he was ostensibly writing only about number concepts, not about "primitive" thinking in general, his long-range intentions were just as ambitious as Lévy-Bruhl's. Immediately after the example of "the preponderance of form" just cited, Wertheimer offered another: "a somewhat blunted triangle is a triangle, not a rectangle or a hexagon, as it would have to be called from a merely mathematical point of view" (Wertheimer 1912a: 326). There is nothing concretely functional about a figure drawn on a piece of paper, and Wertheimer did not claim that we perceive the triangle in this way because we have learned to do so, or because it is in our biological interest. The blunted triangle *is* a triangle—that is, it is immanent in the phenomenon that it is perceived in this way. In such observations Wertheimer expounded a new epistemology, a form of psychological realism which I have elsewhere called "immanent structuralism" (Ash 1982). His implicit message was that true philosophy must be based on this particular conception of lived reality. Given that message, it is understandable that Wertheimer did not construct an evolutionary sequence from "primitive" to abstract thinking.

In his paper on apparent movement, published only a few months later, Wertheimer presented what he took to be experimental confirmation of his viewpoint and hypothesized the existence of neurological "short circuits," or structured brain events corresponding to perceived movement-structures (Wertheimer 1912b). In 1915 Koffka carried these claims still further, articulating the principles of Gestalt theory as a unified system. Perception, action, and the psychiological processes underlying both, he maintained, are all structured in the same way; and all are united in a total, structured experience which is in turn part of the organism's interaction with real objects in the external world (Koffka 1915: esp. 57 ff.). This conception of experience—particularly Koffka's emphasis upon organism-environment interaction, his designation of the stimulus as a real object (not, e.g. a pattern on the retina) and his extension of the Gestalt principle to action—was reminiscent of American functionalist psychology; and he cited Dewey's *Essays in Experimental Logic* (1916) directly.

There was, however, one important difference. Dewey treated psychology as "the natural history of thought;" its purpose for him was "to locate the particular situation in which each structure [of thought and behavior] has its origin," and to trace "the successive modifications through which, in its response to changing media, it has reached its present conformation" (Dewey 1916: 93, 95). Wertheimer had suggested such a perspective in his distinction between "natural" and arithmetical number concepts. But he had given no indication that he thought of the movement from one to the other as an evolutionary sequence. For Koffka, too, evolutionary history was apparently less significant thant epistemology. In his 1915 paper he cited Edinger's neuroanatomical work only as a source of examples for the universal presence of "Gestalt stimuli." As if to underscore the point, the behavior he chose was that of the snapping fish described above, an "old brain" rather than a "new brain" creature. The implication for any general theory of development was clear, though Koffka did not state it explicitly in 1915. "Elementary" sensations are neither psychologically nor historically primary. Edinger's mechanistic model of behavioral evolution could be retained only by reformulating its epistemological underpinnings on the basis of Wertheimer's Gestalt theory.

Wolfgang Köhler proposed just such a reformulation at the end of his study of so-called "structural functions" in anthropoid apes and chickens. The central finding of that study was that both higher and lower animals on the evolutionary scale were capable of perceiving and learning relationships. Such findings, and Edinger's observations that even frogs and lizards react to structured stimuli, showed, in Köhler's opinion, that "only a portion, and hardly the essential portion of the reactions of even the lowest organisms can be understood as mere juxtapositions and sucessions of absolute stimulus influence in isolation." It followed that models of "developmental history" based on sensationalist or empiricist epistemology were "worthless" (Köhler 1918: 37–38). He made it clear, however, that he did not wish to dismiss either evolutionary theory or the idea of "developmental history," but to reconstruct the latter on a new basis.

In his philosophical masterwork, Köhler then provided that new basis. Even the physical world, he claimed, contains articulated physical systems, the behavior of which cannot be explained as summations of isolated events (Köhler 1920). If such systems exist in the external world, there was no reason to deny their existence in the brain. Köhler went on to suggest that "the osmatic field could just as well be one physical system," and to postulate an "*objective similarity* between the Gestalt characteristics of psychophysical events and those of the phenomenal field—*not only in general,* in the sense that we are dealing with Gestalten in both cases, *but in the specific character of every Gestalt in each individual case*"(1918: 176–177, 192–193; emphasis in the original). Köhler did not draw out the implications of this claim for general biology until the mid-1920s. But it was already clear enough to readers like Koffka in 1921 that if Köhler's claim were correct, "the opposition of mechanism and vitalism has been overcome" (Koffka 1921: 414).

Here again, this time more explicitly, we have what we might call the primacy of epistemology, or even of ontology, over evolution. Köhler continued to make the same point throughout his life—for Gestalt theory, the issue is not the acceptance or rejection of evolution, but what it is that evolves (Köhler 1971). Perhaps now we can begin to understand why Koffka, when he was asked to write a summary of Gestalt theory that could be useful to teachers, titled the result not "principles of developmental psychology" but "the foundations of psychical development." It is to his exposition of these foundations that we now turn.

Koffka's synthesis: a Gestalt theory of development

By 1914, Koffka had been confronted with Edinger's preformationist model of the evolution of behavior and Lévy-Bruhl's conception of the radical otherness of "primitive" thinking, with its implications for a theory of cultural evolution. Shortly thereafter, he had assisted in the emergence of Gestalt theory. In *The Growth of the Mind*, he then attempted to weave these strands together with a wealth of observations from the work of many others into a coherent general theory of psychical development. In order to understand and assess this attempt, we will begin with his treatment of Edinger's model.

Koffka called Edinger's model of "developmental history," in particular the distinction between "old brain" and "new brain" functions, "a valuable heuristic principle" (Koffka 1925: 55). Most significant to him was the fact, also emphasized by Edinger, that the human cerebral cortex continues to develop after birth. Evidence about the perception of motion in infants indicated, for example, that this is "a performance which improves during the course of life," largely due to growth in the optic sector. If this is the case, then "it is not 'experience' which accounts for the gradual increase ... but, evidently, a physiological alteration of the organ which ... we have called *maturation*" 1925: 64). When Koffka extended the point to development in general, however, he added an important twist: "We must think of development in terms of a process of maturation, in the course of which certain regions of the nervous system attain the capacity of forming fixed configurations which at first they do not possess; *this process of maturation being dependent upon functional employment*" of the organ in question (1925: 285; emphasis mine).

To put it briefly: for Koffka, development is only partly the realization of preformed anatomical potential; it is maturation aided by practice.

The introduction of functionalistic thinking meant that Koffka could treat learning, too, as "essentially a type of development" (1925: 51; 38–39). It was at this level that he differed most clearly with Edinger; for he had come "to a quite different conclusion as to the nature of these ["new brain"] activities" and of the brain functions underlying them (1925: 55). Wolfgang Köhler's demonstration of "insight" in anthropoid apes had shown, he maintained, that learning is not, or not only, the gradual assemblage of associative connections; it can also occur in a single, "nonheritable achievement" (1925: 152). But even such achievements have roots. Just as perception and action become, with practice, "an integrated sensory-motor process ... an interconnected system ... uniting phenomena and movements in one total form of behavior" (1925: 146–148), so too in learning "the total situation becomes organized ... an intelligent construction of the field takes place with respect to the goal" (1925:172,209).

As early as 1913, Max Wertheimer had presented, in lectures, a conception of "the epistemological process" as "a process of 'centering', of 'structuring', or of grasping that particular aspect which provides the key to an orderly whole, a unification of the particular individual parts that happen to be present" (cited in von Wartensleben 1914: 1–2; cf. Michael Wertheimer 1980: 14, and Ash 1982: 302). Evidently Koffka had adapted Wertheimer's conception of the "knowledge process" to cover the structure of all behavior, both instinctive and intended. He did the same for the relationship of learning to maturation. Just as the functional employment of an organ aids the maturation of the behavior of that organ, so "the maturation of a performance improves with practice" (1925: 151); and "practice means the formations of a figure, rather than the strengthening of bonds of connection" (1925:234).

Koffka could confidently extend such metaphors so far, because he had accepted Köhler's philosophy of nature. This was most obvious in his discussion of instinct. Citing Köhler's discussion of the second law of thermodynamics at the end of *Die physischen Gestalten,* he asserted that there are events in the physical world which "shape themselves," as it were toward a very definite end, that of the simplest organization consistent with the given conditions. Goal-directedness is thus not confined to living matter. If we seek an explanation for instinctive behavior, we should therefore not attribute it to any vital principle or "entelechy," nor to "an inherited system of conncected neurones." Rather, we should "investigate what kind of physicochemical 'closure' produces these astonishing types of behavior, and under what conditions." He admitted that "instinct is still a riddle;" but "at least it is no longer one that forces upon us the acceptance of psycho-vitalistic principles" (1925: 106). Since both instinctive and learned responses are present in the same individual, and since both have essentially the same structure, Koffka thought it unnecessary to choose sides in the heredity-environment controversy. A decision was not possible on this issue in any case, he wrote, without clarity about the nature of experience itself (1925: 52). Having achieved that clarity, he could accept a role for practice in the development of behavior, because he subsumed both the function-aided maturation of instinctive behavior and the practice-aided maturation of "performances" in learning under the same physical teleology. He could thus portray even Köhler's "insight" as a result of development, and make frequent use of Claparéde's term "construction" in an essentially maturational theory.

To make this view more plausible Koffka worked out a number of hypothetical developmental sequences. The most extensive of these was for the development of color vision (1925: 264 ff.) This he described as "the gradual construction of new color configurations" by a process akin to that exhibited in Köhler's experiments with "structural functions" in animals (1925: 272). The differnce between figure and ground already investigated by Edgar Rubin he termed the "most primitive" phenomenon of visual perception. Transferred to color vision, this meant that the first stage of development would be the distinction between chromatic and achromatic colors. This would be followed by the differentiation first of the "warm" and "cold" colors—more exactly of the reds and blues, or of red and "not-red"—then of the spectral colors, and finally of intermediate hues. A child who earlier saw only blue and red, for example, could later come to distinguish lilac in relation to blue as "not-blue." On this basis it could gradually develop a wide range of color phenomena before it learned their common names. Koffka offered a variety of observations in support of this hypothetical sequence, but admitted that much of it remained speculative; and he did not attempt to work out a more complete stage theory of the kind that Piaget would soon develop. In fact, the schema was, at bottom, a deduction from Wertheimer's and Köhler's work and the known facts about the visual spectrum.

In effect, Koffka transformed Edinger's model of "developmental history" by combining it with functionalism, then subordinating the result to Wertheimer's epistemology and Köhler's physical teleology. Because of his claim that practice could modify or complete the development even of preformed behavioral schemata, he was open to the charge of attempting to revive Lamarckism. This was not his aim. Köhler's physical "Gestalt laws" are not acquired characteristics that can then be inherited, but invariant structural principles for physical and psychical events, inherited and acquired behaviors. In one sense this style of theorizing is similar to that of Driesch, for both describe development as a realization of inherent potential. However, the location of that potential is fundamentally different. For the vitalists, it was exclusively within the organism; for Koffka, it was in the organism-environment interaction, which works as it does because behavior, reflected experience, and the objects to which they are directed are subject to the same structural laws.

However, in all of this Koffka referred primarily to the development of individuals. Early in the book he raised the issue of ontogeny and phylogeny. After reviewing the recapitulationist and "utilitarian" or neo-Darwinist alternatives, he accepted the "correspondence" theory held by Claparéde and Dewey, among others. This, the view "that the general characteristic of development are the same for both the individual and the species," he called "far more cautious than either of the other two" theories; it holds the way open for further hypotheses (1925: 46–47). As he proceeded, it became clear that this was insufficient. If his system were to be complete and consistent, and also applicable to pedagogy, he had to provide explicitly for the social dimension.

It was here that Lévy-Bruhl entered the picture. Koffka integrated Lévy-Bruhl's thinking into his argument in the final chapter of the book, entitled "The World of the Child." In general he retained the formulations about the thought of "primitive" peoples already cited, simply transferring them from the so-called "primitive" mind to that of the child. There was, however, one fundamental difference. The claims expressed by both Lévy-Bruhl and Wertheimer in universalist terms appear here in historicized form. There is indeed a "child-world" which is different from that of adults, and persists for a time alongside it. However, Koffka wrote, "we are dealing here not with an unchanged child-soul, but with a world-view which continually undergoes a process of transformation" (1925: 336–337). In part this process is one of maturation, during which inanimate objects become distinct from animate ones, objects in general acquire the quality of things with attributes, and appearance is distinguished from reality. But the shape of the process "depends upon the total environment, and above all upon the sociological conditions of this milieu ... man's entire development, including, of course, his perceptions, is dependent upon society" (1925: 339–340).

This is obvious for both children and adults in primitive society, where social bonds appear to be much stronger than in "civilized" society. In the case of children, however, it is difficult to discover the phenomena and structures of the "child-world," precisely because it is "constantly influenced by association with adults and hence [is] not stable enough to show its worth in performance," except perhaps in play (1925: 335). Max Wertheimer had said in 1912 that in such a situation it was often understandable that children or members of other cultures resisted the demands of teachers from "outside" (Wertheimer 1912a: 349n.). Koffka put it this way:

The release from [immediately perceived] reality which is possible and easy to our mode of thinking is a specific product of our civilization. The child must go a tremendously long way in a short time in order to learn to think as adults do, in a manner which is not at all natural to him. To lead him along this way, so that his advancement may be vital to him, is the difficult but thankful task of the teacher (1925: 335).

At the very least, "respect" was due to children for all that they manage to achieve in their earliest years (1925: 319).

In passages such as these, Koffka appears to become an advocate of the "natural" child, much like the proponents of Deweyite progressive education, which was becoming fashionable in the United States at the time. Teachers appear here as agents of alienation working on behalf on an adult "civilization" with goals fundamentally different from those of the child. However, the opposition is not as simple as that. The intervention of teachers and parents in the maturation process is also a necessary aspect of the development of culture, and of the development of the child within that culture. According to this view, then, the child cannot be simply left to itself. Even the teaching strategies that declare this to be their goal are interventions. Though Koffka sought both to explain the development of reason and to make development reasonable, the end result has the tragic cast of Freud's *Civilization and its Discontents*. Nonetheless, it is clear that Koffka had begun with such statements to approach a historico-cultural conception of development.

Conclusion

However, Koffka did not pursue these beginnings further; nor did he produce the developmental social psychology that might have emerged from them. He had asserted that mental development proceeds the same way at all levels; it is "not the bringing together of separate elements, but the arousal and perfection of more and more complicated configurations in which both the phenomena of consciousness and the functons of the organism go hand in hand" (1925: 356). But he had not shown in any detail whether or how the functional interaction he would constently have to posit between the developing individual and society—or its agents, teacher's and parents, takes place. Nor was there any discussion of the development of social interactions among children. Without such discussions, the usefulness of the book to teachers was limited.

More important to psychologists, probably, were other difficulties. Despite the wealth of detail Koffka packed into his account, many of his generalizations were deductions from general principles, not inductions from research results. Though these generalizations were framed in such a way that they might beomce testable experimentally, he did not carry out such tests himself. He continued his running debate with Thorndike in later discussions of the law of effect, and students of Gestalt theory, especially Americans who studied in Berlin in the late 1920s such as N.R.F.Maier and D.F.Adams, attempted to apply Gestalt principles to learning theory. Through this work, and Koffka's dialogue with E.C.Tolman, Gestalt theory exerted a not insignificant influence on the development of learning theory, and thus indirectly on developmental psychology in the United States. However, the fact remains that Koffka had no children of his own to observe, and did not set up a laboratory dedicated to child studies; his research interests lay elsewhere. Though many of the principles in his 1921 (1925) text were restated and elaborated in his 1935 classic, *Principles of Gestalt Psychology,* there was little direct discussion either of developmental or of child psychology there. Perhaps this ommission accounts in part for the fact that Koffka's work had either slight or only a negative reception among developmental psychologists in the United States. It was not clear how these principles could lead to further experimentation in the field, and the suggested schemas and stages of development in particular areas, such as color perception, were not worked out extensively enough to be of direct pedagogical use. The hints Koffka dropped about the determining roles of society and history were taken up most enthusiastically in Russia by the so-called cultural-historical school led by Lev Vygotsky (Scheerer 1981).

In Western Europe and the United States, developmental psychology went other ways. In his contribution to this volume, Kurt Danziger shows how the conceptual fruits of attempts to develop a common theoretical conception for socialization and for cognitive development by thinkers such as James Mark Baldwin and Piaget were later divided among two specialties, developmental and social psychology. After the above account it is clear that Gestalt theory also belongs to this history. It, too, was one of the last attempts to hold the dimensions of psychological reality together, in this case by referring them to a common ontological base. The substantive issues Koffka raised in that attempt—the problem of the physical and biological realities underlying cognitive and behavioral development, and the relations of

356   Ash

individual development to its cultural and social context, remain central today.

References

Allen,G.E. (1975) *Life science in the twentieth century.* New York: Wiley.
Ash,M.G. (1982) The emergence of Gestalt theory: experimental psychology in Germany, 1890–1920. Unpublished Doctoral Dissertation, Harvard University.
Casaneuve,J. (1973) *Lucien Lévy-Bruhl.* New York: Harper and Row.
Cassirer,E. (1969) *The problem of knowledge: philosophy, science and history since Hegel.* New Haven: Yale University Press.
Dewey,J. (1916) *Essays in experimental logic.* Chicago: University of Chicago Press.
Edinger,L. (1908) The relations of comparative anatomy to comparative psychology. *Journal of Comparative Neurology and Psychology* 18: 437–457.
—(1909) Die Beziehungen der vergleichenden Anatomie zur vergleichenden Psychologie. Neue Aufgaben, *Bericht über den III. Kongress für experimentelle Psychologie...1908.* Leipzig: Barth.
—(1911) *Vorlesungen über den Bau der nervösen Zentralorgane der Menschen und der Tiere.* (8th ed. 2 vols.) Leipzig: Vogel.
Köhler,W. (1918) Nachweis einfacher Strukturfunktionen beim Schimpansen und beim Haushuhn, *Abhandlungen der königl. Preuss. Akad. der Wissenschaften,* phys.-math. Kl., Nr. 2.
—(1920) *Die physischen Gestalten in Ruhe und im stationären Zustand. Eine naturphilosophische Untersuchung.* Braunschweig: Vieweg.
—(1971) Psychology and evolution. In Mary Henle (Ed.), *The Selected Papers of Wolfgang Köhler.* New York: Liveright.
—(1912) Ein neuer Versuch eines objektiven Systems der Psychologie, *Zeitschrift für Psychologie* 61: 266–278.
—(1914) Review of Lévy-Bruhl (1912). *Zeitschrift für Religionspsychologie* 1: 267–278.
—(1915) Zur Grundlegung der Wahrnehmungspsychologie. Eine Auseinandersetzung mit V.Benussi. *Zeitschrift für Psychologie* 73: 11–90.
—(1921) Review of Köhler (1920). *Die Naturwissenschaften* 9: 413–414.
—(1925) *The growth of the mind: an introduction to child-psychology* (1921). Trans. R.M.Ogden. New York: Harcout, Brace.
—(1935) *Principles of Gestalt psychology.* New York: Harcourt, Brace.
Koffka,K and Stählin,W. (1914) Zur Einführung. *Zeitschrift für Religionspsychologie* 1: 1–9.
Lévy-Bruhl,L. (1912) *Les fonctions mentales dans les sociétés inférieures* (1908). (2d ed.) Paris: Alcan.
Scheerer,E. (1980) Gestalt Psychology in the Soviet Union I: The Period of Enthusiasm, *Psychological Research* 41: 113–132.
Spencer,H. (1867) *First Principles.* 2d ed. London: Williams and Norgate.
Vogt,W.P. (1976) The Uses of Studying Primitives: A Note on the Durckheimians 1890–1940. *History and Theory* 15: 33–44.
Wartensleben,G.von (1914) *Die christliche Persönlichkeit im Idealbild. Eine Beschreibung sub specie psychologica.* Munich: Kempton and Kösel.

Wertheimer, M. (1912a) Über das Denken der Naturvölker I. Zahlen und Zahlengebilde. *Zeitschrift für Psychologie* 60: 321–378.

—(1912b) Experimentelle Studien über das Sehen von Bewegung. *Zeitschrift für Psychologie* 61:

Wertheimer, Michael (1980) Max Wertheimer: Gestalt Prophet. *Gestalt Theory* 2: 3–17.

The Role of Film in John B. Watson's Developmental Research Program: Intellectual, Disciplinary, and Social Influences

by Benjamin Harris

Within the history of psychology, John B. Watson is most often remembered as the founder of behaviorism. His career is chiefly remembered as having been established in the field of animal behavior, as having paused briefly in the nursery to condition the child "little Albert," and then having ended in commercial advertising and popular advice-giving (Buckley 1982; Morawski and Harris 1979; Cohen 1979; Lomax, Kagan, and Rosencrantz 1978). What is rarely appreciated is that by 1917 Watson had completely shifted the focus of his research to the human infant, and that this research marked the first experimental use of motion pictures by a psychologist in the United States.

Although the filmed record of Watson's infant research has long been presumed to be lost (Cohen 1979; Watson 1919a), a copy of it was recently unearthed and is now being made available to interested scholars.[1] In conjunction with this film's distribution, this essay has two functions. First, it describes Watson's research with human infants. Second, it analyzes the historical influences that contributed to Watson's position as a pioneer film maker in psychology.

Watson's infant research

In late 1916, at the height of Watson's career at Johns Hopkins University, he obtained an invitation from his colleague Adolf Meyer to shift his laboratory to the newly established Phipps psychiatric clinic (Samelson 1980). There, Watson began observations of newborn infants, and behavioral tests of infants up to one year old (Blanton 1917; Watson 1917a, b; Watson and Morgan 1917). Eventually, Watson expanded his pool of subjects to include infants from a local orphanage and some from weatlhy families; both of these populations were used for repeated testing over periods of many months (Watson 1919b).

Watson's purpose in this research was to investigate patterns of young infants' instinctual behavior, and to observe their acquisition of new behaviors or "habits." This was in keeping with the behaviorist idea that psychology should be science of stimuli and responses, and that all human responses were either instinctual or the result of habit formation (Watson 1917a).

Separating instinctual behavior from habit was crucial for Watson, because his expressed goal was social control through the adjustment of humans' relation to their environment (1917a: 329). As Watson saw it, this would often demand the remolding of individuals' behavior (what might be called behavior modification today), and those attempting such remolding would need to know how much the individual's behavior was instinctual, how much was the result of habit, and how the habits developed. To Watson, the surest way to see how habits developed was to make a developmental survey of hundreds of human infants.

In this developmental survey, Watson was interested in both motor and emotional responses. To illustrate how Watson investigated the former type of behavior, it is useful to look at his attempts to determine the origins of infants' hand preference—a topic of debate in early twentieth-century psychology (e.g. Lashley 1917, Meyer 1913, Wooley 1910).

According to behaviorist theory, few innate behavior patterns existed in humans, apart from life-sustaining, unconditioned reflexes and the so-called manipulation instinct. In the case of handedness, Watson reasoned that adults most often place objects in a baby's right hand, thus it develops a preference for using that hand.[2] Based on this reasoning, Watson believed that careful determination of young infants' hand use would show them to have not yet developed a stable hand preference.

To test this belief, Watson determined infants' handedness, using four different techniques. First, he suspended infants from either their right or left hands, recording their weight and how long they could support themselves. Second, he constructed and used a device which made cumulative records of the activity of infants' right and left hands. Third, he made anthropomorphic measurements of infants' right and left biceps, forearms, wrists, and palms. Finally, Watson tested older infants (150 days to 1 year old) on a weekly basis to see which hand they used to reach for a candle or a stick of candy.[3]

Watson's tests of other types of motor behavior are shown in the film and described in his 1919 book: *Psychology from the Standpoint of a Behaviorist.* In addition to such motor tests, he attempted to assess young infants' instinctive (unconditioned) emotional reactions to stimuli such as loud noise, animals, and toys; and to physical manipulation by Watson. As is widely known, the results of these tests were consistent with Watson's theory of human emotional development (i.e. which included the prediction that infants do not innately fear animals or objects). This theory was also supported by Watson's later conditioning of the infant Albert B.—at least according to the story as Watson told it in later years (see Harris 1979).

The significance of Watson as Filmmaker

Recently, much has been written on the significance of this work of Watson's, including methodological criticism of the research[4] and historical analyses of Watson's role as developmentalist and scientific expert (Cornwell and Hobbs 1976; Harris 1983; Lomax et al. 1978). What has not been discussed, however, are the historical factors that led to Watson's pioneering use of cinema in psychological research (preceding other researchers in, for example, child development by five to ten years).[5]

Beginning on the question of scientific methodology, the initial significance of Watson's filmmaking was in regard to his own research. That is, the first reason that Watson pioneered the use of film is that it was an appropriate methodology for a behaviorist research program. Watson, after all, was the most vocal advocate of transforming psychology into a science of observable stimuli and responses. To the extent that he put this idea into practice, cinematic recording was a natural method for the preservation of observable events in the laboratory.

Thus Watson initially developed a form of *camera obscura* which projected the image of a maze-running rat onto a piece of paper for tracing (Watson 1914). Then as he moved to primates, he used still photography to illustrate monkeys' body movements and emotional expressions (Lashley and Watson 1917). Finally, as Watson adopted classical conditioning as the basis of his learning theory, it became necessary to devise a method that would allow Watson to capture sudden changes in reflexive behavior such as breathing, muscle tensing, or blinking. By the turn of the century, it was clear that motion picture technology offered such advances over previously-used still photography (Gilman 1978, 1979), and that it could be brought into the psychological laboratory. Not only could cinema record and reproduce movements (e.g. Marey 1894), but it could free the experimenter from the role of data recorder, allowing him to attend to other tasks such as keeping infants from drowning or falling on their heads (Watson 1919).

Of course, it is important to avoid an idealist or completely "internalist" view of how Watson developed the idea of using cinema; it was his colleagues and contemporaries as much as his experimental needs that suggested motion pictures to Watson. Specifically, Watson's correspondence credits the physiological psychologist S.I. Franz with inspiring Watson to think that he could make a cinematic record of infant behavior (Watson 1919). No doubt Franz had seen some of the pioneering neurology and psychiatry films of the early twentieth century—which allowed detailed observation of, for example, patterns of muscle activity in epileptic, neurotic, and psychotic patients (Chase 1905, Hennes 1910, Thomalla 1919b, Weisenburg 1912). Also, it is likely that Watson himself was familiar with the time-motion study films made by industrial efficiency experts (Gilbreth 1926), and with early commercial films that portrayed the "baby's day" (Niver 1967: 71).

In addition to Watson being influenced by his colleagues in psychiatry and medicine, it is possible to see him responding to another type of disciplinary factor. As Watson explained to his university's president, he wanted a film record of his pioneering research because the politics and funding which allowed this research to occur might change. Here, Watson was saying that he wanted to use film to preserve his social status within the field, just as scientists more generally use journal publications.[6]

In addition to the intellectual and disciplinary reasons for Watson's filmmaking, there is a final influence worth mentioning and that is Watson's relationship to the general culture and to institutions beyond the laboratory and university.

As a prototypic scientific expert of the post-First World War period, Watson knew well the importance of speaking to child study societies, charitable foundations, and to the general public. Thus, Watson confided to the president of Johns Hopkins, the final reason for him to become a film director was the public visibility that a film would bring to his work (Watson 1919). As Watson saw it, copies of his proposed film could be both sold for educational use, and also be shown by Watson himself as part of his frequent public lectures. The former use would encourage more infant research, he felt, and having a film that he could show to child study clubs and other organizations might help Watson elicit enough donations to fund further research—such as the creation of a laboratory for the extended study of a small group of children from birth to adolescence.

Also mentioned by Watson was the general "propaganda" value that this film could have, helping mothers see their responsibility for shaping the emotional lives of their young children. It is noteworthy that Watson had personal knowledge of the use of cinema as propaganda, since he and Karl Lashley had just begun work on the effects of anti-Veneral disease films on public attitudes toward social hygiene (Lashley and Watson 1921).

In summary, Watson's production of one of the first psychology films in the United States seems to have been the product of a variety of factors, which can be characterized as intellectual, disciplinary, and social. I will close by noting that these factors have been separated here only for purposes of illustration. In reality, Watson's career and motivation were influences by a complex interaction of these factors; they themselves cannot be assessed independently of one another, making it impossible to establish unidirectional causality.

This point is exemplified by the relationship of Watson's film to the industrial uses of film by experts in time-motion study such as the Gilbreths. Their similar interests (in the careful analysis of human movements) and chronological proximity may have been due to Watson's having seen a newsreel of the Gilbreths' efficiency-based household at a time when Watson was becoming interested in the psychology of children and the family (Gilbreth and Carey 1948).

It is more likely, however, that the appearance of both of these types of film was related to three factors. First was their creators' shared interest in the social control of patterns of simple human behavior—in one case, applied to industry and in the other, to the psychology laboratory. Second was the Gilbreths' and Watson's joint willingness to comply with the public's desire for scientific experts of demonstrable competence. Finally, the production of films by both a behaviorist and by a team of efficiency experts was facilitated by the generally high level of industrialization and technological development of certain sectors of American business in the early twentieth century. After the turn of the century, it was investments in technology and science that helped the film industry grow quickly, and to expand into new areas such as psychological research.[7] At the same time, widespread industrialization and the accompanying rationalization of labor created new social relations throughout urban society (e.g. the role of the scientific expert) that were just as necessary for the development of film into an intructional tool of scientists and other experts. In the case of Watson, these factors provided him, as a psychologist, ample opportunity to develop an innovative research applicaton of motion picture technology. They also provided him, as an expert, with the opportunity to take the film that he had made and use it as propaganda for a scientifically managed, fearless way of life (see *Harris* 1983).

Notes

1   Videotape copies of Watson's film have been produced under the sponsorship of the Wellesley History of Psychology Workshop. Information on their availability can be obtained by writing Dr. Ben Harris, Department of Psychology, Vassar College, Poughkeepsie, NY 12601, USA.
2   Both Watson's idea as to the origin of handedness, and his fourth method of assessing it appeared initially in the writing of S.I.Franz (1917). The careers of Watson and Franz seemed to have many connections, including their having served together on the APA's Committee on Psychology and Medical Education (see Franz 1913).
3   According to Watson's later reports (Watson 1919b, Watson and Watson 1921) he found no reliable differences in young infants' hand preferences; this was consistent with Watson's belief that handedness was learned rather than genetically determined.
4   For those interested in the internal validity of Watson's work on emotional development, I recommend a careful reading of Watson and Rayner's (1920) *Journal of Experimental Psychology* article, together with an examination of the film record of their research. Of course, apart from the internal validity of Watson's work, interesting questions of generalizability (external validity) also can be posed. For example: how much was Watson's theory valid only for institutionally-raised infants?—since they made up the vast majority of Watson's sample.
5   In 1915, the psychologist Hugo Münsterberg began making films on a number of psychological topics (e.g. attention, facial recognition, imagination). However, these films do not seem to have been integrated into Münsterberg's research; they were designed for entertainment purposes, allowing audiences to "test their minds" on cinematographically presented tasks (Daypho-Bray 1921, Hale 1980). For information on subsequent uses of film in developmental psychology, see articles by Gesell (1935, 1952), Irwin (1931), and Beck (1938).
6   Interestingly, a similar motivation was claimed at roughly the same time by another pioneer in scientific cinematography, the German physician Curt Thomalla. Thomalla said that it was the absence of scientific congresses during the First World War that induced him to propose the creation of a psychiatric film archive in 1919, so that interesting cases could be shared with colleagues at a later time (Thomalla 1919a, 1929).
    Ash (1982) has pointed out that in discussing his filmed observations of apes, Wolfgang Köhler (1921/1971), also mentioned the need for a film record that could be shown

to colleagues. Köhler emphasized that a film record is helpful in combating others' *a priori* biases concerning animal behavior and their suspicions about Köhler's own observations.

[7] An important subject for further research is the precise relationship that existed between film companies and scientists such as Münsterberg and Watson. Specifically, to what extent did these companies market their equipment and techniques in the 1910's, partially sponsoring the work of well-known scientists in order to gain publicity and credibility for themselves and their industry?

References

Ash, M. (1982) Personal communication to author, October 1, 1982.

Beck, L. F. (1938) A list of sixteen millimeter films in psychology. *Psychol. Bull.* 35: 127–169.

Blanton, M. G. (1917) The behavior of the human infant during the first thirty days of life. *Psychol. Rev.* 24: 456–483.

Buckley, K. W. (1982) Behaviorism and the professionalization of American psychology: a study of John Broadus Watson, 1878–1958. Unpublished Doctoral Dissertation, University of Massachusetts.

Chase, W. G. (1905) The use of the biograph in medicine. *Boston Med. Surg.* 153(21): 571–572.

Cohen, D. (1979) *J. B. Watson.* Boston: Routledge and Kegan Paul.

Cornwell, D and Hobbs, S. (1976) The strange saga of little Albert. *New Society,* 18 March, pp. 602–604.

Franz, S. I. (1917) Observations on the preferential use of the right and left hands by monkeys. *J. Animal Behav.* 3: 140–144.

—(1913) On psychology and medical education: *Science* 38: 555–566.

Gesell, A. (1935) Cinemalysis: A method of behavior study. *J. Genet. Psychol.* 47: 3–15.

Gilbreth, Lillian M. (1926) *The quest for the one best way; sketch of the life of Frank Bunker Gilbreth.* Chicago: Society of Industrial Engineers.

Gilbreth, F. B., Jr. and Carey, E. G. (1948) *Cheaper by the dozen.* New York: Thomas Y. Crowell.

Gilman, S. (1978) Zur Physiognomie des Geisteskranken in Geschichte und Praxis. *Sudhoffs Archiv* 62: 209–234.

—(1979) Darwin sees the insane. *J. Hist. Beh. Sci.* 15: 253–262.

Hale, M. (1980) *Human science and social order: Hugo Münsterberg and the Origins of applied psychology.* Philadelphia: Temple University Press.

Harris, B. (1979) Whatever happened to Little Albert? *Amer. Psychol.* 34: 151–160.

—(1983) "Give me a dozen healthy infants. . .": John B. Watson's popular advice on child rearing, women, and the family. In M. Lewin (Ed.), *Mistaken identity: psychology views the sexes, 1800–1980.* New York: Columbia University Press.

Hennes, H. (1910) Die Kinematographie im Dienste der Neurologie und Psychiatrie nebst Beschreibung einiger selteneren Bewegungsstörungen. *Med. Klin* 6: 2010–2014.

Irwin, O. C. (1931) A cold light for photographing infant reactions with a high speed motion picture camera. *Child Devel.* 2: 153–155.

Köhler, W. (1971) Methods of psychological research with apes. In M. Henle (Ed.). *The selected papers of Wolfgang Kohler.* New York: Liveright (Originally published in German, in 1921).

Lashley, K.S. (1917) Modifiability of the preferential use of the hands in the rhesus monkey. *J.Animal Behav.* 1: 178–186.

Lashley, K.S. and Watson, J.B. (1917) Notes on the development of a young monkey. *J. Animal Behav.* 3: 114–139.

—(1921) The psychological study of motion pictures in relation to venereal disease campaigns. *Social Hygiene 7:* 181–272.

Lomax, E.M.R., Kagan, J. and Rosencrantz, B.G. (1978) *Science and patterns of child care.* San Francisco: W.H.Freeman.

Marey, M. (1894) Des mouvements que certains animaux exécutent pour retomber sur les pieds, lorsqu'ils sont precipités d'un lieu élève. *Compt. r. Acad. Sci.* 119: 714–717.

Meyer, A. (1912) The value of psychology in psychiatry. *J. Amer. Med. Assoc.* 58: 911–914.

Meyer, M. (1913) Left-handedness and right-handednes in infancy. *Psychol. Bull.* 10: 52–53.

Morawski, J. and Harris, B. (1979) John B.Watson's predictions for 1979. Paper presented to the meeting of the Eastern Psychological Association, Philadelphia.

Niver, K. (1967) *Motion pictures from the Library of Congress paperprint collection, 1894– 1912.* Berkeley, California: University of California Press.

Samelson, F. (1980) J.B.Watson's Little Albert, Cyril Burt's Twins, and the need for a critical science. *Amer. Psychol.* 35: 619–625.

Thomalla, C. (1919a) Verwertungsmöglichkeiten des medizinischen Lehrfilms. *Wiener Klin. Wochensch.* 32: 883–886.

—(1919b) Wissenschaftliche Kinematographie. *Berlin. Klin. Wochensch.* 56: 321–325.

—(1929) The development of the medical film and of those dealing with hygiene and general culture in Germany. *Internat. Rev. of Ed. Cinemat.* 1: 440–454.

Watson, J.B. (1913) Psychology as the behaviorist views it. *Psychol. Rev.* 20: 158–177.

—(1914) A circular maze with camera lucida attachment. *J. of Animal Behav.* 4: 56–59.

—(1917a) An attempted formulation of the scope of behavior psychology. *Psychol. Rev.* 24: 329–352.

—(1917b) Practical and theorectical problems in instinct and habits. In H.S.Jennings, J.B.Watson, A.Meyer, W.I.Thomas (Eds.), *Suggestions of modern science concerning education.* New York: Macmillan.

—(1919) Letters to F.J.Goodnow, 27 October and 13 November 1919. (From the Papers of the Office of the President, Hamburger Archives, Johns Hopkins University, Baltimore, Md.)

—(1919a) Experimental investigation of babies (Film). Chicago: Stoelting. (*Psychol. Abstr.* (1937) 11: no. 6061.)

—(1919b) *Psychology from the standpoint of a behaviorist.* Philadelphia: Lippincott.

Watson, J.B. and Morgan, J.J.B. (1917) Emotional reactions and psychological experimentation. *Amer. J. of Psychol.* 28: 163–174.

Watson, J.B. and Rayner, R. (1920) Conditoned emotional reactions. *J. of Exper. Psychol.* 3: 1–14.

Watson, J.B. and Watson, R.R. (1921) Studies in infant psychology. *Sci. Month.* 13: 493–515.

Weisenburg, T.H. (1912) Moving picture illustrations in medicine. *J. Amer. Med. Assoc.* 59: 2310–2312.

Wooley, H.T. (1910) The development of right-handedness in a normal infant. *Psychol. Rev.* 17: 37–41.

Martha Muchow: A Tribute to a Pioneer in Environmental Child Psychology

by Joachim F. Wohlwill

September, 1983 marked the 50th anniversary of the tragic death of Martha Muchow, one of the most promising and creative of the students of William Stern and Heinz Werner during the pre-war period at the University of Hamburg. Although her work is hardly well known, even to psychologists in her native country, and her untimely death cut short a highly promising career before she had had an opportunity to establish herself and her thinking on the psychological scene, her contribution deserves rather more than a footnote in the history of German developmental psychology. For, as we shall see, Muchow managed to combine, in a highly inventive and imaginative fashion, features of the developmental psychology of Stern and Werner with the essentials of a highly perceptive observational approach that marks her as a clear forerunner of the ecological psychologists' approach to the study of child behavior.

But let us attempt at the outset to sketch briefly the historical context for her life and work. It took place almost entirely in the setting of the Psychological Institute at the University of Hamburg that Stern had founded in 1919, bringing with him an interest in experimental and diagnostic techniques, and contributing greatly to the development of intelligence tests.[1] Beyond that, Stern was one of the very first "compleat" developmental psychologists, as shown in his comprehensive text of child psychology, *Psychologie der frühen Kindheit,* first published in 1914. Stern was instrumental, furthermore, in bringing to this Institute a number of other important figures in developmental psychology, of whom the most notable was Heinz Werner, whose influence of Muchow's work and thought proved considerable, as we will see.

All this made for an intellectually lively atmosphere indeed, enriched by the ideas of the philosopher Ernst Cassirer, the biologist Jakob von Uexküll, and others from diverse fields with whom Muchow undoubtedly had contact. And at the same time the Institute, under Stern's leadership, seemed to have been marked by a strong sense of responsibility to the social milieu of the city of Hamburg in which it was placed—particularly that of the families inhabiting the working districts of the city of Hamburg during and following the years of World War I, with its severe economic and social problems. Thus and interest in viewing the child in its family setting, and in applying the results of research on child development to issues of both pedagogy and social welfare came naturally to Stern and his associates, and the Martha Muchow in particular.

Martha Muchow came to psychology, and to Stern's Institute, from the field of education, having taught both elementary and high school between 1912 and 1919, that is, when she was in her twenties.[2] This experience was for her much more than a mere way-station to more advanced study and research; her primary identification, it seems, remained with the field of early childhood education, and she was very active in a movement concerned with problems of preschool and early primary-school education connected with the noted nine-teenth-century pedagogue Friedrich Froebel, the founder of the kindergarten movement. Both professionally and in her writings, many of which appeared in educational and pedagogical journals, this remained her field of primary interest to the end of her life. And beyond the specific area of early-childhood education, she maintained an active concern for problems of child care, for the then-growing German youth movement, and for social issues affecting children and adoles-cents in their family settings—issues that remained intertwined with her academic career.

Yet, from 1919 on, when she enrolled as a student at the University of Hamburg, Martha Muchow managed to combine, and indeed to integrate a diversified and successful career as a researcher, instructor, and academician with the aforementioned interests and concerns. Her field of study is described as "Psychology, philosophy, German philology and history of literature"—rather rich are by today's standards of specialization, and one that broght her into contact, not only with her chief mentor, William Stern, but with such notable figures as the philosopher Ernst Cassirer, and the biologist and animal ecologist Jakob von Uexküll. William Stern seems to have been impressed with her rather strongly, for after she had been a student for just one year (thus at the beginning of what we in the United States would call her sophomore year) she became both his research and his teaching assistant. Graduating in 1923 with the approximate equivalent of our Master's degree (based on a thesis on the psychology of the teacher), Muchow stayed on with Stern, conducting a series of studies on child cognition and intelligence, and collaborating with Heinz

Werner on research on infant behavior, and on magical forms of behavior in children. In addition she was writing on such topics as child play, on Montessori and Froebel, on problems of questionnaire- and test-construction, and even on parent education in the U.S., based on publications and activities of the Child Study Association.

Her interest in what was taking place in the U.S.A. led in 1931 to a four-month long tour to centers for child-development research in twelve different U.S. cities, which served both to acquaint her with American psychologists and persons from child development and education and their works, and to present her own work to American audiences, in the form of a series of 17 colloquia. She was quite tempted to remain in the U.S. for a while, which she had the opportunity to do through several offers of employment that came her way. She resisted these temptations, however, in large part it seems because she did not feel that she could readily move her work, and her life, to this country.

Muchow returned to Germany to a seemingly hectic pace of academic and professional activity, perhaps in part as a reaction to her growing disturbance, and sense of helplessness about the darkening clouds on the political horizon, which to her and most of her associates' dismay culminated in March of 1933 in the triumph of Hitler and the Nazis.

Her apprehension proved all too well founded, for by mid-April the Nazis had passed laws that resulted in the immediate dismissal of all Jews employed in public service positions, among them of course the universities.[3] Thus William Stern, Heinz Werner, and others with whom Muchow had worked were immediately barred from further participation in the work of the Institute of Psychology, and indeed from physical access to the Institute itself. In spite of the shattering impact that these events must have had on her, she managed to keep going, devoting much of her efforts to helping those among her associates who had immediately, for political reasons or because of their Jewishness, become the target of persecution at the hands of the Nazis. But on her forty-first birthday, 25 September, 1933, came the culminating blow: the disbanding of the Institute of Psychology, as she had known it, and its transfer to a party hack handpicked by the Nazis, who was to turn it into an instrument for education in Nazi ideology. To add insult to injury, on Martha Muchow befell the onerous task of presiding at the ceremony at which Stern's successor took over, in spite of the fact that she herself had by then been "transferred out" of the Institute, because of her close association with Stern and Werner, and had been ordered to resume her work as a school teacher.

It is hardly surprising that all this became too heavy a burden for her to bear. Two days later Martha Muchow took her own life. Characteristically, the Nazis barred William Stern from her funeral, and ordered her brother, much against his will, to hoist the Swastika at her burial.

As noted earlier, Muchow published extensively in the areas of pedagogy, and of infancy and early childhood development, including expository and theoretical writings, as well as empirical research. Among the latter we may cite a study (Muchow 1926) of 10-year old children's performance on tasks of attention, memory and psychomotor skill at the seashore, as affected by weather conditions (e.g. high winds) as well as by their own activities (e.g. following swimming or sunbathing). A study of a very different kind (Muchow 1949) and one that reveals very directly the influence of Heinz Werner, dealt with children's reproductions of geometric designs; it consists predominantly of qualitative phenomenologically tinged interpretation of their mode of response and verbalizations (e.g. a child reacting to a highly angular design with expressions of disgust, remarking on the "prickly" nature of the figure, or another insisting that a figure made up of a semicircle open on top, with a small dot inside it, must be upside-down, else the dot would fly up into space).

Muchow's major contribution, however, was her monograph *Der Lebensraum des Grosstadtkindes (The Lifespace of the Urban Child)*, written with the collaboration of her brother, Hans Muchow, who arranged for its publication after her death (Muchow and Muchow 1935). It was a comprehensive study, carried out over a period of several years, of children's knowledge and use of different areas and locales in their environment, based on a combination of interviews, an pencil-and-paper measures designed to reveal the extent of geographic space frequented by children for regular play, or familiar to them from more limited forays, along with observations of children's actual use of selected sites in their surroundings. The setting was a large working-class district in the city of Hamburg, and the children ranged in age from nine to 14, in the case of the measures obtained in the schools through interviews and structured testing. (The observational work included children of whatever age happened to be seen at the sites selected, generally ranging from preschool to adolescence.)

This monograph of the Muchows' has attracted the interest of contemporary workers on environmental cognition in children, but has become known largely through the extensive reference made to it by Muchow's mentor, Heinz Werner in his *Comparative Psychology of*

Mental Development. Indeed, there is a strong Wernerian flavor to some parts of this work, and to the Muchows' conclusions in particular, which emphasize the child's phenomenological world as quantitatively and qualitatively different from that of adults, selecting out particular features of an environment in terms of their significance for the child, e.g. a fence for climbing on or over, a quiet street for playing certain games, etc. (cf. Wapner, in press). Yet the work is fully as relevant from a very different perspective, that of the behavioral ecologists. For it is based on highly detailed analysed of the environmental features of the sites frequented by the children, and of the manner in which they were used, in a manner quite congruent with the behavior-setting views of the Kansas group, and with the concept of behavior-environment synomorphy in particular (cf. Schoggen, in press). The work, furthermore, anticipates much more recent work on territorial range in children (Moore and Young 1978), and indeed amplifies some aspects of that work, in demonstrating, for instance, that the commonly found sex differences in territorial range apply to the children's "roaming space," i.e. the area known to them from occasional traversals or forays, while the narrow zone of the children's "play space" is similar in magnitude for the two sexes.

In its combination of observational and interventive methodologies, and in its broad-ranging scope, from cognition to affect to use of the environment, the Muchows' monograph foreshadows Hart's (1979) much more recent, and justly acclaimed field study of children in a small Vermont village, which it complements in dealing with the urban environment. Indeed, it seems that part of Muchows' interest in this topic derived from a concern for urban children as possibly different from rural children, and for the impact of urban environmental conditions on them. Here is where yet a further important influence on Muchow's work becomes discernible, that of Friedrich Froebel, the nineteenth-century pedagogue, in whose ideas Muchow displayed a life-long interest. For Froebel had made observations of rural children's activities in their natural environments, emphasizing the ways in which those children make use of them for the development of various skills, and for imposing new challenges on themselves, through diverse athletic feats, as in fording a river, climbing a tree, or exploring a cave. Muchow displayed a very observant eye for the forms that such activity took when translated onto the urban setting. Thus, she goes into great length in detailing the diverse ways in which children respond to a fence separating a street from a landing area below. The fence, which for adults acts as a barrier, represents instead a challenge to them, as a testing ground for their agility, skill and strength, and as a stimulus to their ingenuity in devising new ways to climb along, over or through it. It thus allows them to display as well as build their sense of competence and mastery of the environment.

Nor are her observations in this regard confined to motor and athletic exploits: the theme is similarly in evidence in her fascinating account of the stratagems devised by children to transcend a human barrier, in the form of a guard posted at the entrance to a department store for the express purpose of keeping out children. Surely the ingenuity demonstrated by the children in outwitting or eluding the guard represents as much an example of the mastery of their environment as the behaviors they engaged in vis-à-vis the fence, or for that matter inside the department store, in riding the escalator in the wrong direction.

In short, the monograph displays a sensitive, understanding, and sympathetic eye and ear to the world of children, and to their development. Had Muchow lived, and been allowed to continue her so very promising career, it is easy to imagine her developing this combined developmental and ecological focus in her work into a highly significant and potentially most influential contribution to the field of child psychology and development. But the advent of Nazism not only robbed Martha Muchow of an opportunity to fully realize that promise, but stopped German psychology virtually dead in its tracks (with the limited exception of some Gestaltists who somehow were able to continue their work). Furthermore, as Zinnecker (1978) has observed, post-was German psychology proved on the whole unreceptive to the Stern-Werner tradition. While Zinnecker may be somewhat unjust in talking of developments in what he calls *Milieupsychologie* as a deadend street (cf. Walter and Oerter 1979), it is true that the kind of meticulous and insightful eye to the features of the physical environment that we find in the Muchow and Muchow monograph is absent from the work of contemporary German child and developmental psychology. All the more reason then for taking satisfaction in the interest that Muchow's work appears to be attracting, belatedly, in the United States, notably on the part of a group of geographers and environmental psychologists concerned with children's environmental cognition (Hart 1979, Hart and Moore 1973), as well as among developmental and ecological psychologistis more generally (Schoggen, in press; Siegel, in press; Wapner, in press). It appears that the relevance of her thought and her approach for psychologists today is being increasingly appreciated, and that the thread of her pioneering efforts so tragically cut short fifty years ago is being picked up in contemporary research and thinking on the child's environmental experience.

Notes

[1] Hardesty (1976) has given a thorough account of Williams Stern's work and achievement as Director of the Institute of Psychology at Hamburg.

[2] The following brief sketch of Muchow's academic career is based on the more extended accounts provided by Strnad (1949) and Zinnecker (1978). The latter also gives a comprehensive bibliography of publications by and about Muchow.

[3] An adequate treatment of the impact of the advent of the Nazi regime on German psychology remains to be written. But the effects of the 1933 takeover were sudden and dramatic, not only because of the dismissal of all Jews and politically suspect persons from university positions, but also through the immediate restructuring of the educational and scientific apparatus, to serve the ends of the new Nazi ideology. This impact is convincingly demonstrated by a persual merely of the table of contents of one of the leading German psychological journals, *Archiv für die gesamte Psychologie,* for the years 1932 through 1935. Virtually overnight that journal was transformed from one of the leading media for the dissemination of major advances in basic research in psychology to a vehicle of nationalist and racist propaganda and of politically tinged applied research of dubious scientific merit.

References

Hardesty, F.P. (1976) Louis William Stern: A new view of the Hamburg years. In K. Salzinger (Ed.), *Psychology: Works in progress. (Annals of the New York Academy of Sciences,* vol. 270). New York: New York Academy of Sciences, pp. 30–44.

Hart, R. (1979) *Children's experience of place.* New York: Irvington.

Hart, R. and Moore, G.T. (1973) The development of spatial cognition: A review. In R.M. Downs and D. Stea (Eds.), *Image and environment.* Chicago: Aldine, pp. 246–288.

Moore, R. and Young, D. (1978) Childhood outdoors: Toward a social ecology of the landscape. In I. Altman and J.F. Wohlwill (Eds.), *Children and the environment. (Human Behavior and Environment.* vol. 3). New York: Plenum, pp. 83–130.

Muchow, M. (1926) Psychologische Untersuchungen über die Wirkung des Seeklimas auf Schulkinder. *Zeitschrift für Pädagogische Psychologie 27:* 18–31.

—(1949) *Aus der Welt des Kindes: Beiträge zum Verständnis des Kindergarten- und Grundschulalters.* Ravensburg: O. Maier.

Muchow, M. and Muchow, H. (1935) *Der Lebensraum des Grossstadtkindes.* Hamburg: M. Riegel. (Reprinted ed., Bensheim, Germany: Päd. Extra, 1978).

Schoggen, P. (in press) Martha Muchow: Precursor to ecological psychology. *Human Development.*

Siegel, A.W. (in press) Martha Muchow: Anticipations of current issues and developmental psychology. *Human Development.*

374   Wohlwill

Strnad, E. (1949) Martha Muchow in ihrer Bedeutung für die sozialpädagogische Arbeit. In M. Muchow, *Aus der Welt des Kindes: Beiträge zum Verständnis des Kindergarten- und Grundschulalters.* Ravensburg: O. Maier, pp.7–18.

Walter, H. and Oerter, R. (Eds.) (1979) *Ökologie und Entwicklung.* Donauwörth (Germany): Auer.

Wapner, S. (in press) Martha Muchow and organismic-developmental theory. *Human Development.*

Zinnecker, J. (1978) Recherchen zum Lebensraum des Grossstadtkindes: eine Reise in verschüttete Lebenswelten und Wissenschaftstraditionen. In M. Muchow and H. Muchow, *Der Lebensraum des Grossstadtkindes.* (B. Schonig and J. Zinnecker, eds.). Bensheim, Germany: Päd-extra, pp.10–52.

The Idea of Development in the Writings of Eino Kaila

by Manu Jääskeläinen

The idea of a continuing, directed, adapted, resilient, and progressive change of the world—the idea of evolution was rationally formulated for the first time in the history of Western civilization by the Pre-socratic philosophers (Burnet, 1965):

> Anaximander (c.565 B.C.) has been called a precursor of Darwin by some ... It is clear ... that Anaximander had an idea of what is meant by adaptation to the environment and survival of the fittest, and that he saw the higher mammals could not represent the original type of animal. For this he looked to the sea.

However, a scientifically competent integration of the concepts "change", "invariance" and "direction" was first possible in Galileian physics. This scientific development was made possible, as shown by Bernal (1969), by a decisive change in the general social and philosophical outlook which did emphasize the significance of the time dimension in a new way. With this change, the new ways of production and commerce were closely connected.

The Age of Enlightenment transferred the idea of evolution into the geological, biological, sociological, and psychological spheres of reality. In this way the modern theory of evolution was born in its contemporary meaning, as the works of Goethe, Rousseau, Herder, Carus, Humboldt, Buffon, Lamarck, Kant and Hegel and many others have shown. Charles Darwin's impact is, of course, a decisive one. According to Murphy and Kovach (1972):

> Almost never, until the eighteenth century, does one have any psychology of childhood at all. The eighteenth century began to put children on the map: the twentieth century was moved them toward the center of the map ... It is partly Darwinism that has taught us to use the time dimension. But to think in developmental terms is characteristic of our whole way of life.... Indeed, practically all "behavior models" of today bristle with time-dependent measures of differentiation and integration.

Child psychology began with Comenius, Rousseau, Pestalozzi, Froebel and Herbart. According to Murphy and Kovach (1972):

> As early as 1787, Tiedemann had kept records of small children's growth, and later Charles Darwin made sensitive observations on the development of his infant son—these notes laid the foundation for an experimental child study

which began with Preyer (1882) and a widespread enthusiasm in Germany for the study of the child at home and at school: a study of children's drawings, play and conversation.

The idea of evolution was formulated for the first time in the history of Finnish psychology by the philosopher Johann Wilhelm Snellman, in terms of a Hegelian philosophy. In his work *Versuch einer speculativen Entwicklung der Idee der Persönlichkeit*, (1841) he stated:

> So hat die Philosophie des objectiven Geistes die wesentliche Seite, daß sie nicht nur eine Entwicklung der Begriffe des Rechts u.s.f. enthält, sondern zugleich das Sichbestimmen des Persönlichen Geistes, d.h. eine Entwicklung des persönlichen Selbstbewußtseyns ausmacht ... Bekanntlich hat Hegel in der Phänomenologie eine solche Entwicklung des Selbstbewußtseyns an den objektiven Gestaltungen des Geistes durchgeführt...

As all students of Hegel know, psychology is a part of the science of the Subjective Spirit and emerges in a dialectical process from Anthropology and Phenomenology (Stace, 1955):

> *Mind*, as treated in *psychology* is the return into itself of the subjective spirit, its return enriched from its going forth into consciousness. It is the subjective spirit 'in and for itself'.

Snellman states that the philosophy of the objective spirit contains the idea of the evolution of social conceptions (i.e. the idea of right and wrong). Other evolutionary topics include the development of perso-

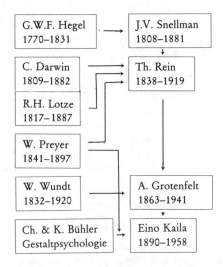

Fig. 1. Main phases in the development the concept of evolution in Finnish psychology

nality or selfconsciousness. For Snellman, unlike Hegel, the concept of personality takes a central place in his thinking. At a somewhat later time, Finnish psychology became an explicitly experimental, natural science. In this transformation process, Lotze played a decisive role (Jääskeläinen, 1983).

Preyer's work was presented at the turn of the century by Bruno Boxström in his textbook on The *Pedagogical Doctrine of the Mind* (1909). Professor Thiodolf Rein, a student of Snellman and originally a Hegelian, was influenced by the development of the natural sciences and the general scientific spirit of the period.* His *Textbook of Psychology* (1884, 1910) presented the theory of evolution in its modern Darwinian form. Rein was the teacher of Arwid Grotenfelt, who published his dissertation, *Das Weber'sche Gesetz und die physische Relativität,* in 1888. Grotenfeld had visited Leipzig and Wundt's laboratory and possessed a thorough knowledge of psycho-physics. In his later life, Grotenfeld became more interested in the history of philosophy, although he remained interested in the possibility of developing a scientific psychology in Finland. He also was the teacher of Eino Kaila of Helsinki University and remained his chief supporter in the faculty of philosophy.

Eino Kaila (1890–1958) is the founding-father of scientific psychology in Finland. However, he did not act in a historical vacuum. Kaila's views of the idea of evolution, as we shall see, illustrate the *contextual uses of a concept* over an extended period of time.

Early Evolutionary Influences

Kaila became influenced by the idea of evolution early in his career. Darwin's main work, *The Origin of Species* (1859), was translated into Finnish and published only in 1913. Kaila reviewed the book and published a lengthy paper about Darwin's central ideas and his own evaluation of these views (1916). First, he emphasized that Darwin's theory of evolution is not a general theory. It is no matter of "opinions" or "attitudes" because it is founded on detailed scientific studies. According to Kaila, Darwin's theory does not merely reflect the *Zeitgeist.* Darwin had predecessors, and he had to fight for his ideas against the academic and social elite of his time.

Kaila also focused on the religious development of Darwin, whom he characterized as an "intellectual and emotional agnostic." Following

Huxley, Kaila also addressed himself to the reception of Darwin's work. In this connection, Eino Kaila emphasizes the personal transformation in Huxley's own thinking and the hard and, in many cases, unjustified criticism of Darwinism by intellectual leaders in England, in continental Europe, and overseas. Kaila focused on some weak points in Darwin's theory, especially some statements about heredity which had already become outdated by the beginning of the 19th century, and concluded (1916):

> Anyone, who has not yet acquainted himself with Darwin's work and reads it for the first time, will be surprised by the vigor of his arguments.

Kaila first became familiar with Darwin's ideas even before his review of Darwin's major work. In 1913 he published a lengthy paper on *Culture and the Theory of Evolution*. In this essay he presented ideas from the writings of the Norwegian writer C.Collin (1912). Collin distinguished three stages in the formation of the theory of evolution. The romantic period is represented by the works of Buffon, E.Darwin, Lamarck, Goethe and Saint-Hilaire. The period of the evolutionary theory proper relates to Darwin's *Origin of Species* and to the writings of A.R. Wallace (1858). The third phase begins with Darwin's *Descent of Man* (1871). Collin sharply criticized the theory of "survival of the fittest" from a social point of view and emphasized that this perspective leads to an inhuman and irrationalist conception of social Darwinism. Collin also focused at length on the second phase in the development of evolutionary thinking. He points out that Darwin presented an analysis of the human side of nature in *The Descent of Man*. He notes that nature and society provide many examples of the increasing significance of cooperation, group-work, division of labor, coordination, altruism, etc. Both Collin and Kaila supported their views further by the then popular writings of Kropotkin. Kaila also attempted a synthesis between the optimistic evolutionary conception of the Enlightenment and the pessimism and nihilism of Social Darwinism. Kaila regarded both extremes as unscientific. Collin and Kaila were convinced that the gradual evolution of human culture lead to a similar growth in human altruism. This development, however, is not direct and linear but full of conflict and disagreement. There will always be conflict between the egoistic and altruistic elements in human culture and society and between individuals who adhere to these extreme positions. Nevertheless, Kaila and Collin were convinced that individual personalities and entire social and cultural systems could change over time in a "progressive" direction.

In summary, the idea of evolution became a stable element in the monistic world-view of Eino Kaila: 1. The theory of evolution is a scientifically sound and valid theory for him, although he was fully aware that the theory of evolution was not as "closed" and "final" a system as Newton's *General Mechanics*. 2. Kaila understood the idea of evolution monistically and consequently believed that the process of evolution continued at the psychological and social levels of reality. 3. The idea of the survival of the fittest must not lead to unrestricted egotism in the human sphere but can also promote greater cooperation and altruism. In contrast to the predictions of Malthus, human evolution has already taken a decisive turn towards altruism. The evolution in this direction requires a continuous battle against egoistic and other negative elements in man.

Criticism of Vitalistic Theories

Kaila dealt with the theory of evolution once again in a 1920 work which can be translated as *Mental Life as a Biological Phenomenon*. At executed and written in the spirit of the Würzburg-School (Boring, 1950). It comes as quite a surprise to note that the theoretical concepts and structures which Kaila utilized in this work were rather mechanistic. Only the concepts of association and reproduction were used as explanatory terms (1916):

> Bei der kausalen Erklärung brauchen wir also durchaus nicht unsere Zuflucht zu einem Verstand oder dergl. zu nehmen.

The concept of "reason" is like the concept *"virtus dormitiva"* in the medicine of the middle ages. Both are, in Kaila's views, equally useless as scientific explanations.

Kaila dealt with the theory of evolution once again in a 1920 work which can be translated as *Mental Life as a Biological Phenomenon*. At that time the famous biologist Gustav Wolff wanted to refute Darwin's theory of evolution. According to Wolff, phenomena which exhibit self-regulatory traits in nature, are not compatible with Darwin's theories. Wolff, like Driesch later on, hypothesized the existence of a special "vital energy", which can be used to explain the adaptability and plasticity of organic behavior. In addition, Wolff argued that the second law of thermodynamics was not valid for living organisms.

Kaila, in turn, argued that psychological phenomena can be fully explained by neurophysiological concepts. This outlook, however, reflects a monistic and not a eductionistic orientation! For Kaila there were no purely psychological states of personality but only psychophysiological conditions. Consequently, the conflict between mechanism and vitalism existed also in psychology.

Driesch believed that one cannot really talk about "animal psychology". Animals at most exhibit "psychoid" (psychology-like) behaviors which can studied by means of psychological analogues. Driesch further used the concept of "entelechy" to avoid charges of anthropomorphism. Thus, his position is basically an interactionistic one. Hence conflicts with Kaila's basic monistic views could not be avoided.

Kaila took the position that the "mechanistic principle" is valid in psychology. Hence, there was no need for the special presuppositions of vitalism or for the typical explanatory concepts of this school of thought (i.e. psychoid, entelechy, vital energy, life force, etc.). It must be noted that Kaila opposed the "vulgar materialism" of Haeckel and Ostwald. For him the facts of psychological development were explainable within a general, monistic frame of reference.

Finally, Kaila analyzed the problems of self-regulatory processes. He gave the vitalists credit for the quality of their observations. However, he tried to explain these phenomena in the psychological sphere by the concept of "ideational coordination" *(Ideatorische Koordination)*. In this sense psychological evolution is directly connected with neurophysiological development. New psychological patterns *(Ganzheiten)* emerge on the basis of new psychophysical formations (ideational coordinations). New coordinations between associations and psychological reproductions emerge because all (human) processes of organisms are psychophysiological by nature.

It should be stressed that Kaila soon afterwards gave up this conception of the idea of evolution. The concept of "ideational coordination" was obviously much too simple. The modern reader, of course, is fully aware that "assocation" and "reproduction" cannot sufficiently explain most psychological processes.

Kaila's basic, monistic attitude with its emphasis on the continuity between biological and psychological patterns of development, is an enduring element of his thinking. His sharp opposition to vitalism and dualism cannot be overlooked. Other important features of Kaila's theories at that time include his search for biological correlates of behavior and the accpetance of the importance self-regulatory mechanisms.

Psychological Development during Early Childhood

In 1932 Kaila published a monograph, *Die Reaktionen des Säuglings auf das menschliche Gesicht* (Reactions of infants to the human face). It is quite apparent that his views had changed during the 1920s. The most important difference is now the rejection of associationism as an explanatory principle. Its place is taken by Gestalt theory. Consequently, Kaila's view of evolution was radically altered. His central concern is nor how undifferentiated configurations emerge and develop into differentiated and articulated *Gestalten*. Nevertheless, Kaila still remained strongly interested in the question of evolution, even though personal "scientific revolutions" had occured. Kaila himself described his new work (1932):

> ... Ich wollte anfänglich hauptsächlich nur die mimischen Reaktionen des Säuglings (im zweiten Vierteljahr) untersuchen, wobei insbesondere eine Nachprüfung derjenigen in der gegenwärtigen Kinderpsychologie vertretenen Ansicht erstrebt wurden, dass die Säuglinge schon im angegebenen Alter fähig sein sollten, die gesehene (stumme) Mimik des Partners 'reflektorisch zu übertragen' und Gesichtsbewegungen 'instinktiv nachzuahmen'. Es gelang mir aber im Laufe der Untersuchung, einige Entdeckungen zu machen, die auch die mimischen Reaktionen in ein neues Licht stellten; die Untersuchung mußte deswegen auf den gesamten Bereich der Reaktionen des Säuglings auf das menschliche Gesicht ausgedehnt werden.

Kaila conducted his observations and experiments at the Institute for Child Care of the City of Vienna, which was founded by Charlotte Bühler. He also received encouragement and assistance with his research from Karl Bühler.

It is Kaila's view that the social contact, which was created by non-verbal, visual communications between infant and adult and which lead to the child's imitatory behavior, produced a special psychological state in the young child. The child experienced for the first time in life a feeling of *joy*. Kaila suggested that this is a special type of cortical stimulation *(kortikaler Zustand)* which contained the beginnings for the differentiation of the phenomenological experiential field. The fact that this first experience of pleasure or joy was produced by human contact is of special importance for the social development of man.

Kaila now posed the question: What factors in the psychological field make this reaction happen? In his answer he emphasized the role of the visual configuration of the upper part of the adult face (excluding the mouth, the cheeks and the hair). Is must be admitted that Kaila's procedures are more anecdotal than experimental. Nevertheless, his general methods and results are still important for the understanding of his theory of evolution.

According to Kaila, the analysis of the perceptual processes of infants reveal that a process of differentiation occurs which proceeds from general and diffuse configurations to more detailed and articulated *Gestalten*. Development does not consist in the mere summation of elementary associations. This finding applies to all types of evolutionary processes, even to the micro-genetic situation *(Aktualgenese)*, as Koffka, Köhler, Wertheimer and other Gestaltists have demonstrated. The principle was formulated most cogently by Heinz Werner: "Development proceeds through analysis, not through synthesis."

In his monograph, Kaila also addresses himself to the topic of mimic imitation. In this context, he commented on the earlier work by Preyer. Preyer had observed imitation in children already during the first and second quarter of their first year. He believed that infants could imitate behavior even earlier than had been shown (1882). For example, small children could imitate movements of the lips and mouth spontaneously, as long as these were demonstrated to them rather frequently. Kaila noted that Preyer had correctly concluded that these "games" occurred within a social context and differ from purely spontaneous mimic activity by the child.

Kaila also discovered that these social reactions of children may somewhat later on cease in children. Preyer had noted that these behavior patterns take definite shape during the seventh month of life. In Kaila we find the following interpretation (1932):

> Was Preyer hier beobachtet hat, ist sehr charakteristisch: Am Anfang des zweiten Vierteljahres kommen zuweilen sogar reichliche, scheinbare Nachahmungen vor; am Ende desselben Vierteljahres zeigen sich Tendenzen zu wirklichen Nachahmungen, die aber erfolglos bleiben. Der Säugling weiß, was er will, kann es aber nicht. Es wird sich zeigen, daß Preyer hier einem allgemeinen Sachverhalt auf die Spur gekommen ist.

Kaila's explanation of the emergence of mimic imitation behavior is summarized in Figure 2.

(1) Perceived movements of adult mouth in connection with the social contact with the infant	(2) Spontaneous innervations of infant's mouth in connection with the social contact (smiling, gurgling, etc.)
(3) Spontaneous mouth-play i.e. tendency to mimic imitation	(4) Spontaneous mouth-play i.e. social mouth-reactions

Fig. 2. Explanatory scheme of imitatory behavior of infants according to Eino Kaila (1932)

Finally, Kaila noted that social-mimic imitation of the infant are restricted to a certain age of life. These behaviors may disappear within the time periods, mentioned above, only to return later. The development of speech and the gradual emergence of symbolic functions in man make these elementary forms of social, non-verbal communication obsolete and unnecessary. They are replaced by more developed forms of communication, learning and self-expression.

Kaila's research on smiling in children was briefly mentioned in Piaget's and Inhelder's classic, *La Psychologie de l'Enfant* (1966). Unfortunately, his original contributions do not seem to have been fully understood. Kaila's views were identified with those of C. Bühler and Piaget and Inhelder incorrectly concluded that these authors perceived a special reaction of the infant in the face of another, adult person.

Acutally, Kaila does not interpret his findings as evidence for a direct and specific reaction on the face of another (adult) person. Kaila does not believe that the response of the child was genetically conditioned or instinctive, as Piaget and Inhelder seem to have inferred. Quite to the contrary, he explicitly rejects the instinct-theoretical interpretation of his findings. However, he seems to take the view that the child's imitational behavior is *biologically conditioned.* According to Kaila, Preyer had noted that the phenomenon of mimic imitation is important because it gives clear evidence of the activity of the human brain. Kaila points out that the infant can reflect (Widerspiegelt) the facial expressions he sees only when it is able to *perceive* in the full sense of the word. Adequate perception, in turn, is possible only if the corresponding cortical processes function satisfactorily. Furthermore, these instinctual behavior, similar to that of bees, would be possible *(bienenhaft differenziert).*

Kaila explains the perception of the adult face by the child by referring to the invariance of eye contact between adult and child. While the oral part of the face is in a state of constant movement, the visual part of the face *(Augenpartie)* virtually remains the same. Specifically, Kaila makes the following points (1932):

> Wenn wir nun weiter bedenken, daß, falls ein Gegenstand erkannt wird, er selbstverständlich aufgrund seiner Invarianzen erkannt wird, so kommen wir zum folgenden Ergebnis auf Grund unserer Überlegungen: Das menschliche Gesicht wird vom Säugling beim Übergang vom ersten zum zweiten Vierteljahr aufgrund der Invarianz des Blicks, d.h. der Augenpartie erkannt ... Der Blick des Erwachsenen wird für den Säugling zum allerersten phänomenalen Gegenstand ... deshalb, weil der Säugling das entsprechende Sehding in der für ihn wichtigsten biologischen Situation in annähernd invarianter Form vor sich sieht.

In this statement Kailas presents the theory of invariance as an explanation for the emerging conception of the human face. This is the first time in his work where the Theory of Invariance finds such a clear expression. The same formulation played a remarkable role in his later intellectual development. In this example, the "look" of the adult is the very first phenomenal "object" from the infant's point of view. As a rule, this is, of course, the face of the mother. However, in the infants, studied by Kaila, this was not the case. Kaila was fully conscious of the social and human situation of the children studied by him. Clearly, Kaila's interpretation differs radically from the conclusions which Piaget and Inhelder drew from his work.

Since 1932 the concept of invariance and the Gestalt principle form an organic and coherent part in Kaila's general work and in his specific writings about evolutionary matters.

The Development of the Human Personality

Kaila's major psychological publication is his book, *Personality* (1934) which at that time was regarded as the earliest work offering an integrated view of the human personality on the basis of modern psychological research. The famous classic by Gordon Allport, *Personality: a psychological interpretation,* was published somewhat later (1937). Eino Kaila's book was translated into Swedish and Danish. It influenced the psychological thinking in Scandinavia in a remarkable way. It contains a chapter on the "Birth of mental life", in which problems of developmental psychology are analyzed and discussed within the context of Kaila's psychology of personality. Kaila begins his presentation of developmental psychology by studying in detail a "common sense" theory which he called "Cartesian conceptions." According to this view, the concept of reality is founded on the existence of one's own consciousness. This way of thinking leads to an egocentric theory of development of the human personality. Kaila regards this theory as false quoting Nietzsche in support of his views: "Das Du ist älter als das Ich" (The concept of the other is older than the concept of the ego). In Kaila's view the self develops as the result of social interaction and primarily reflects this interaction. According to Kaila, human consciousness is no *tabula rasa* either. Human preceptions are active cognitive processes and not merely passive reflections of objective reality. He criticized Piaget's view that the young child develops from an egocentric view of life to an objective perception of reality. Specifically, Kaila distinguished between two types of egocentrism. First, there is "functional egocentrism." In addition, we have "phenomenological egocentrism." Whenever these two orientations occur in the same personality, the result is autism. The normal child lives in a world which is totally *objective.* The child's behavior can be interpreted as egocentric from the perspectives of an adult. However, the objects in the child's world *are* childish. This view is very different from the charge that the child views the world egocentrically. Psychological development leads to a differentiation between the "Self" or "I" and the outside world which is "there" and which has the phenomenological property of "objectivity." A primitive world is *not* egocentric but mental, psychical or spiritual *(beseelt)* which is a totally different perspective.

In this process of increasing differentiation and objectivization of human consciousness, the symbol function plays an important role. A biological continuity exists between signal and symbol function. However, only the symbol function is a specifically human characteristic. The birth of mental life, in the human sense of the word, means that a decisive, irreversible, and total existential transformation from the signal function to the symbol function occurs. This change is neurobiologically anchored in the cortical system of man. With the help of symbols man can comprehend the existing world. Consequently, the human personality is "freed" from the slavery of immediacy as the symbol function increases in importance in the individual life and the world becomes more comprehensible. The development of the concept of time plays an important role in this context.

Eino Kaila analyzes the meaning of human and social value from the point of view of the theory of evolution. According to Kaila, there is a clear direction of evolutionary development towards increased altruism in human society and personality. This "law" is valid on the individual and the cultural level. It should be apparent that Kaila remained faithful to his basic conviction throughout the 1920s that the evolution of man is meaningful and leads towards increased altruism. However, during the war and the immediately following period, Kaila's belief in the positive potential of human development was put to a hard test, as many works from this period show. Still, the idea of evolution remained an intellectual and, possibly, emotional cornerstone in this thinking. Kaila presented these views once more in the 1948 essay *The Humanistic World-View*. In this paper he focused on the role of rational and irrational forces in the development of the individual and mankind as as whole. Kaila concluded that rational motives still continue to have a *chance* to affect life. It is this chance or opportunity which is important for mankind, as long as it survives. All possible efforts in the fields of psychological, philosophical, scientific, social and pedagogical research and thought are needed to increase to opportunities for the altruistic development of the human personality. We can prevent the outbreak of irrational and aggressive motives of man only by concentrating on the positive forces of human reason.

It may be concluded that the theory of evolution and the evolutionary and developmental psychology, which resulted from it, had a major impact on the theoretical and methodological orientation of Finnish psychology. The idea of Continental psychology reached Finland directly and rather speedily. The ideas of Hegel and his disciples, of Lotze, Wundt, Fechner, Preyer and Darwin were not just copied but were subtly and originally adapted to the Finnish academic and intellectual situation. The German ideas were actively debated and changed and original ideas about the development of mind were proposed in Finland. Today one finds many developmental psychologists in Finland who focus on specialized research topics in developmental psychology (i.e. development of social interaction, intellectual maturation etc.).

References

Bernal, J.D. (1969). *Science in history* (Vols. 1–4). Middlesex, England: Penguin Books.

Boring, E.G. (1950). *A history of experimental psychology*. New York: Appleton.

Burnet, J. (1892). *Early Greek philosophy*. Cleveland: Meridian.

Collin, C. (1912). *Brorskabets religion og den nye livs videnskab. Med en historisk belysning av darwinismen*. Kristiania.

Jääskeläinen, M. (1983). From Hegel to scientific psychology. A change of paradigm in Finnish psychology during the end of the 19th and the beginning of the 20th century. Unpublished manuscript.

Kaila, E. (1913). Kultuuri ja kehitysoppi I—II (Culture and evolution). Uusi Suomi, September 7 and 12.

—(1916). "Lajien synty" suomeksi (The origin of species, in Finnish). Uusi Suomi, May 3.

—Über die Motivation und die Entscheidung. Eine experimentelle psychologische Untersuchung. Helsinki: Academic Dissertation.

—(1920). *Sielunelämä biologisena ilmiönä* (Mental life as a biological phenomenon, in Finnish). Helsinki: Otava.

—(1932). Die Reaktionen des Säuglings auf das menschliche Gesicht. *Annales Universitatis Aboensis, Jääskeläinen, Kaila*, 1984 Series B, *12*.

—(1934) *Persoonallisuus* (Personality, in Finnish). Helsinki: Otava.

—(1948) *Humanistinen elämänöäkemys* (Humanistic World-Views, in Finnish). Ylioppilaslehti.

Murphy, G. and Kovach, J.K. (1972). *Historical introduction to modern psychology* (6th ed.). London: Routledge and Kegan, Paul.

Preyer, W. (1882). *Die Seele des Kindes*. Leipzig: Grieben.

Piaget, J. and Inhelder, B. (1966) *The psychology of the child*. London: Routledge, Kegan, Paul.

Sants, J. (Ed.) *Developmental psychology and society*. New York: St. Martin's Press.

Snellman, J.V. (1981). *Die Persönlichkeit*. Sankt Augustin: Richarz (1841).

Stace, W.T. (1955). *The philosophy of Hegel*. New York: Dover (1924).

Trevarthen, Colwyn (1980) *Neurological Development and the Growth of Psychological Functions*. In: Sants.

Wilenius, R. (1981) *Einleitung* (Introduction to Snellman's Die Persönlichkeit Hans Richarz, Sankt Augustin).

Epilogue

This book has presented a series of research papers which were prepared initially for the International William T.Preyer Symposium at Friedrich-Schiller-Universität in Jena, German Democratic Republic, during the early fall of 1982. The centenary of the publication of Preyer's classic, *Die Seele des Kindes* (The Mind of the Child, 1882), brought historians of science, psychology, and philosophy together with developmental psychologists and educators from many countries to share their views about the origin of the concept of "development" and the establishment of developmental psychology as a scientific discipline.

The concept of development becomes one of the most fascinating research questions in history, when we trace its metamorphoses from the *panta chorei* of Heraclitus to contemporary formulations. The papers in our publication address the entire spectrum, with emphasis placed on nineteenth century and early twentieth century viewpoints. While philosophers have been interested in evolutionary change for nearly three millenia, developmental thinking reached one peak in the eighteenth and early nineteenth century in geology (Charles Lyell), biology (Charles Darwin) and, as we recognize, also in psychology.

This volume has tried to reconstruct some of the sources which introduced developmental thinking into modern psychology. In this respect our book reveals how basic research in the history of science can benefit those disciplines which are concerned with matters of change. We also believe that this collection illustrates a wide range of historiographic principles and techniques, which are available to contemporary scholars in the field.

History is the open book of human development. Historical sophistication is necessary to understand the past, to have impact on the present, and to prepare for the future. An understanding of historical factors permits us to reconstruct ideas, conditions, and events to a greater or lesser degree. Thus, history enables us to evaluate contemporary events, problems, and ideas in science. We are also better prepared to identify mere "scientific fashions" and to gain the necessary distance from the so-called *Zeitgeist*. Familiarity with the history of the research problems of a scientific discipline can make it possible for us to rediscover and reactivate forgotten ideas. In this respect, the comparison of past and present times may lead to a reevaluation of both contemporary and traditional thought.

The historical analysis of scientific investigations continues to provide information for the analysis and understanding of creative processes, which in turn, can help in the planning and execution of new scientific research projects. The history of science shows how interconnected and complex roads lead to discovery, how much time is needed and how many detours have to be made before new discoveries occur. History teaches us that potentially significant discoveries can be anticipated and planned only to a very limited degree and that originality does not yield readily to force. The sentiment that, "if experimental scientists had read more, they would have discovered less," contains, of course, an aphoristic exaggeration. It is more likely that a solid education in the history of one's scientific discipline would result in the formulation of better hypotheses for empirical research and would, hopefully, reduce the number of poorly planned and incompetently executed experiments. Research in the historiography of science, therefore, can help correct the excessive emphasis on mere data collection and the equally questionable adherence to obtuse theoretical models, which characterize much present research in the social and natural sciences.

The basic question "Why should we study the history of psychology?" (Wertheimer 1983) and the recent, extensive publication of collections of empirical research and theoretical discussions in the history of psychology (Bringmann and Tweney 1980, Brozek and Pongratz 1980, Eckardt and Sprung 1983, Meischner and Metge 1980 Woodward and Ash 1982) play an important role in the planning of experimental research and even of diagnostic investigations in the clinical field (Sprung and Sprung, 1983). Research in the history of psychology, like in any other field of science, must be carried out by specialists within the respective discipline in cooperation with scholars from related fields of study (Parthey and Schreiber 1983). The present volume is the joint endeavor of historians of science, of experimentalists with a historical bent, of theoreticians of science, and of philosophers and methodologists. Consequently, the "microscopic" perspective of the various specialists is complemented by the "telescopic" vision of the philosopher.

Much has been written about the differences in research methods of historians and experimental scientists. The essays in this volume make it, at least, implicitly clear that many communalities do exist. The careful analysis of documents can be viewed as a retrospective examination of the products of human behavior (i.e. scientific writings, letters, diaries, works of art). The reconstruction of the original behavior from the archival and documentary sources and the identification of the conditions under which these events occurred in the first place are skills which do not belong exclusively to the repertoire of the historian. The search for the relevant literature, the formulation of testable hypotheses, and the theoretical deliberations of the experimentalist are guided by similar principles and techniques as the work of the historian. Such agreements in approach include "internal *vs.* external" criticism of documents as well as the methodological principle of the "replicability" of all conditions under which the data were collected and analyzed. Further important parallels can be found in the distinction between the conditions which are "necessary" and "sufficient" to explain a phenomenon, the emphasis on a "normative viewpoint" in the selection and evaluation of research results and, finally, the necessity for the special "subject-method-object" relationship pertinent to any psychological research (Sprung and Sprung 1983).

The truism—history is made by man—applies, of course, to the sciences and their history. The papers contained in this book illustrate the history of evolutionary and developmental thinking by the psychographic reconstruction of the lives and accomplishments of important personalities. This observation is particularly true as far as William T. Preyer is concerned. The reconstruction of the lives, work, and impact of seminal personalities within the economic, sociological, political, and cultural contexts of their times, provides us with direct access to the process of scientific development and discovery. The reconstruction of this genetic process enables us to better understand the current situation in any given field of study and to anticipate directions of future development. Thus, historians of science can influence, quite directly, current and future experimental investigations in the sciences. It is the strong hope of the authors and editors of the present volume that our work will be a worthwhile contribution to modern psychology and the related disciplines, which share our fascination with questions about the origin and development of behavior.

Helga Sprung

References

Bringmann, W.G. and Tweney, R.D. (Eds.) (1980) *Wundt studies.* Toronto: Hogrefe.
Brozek, J. and Pongratz, L.J. (Eds.) (1980) *Historiography of modern psychology.* Toronto: Hogrefe.

Eckardt, G. and Sprung L. (Eds.) (1983) *Advances in the historiography of psychology.* Berlin, GDR: Deutscher Verlag d. Wissenschaften.

Meischner, W. and Metge, A. (Eds.) (1980) *Wilhelm Wundt—Progressives Erbe, Wissenschaftsentwicklung und Gegenwart.* Leipzig: Karl-Marx-Universität.

Parthey, H. and Schreiber K. (Eds.) (1983) *Interdisciplinarität in der Forschung—Analysen und Fallstudien.* Berlin, GDR: Akademie Verlag.

Preyer, W. (1882) *Die Seele des Kindes.* Leipzig: Grieben.

Sprung, L. and Sprung, H. (1983) The communication-theoretical approach: historical developments and new foundations of a theory of psychological methods. In G. Eckardt and L. Sprung (Eds.) *Advances in the historiography of psychology.* Berlin, GDR: Deutscher Verlag d. Wissenschaften.

Wertheimer. (1983) Why should we study the history of psychology? In G. Eckardt and L. Sprung (Eds.) *Advances in the historiography of psychology.* Berlin, GDR: Deutscher Verlag der Wissenschaften.

Woodward, W. R. and Ash, M. G. (1982) *The problematic science: psychology in nineteenth-century thought.* New York: Praeger.

About the Authors

MITCHELL G.ASH is an Assistant Professor of History at the University of Iowa. He is co-editor, with William Woodard, of *The Problematic Science: Psychology in Nineteenth Century Thought* (New York, 1982). His articles have appeared in *Central European History, Psychological Research, Wundt Studies* (ed. by Wolfgang G.Bringmann and Ryan D.Tweney, Toronto, 1980). and in the annual, *Sociology of the Sciences.* He is currently working on a study of German-speaking psychologists in the United States after 1933. Dr. Ash holds a B.A. from Amherst College, where he studied philosophy, psychology, and intellectual history, and the A.M. and Ph.D. degrees in history from Harvard University.

WILLIAM BALANCE received his Ph.D. from the University of Alabama and is currently a Professor at the University of Windsor. He is a clinician in terms of background and primary interests. In addition to his contributions to the history of psychology, he has published in the areas of affective responses to media, feedback from psychological assessment, therapy, and most recently, the verification of theories regarding suicide through the study of suicide notes. His writings in the history of psychology have focused on biographical studies of nineteenth-century precursors and founders of experimental psychology.

PETER J.BEHRENS is an Assistant Professor of Psychology at the Alltentown Campus of Pennsylvania State University. His research on the first dissertation in experimental psychology from Wundt's laboratory and a comparison of the Leipzig program with the first American Ph.D. program in psychology at Johns Hopkins University have appeared in *Psychological Research* and other publications devoted to the history of psychology. Dr.Behrens holds a Ph.D. in Experimental Psychology from Lehigh University.

NORMA J.BRINGMANN completed her B.A. in German at the University of Windsor in Canada. She has evolved an independent interest in the history of nineteenth-century German psychology. Her publications have appeared in *Wundt Studies* (1983), *Studies in the History of Psychology and the Social Sciences* (1983), and *Advances in the Historiography of Psychology* (1983). Her current research interests include the merging and diverging approaches of anthropology and psychology and their respective contributions to the cross-cultural study of child-rearing methods and ideologies.

WOLFGANG G.BRINGMANN is a Professor of Psychology at the University of South Alabama. A clinical psychologist by training, he holds the M.A. and Ph.D. from the University of Alabama. His research in the history of psychology has concentrated on the development of psychology as an autonomous science in nineteenth century Germany, the use of archival and documentary research methods and the life and work of Wilhelm Wundt. Dr. Bringmann is the author of three books and more than one hundred publications in the history of psychology, clinical psychology, and experimental-social psychology. His writings have appeared in journals like the *American Psychologist,* the *Canadian Psychological Review, Contemporary Psychology,* the *Journal of the History of Behavioral Sciences, Isis, Psychologische Beiträge, Psychologie Heute,* and *Storia e Critica della Psicologia.* His current projects include a documentary biography of Hermann Ebbinghaus and a collection of Fechner's writings.

URIE BRONFENBRENNER is a Jacob Gould Schurman Professor of Human Development, Family Studies, and Psychology at Cornell University. Born in Moscow, Professor

Bronfenbrenner graduated from Cornell with an AB in Psychology and Music, received his Ed.M. from Harvard and a Ph.D. in Developmental Psychology from the University of Michigan. He was a psychologist with the U.S. military services during World War II and taught for two years at the University of Michigan before joining the Cornell Faculty in 1948. His studies of children and families have taken him to England, Israel, Switzerland, the People's Republic of China and the Soviet Union. Part of his cross-cultural research on child-rearing was published in 1970 under the title *Two Worlds of Childhood: US and USSR*. Professor Bronfenbrenner's most recent volume was published in 1979 under the title *The Ecology of Human Development: Experiments by Nature and Design*. He is currently working on a new book entitled *On Making Human Beings Human*. Professor Bronfenbrenner is one of the founders of Headstart. He has served on the Committee on Child Development Research and Public Policy of the National Research Council of the National Academy of Sciences and the Scientific Advisory Board for Educational Research of the Max-Planck-Institut in West Berlin. Professor Bronfenbrenner holds three honorary doctorates (Brigham Young, USA; Münster, West Germany; Göteborg, Sweden) and has received numerous honors and awards for his research in child development.

JOHN C. CAVANAUGH is an Assistant Professor of Psychology at Bowling Green State University. He was a postdoctoral trainee at the University of Minnesota. Dr. Cavanaugh is the author of several articles in the area of life-span cognitive development as well as the history of developmental psychology. He is currently working on a history of the concepts and data used to describe cognitive development in children. He holds the B.A. from the University of Delaware and an M.A. and Ph.D. from the University of Notre Dame.

KURT DANZIGER is a Professor of Psychology at York University in Toronto, Canada. He has published two books, *Socialization*, and *Interpersonal Communication*, as well as numerous articles in the areas of social psychology, child development, sociology of knowledge, and history of psychology. These articles have appeared in such publications as *Journal of Genetic Psychology, British Journal of Social Psychology, British Journal of Sociology, History of Science, Psychological Research*, and *Journal of the History of the Behavioral Sciences*. Dr. Danziger holds a doctorate from the University of Oxford.

ROGER A. DIXON is a Research Scientist in the Center for Psychology and Human Development at the Max Planck Institute in West Berlin. In conjunction with his work on cognitive development in adulthood he has published in *Developmental Psychology, Journal of Gerontology, Journal of Verbal Learning and Verbal Behavior, and Life-span Development and Behavior*. His work on history and theory of developmental psychology has appeared in several edited volumes. He holds an M.A. in the history and the philosophy of the social sciences from the University of Chicago and an M.S. and Ph.D. in life-span developmental psychology from Penn State University.

GEORG ECKARDT is an Assistant Professor of Psychology at Friedrich Schiller University in Jena, German Demorcratic Republic (GDR), where he completed his education with a Ph.D. in Psychology. Dr. Eckardt specializes in the teaching of child psychology and the history of psychology. His published research has concentrated on problems in the history of social psychology, the development of child psychology as a modern science and research methodology in the social and behavioral sciences. Dr. Eckardt has held visiting appointments at Moscow and Tiflis universities in the USSR and is the President of the Historical Commission for Psychology of the GDR.

CHRISTINA FRITSCHE is a psychologist who received her education at Humboldt

University in Berlin and at Karl Marx University in Leipzig, GDR. After receiving her doctorate, she became a member of the Wundt Research Project at Karl Marx University and in this function assisted in the preparation of the XXII International congress for Psychology. Dr.Fritsche holds a research appointment at the Karl Sudhoff Institute for the History of Medicine and the Natural Sciences. She has published about Wilhelm Wundt's relationship with the academic philosophy of his time, the "crisis of psychology," and is currently involved in a long-term research project dealing with the history of psychotherapy in Germany.

HOWARD E.GRUBER is a Professor of Psychology at the University of Geneva in Switzerland and at Rutgers University in the USA. He is the author and/or editor of *Darwin on Man, a Psychological Study of Scientific Creativity* (1974, 2nd. ed., 1981); *The Essential Piaget* (with J.Voneche, 1977); and various other books. *Darwin on Man* received the Phi Beta Kappa Award for books in science, and other awards. Dr.Gruber has published many papers on visual perception, creative thinking, history of science, and education. He is interested in applications of psychology to ensuring human survival, especially against the threat of nuclear war. He has been a faculty Fellow of the Ford Foundation, a Special Fellow of the National Institutes of Mental Health, a John Simon Guggenheim Fellow, and a Member of the Institute for Advanced Study (Princeton). He holds a B.A. from Brooklyn College and a Ph.D. from Cornell University (1950).

BEN HARRIS, a clinical psychologist, received his B.S. from Hampshire College and his Ph.D. from Vanderbilt University, completing his internship at the Baylor College of Medicine. He has been an Assistant Professor of Psychology at Vassar College since 1978, and spent the 1982–83 academic year as Visiting Scholar in the University of Pennsylvania's Department of the History and Sociology of Science. His research is on the ideology of social science in the United States between the World Wars. He is a member of a variety of professional organizations, including the Group for a Radical Human Science, and the Benjamin Rush Society. In 1983, he was appointed Chair of the Ad Hoc Committee on History of the Society for the Psychological Study of Social Issues.

MANU JÄÄSKELÄINEN is the Chief of Educational Affairs for the Finnish Medical Association. Previously, he worked as a research psychologist at the Institute for Occupational Health. His publications include works in the fields of medical education, history of psychology, history of medical education, organizational psychology, and the behavioral foundations of health care and health care planning. His main work is his doctoral dissertation (in Finnish). He is also the author of *Advanced Medical Education in Finland,* and the coauthor of *Structure and Functions of Health Care Centers.* He received his Ph.D. in psychology from the University of Helsinki in Finland.

SIEGFRIED JAEGER is a Research and Teaching Associate of the Psychological Institute at the Free University of Berlin. Dr.Jaeger is co-author, with Irmingard Staeuble, of *Die gesellschaftliche Genese der Psychologie* (Frankfurt, 1978). He has also published research on eighteenth and nineteenth century history of psychology. He holds a diploma in psychology and the Ph.D. from the Free University of Berlin.

ROBERT KEEGAN received his B.A. in psychology at Montclair State College, his M.A. from the Graduate Faculty of the New School for Social Research in New York City, and expects his Ph.D. in psychology in 1984 from the Institute for Cognitive Studies of Rutgers University. From 1979–1984 he served in various capacities as lecturer, instructor, and teaching assistant. His research experience includes case studies of highly creative individuals, archival research on Charles Darwin, and experimental work on the nature of memory traces. He has served as co-editor of a special issue of the *Journal of the History of the Behavioral Sciences* (1983) on Charles Darwin and has published a commemorative book with Howard Gruber for the Darwin centennial. He is presently working on another book on Darwin's thinking and plans to publish Darwin's diary of his first child, William Erasmus.

URSULA E.KÖHLER is a retired Professor of Industrial and Occupational Psychology at the Technological University in Dresden, GDR. After completing her education in biology, mathematics, and psychology, Professor Köhler has been an academic teacher for more than thirty years, focusing her teaching on the theory and history of developmental psychology and its practical applications to child-rearing. Influenced by the activity theories of Rubinstein, Leontjew, and Straub, especially as they pertain to cognitive problems, she has concentrated in recent years on methodological issues and their application to the industrial situation. Dr.Köhler's dissertation research dealt with the psychology of preschool children. Her later writings have primarily focused on methodological issues.

RICHARD M.LERNER is a Professor of Child and Adolescent Development at Pennsylvania State University in the United States. Dr.Lerner has written or edited more than 10 books and over 100 articles and chapters in the area of developmental psychology, specifically on topics such as concepts and theories of development, developmental methodology, and personality and social development. He is on the editorial board of *Child Development*, is an Associate Editor of the *International Journal of the Behavioral Sciences* and is currently co-editor of the annual series, *Life-Span Development and Behavior*. He received his B.A. and M.A. degrees from Hunter College of the City University of New York, and his Ph.D. degree from the City University of New York.

RICHARD LOWRY is Professor of Psychology at Vassar College. His publications include *The Evolution of Psychological Theory: A Critical History of Concepts and Presuppositions; A.H. Maslow: An Intellectual Portrait; Dominance, Self-Esteem, Self-Actualization;* and *The Journals of A.H. Maslow* (two volumes). He is currently working on a book to be entitled "The Dark Side of the Soul: Psychological Reflections on the Problem of Evil." Professor Lowry holds a Ph.D. from Brandeis University.

ALEXANDRE MÉTRAUX works at the Psychological Institute of the University of Heidelberg in the Federal Republic of Germany. During 1974/75 he was a Visiting Assistant Professor of Philosophy at the Graduate Faculty of the New School for Social Research in New York City. Dr.Métraux has published in the area of philosophy, the history of psychology, the theoretical foundations of the social sciences, and the philosophy of law. His publications include *Max Scheler ou la phenomenologie de valeurs* (Paris: Seghers, 1973) and Kurt Lewin, *Wissenschaftstheorie I* (1981). He is co-editor with Horst Gundlach of *Kinesis—Studies in the Theory and in the History of Psychology.* He received his Ph.D. from the University of Basel in Switzerland.

PAUL MITZENHEIM is a Professor of the History of Education at Friedrich Schiller University in Jena, GDR. He has published books and articles about the history of the reform education movement in Germany, about Friedrich Fröbel, the development of education in Thuringia, and the teaching of pedagogy at Jena University.

FRANK ORTMANN is a Research and Teaching Associate at the Institute for the History of Medicine and the Natural Sciences (Ernst Haeckel Haus) at Friedrich Schiller University in Jena, GDR. He also holds an appointment as a specialist in internal medicine. Dr.Ortmann's main fields of research are the history of medicine in Jena and the history of psychiatry. He studied medicine at Karl Marx University in Leipzig and holds a diploma and a doctorate in medicine from Friedrich Schiller University.

ROBERT J.RICHARDS is an Associate Professor in the History of Science, the Conceptual Foundations of Science, and Biopsychology at the University of Chicago. He also serves as Director of the Program in History, Philosophy, and Social Studies of Scienes and Medicine in the College. Dr.Richards has published in the *British Journal of the History of Science, Journal of the History of Biology, Journal of the History of the Behavioral Sciences, Proceedings of the American Philosophical Society,* and many other journals. His book, *Darwin and the Emergence of Evolutionary Theories of Mind and Behavior,* will be published by the University of Chicago Press. He holds advanced degrees in biological psychology, philosophy, and history of science.

ECKART SCHEERER is a Professor of Psychology at the University of Oldenburg in the Federal Republic of Germany. He was a Research Fellow at the Center for Visual Science at the University of Rochester. Dr.Scheerer has published in the area of experimental psychology and in the history and theory of psychology. His publications include *Die Verhaltensanalyse* (Berlin, Heidelberg, New York: Springer, 1983), the first volume of a projected series *Theorien der Psychologie.* He is coordinating editor of *Psychological Research,* an international journal of cognitive psychology which was founded as *Psychologische Forschung.* In addition, he is sectional editor for psychology/biology/medicine of the *Historisches Wörterbuch der Philosophie* (Basel, Stuttgart: Benno Schwabe). He holds a Diploma and a Ph.D. in psychology, both from Ruhr University in Bochum (Federal Republic of Germany).

HANS-DIETER SCHMIDT is a Professor for Developmental Psychology at Humboldt University in Berlin, German Democratic Republic. Dr.Schmidt has published in the area of developmental psychology and on the psychology of personality. Many of his articles have appeared in the *Zeitschrift für Psychologie.* He is the author of *Allgemeine Entwicklungspsychologie* (1982), and co-editor of *Evolution and Determination of Animal and Human Behavior.* Professor Schmidt holds a doctorate in science from Humboldt University in Berlin.

HELGA SPRUNG is a private researcher in psychology and the history of psychology in Berlin, GDR. Dr.Sprung has published extensively in the areas of experimental psychology (psychophysiology of hypertension, psychopharmacology), clinical psychology, research methodology, philosophy of sciences, psychodiagnosis and history of psychology (psychophysics, the theoretical foundations of psychology, scientific institutions, theory and methods in the history of psychology, nineteenth century German intellectual history). Her publications have appeared in *activitas nervosa superior, Zeitschrift für Psychologie, Probleme und Ergebnisse der Psychologie, studia psychologica, Revista Latinoamericana de Psicologia,* and *Revista de Historia de la Psicologia.* She is a co-author, with Lothar Sprung, of *Grundlagen der Methodologie und Methodik der Psychologie—Eine Einführung in die Forschungs- und Diagnosemethodik für empirisch arbeitende Humanwissenschaftler* (Berlin, 1984). Dr.Sprung holds a Diploma in Psychology from Humboldt University in Berlin and a Ph.D. in Science from the same institution.

LOTHAR SPRUNG is an Assistant Professor of Psychology at Humboldt University in Berlin, GDR. Dr.Sprung has many publications, in experimental psychology (concept formation, memory, experimental psychopathology), research methodology, philosophy of science, psychodiagnostics, cognitive psychology and the history of psychology (psychophysics, scientific institutions, theories and methods, 19th century intellectual history in Germany). His work has appeard in journals like *Zeitschrift für Psychologie, Probleme und Ergebnisse der Psychologie, Das Deutsche Gesundheitswesen, folia ophthalmologica, studia psychologica, Revista Latinoamericana de Psicologia,* and *Revista de Historia de la*

Psicologia. He is co-editor with Georg Eckardt of *Advances in the Historiography of Psychology* (Berlin, 1983) and co-author with Helga Sprung of *Grundlagen der Methodologie und Methodik der Psychologie* (Berlin, 1984). Dr.Sprung has held visiting appointments at academic institutions in Warsaw (1970), Moscow (1976), Jena (1978), and Paris (1983). He is a graduate of the Ph.D. program in Experimental Psychology at Humboldt University in Berlin, GDR.

IRMINGARD STAEUBLE is a Professor of Psychology at the Free University in Berlin, FRG. She has published in the area of social psychology and the history and critique of psychology and the social sciences. She is co-author, with Helmut Nolte, of *Zur Kritik der Sozialpsychologie* (München: Hanser, 1972) and, with Siegfried Jaeger, of *Die gesellschaftliche Genese der Psychologie* (Frankfurt: Campus, 1978). Professor Staeuble holds a diploma in Psychology and a Ph.D. in Philosophy from the Free University of Berlin.

ETHEL TOBACH holds an appointment as Curator of Comparative Psychology at the American Museum of Natural History in New York and Professorial positions in Biology and Psychology at the City University of New York and New York University. Professor Tobach has published several books and numerous articles and chapters in the fields of comparative psychology, developmental psychology, evolution theory, the psychology of women and the history of psychology. She has received many academic and professional honors including membership in major APA committees, and an appointment to the New York State Board for Psychology.

RYAN D.TWENEY is Professor of Psychology at Bowling Green State University, Bowling Green Ohio, USA. He has published extensively in the fields of psycholinguistics, cognitive psychology, and the history of psychology. He is co-editor, with Wolfgang Bringmann, of *Wundt Studies,* and, with M.E. Doherty and C.R. Mynatt, of *On Scientific Thinking.* He is currently working on a cognitive analysis of Michael Faraday's research methods. He tolds the doctorate in psychology from Wayne State University, and the B.S.in psychology from the University of Chicago.

MICHAEL WERTHEIMER was educated at Swarthmore, Johns Hopkins, and Harvard. After teaching for three years at Wesleyan University, he went in 1955 to the University of Colorado, where he has remained since, becoming a full professor in 1961. Early research concentrated on perception, cognition, and psycholinguistics; more recently he has focused on general psychology, philosophical psychology, and the history of psychology. A past president of the American Psychological Associations's Divisions of General Psychology, The Teaching of Psychology, Philosophical Psychology, and the History of Psychology, he was the 1983 recipient of the American Psychological Foundation's Award for Distinguished Teaching in Psychology.

KARL-FRIEDRICH WESSEL is a Professor of Philosophy and Head of the Division for the Philosophical Problems of Science, Technology and Mathematics at Humboldt University in Berlin, GDR. His research interests include the history of science, philosophical problems and the history of psychology, and the historical relationship between philosphy and sience. Professor Wessel is the author or numerous articles and the follwing recent books: *Kritischer Realismus und dialektischer Materialismus* (1971), *Pädagogik in Philosophie und Praxis* (1975), (with Hörz) *Philosophische Entwicklungstheorie* (1983), and, (with Hörz, Pölltz, Röseberg, and Parthey) *Philosophische Probleme der Physik.* Dr.Wessel holds a Ph.D. in Philosophy from Humboldt University where he qualified in 1971 as a full-time academic teacher.

JOACHIM WOHLWILL is a Professor of Human Development at Penn State University. Dr.Wohlwill has worked as a post-doctoral Fellow with Jean Piaget at the

University of Geneva and as Director of the Graduate Program in Developmental Psychology under Heinz Werner at Clark University. He is the author of *The Study of Behavioral Development*, and has published on diverse topics in perceptual and cognitive development, on environmental psychology, and on psychological aesthetics. His current interest is in creativity and the role of environmental stimulation on development. Dr. Wohlwill has a B.A. from Harvard University and a Ph.D. from the University of California at Berkeley.

WILLIAM R. WOODWARD is an Associate Professor of Psychology at the University of New Hampshire and co-director of the Graduate Program in History and Theory of Psychology. He is currently working on an intellectual biography of the German Philosopher and psychologist, Rudolf Hermann Lotze. He edited, with Mitchell G. Ash, *The Problematic Science: Psychology in Nineteenth Century Thought* (NY: Praeger: 1982) and contributed the introduction to *Essays in Psychology* in *The Works of William James* (Cambridge: Harvard, 1983). Dr. Woodward received his Ph.D. in History of Science and Medicine from Yale University in 1975.

Index